EMPLOYER AND EMPLOYEE

EMPLOYER

AND

EMPLOYEE

by

G. BARRIE MARSH, LL.B.,
Solicitor

A complete and practical guide to the
modern law of employment

LONDON:
Printed and Published by
SHAW & SONS LTD.
Shaway House, SE26 5AE
1977

Published   -   -   -   February 1977

ISBN 07219 0740 7

CONTENTS

PAGE

PREFACE xiii
TABLE OF STATUTES xv
TABLE OF CASES xxiii
LIST OF ABBREVIATIONS xxxi
INTRODUCTION xxxiii

PART I

BEFORE THE EMPLOYMENT COMMENCES

CHAPTER 1—ENGAGING AN EMPLOYEE 3

Discrimination in Engagement of an Employee ... 3
    Sex Discrimination 3
        Forms of sex discrimination 4
        Exceptions 7
    Racial Discrimination 11
        Forms of racial discrimination 12
        Exceptions 13
    Practical Implications for the Employer 15
        Sanctions 15
        Avoiding the pitfalls 21
        Questionnaires for use prior to proceedings... 24
        Employers' responsibility for managers and
            other employees 25
    Rehabilitation of Offenders Act 1974 26
    Disabled Persons (Employment) Act 1944 28

PART II

THE EMPLOYMENT ITSELF

CHAPTER 2—THE CONTRACT OF EMPLOYMENT 30

The Terms of Employment 31
    Express Terms 31
    Implied Terms 32
    Collective Agreements 33
    Works Rules 34
    Statutory Rights 35
The Contracts of Employment Act 1972 36
    The required particulars 36
    Method of time and communication 41
    Changes in terms of employment 42
    Changes in the law 43
    Excluded categories of employees 44
    Sanctions 46

PAGE

CHAPTER 3—EQUAL PAY 48

The Equal Pay Act 1970 49
The equality clause 49
What does the Act cover? 49
Who is entitled to the benefit of the Act? ... 50
What is " like work "? 51
What is work of " equivalent value "? 52
The employee's remedies 53
Central Arbitration Committee 54
Examples of decided cases under the Equal Pay
Act 54

CHAPTER 4—DISCRIMINATION DURING EMPLOYMENT ... 59

Sex Discrimination 59
Discrimination in terms of employment 59
Promotion, transfer and training 60
Benefits, facilities and services 62
Other detriment 62
Sanctions 63
Victimisation 63

Racial Discrimination 64

Practical Implications for Employers 65

PART III

DURING THE EMPLOYMENT

THE OBLIGATIONS OF THE EMPLOYER AND
THE RIGHTS OF THE EMPLOYEE 66

CHAPTER 5—THE EMPLOYER AND THE TRADE UNION ... 68

Union Recognition 68

Disclosure of Information 75
Disclosure under the Code of Practice 75
Disclosure under the Employment Protection Act
1975 75
Failure to disclose 79
Disclosure under the Industry Act 1975 80

The Closed Shop 83

Terms and Conditions of Employment 86
Recognised terms and conditions 87
General level of terms and conditions 87
Who can make the claim? 88
The Advisory Conciliation and Arbitration Service 89
The Central Arbitration Committee 89

Inducement of a Breach of Contract 90

Other Matters 94

CHAPTER 6—THE EMPLOYEE AND THE TRADE UNION ... 96

Trade Union Membership and Activities 96
Excluded categories of employees 98
Sanctions 98
The 1972 Code of Practice 99

Time off for Union Members 99
Excluded categories of employees 100
Sanctions 101

PAGE

Time off for Union Officials 101
    Excluded categories of employees 102
    Sanctions 102
Unfair Dismissal 103

CHAPTER 7—MATERNITY RIGHTS 104
    Dismissal on Grounds of Pregnancy 104
    Offer of suitable alternative employment 105

    Right to Maternity Pay 108
    Excluded employees 108
    Conditions of entitlement 108
    Amount of maternity pay 110
    When is maternity pay due? 111
    Sanctions 111
    The Maternity Pay Fund 112

    The Right to Return to Work 113
    Conditions of entitlement 114
    The right to return 114
    The job itself 116
    Temporary replacements 117
    Sanctions 117

    Contracting out 119

CHAPTER 8—MEDICAL SUSPENSION PAY 120
    Conditions of entitlement 120
    Exclusions 121
    The amount of pay 123
    Dismissals 123
    Sanctions 124

CHAPTER 9—ITEMISED PAY STATEMENT 125
    Excluded categories of employees 126
    Sanctions 127

CHAPTER 10—TIME OFF FOR PUBLIC DUTIES 129
    Conditions 129
    The time off 130
    Excluded categories of employees 131
    Sanctions 132

PART IV

THE EMPLOYER IN A CHANGING BUSINESS

CHAPTER 11—LAY-OFF AND SHORT-TIME 133
    Lay-Off 133
    Short-Time 140

    Rights to a Redundancy Payment by Reason of Lay-off
    or Short-Time 142
    Lay-off 143
    Short-time 143
    The right to a redundancy payment 145
    The position of the employer 146

CHAPTER 12—GUARANTEED PAY 149
    Guaranteed Pay Agreements 149

PAGE

Statutory Guarantee Payments 150
The right itself 151
The amount of the payment 152
Limitations on guarantee payments 153
Where the right is lost 153
Guarantee agreements 154
Sanctions 155

CHAPTER 13—REDUNDANCY 156

The Basic Principle of Redundancy 157

Who is Protected by the Act? 157
Excluded employees 158
Conditions 162

Dismissal 163

What is Redundancy? 163
Proof of redundancy 164

Types of Redundancy 166
Cessation of the business 166
Moving the place of business 167
Reduction in work 169

Non-Redundancy Reasons for Dismissal 170

Offer of Alternative Employment 172
The offer 172
Refusal of offer of new employment 173
What is " suitable employment "? 174
Acceptance of offer of new employment 176
The trial period 177

Transfer of Business 179

Claims for Redundancy Payments 183

The Amount of the Redundancy Payment 185

The Employer's Rebate 187

Contracting Out 189

CHAPTER 14—REDUNDANCY CONSULTATION 191

The Code of Practice 191

Consultation under the Employment Protection Act
1975 193
The duty to consult 193
Larger scale redundancies 193
Notification to Secretary of State 196
Excluded Employees 196
Sanctions—the protective award 197
What is the position of the individual em-
ployee? 199
Sanctions—the Secretary of State 200
Collective agreements 201
Contracting out 201

Time Off to Look for Work 201
Conditions 201
The terms 202
Sanctions 203
Excluded categories 204

PAGE

Chapter 15—INSOLVENCY OF THE EMPLOYER 205
    Priority of debts 206
    The employee's rights on insolvency 207
    The remedies of the employee 210
    Excluded categories 210

PART V

TERMINATION OF EMPLOYMENT

Chapter 16—DISMISSAL 212
    Statutory definition 212
    Termination with or without notice 213
    Non-renewal of a fixed-term contract 216
    Constructive dismissal 216
    Resignations 219
    Dismissal by operation of law 220
        Redundancy 220
        Frustration 221

Chapter 17—WRONGFUL DISMISSAL 226
    Termination by notice 226
    The statutory minimum periods of notice ... 227
    Conduct justifying summary dismissal 229
    Remedies for wrongful dismissal 231
        The employee's loss 232
        The employer's claim 235
        The employee's claim 236
    Inter-relationship of wrongful dismissal and unfair
    dismissal 238

Chapter 18—REASONS AND REFERENCES 240
    The Reason for the Dismissal 240
    At common law 240
    The statutory position 241
    The right to a written statement of reasons for
    dismissal 241
    Excluded categories of employees 243
    References 244

Chapter 19—UNFAIR DISMISSAL—THE RIGHTS OF THE EM-
    PLOYEE 246
    The right not to be unfairly dismissed 247
    Excluded categories of employees 247
    Contracting out 253
    Dismissal 256

Chapter 20—UNFAIR DISMISSAL—WHEN IS A DISMISSAL
    UNFAIR? 257
    Burden of proof 257
    How can the employer show that a dismissal
    was not unfair 257
    Automatic unfair dismissal 259
    Inadmissible reasons—the statutory definition 259
    Inadmissible reasons in practice 261
    Interim relief for employees 262
    Dismissal which is automatically fair 267

PAGE

Chapter 21—UNFAIR DISMISSAL—THE REASON FOR THE
DISMISSAL 271
Capability or Qualifications 274
Definitions 274
Skill or aptitude 275
Qualifications... 277
Health and sickness 278
Pregnancy 281
Conduct 282
Disobedience to instructions 282
Lack of co-operation 284
Dishonesty 285
Violence, swearing and drinking 288
" Off-duty " conduct 289
Redundancy 290
Selection for redundancy due to an inadmissible
reason 291
Selection for redundancy in contravention of a
customary arrangement or agreed procedure ... 292
Where dismissal for redundancy is unreasonable 293
Breach of a Statutory Duty or Restriction 296
Some Other Substantial Reason... 297

Chapter 22—UNFAIR DISMISSAL—DID THE EMPLOYER ACT
REASONABLY? 300
The Code of Practice 302
Warnings 304
Will a breach of the Code make dismissal unfair? 306
Reasonableness and other factors 309

Chapter 23—UNFAIR DISMISSAL—THE EMPLOYEE'S REME-
DIES 311
The application to the Tribunal... 311
The Remedies 315
Reinstatement and Re-engagement 315
Reinstatement 316
Re-engagement 317
Non-compliance with the Tribunal's Order ... 319
Compensation 321
Basic award 322
Compensatory award 323
Contributory fault 327
Mitigation 329

PART VI

INDUSTRIAL TRIBUNALS

Chapter 24—THE INDUSTRIAL TRIBUNAL—BEFORE, DURING
AND AFTER 333
Settling " out of court " 333
The Conciliation Officer 335
The Industrial Tribunal 337
The employee's application 339
The employer's reply 340
Preliminary matters 341

PAGE

The hearing 342
Costs 344
After the decision 345
Application for a review 345
Appeal 348

APPENDIX I—Extract from: THE SEX DISCRIMINATION (QUES-
TIONS AND REPLIES) ORDER 1975:
Questionnaire of person aggrieved 350
Reply by respondent 351

APPENDIX II—CALCULATION OF PERIOD OF EMPLOYMENT:
Continuous employment 352
Normal working week 353
Breaks in employment 355

APPENDIX III—NORMAL WORKING HOURS AND CALCULA-
TION OF A WEEK'S PAY:
Normal working hours 360
A week's pay 361

APPENDIX IV—DISCIPLINARY PRACTICE AND PROCEDURES:
Draft Code of Practice issued under the Employment
Protection Act 1975 364
Essential features of disciplinary procedures ... 365
The procedure in operation 366

APPENDIX V—TIME OFF FOR TRADE UNION DUTIES AND
ACTIVITIES:
Draft Code of Practice 368

APPENDIX VI—SUMMARY OF RIGHTS OF EMPLOYEES ... 372

ALPHABETICAL INDEX 383

PREFACE

" A man-cub is a man-cub and he must
learn all the Law of the Jungle "

THE JUNGLE BOOK—RUDYARD KIPLING.

The Duke of Argyll is reputed on one occasion to have said—

" As far as I'm concerned there are only two kinds of people in the world—those who are nice to their servants and those who aren't ".

Although it may still be possible to divide employers into these same two categories, the difference to-day is that the law itself has a much greater " say " in whether or not an employer is " nice " to his employee.

The aim of this book has been to provide a compact and yet comprehensive study of *all* aspects of the present law of employment. This sphere of the law has, of course, changed dramatically since 1972 and within the last twelve months alone five further major Acts of Parliament have reached the statute book.

It is not surprising that businessmen, employees and trade union leaders—let alone lawyers !—have become confused as to their rights and obligations. It is hoped that within one single volume this book will help to guide all these people through the present morass of legislation.

Publication has been delayed until now so that full consideration might be given to the Race Relations Act 1976, to all the practical implications of the Equal Pay Act 1970 and the Sex Discrimination Act 1975 in the light of the various decided cases under those Acts.

[xiii]

It has also been possible to deal with the new rights contained in the Employment Protection Act 1975, the respective dates on which it is now known that they will come into force and the various guidelines now laid down by the most recently decided cases of Industrial Tribunals and of the Employment Appeal Tribunal.

The law is stated as at 1st January 1977, although it has also been possible to give subsequent dates in 1977 when certain of the Employment Protection Act rights become effective.

I would like to acknowledge with gratitude all the encouragement and assistance given to me by Gordon Morris of my publishers and I must also thank Dorothy Ryan and Barbara Edge for all that they have done in transferring a mass of " scribbled " manuscript into an organised and legible proof.

Finally—and by no means least—I thank my wife for her great patience and forbearance—particularly during the " long hot summer " of 1976.

G. BARRIE MARSH, LL.B.

1st January 1977.

19 WATER STREET,
LIVERPOOL,
L2 0RP.

TABLE OF STATUTES

PAGE

Bankruptcy Act 1914 ... ... 206, 207

Calculation of Redundancy Payments Order 1974 185

Companies Acts 1948-1967 ... ... 75, 206, 207

Contracts of Employment Act 1963 ... ... 36, 46, 228

Contracts of Employment Act 1972—
s. 1 229
   (3) 229
   (6) 229
  4 ... ... 36, 372, 380
   (1) 37
   (2) 36
   (3) 39
   (5) 33, 41
   (7) 44
  5 ... ... 37, 42, 43
  6 42
  9 45
   (2) 45
   (3) 45
Schedule 1 ... ... 37, 352
       para. 3 353
           4 353-355
           5 (1) 355
           5 (1) (b) 134
           5 (1) (c) 357
           5(2) 355
           6 358
           7 358
           8 357
           9 ... ... 38, 358
           9 (2) 180
           10 38
           11 (2) 354

Disabled Persons (Employment) Act 1944—
s. 9 28
   (2) 28
   (5) 29
  11 28
  14 29

Disabled Persons (Standard Percentage) Order 1946 28

Dock Workers (Regulation of Employment) Act 1946 ... 196, 204, 210, 243, 252, 382

Employment Appeal Tribunal Rules 1976 ... ... 348, 349

Employment Protection Act 1975—
s. 1 335
  2 (4) 335

[xv]

Employment Protection Act 1975—*continued*   PAGE

s. 6	...	...	...	...	...	...	...	...	...	335
(1)	...	...	...	...	...	...	...	...	302, 303, 364
(3)	...	...	...	...	...	...	...	...	72, 364
7	...	...	...	...	...	...	...	...	...	68
8	...	...	...	...	...	...	...	...	...	68
10	...	...	...	...	...	...	...	...	...	73
11	...	...	...	...	...	...	...	...	71-74, 261
12	...	...	...	...	...	...	...	...	71-74, 261
15	...	...	...	...	...	...	...	...	71-74, 261
16	...	...	...	...	...	...	...	...	71-74
17-21	...	...	...	...	...	...	...	...	75-80
18	...	...	...	...	...	...	...	...	78-79
22	...	...	...	...	...	...	...	...	150, 376
(1)	...	...	...	...	...	...	...	...	151
(2)	...	...	...	...	...	...	...	...	152
24	...	...	...	...	...	...	...	...	152
25	...	...	...	...	...	...	...	...	153
26 (1)	...	...	...	...	...	...	...	...	152
27 (3)	...	...	...	...	...	...	...	...	155
28	...	...	...	...	...	...	...	...	154
29-33	...	...	...	...	...	...	...	...	120, 376
32 (2)	...	...	...	...	...	...	...	...	124
33	...	...	...	...	...	...	...	...	124
34	...	...	...	...	...	...	...	...	104, 107, 281
(1)	...	...	...	...	...	...	...	...	105
(1) (a)	...	...	...	...	...	...	...	...	105
(2)	...	...	...	...	...	...	...	...	105
(3)	...	...	...	...	...	...	...	...	106
(6)	...	...	...	...	...	...	...	...	253
35	...	...	...	...	...	...	...	...	108, 113, 376
39	...	...	...	...	...	...	...	...	112
39-47	...	...	...	...	...	...	...	...	112
48	...	...	...	...	...	...	...	...	113, 116
(5)	...	...	...	...	...	...	...	...	117
49	...	...	...	...	...	...	...	...	113, 115
50	...	...	...	...	...	...	...	...	113, 118
53	...	...	...	...	...	...	...	...	96, 374
(1)	...	...	...	...	...	...	...	...	96
(6)	...	...	...	...	...	...	...	...	97
57 (1)	...	...	...	...	...	...	...	...	101, 368, 374
58	...	...	...	...	...	...	...	99, 100, 368, 374
(3)	...	...	...	...	...	...	...	...	100
59	...	...	...	...	...	...	...	...	129, 374
(4)	...	...	...	...	...	...	...	...	130
60 (1)	...	...	...	...	...	...	...	...	132
61	...	...	...	...	...	...	...	...	201, 203, 374
(1)	...	...	...	...	...	...	...	...	202
(7)	...	...	...	...	...	...	...	...	203
63-69	...	...	...	...	...	...	...	...	206
63	...	...	...	...	...	...	...	...	206
(2)	...	...	...	...	...	...	...	...	208
64	...	...	...	...	...	...	...	...	380
65	...	...	...	...	...	...	...	...	208
68	...	...	...	...	...	...	...	...	209
69 (1)	...	...	...	...	...	...	...	...	207
70	...	...	...	...	...	...	...	...	165, 241, 380
71	...	...	...	...	...	...	...	...	315
(8)	...	...	...	...	...	...	...	...	316

Employment Protection Act 1975—*continued*   PAGE
s. 72   ...   .   315, 319
    (5)   321
73 (6)   321
74 (7)   323
76   ...   . 315, 323, 324
    (4)   329
    (5)   324
    (6)   327
77   ...   .   17, 323
78   ...   .   103, 262
79   ...   .   103, 262
80   ...   .   103, 262
81   ...   .   125, 374
83   126
84   127
    (3)   127
    (5)   127
85   360
98   86
99 (1) 193, 378
    (3)   193
    (5)   194
    (7)   194
    (8)   195
101 (2)   197
102   198
106 (1)   193
107   201
108 (3)   336
109   ...   . 47, 238, 338
116   95
118   ...   . 97, 119, 201, 335
126 (1)   68
    (5)   352
Schedule 2 ...   .   120, 121
Schedule 3 ...   .   118, 119
Schedule 4 ...   . 110, 123, 144, 152, 157, 186, 242, 360-363
Schedule 11   ...   .   86, 87, 90
Schedule 15   95
Schedule 16, Part I—
        para. 2   173
             3   ...   .   163, 212
             9   184
        Part II 36, 44, 228, 352
        para. 4 (*b*)   39
             5 (*b*)   32
             7   44
             8   44
            10 (*b*)   45
            13   353
            14   353
            17   116
            19   38
        Part III—
        para. 8   220
             9   220
            11   259
            12   259
            21   314

PAGE

Equal Pay Act 1970—
s. 1 (1) 49, 372
   (4) 51, 58
   (5) 52
   (6) 50
  2 (1A) 53
Health and Safety at Work, etc., Act 1974 ... ... 95, 121
Income and Corporation Taxes Act 1970 185
Industrial Relations Act 1971... ... 31, 40, 69, 72, 83, 91, 96, 99, 246, 302
Industrial Training Act 1964 337
Industrial Tribunal (Labour Relations) Regulations 1974... ... 338, 341, 346
Industrial Tribunals (Labour Relations) (Amendment) Regulations 1976 321
Industry Act 1975 ... ... 75, 80-82
Insolvency Act 1976 ... ... 206, 207
Law Reform (Limitation of Actions, etc.) Act 1954 236
Limitation Act 1939 236
Merchant Shipping Act 1894 45
Merchant Shipping Act 1970 31
Mines and Quarries Act 1954... 10
Race Relations Act 1976—
s. 1 (1) (a) 12
  1 (1) (b) 12
  1 (2) 12
  3 (1) 12
   (4) 12
  4 13
   (2) 64
  5 13
   (3) 14
   (4) 14
  6 14
   (1) 13
  9 14
  14 17
  16 14
  29 13
  32 26
   (3) 26
  33 18
  34 14
  35 14
  37 14
  38 14
  39 14
  41 15
  42 15
  50 18
  53 15
  54 15
  56 16
   (4) 16
  57 16
   (4) 17
  58-61 19

Race Relations Act 1976—*continued* PAGE

s. 63 20
64 (1) 20
65 25
66 17
68 (6) 15, 23
(7) 15
70 18

Redundancy Payments Act 1965—

s. 1 (1) 157, 162, 166
(2) 164
2 ... ... 172, 178
(2) 171
(3) 173
(4) 121
(5) 173
3 (1) 214
(2) 163, 212
(2) (c) 137, 141
(3) 176
(5) 177
(9) 183, 213
4 215
5-7 ... ... 135, 140, 142
5 (1) 133, 143
(2) 140, 143-145, 148
6 145
(3) (b) 146
(4) 147
7 (1) 147
(3) 145
9 (2) (a) 352
(b) 164
11 190
13 179
15 190
(2) 160
17 (1) 161
18 183
19 (1) 161
21 183
22 (1) 220
25 (1) 157, 180
32 205
48 (4) 179
Schedule 1 ... ... 157, 160, 352
Schedule 2 144
Schedule 4 179

Redundancy Payments Rebates Regulations 1965 188

Rehabilitation of Offenders Act 1974—

s. 4 (2) 27
(3) (a) 27
(b) 26, 28, 290
(4) 27

Sex Discrimination Act 1975—

s. 1 (1) (b) 5
2 4
(1) 61
(2) 8

Sex Discrimination Act 1975—*continued* PAGE

										PAGE
s. 3 (1) (*b*) ...	...	...	...	...	...	...	...	...	...	6
4 ...	...	...	...	...	...	...	...	...	...	63
5 (3)	...	...	...	...	...	...	...	...	...	5
6 (1)	...	...	...	...	...	...	...	...	...	4, 59
(2) (*a*) ...	...	...	...	...	...	...	...	...	...	60
(*b*) ...	...	...	...	...	...	...	...	...	60, 61, 62	
(3)	...	...	...	...	...	...	...	...	...	7
(4)	...	...	...	...	...	...	...	...	...	8
(5)	...	...	...	...	...	...	...	...	...	60
(6)	...	...	...	...	...	...	...	...	...	60
(7)	...	...	...	...	...	...	...	...	...	62
7 ...	...	...	...	...	...	...	...	...	...	8
8 (5)	...	...	...	...	...	...	...	...	...	60
15	...	...	...	...	...	...	...	...	...	17
17	...	...	...	...	...	...	...	...	...	10
18	...	...	...	...	...	...	...	...	...	10
19	...	...	...	...	...	...	...	...	...	10
20	...	...	...	...	...	...	...	...	...	10
21	...	...	...	...	...	...	...	...	...	10
38	...	...	...	...	...	...	...	...	...	6
(3)	...	...	...	...	...	...	...	...	...	6
(5)	...	...	...	...	...	...	...	...	...	7
41	...	...	...	...	...	...	...	...	...	26
(3)	...	...	...	...	...	...	...	...	...	26
42	...	...	...	...	...	...	...	...	...	18
43	...	...	...	...	...	...	...	...	...	10
44	...	...	...	...	...	...	...	...	...	10
45	...	...	...	...	...	...	...	...	...	10
59	...	...	...	...	...	...	...	...	...	18
62	...	...	...	...	...	...	...	...	...	15
63	...	...	...	...	...	...	...	...	...	15
65	...	...	...	...	...	...	...	...	...	16
(3)	...	...	...	...	...	...	...	...	...	16
66	...	...	...	...	...	...	...	...	...	16
(4)	...	...	...	...	...	...	...	...	...	17
67-70	...	...	...	...	...	...	...	...	...	19
72	...	...	...	...	...	...	...	...	...	20
73 (1)	...	...	...	...	...	...	...	...	...	20
74	...	...	...	...	...	...	...	...	24, 350-351	
(2) (*b*)	...	...	...	...	...	...	...	...	...	24
75	...	...	...	...	...	...	...	...	...	17
76 (5)	...	...	...	...	...	...	...	...	...	15, 23
(6)	...	...	...	...	...	...	...	...	...	15
85	...	...	...	...	...	...	...	...	...	10

							PAGE
Sex Discrimination (Questions and Replies) Order 1975 ...				...		...	24, 25, 350
Social Security Act 1975	...	...	...	...	...	...	110
Social Security (Unemployment, Sickness and Invalidity Benefit) Amendment (No. 2) Regulations 1976 ...		...	...	...	...	...	326
Terms and Conditions of Employment Act 1959	...	...	...	...		86, 87
Trade Disputes Act 1906	...	...	...	...	...	...	91

Trade Union and Labour Relations Act 1974—

									PAGE
s. 1 (2)	...	...	...	...	...	...	...	...	246
13	...	...	...	...	...	...	...	91, 92, 93	
14	...	...	...	...	...	...	...	...	93
29 (1)	...	...	...	...	...	...	...	...	71, 91

Trade Union and Labour Relations Act 1974—*continued*   PAGE

s. 30 (1) 68, 83-84, 102, 247
    (1) (*c*) 85
  39 (1) 247
Schedule 1—
   para. 1 (2) 302
         3 302
         4 (1) 247, 380
         5 (2) 212
           (2) (*c*) 137, 141
           (5) 213
           (6) 214, 248
         6 (1) (*b*) 241, 258, 297
           (2) 241, 258, 296
           (2) (*a*) 274, 275, 278
               (*b*) 282
               (*c*) 290
           (4) 103, 259-260
           (4A) 262
           (5) 85, 259-260, 262, 268
           (5A) 268
           (6) 259-261
           (7) 292
           (8) 117, 124, 244, 274, 293, 300
           (9) 274
           (9) (*a*) 278
               (*c*) 290
         7 (2) 269
         9 (1) (*b*) 250
        10 107
           (*a*) 355
        13 255
           (2) 255
        18 (1) 270
        19 324
        20 (1) 319
        21 (4) 311
        26 (2) 336
           (4) 334
        30 (1) 352
           (2) 352
        32 (1) 253, 334
           (1) (*b*) 255
           (2) (*d*) 334
        33 247
Trade Union and Labour Relations (Amendment) Act 1976 ... 83, 259, 262
  s. 1 (*e*) 259
    3 (2) 91
      (5) 259

TABLE OF CASES

A

PAGE

Abernethy v. Mott, Hay & Anderson [1974] I.C.R. 323; 118 S.J. 294; [1974] I.T.R. 251; 16 K.I.R. 277; [1974] I.R.L.R. 213, C.A.; affirming [1973] I.T.R. 228; [1973] I.R.L.R. 123, N.I.R.C. ...   165, 273

Allen v. Flood [1898] A.C. 1   3

Amalgamated Union of Engineering Workers v. Sefton Engineering Co. [1976] I.R.L.R. 318, Industrial Tribunal   197

B

Barrel Plating and Phosphating Co. Ltd. v. Danks [1976] I.T.R. 148; [1976] 1 W.L.R. 879, Employment Appeal Tribunal   250

Basnett v. J. & A. Jackson [1976] I.C.R. 63   ...   . 233, 234, 330

Bateman v. British Leyland (U.K.) Ltd. [1974] I.C.R. 403; [1974] I.T.R. 266; 16 K.I.R. 284; [1974] I.R.L.R. 101, N.I.R.C.; affirming [1973] I.R.L.R. 265, Industrial Tribunal   346

Bedwell & Others v. Hellerman Deutsch Ltd. [1976] I.R.L.R. 98, Industrial Tribunal   57

Bentley Engineering Co. Ltd. v. Crown and Miller [1976] I.C.R. 225   ...   184, 356

Bernstein v. Bernstein Bros. [1969] I.T.R. 106, Industrial Tribunal   ...   161

Bessenden Properties Ltd. v. Corness [1974] I.R.L.R. 338, C.A.; affirming [1974] I.T.R. 128; [1973] I.R.L.R. 365, N.I.R.C.   293

Blackman v. Post Office [1974] I.C.R. 151; [1974] I.T.R. 122; [1974] I.R.L.R. 46, N.I.R.C. 275, 277

Blackwell v. G.E.C. Elliott Process Automation Ltd. [1976] I.R.L.R. 144, Employment Appeal Tribunal   330

Boston Deep Sea Fishing and Ice Co. v. Ansell (1888) 39 Ch.D. 339   ...   240

Breach v. Epsylon Industries Ltd. [1976] I.C.R. 316; [1976] I.R.L.R. 181, Employment Appeal Tribunal 138, 218

Brindley v. Tayside Health Board [1976] I.R.L.R. 364   21

British Broadcasting Corporation v. Ioannou [1975] Q.B. 781; [1975] I.C.R. 267; [1975] 3 W.L.R. 63; 119 S.J. 337; [1975] 2 All E.R. 999; [1975] I.T.R. 88; 18 Man. Law 19; [1975] I.R.L.R. 184, C.A.; affirming sub nom. Ioannou v. British Broadcasting Corporation [1974] I.C.R. 414; sub nom. British Broadcasting Corporation v. Ioannou [1974] I.T.R. 213; [1974] I.R.L.R. 77, N.I.R.C.   ...   160, 216, 254

Brodie v. Startrite Engineering Co. Ltd. [1976] I.R.L.R. 101, Industrial Tribunal 56, 58

PAGE

Buckland *v.* Dowty Rotol Ltd. [1976] I.R.L.R. 162, Industrial Tribunal   57

Budgen & Co. *v.* Thomas (C.) [1976] I.C.R. 344; [1976] I.R.L.R. 174, Employment Appeal Tribunal   307

C

Camellia Tanker Ltd. S.A. *v.* International Transport Workers Federation & Nelson [1976] I.C.R. 274; [1976] I.R.L.R. 183, 190, C.A.   ...   92-94

Capper Pass Ltd. *v.* Lawton [1976] I.R.L.R. 366; *The Times*, October 20, 1976, Employment Appeal Tribunal   51

Chapman *v.* Goonvean & Rostowrack China Clay Co. Ltd. [1973] I.C.R. 310; [1973] 1 W.L.R. 678; 117 S.J. 416; [1973] 2 All E.R. 1063; [1974] I.T.R. 379; 14 K.I.R. 382, C.A.; affirming [1973] I.C.R. 50; [1972] 1 W.L.R. 1634; 116 S.J. 967; [1973] 1 All E.R. 218; [1972] I.R.L.R. 124; 13 K.I.R. 308; [1973] I.T.R. 77, N.I.R.C.   ...   171

Chappell *v.* Times Newspapers [1975] I.C.R. 145; [1975] 1 W.L.R. 482; 119 S.J. 82; [1975] 2 All E.R. 233; [1975] I.R.L.R. 90; 18 Man. Law 5, C.A. 220, 231

Clarkson International Tools Ltd. *v.* Short [1973] I.C.R. 191; 14 K.I.R. 400; [1973] I.T.R. 185; [1973] I.R.L.R. 90, N.I.R.C.   296

Coleman *v.* Magnet Joinery Ltd. [1975] I.C.R. 46; [1975] K.I.L.R. 139; [1974] I.R.L.R. 343, C.A.; affirming [1974] I.C.R. 25; [1974] I.T.R. 74, N.I.R.C.   316

Collier *v.* Sunday Referee Publishing Co. Ltd. [1940] 2 K.B. 647   ...   138

Cooper *v.* British Steel Corporation [1975] I.C.R. 454; 119 S.J. 743; [1975] I.T.R. 137; [1975] I.R.L.R. 308   328

Costain Civil Engineering Ltd. *v.* Draycott (1976) *The Times*, November 12, 1976, Employment Appeal Tribunal   162

Coulson *v.* City of London Polytechnic [1976] 1 W.L.R. 834; [1976] 3 All E.R. 234; [1976] I.T.R. 121, Employment Appeal Tribunal   ...   249, 354, 355

Council of Engineering Institutions *v.* Maddison [1976] I.R.L.R. 389; *The Times*, August 3, 1976, Employment Appeal Tribunal   334

Cox *v.* Philips Industries Ltd. [1976] I.C.R. 138; [1976] 1 W.L.R. 638; [1976] 3 All E.R. 161   ...   .   17, 219, 232

Crompton *v.* Truly Fair (International) Ltd. [1975] I.C.R. 359; [1975] I.T.R. 114; [1975] I.R.L.R. 250   181

Cuthbertson *v.* A.M.L. Distributors [1975] I.R.L.R. 228, Industrial Tribunal   237

D

Da Costa *v.* Optolis [1976] I.R.L.R. 178, Employment Appeal Tribunal   273, 287

Dacres *v.* Walls Meat Co. Ltd. [1976] I.C.R. 44   349

Dada *v.* Metal Box Co. Ltd. [1974] I.C.R. 559; [1974] I.T.R. 390; [1974] I.R.L.R. 251, N.I.R.C.   342

PAGE

Dedman v. British Building and Engineering Appliances Ltd. [1974]
I.C.R. 53; [1974] 1 W.L.R. 171; (1973) S.J. 938; [1974] 1 All E.R.
520; [1974] I.T.R. 100; (1973) 16 K.I.R. 1; [1973] I.R.L.R. 379,
C.A.; affirming *sub nom.* British Building & Engineering Appliances
v. Dedman [1973] I.C.R. 82; [1973] I.T.R. 130, N.I.R.C.   313

De Francesco v. Barnum (1890) 43 Ch.D. 165   231

Devis (W.) & Sons Ltd. v. Atkins [1976] I.R.L.R. 428, *The Times*,
November 2, 1976, C.A.; affirming [1976] 1 W.L.R. 393; [1976]
2 All E.R. 822; [1976] I.R.L.R. 16   272

Dixon v. Stenor Ltd. [1973] I.C.R. 157; [1973] I.R.L.R. 28; [1973]
I.T.R. 141, N.I.R.C.   215

Dugdale and Others v. Kraft Foods Ltd. [1976] I.R.L.R. 368; *The
Times*, October 29, 1976, Employment Appeal Tribunal   58

Dunning (A. J.) & Sons Ltd. (Shop Fitters) v. Jacomb [1973] I.C.R. 448;
[1973] I.T.R. 453; 15 K.I.R. 9; [1973] I.R.L.R. 206, N.I.R.C. ...   308

E

Earl v. Slater and Wheeler (Airlyne) [1972] I.C.R. 508; [1973] 1 W.L.R.
51; 117 S.J. 14; [1973] 1 All E.R. 145; [1973] I.T.R. 33; (1972)
13 K.I.R. 319; [1972] I.R.L.R. 115, N.I.R.C., affirming [1972] I.T.R.
387, Industrial Tribunal 272, 307, 308

Evenden v. Guildford City Association Football Club Ltd. [1975] Q.B.
917; [1975] I.C.R. 367; [1975] 3 W.L.R. 251; 119 S.J. 460; [1975]
3 All E.R. 269; [1975] I.T.R. 95; [1975] I.R.L.R. 213, C.A.;
reversing [1974] I.C.R. 554; [1974] I.R.L.R. 285, N.I.R.C.   182

Everwear Candlewick Ltd. v. Isaac [1974] I.C.R. 525; [1974] 3 All E.R.
24; [1974] I.T.R. 334; 17 K.I.R. 70, N.I.R.C.   330

F

Fanshaw v. Robinson & Sons Ltd. [1975] I.R.L.R. 165, Industrial
Tribunal   218

Farmeary v. Veterinary Drug Co. Ltd. [1976] I.R.L.R. 322, Industrial
Tribunal   263

Ferguson v. John Dawson & Partners (Contractors) Ltd. [1976] I.R.L.R.
346; *The Times*, July 23, 1976   158

Ferrybridge Six, the case of, *see* Sarvent v. C.E.G.B.

Fielding (Harold) Ltd. v. Mansi [1974] I.C.R. 347; [1974] 1 All E.R.
1035; [1974] I.T.R. 208; [1974] I.R.L.R. 79, N.I.R.C.   359

Flint v. Eastern Electricity Board [1975] I.C.R. 395; [1975] I.T.R. 152;
[1975] I.R.L.R. 277 ... ... 346, 347

Fougère v. Phoenix Motor Co. Ltd. [1976] I.R.L.R. 259; *The Times*,
July 7, 1976, Employment Appeal Tribunal   325

G

Gascol Conversions Ltd. v. Mercer [1974] I.C.R. 420; 118 S.J. 219;
[1974] I.T.R. 282; [1975] K.I.L.R. 149; [1974] I.R.L.R. 155, C.A.   186

Gilbert v. I. Goldstone Ltd. [1976] I.R.L.R. 257, Employment Appeal
Tribunal   218

PAGE

Gorfin v. Distressed Gentlefolks Aid Association [1973] I.R.L.R. 290,
   Industrial Tribunal   298
Graham v. Todd (Anthony) (Haulage) Ltd. [1975] I.R.L.R. 45, Industrial
   Tribunal   32
Grundy (Teddington) Ltd. v. Willis [1976] I.C.R. 323; [1976] I.R.L.R.
   118   295

H

Hamblin v. London Borough of Ealing [1975] I.R.L.R. 354, Industrial
   Tribunal   275
Hammond v. Haigh Castle & Co. Ltd. [1973] I.C.R. 148; [1973] 2 All
   E.R. 289; [1973] I.T.R. 199; 14 K.I.R. 407; [1973] I.R.L.R. 91,
   N.I.R.C. 312, 314
Hare v. Murphy Brothers Ltd. [1974] I.C.R. 603; 118 S.J. 596; [1974]
   3 All E.R. 940; [1975] K.I.L.R. 31; [1974] I.R.L.R. 342; [1975]
   I.T.R. 1, C.A.; affirming [1973] I.C.R. 331; [1973] I.T.R. 458;
   16 K.I.R. 57, N.I.R.C.   222
Harris & Russell Ltd. v. Slingsby [1973] I.C.R. 454; [1973] 3 All E.R.
   31; [1973] I.T.R. 433; 15 K.I.R. 157; [1973] I.R.L.R. 221,
   N.I.R.C.   285
Hebden v. Forsey & Son [1973] I.C.R. 607; [1973] I.T.R. 656; 15 K.I.R.
   161; [1973] I.R.L.R. 344, N.I.R.C.   224
Hedley Byrne & Co. v. Heller & Partners [1964] A.C. 465; [1963] 3
   W.L.R. 101; 107 S.J. 454; [1963] 2 All E.R. 575; [1963] 1 Lloyd's
   Rep. 485, H.L.; affirming [1962] 1 Q.B. 396; [1961] 3 W.L.R.
   1225; 105 S.J. 910; [1961] 3 All E.R. 891; [1961] C.L.Y. 518, C.A.;
   affirming The Times, December 21, 1960; [1960] C.L.Y. 186   ...   244
Hill v. Parsons (C. A.) & Co. Ltd. [1972] 1 Ch. 305; [1971] 3 W.L.R.
   995; 115 S.J. 868; [1971] 3 All E.R. 1345, C.A.   231
Hopkinson v. E.P. Publishing Ltd. [1976] I.R.L.R. 99, Industrial Tribunal   55

J

Jacobs v. Norsalka Ltd. (1976) The Times, July 5, 1976, Employment
   Appeal Tribunal   239
James v. Waltham Holy Cross U.D.C. [1973] I.C.R. 398; [1973] I.T.R.
   467; 14 K.I.R. 576; [1973] I.R.L.R. 202, N.I.R.C. 305, 306
Jones v. Sherman (Harry) Ltd. [1969] I.T.R. 63, Industrial Tribunal   ...   136

K

Kenmir v. Frizzell [1968] 1 W.L.R. 329; [1968] 1 All E.R. 414; [1968]
   I.T.R. 159; 3 K.I.R. 240, D.C.   180

PAGE

L

Ladd v. Marshall [1954] 1 W.L.R. 1489; 98 S.J. 870; [1954] 3 All E.R. 745, C.A.   346

Langston v. Amalgamated Union of Engineering Workers [1974] I.C.R. 180; [1974] 1 W.L.R. 185; (1973) 118 S.J. 97; [1974] 1 All E.R. 980; (1973) 16 K.I.R. 139; *sub nom.* Langston v. Amalgamated Union of Engineering Workers (Engineering Section) and Chrysler United Kingdom [1974] I.R.L.R. 15, C.A.; reversing [1973] I.C.R. 211; [1973] 1 W.L.R. 521; 117 S.J. 185; [1973] 2 All E.R. 430; 14 K.I.R. 417; *sub nom.* Langston v. Amalgamated Union of Engineering Workers and Chrysler (U.K.) [1973] I.R.L.R. 82, N.I.R.C.   138

Lesney Products & Co. Ltd. v. Nolan; Lesney Products v. Nolan (1976) *The Times*, October 21, 1976, C.A.   171

Lewis Shops Group v. Wiggins [1973] I.C.R. 335; [1974] I.T.R. 55; 14 K.I.R. 528; [1973] I.R.L.R. 205, N.I.R.C.; reversing *sub nom.* Wiggins (F.) v. Lewis Shops Group, The [1973] I.R.L.R. 114, Industrial Tribunal   307

Lloyd v. Brassey [1969] 2 Q.B. 98; [1969] 2 W.L.R. 310; 112 S.J. 984; [1969] 1 All E.R. 382; [1969] I.T.R. 100; 5 K.I.R. 393, C.A.; reversing [1968] 2 Q.B. 832; [1968] 3 W.L.R. 526; [1968] 2 All E.R. 1228; (1968) 112 S.J. 638; [1968] I.T.R. 324; 5 K.I.R. 10, D.C. ...   157

Lowndes v. Specialist Heavy Engineering Ltd. [1976] I.R.L.R. 246, Employment Appeal Tribunal   308

M

McCarthy v. Burroughs Machines Ltd. [1975] I.T.R. 46, Industrial Tribunal   136

McDonald v. Applied Art Glass Co. Ltd. [1976] I.R.L.R. 130, Industrial Tribunal 21, 22

McGregor v. Gibbings Amusements Ltd. [1975] I.T.R. 64, Industrial Tribunal   347

Maher v. Fram Gerrard Ltd. [1974] I.C.R. 31; (1973) 117 S.J. 911; [1974] 1 All E.R. 449; [1974] I.T.R. 36; (1973) 16 K.I.R. 62, N.I.R.C.   168

Maris v. Rotherham Corporation [1974] I.C.R. 435; [1974] 2 All E.R. 776; [1974] I.T.R. 288; 16 K.I.R. 466; [1974] I.R.L.R. 147, N.I.R.C.   328

Marler (E. T.) Ltd. v. Robertson [1974] I.C.R. 72, N.I.R.C.   345

Marriot v. Oxford and District Co-operative Society Ltd. [1970] 1 Q.B. 186; [1969] 3 W.L.R. 984; 113 S.J. 655; [1969] 3 All E.R. 1126; 7 K.I.R. 219; [1969] I.T.R. 377, C.A.; reversing [1969] 1 W.L.R. 254; 113 S.J. 34; [1969] 1 All E.R. 471; 6 K.I.R. 479; [1969] I.T.R. 125, D.C.   219

Marshall v. Harland & Wolff Ltd. [1972] 1 W.L.R. 899; 116 S.J. 484; [1972] 2 All E.R. 715; [1972] I.T.R. 132; [1972] I.C.R. 101; [1972] I.R.L.R. 90, N.I.R.C. 223, 234, 279

Maulik v. Air India [1974] I.C.R. 528; [1974] I.T.R. 348, N.I.R.C.; affirming [1974] I.T.R. 257, Industrial Tribunal   251

Mercia Rubber Mouldings Ltd. v. Lingwood [1974] I.C.R. 256; [1974] I.R.L.R. 82, N.I.R.C.   298

PAGE

Merseyside and North Wales Electricity Board *v.* Taylor [1975] I.C.R.
185; 119 S.J. 272; [1975] I.T.R. 52; [1975] I.R.L.R. 60   281

Modern Injection Moulds Ltd. *v.* Price (J.) [1976] I.C.R. 370; [1976]
I.R.L.R. 172, Employment Appeal Tribunal   296

Morris *v.* Scott & Knowles [1976] I.R.L.R. 238, Industrial Tribunal ...   62

Morton Sundour Fabrics *v.* Shaw [1967] I.T.R. 84; (1966) 2 K.I.R. 1;
[1966] C.L.Y. 4472, D.C. 166, 214

N

Norton Tool Co. Ltd. *v.* Tewson [1972] I.C.R. 501; [1973] 1 W.L.R.
45; 117 S.J. 33; [1973] 1 All E.R. 183; (1972) 13 K.I.R. 328;
[1973] I.T.R. 23, N.I.R.C. 238, 324, 326

O

O'Brien *v.* Associated Fire Alarms Ltd. [1968] 1 W.L.R. 1916; (1968)
112 S.J. 232; [1969] 1 All E.R. 93; 3 K.I.R. 223; [1968] I.T.R. 182,
C.A.   168

Ord *v.* Maidstone & District Hospital Management Committee [1974]
I.C.R. 369; [1974] 2 All E.R. 343; [1974] I.T.R. 243; [1974]
I.R.L.R. 80, N.I.R.C.   250

P

Peskett *v.* Robinsons (Woking) Ltd. [1976] I.R.L.R. 134, Industrial
Tribunal   56

Portec (U.K.) Ltd. *v.* Mogenson [1976] I.C.R. 396; [1976] I.R.L.R. 209,
Employment Appeal Tribunal   251

R

Rowbotham *v.* Lee (Arthur) & Sons Ltd. [1975] I.C.R. 109; [1975]
I.T.R. 145; [1974] I.R.L.R. 377   168

S

St. Anne's Board Mill *v.* Brien [1973] I.C.R. 444; [1973] I.T.R. 463;
sub nom. St. Anne's Board Mill *v.* Brien, Kelly, Rees & Grace [1973]
I.R.L.R. 309, N.I.R.C.   308

Sanders *v.* Neale (Ernest A.) Ltd. [1974] I.C.R. 565; [1974] 3 All E.R.
327; [1974] I.T.R. 395; [1975] K.I.L.R. 77; [1974] I.R.L.R. 236,
N.I.R.C.   231

Sarvent & Others *v.* Central Electricity Generating Board [1976] I.R.L.R.
66, Industrial Tribunal 85, 262, 268

Scottish Co-operative Wholesale Society Ltd. *v.* Lloyd [1973] I.C.R. 137;
[1973] I.T.R. 178; [1973] I.R.L.R. 93, N.I.R.C. 306, 307

PAGE

Secretary of State for Employment *v.* ASLEF (No. 2) [1972] 2 Q.B. 455;
[1972] 2 W.L.R. 1370; 116 S.J. 467; [1972] 2 All E.R. 949; [1972]
I.C.R. 19; 13 K.I.R. 1, C.A.; affirming *sub nom.* Secretary of State
for Employment *v.* ASLEF [1972] 2 Q.B. 443; [1972] 2 W.L.R.
1362; 116 S.J. 333, 434; [1972] 2 All E.R. 853; [1972] I.C.R. 7,
N.I.R.C. 35, 284

Sharp and Lister *v.* Mogil Motors (Stirling) Ltd. [1976] I.R.L.R. 132,
Industrial Tribunal 56

Simmons *v.* Hoover [1976] I.R.L.R. 266; *The Times*, July 20, 1976,
Employment Appeal Tribunal 172

Singh *v.* London Country Bus Services Ltd. [1976] I.R.L.R. 176, Employment Appeal Tribunal 278, 287

Spelman *v.* Garnham (George) [1968] I.T.R. 370, D.C. 141

Stock *v.* Frank Jones (Tipton) Ltd. [1976] I.C.R. 237; I.T.R. 63 ... 269

Stocks *v.* Magna Merchants Ltd. [1973] 1 W.L.R. 1505; [1973] I.C.R.
530; 117 S.J. 760; [1973] 2 All E.R. 329 234

T

Tan *v.* Berry Bros. and Rudd [1974] I.C.R. 586; [1974] I.R.L.R. 244,
N.I.R.C. 279

Tarmac Roadstone Holdings Ltd. *v.* Peacock [1973] I.C.R. 273; [1973]
1 W.L.R. 594; 117 S.J. 186; [1973] 2 All E.R. 485; (1973) 14 K.I.R.
277; [1973] I.T.R. 300; *sub nom.* Tarmac Roadstone Holdings *v.*
Peacock, Lockwood, Young [1973] I.R.L.R. 157, C.A. 186

Thomas Wragg & Sons [1976] I.C.R. 313; [1976] I.R.L.R. 145, Employment Appeal Tribunal 176

Thompson & Others *v.* Eaton Ltd. [1976] I.C.R. 336; *The Times*, May
19, 1976, Employment Appeal Tribunal 269

Times Newspapers Ltd. *v.* Bartlett [1976] I.T.R. 106, Employment
Appeal Tribunal 168

Treganowan *v.* Knee (Robert) & Co. Ltd. [1975] I.C.R. 405; 119 S.J.
490; [1975] I.T.R. 121; [1975] I.R.L.R. 247; affirming [1975]
I.R.L.R. 112, Industrial Tribunal 238, 298

Tzoukka *v.* Potomac Restaurants Ltd. [1968] I.T.R. 260 187

U

United Kingdom Atomic Energy Authority *v.* Claydon [1974] I.C.R.
128; [1974] I.T.R. 185; (1973) 16 K.I.R. 94; [1974] I.R.L.R. 6,
N.I.R.C. 167

V

Vokes Ltd. *v.* Bear [1974] I.C.R. 1; [1974] I.T.R. 85; (1973) 15 K.I.R.
302; [1973] I.R.L.R. 363, N.I.R.C. 296

W

Waddington *v.* Leicester Council for Voluntary Service [1977] I.R.L.R. 32; (1976) *The Times*, December 17, 1976   55

Watling *v.* William Bird & Son Contractors Ltd. [1976] I.T.R. 70 ...   338

White *v.* University of Manchester [1976] I.C.R. 419; 120 S.J. 503, Employment Appeal Tribunal   342

Wilson *v.* Maynard Shipbuilding Consultants AB, [1976] I.R.L.R. 385; *The Times*, October 12, 1976, Employment Appeal Tribunal ...   252

Wilson *v.* Racher [1974] I.C.R. 428; (1974) 16 K.I.R. 212; [1974] I.R.L.R. 114, C.A.   229

Wishart *v.* National Coal Board [1974] I.C.R. 460; [1974] I.T.R. 320; N.I.R.C.   357

Woodhouse *v.* Brotherhood (Peter) Ltd. [1972] 2 Q.B. 520; [1972] 3 W.L.R. 215; 116 S.J. 467; [1972] 3 All E.R. 91; [1972] I.C.R. 186; 13 K.I.R. 45, C.A.; reversing on first appeal [1972] 1 W.L.R. 401; (1971) 116 S.J. 142; [1972] 1 All E.R. 1047; 12 K.I.R. 213; *sub nom.* Woodhouse & Staton *v.* Brotherhood (Peter) Ltd. [1972] I.T.R. 110, N.I.R.C.   181

Wragg (Thomas) & Sons *v.* Wood, *see* Thomas Wragg & Sons *v.* Wood.

Y

Yorkshire Engineering and Welding Co. *v.* Burnham [1974] I.C.R. 77; [1974] 1 W.L.R. 206; (1973) 118 S.J. 97; [1973] 3 All E.R. 1176; [1973] I.T.R. 621; [1973] I.R.L.R. 316; N.I.R.C.   234

LIST OF ABBREVIATIONS
used in the text

ACAS — Advisory, Conciliation and Arbitration Service

CAC — Central Arbitration Committee
CBI — Confederation of British Industries
CEA — Contracts of Employment Act 1972

EAT — Employment Appeal Tribunal
EOC — Equal Opportunities Commission
EPA — Employment Protection Act 1975

GOQ — Genuine Occupational Qualification

ICR — Industrial Cases Reports
IRLR — Industrial Relations Law Reports
ITR — Industrial Tribunal Reports
ITF — International Transport Workers Federation

NIRC — National Industrial Relations Court

RPA — Redundancy Payments Act 1965
RRA — Race Relations Act 1976

SDA — Sex Discrimination Act 1975

TUALRA — Trade Union and Labour Relations Act 1974
TUC — Trades Unions Congress

In Chapter 1 the term " the Commission " is used to include both the Equal Opportunities Commission and the Commission for Racial Equality.

INTRODUCTION

Employment Law has undergone enormous changes during the last four years. Indeed, until 1963 (when the first Contracts of Employment Act was passed) there were very few Statutes directly affecting the legal relationship of employer and employee.

The Truck Acts commencing in 1831 had provided that manual workers had to be paid in " current coin of the realm " and the Factories Acts had introduced various measures with a view to providing greater safety at work for employees.

The basic principle, however, was—and in theory still is—that a contract of employment was a matter for negotiation between the parties. The employer and the employee could agree the terms of the contract and there was virtually no limit or restriction on those terms. To-day there are so many statutory exceptions to the basic principle that, for all practical purposes, the principle has been virtually removed. There are now more than seventy Acts of Parliament (quite apart from various statutory instruments and regulations) which affect the relationship of employer and employee.

The latest statutory provisions have changed the whole concept of the Law of Employment and the law now bears very little resemblance to what it was even four or five years ago.

The purpose of this book is to summarise and identify the Law of Employment, as it exists to-day, in the light of this most recent legislation.

This will be done by, as it were, tracing the " history " of an employer/employee relationship from the point of time when the employer decides to advertise for applicants for a particular job, through the appointment and the employment itself and all the problems that may then arise, and ending with the termination of the employment of that employee and a possible appearance before an Industrial Tribunal.

Before embarking on this, what are the recent Acts of Parliament which have brought about these recent major and far-reaching changes in the Law of Employment?

The main Acts are as follows:—

1. **The Contracts of Employment Act 1972** which came into force on 27th July 1972, although the Act in fact only up-dated and consolidated the original Contracts of Employment Act 1963, as amended by subsequent legislation. The CEA (as it will be referred to in the ensuing pages) lays down certain minimum periods of notice to terminate a contract of employment and also requires employers to give to their employees written statements of certain terms of their contracts. Already, the CEA has been amended by subsequent legislation—in particular by the Employment Protection Act 1975.

2. **The Redundancy Payments Act 1965** (to be referred to as the RPA) which became law on 5th August 1965, and provided for employers to make payments to employees who are dismissed because of redundancy or who are, in certain circumstances, laid off or put on short-time. Again, there have been substantial amendments to this Act since 1965—in particular by the Employment Protection Act 1975.

3. **The Trade Union and Labour Relations Act 1974** (to be referred to as the TUALRA) which was enacted on 31st July 1974, although most of its provisions did not come into force until 16th September 1974. For the purposes of this book, the most important part of the Act relates to the right of every employee (with a few exceptions) not to be " unfairly dismissed ". This right has been part of the law since 28th February 1972, when it was introduced under the Industrial Relations Act 1971. The relevant parts of the 1971 Act were re-enacted by section 1(2) and the First Schedule of TUALRA.

The Trade Union and Labour Relations (Amendment) Act 1976 came into force on 25th March 1976, and amends certain parts of TUALRA, the most relevant amendment for these purposes being that relating to the " closed shop " provisions of the Act.

Certain amendments to TUALRA were also introduced by the Employment Protection Act 1975 with effect from 1st June 1976.

4. **The Equal Pay Act 1970** which did not come into force until 29th December 1975, the object of the Act being to prevent discrimination, as regards terms and conditions of employment, between men and women. The Act is amended by and is now set out in full in its amended form in Schedule 1 of the Sex Discrimination Act 1975.

5. **The Sex Discrimination Act 1975** (to be referred to as the SDA) also came into force on 29th December 1975. The Act goes much further than the Equal Pay Act (which only deals with the actual terms and conditions of employment) and it renders unlawful certain kinds of sex discrimination and discrimination on the ground of marriage. The object of the SDA is to promote equality of opportunity between men and women generally and to this end the Equal Opportunities Commission has now been established.

6. **The Employment Protection Act 1975** (to be referred to as the EPA) received the Royal Assent on 12th November 1975 and various parts of the Act come into force at different times—as designated by the Secretary of State. These will be no ed in the relevant chapters. This Act is a substantial piece of legislation. Its aim is to improve industrial relations generally and it introduces a great number of new rights for employees. It also introduces considerable amendments to certain parts of the existing law, *e.g.* with regard to unfair dismissal, redundancies and contracts of employment generally.

7. **The Race Relations Act 1976** (to be referred to as the RRA) received the Royal Assent on 22nd November 1976 and will repeal and replace the earlier legislation on racial discrimination. The Act is framed in very similar terms to the SDA.

It does now seem that there is to be a comparative " lull " in Employment Law legislation. The present Government has indicated that it has achieved its aims with regard to changes in Employment Law, other than with regard to industrial democracy and worker participation (where the report of the Committee of Enquiry under the Chairmanship of Lord Bullock is being considered).

It also seems that there will be some stability for the future, as it is now unlikely that this part of the law will be affected in the foreseeable future by Party politics.

Employer and Employee

PART I

BEFORE THE EMPLOYMENT COMMENCES

CHAPTER 1

ENGAGING AN EMPLOYEE

The basic principle is that an employer can select any employee he requires for a particular job.

At the end of the last century a well known judge in the House of Lords stated:

" An employer may refuse to employ an employee for the most mistaken, capricious, malicious or morally reprehensible motives that can be conceived, but the employee has no right of action against him."[1]

To-day, however, although the basic principle still holds good, it has to be treated with very great care by employers. There are several important statutory exceptions to it and these must now be considered.

DISCRIMINATION IN ENGAGEMENT OF AN EMPLOYEE

Sex Discrimination

Perhaps, the most important exception to the general principle is contained in the **Sex Discrimination Act 1975.**

Under the SDA it is—since 29th December 1975—unlawful to discriminate in employment matters on the grounds of sex or marital status. The Act sets out various exceptions to this general principle and they will be considered later.

---

[1] Lord Davey in *Allen v. Flood* (1898) A.C. 1.

Before we can consider the practical implications of the SDA to the employer, we must first consider the present law as contained in those parts of the Act which deal with employment matters.

Section 6(1) deals with the position both at and prior to the offer of employment. It provides as follows:—

"It is unlawful for a person, in relation to employment by him at an establishment in Great Britain, to **discriminate** against a woman—

 (a) in the arrangements he makes for the purpose of determining who should be offered that employment, **or**

 (b) in the terms on which he offers her that employment, **or**

 (c) by refusing or deliberately omitting to offer her that employment".

Thus, the " problems " begin for an employer even before he takes on a particular employee.

Although section 6 refers to discrimination " against a woman ", the principle applies equally to discrimination against men, section 2 of the Act providing that the relevant parts (II and III) of the SDA " are to be read as applying equally to the treatment of men ". Indeed, the first reported Tribunal case under the SDA was brought by a man (see page 21). It is, however, still lawful for a woman to receive special treatment in connection with pregnancy or childbirth.

Forms of sex discrimination

" **Discrimination** " is defined in some detail by the Act—see sections 1 to 5. The effect of these sections in the employment field is that discrimination can be either direct or indirect and can be either on the ground of sex or marital status.

Direct discrimination arises when a person is treated less favourably than a member of the opposite sex or when a married person of either sex is treated less favourably than an unmarried person of the same sex. It is not, however, unlawful to discriminate against single people as such. The SDA does not say that married people should be treated in the same way, but that people should not be worse off because they are married.

The comparison with the other person must be such " that the relevant circumstances in the one case are the same, or not materially different, in the other " (s. 5(3)).

These words will obviously give rise to arguments in construing the SDA and in cases that may be brought before an Industrial Tribunal. It will be for the Tribunal to decide the facts in each particular case.

Direct discrimination will normally be obvious. Any less favourable treatment is enough to get a claim off the ground. For example, the Airline Company which refuses to employ a male " stewardess " or the shop which refuses to employ a male cashier or shop assistant.

The intention of the employer is not relevant here. It is the **EFFECT** of the discriminatory practice which will be unlawful.

Indirect discrimination arises in the employment field where an employer applies to a specific woman a requirement or condition which applies or would apply equally to a man, but—

    (i) which is such that the proportion of women who **can** comply with it is considerably smaller than the proportion of men who can comply with it **and**

    (ii) which he cannot show to be **justifiable** irrespective of sex **and**

    (iii) which is to the woman's **detriment** because she cannot comply with it.

The typical example is that of a physical requirement such as weight or height which is not really needed for the job but which effectively bans one sex from it.

As indicated previously, the above provisions (which are contained in section 1(1)(b)) apply equally to indirect discrimination against men.

Similar provisions are contained in section 3(1)(*b*) relating to a requirement or condition which is detrimental to a **married person**. In that situation the comparison of the proportion of married persons with the proportion of unmarried persons " who can comply " is made between persons of the **same** sex. As referred to under " Direct discrimination ", however, this provision only relates to married people—**not** to the single person.

In all indirect discrimination cases it is interesting to note that the proportion of persons suffering discrimination has to be **considerably** smaller than the proportion who **can** comply if the discrimination is to be unlawful. In each case the question will be determined by the tribunal hearing the case by reference to all the facts.

In view of these provisions of the SDA, an employer is at risk even before he takes on an employee.

The employer must not discriminate in **recruiting** for the job.

If the employer **advertises** a particular vacancy, he must take care that the advertisement itself is not discriminatory. **Section 38** of the SDA provides that it is unlawful for a person to publish, or place for publication, an advertisement which indicates—or might reasonably be understood as indicating— an intention to do an act which is, or might be, unlawful discrimination.

The SDA specifically provides in section 38(3) that a job description with a sexual connotation, *e.g.* " waiter ", " sales-girl ", " postman " or " stewardess ", **shall** be taken to indicate an intention to discriminate unless the advertisement contains an indication to the contrary. This does not mean that such words cannot lawfully be used in job advertisements. It does, however, mean that where they are used the advertisement must make it clear that no discrimination is intended. This can be done either by using job descriptions applicable to both sexes (" waiter or waitress ") or by actually saying that the job is open to both men and women. A preliminary note issued by the Equal Opportunities Commission already suggests that an advertisement might well refer to—" candidates (men or women) . . . ".

Perhaps, we shall shortly see both in advertisements and on documents, notepaper, invoices, etc., words of reference such as—" An Equal Opportunity Employer ". This is, of course, something which has been common in America for a number of years.

It should be noted that the **publisher** of an advertisement made unlawful under the SDA is also liable, but this liability will not arise if he can show that—

> (*a*) he relied on a statement by the person placing the advertisement to the effect that it was not unlawful **and**
>
> (*b*) it was reasonable for him to rely on that statement.

Here again, however, the employer must take care. If he places an advertisement and knowingly or recklessly makes a materially false or misleading statement to the publisher as to its lawfulness, then he (the employer) can be prosecuted and punished on summary conviction with a fine of up to £400.[1]

Exceptions

The exceptions to the requirement that employers must not discriminate against their employees or against potential employees can be summarised as follows:—

(1) **Private households and small firms**

There will be no discrimination (either on the ground of sex or against married persons) if the employment in question is for the purposes of a private household or if the employer (together with any associated employers) does not employ a total of more than five persons (which will include part-time employees but not persons employed in a private household).[2] If the employer has more than one establishment, it is the total of **all** his employees which will be relevant. The small firms exemption under this head is **not** to be

---

[1] SDA, s. 38(5).
[2] SDA, s. 6(3).

removed by the provisions of the Employment Protection Act 1975 (see page 253).

(2) Pregnancy, childbirth, death and retirement.

It is not unlawful under the SDA for an employer to discriminate:

(a) by offering special treatment to women in connection with pregnancy or childbirth[1] or

(b) in the provision made in relation to death or retirement[2] (*e.g.* retirement age in a pension scheme).

(3) Genuine occupational qualification

Discrimination on the ground of sex by an employer in recruiting for a job (or in providing opportunities for promotion, transfer, training, etc.) will not be unlawful where a person's sex is a **genuine occupational qualification** for the job. This exception does not cover discrimination against married persons.

The SDA sets out in detail in **section 7** the criteria for determining whether a person's sex is a genuine occupation qualification—already popularly referred to as a GOQ.

Establishment of a GOQ, however, is not an automatic exception; the employer must show in each case that the criteria set out do in fact apply to the particular job in question. In addition, a GOQ exception will not apply where the employer already has enough people of the right sex who are capable of doing the job and whom it would be reasonable to employ in order to meet the employer's likely requirements " without undue inconvenience ".

A person's sex is a **genuine occupational qualification** for a job in the following eight cases:—

(a) where the essential nature of the job calls for a man (or woman) for reasons of **physiology** (excluding physical strength or stamina) or in dramatic performances or other entertainment for reasons of **authenticity,** so that in either case the essential nature of the job

---

[1] SDA, s. 2(2).
[2] SDA, s. 6(4).

would be materially different if carried out by a person of the other sex.

(*b*) where considerations of **decency or privacy** require the job to be held by a man (or woman) **either** because it is likely to involve physical contact between the employee and men (or women) in circumstances where they might reasonably object to the employee being of the opposite sex **or** because the employee is likely to work in the presence of people who are in a state of undress or are using sanitary facilities and who might reasonably object to the presence of a person of the opposite sex.

(*c*) where **the nature or location of the establishment** makes it impracticable for the employee to live in premises other than those provided by the employer **and** the only available premises do not provide separate sleeping accommodation for each sex and sanitary facilities which can be used by one sex in privacy from the other **and** it is not reasonable to expect the employer either to equip those premises with accommodation and facilities or to provide other premises for the particular employee.   The standard example invariably given under this head is the lighthouse keeper.

(*d*) where the job is in a **single-sex establishment** (or part of an establishment) for persons requiring special care, supervision or attention and it is reasonable, given the character of the establishment, that the job should be held by someone of the same sex.

Examples here would be employment in prisons and hospitals.   The exception will not automatically apply to all jobs in the establishment; the employer will have to show in relation to any particular job that the character of the establishment requires **that job** to be held by a person of the same sex.

(*e*) where the holder of the job provides individuals with personal services promoting their **welfare or education** and those services can most effectively be provided by a man (or a woman), *e.g.* some probation officers or welfare workers.

(*f*) where there is a **legal bar** or restriction imposed by law and regulating the employment of women, *e.g.* the Factories Act 1961 provisions limiting the times at which women may work in certain places.

(*g*) where the job involves **work outside the United Kingdom** in a country whose laws or customs are such that the job can only be done effectively by a man (or woman) *e.g.* work in an Arab Country.

(*h*) where the job is one of two which are to be held by a **married couple**, *e.g.* golf club steward and wife.

(4) Category or type of employment

Certain particular categories and types of employment are excluded from the general provisions of the SDA. It is not proposed to cover these in detail, but they include **Ministers of religion** where the employment is restricted to one sex only (s. 19) and members of the **Armed Services** (s. 85). Special provisions relate to the **Police** (s. 17) and the **Prison Service** (s. 18). The legal barriers to men becoming **midwives** are removed by section 20, but it is not unlawful for employers to discriminate in selecting or training midwives.

It is still unlawful under the **Mines and Quarries Act 1954** (despite a minor amendment by section 21 of the SDA) for a woman to be employed in job involving the employee spending a significant proportion of his time below ground in an active mine.

(5) General Exceptions

General exceptions from the SDA as a whole include **charities** where the charitable instrument limits benefits to members of one sex only (s. 43); **sports** confined to one sex only (s. 44); **insurance** where proper data to justify the discrimination is relied upon (s. 45); and there is a general exception for acts which are necessary in order to comply with any **statutory requirements** passed before 12th November 1975 (the date the SDA received the Royal Assent).

(6) Positive discrimination

A limited amount of positive discrimination is allowed by the SDA, in particular where an employer gives training for particular work to one sex or encourages one sex to take up that work where in the preceding 12 months there were no (or very few) persons of the sex in question doing that work.

So far we have considered the basic provisions of the SDA in so far as they relate to employment matters **prior** to the actual engagement of the employee. Other aspects of the SDA relating to discrimination during the employment are considered in Chapter 4 (pages 59 to 65, *post*). It must also be remembered that the SDA deals with discrimination in other fields such as education, the provision of goods, facilities, services and premises and various other matters. It is not the purpose of this book to deal with those matters.

Although the SDA itself did not originally provide for the issuing of a Code of Practice, it is now proposed that the Act will be amended to provide for the issue of a Code to assist in the smooth working of the Act. The aim is to give practical guidance aimed at eliminating discrimination and promoting equality of opportunity in the hope that employers, trade unions and individuals will be helped to understand the legislation and their rights and responsibilities. As with the Codes in existence in other spheres of the law, failure to observe any provision of the Code will not itself be unlawful, but the fact will be admissible in evidence before an Industrial Tribunal.

Before considering the practical implications of the SDA for the employer, it is proposed to consider the law of employment as affected by the Race Relations Act legislation.

Racial Discrimination

The second important exception to the general principle that an employer can select any employee he requires for a particular job relates to racial discrimination.

Although the law relating to racial discrimination was originally introduced in an effort to give some protection to coloured immigrants, it now extends much further than discrimination simply on the ground of colour. The Law has also been considerably amended by **the Race Relations Act 1976** (to be referred to as the RRA). That Act repealed the Acts of 1965 and 1968. It fills some of the gaps left by the earlier legislation. For example, under the original Acts proceedings could only be brought by the Race Relations Board. Under the RRA action can be taken by the individual himself. The RRA received the Royal Assent on 22nd November 1976. It is framed in very similar terms to the SDA, and will come into force during 1977 on dates to be appointed by the Secretary of State.

Forms of Racial Discrimination

Direct discrimination against a person by treating that person less favourably on racial grounds is covered by section 1(1)(*a*). **" Racial grounds "** means on the grounds of colour, race, nationality or ethnic or national origins (s. 3(1)). For the purposes of the Act " segregating a person from other persons on racial grounds " is less favourable treatment (s. 1(2)). The **segregation** provisions of the Act do not have comparable provisions in the SDA. The Act here seems to be trying to set a good example as well as providing a remedy for a wrong. If a person is segregated, however, it will be up to him whether he brings any proceedings or not.

Indirect discrimination arises where a person applies to another person a requirement or condition which he also applies equally to persons not of the same racial group but—

(i) which is such that the proportion of persons of the same racial group who can comply is **considerably smaller** than the proportion of persons not of that racial group who can comply with it; **and**

(ii) which he cannot show to be **justifiable** irrespective of the colour, race, nationality or ethnic or national origins of the person to whom it is applied; **and**

(iii) which is to the detriment of that other person because he cannot comply with it (s. 1(1)(*b*)).

Comparison between a member of a racial group and a non-member for this purpose must be between persons in the same or similar circumstances (s. 3(4)).

In the employment field it is unlawful under **section 4** for a person, in relation to employment at an establishment in Great Britain, to discriminate against another—

(a) in the **arrangements** he makes for the purpose of determining who should be **offered** that employment; **or**

(b) in the **terms** on which he offers him that employment; **or**

(c) by **refusing** or **deliberately omitting** to offer him that employment.

It will be noted that these provisions are in almost exactly identical terms to those contained in section 6(1) of the SDA (see page 4, *above*).

Discriminatory advertisements are unlawful as under the SDA (RRA, s. 29).

It is also proposed to issue a **Code of Practice** for race relations with a view to eliminating discrimination in jobs and to promote equality of opportunity in the employment field. The Code—to be drafted by the Commission for Racial Equality—will have the same legal status as the Industrial Relations Code (see page 302).

Exceptions

The **exceptions** to the provisions of the Race Relations Act are more limited than under the SDA. They are as follows:—

(1) Employment for the purposes of a **private household.** There is no exclusion for small firms, as there is in the SDA.

(2) **Genuine occupational qualifications** arise where being a member of a particular racial group is a GOQ for a job.[1] This can only arise in four cases as follows:—

(a) where the job is one in acting or **entertainment** and it needs someone of a particular racial group for authenticity; or

---

[1] RRA, s. 5.

(*b*) where an **artist's or photographic model** is required in the production of a work of art, photograph or film; or

(*c*) where the job involves working in a place where food or drink is provided for the public (for payment or not) in a **particular setting** for which, in that job, a person of that racial group is required for reasons of authenticity; or

(*d*) where the job involves the provisions of **personal welfare services** to members of one racial group and those services can most effectively be provided by a person of that racial group.

The exceptions will not apply if the employer already has employees of the particular racial group who can reasonably be used to carry out those duties without undue inconvenience (s. 5(4)). On the other hand the exceptions can apply where only some of the duties call for a person of a particular group (s. 5(3)).

(3) Employment at an establishment in Great Britain is excluded from the 1976 Act if the person employed is **not ordinarily resident** here and the employment is intended to provide him with training in skills to be exercised by him **wholly outside Great Britain** (s. 6).

(4) There are special provisions in the 1976 Act relating to **seamen** recruited abroad (s. 9); the **Police** (s. 16); **charities** set up for conferring benefits on persons of a class defined by colour (s. 34);

(5) The 1976 Act does not apply to facilities or services to meet the **special needs** of a particular racial group in regard to education, training or welfare (s. 35); nor does it apply to **discriminatory training** and encouragement by particular training bodies where, for example, there is no one of a particular racial group doing particular work in Great Britain (ss. 37 and 38).

(6) **Sport and competitions** are excluded from the provisions of the 1976 Act with regard to selection to represent ones country, place or area (s. 39).

(7) A discriminatory act is not unlawful if it is pursuant to any **statutory authority** (whether before or after 22nd November 1976) (s. 41) or if it is done for the purpose of safeguarding **national security** (s. 42).

Practical Implications for the Employer

Sanctions

What are the possible consequences in the employment field if an employer does discriminate at the very outset either by not offering a job to a particular person or by including in an offer terms and conditions which are discriminatory?

What are the sanctions?

In fact, both the SDA (s. 62) and the RRA (s. 53) provide that a breach of the Act shall incur no penalty (civil or criminal) except as provided by that Act. But there are sanctions in the two Acts.

These must now be considered (both as to sex discrimination and racial discrimination) under three heads.

1. Proceedings before an Industrial Tribunal

An employee (and it should be remembered that this includes a " disappointed " applicant for a job) can apply to an Industrial Tribunal if he has suffered unlawful discrimination (SDA, s. 63, and RRA, s. 54).

The actual procedures relating to an Industrial Tribunal application and the powers of the Tribunal will be considered in more detail in Chapter 24 (page 333, *post*). An application to a Tribunal in those matters must be presented within three months of the act or omission complained of, although there are provisions in both Acts the effect of which may be to extend this time limit where the contract of employment includes an unlawful term (SDA, s. 76(6), and RRA, s. 68(7)), or where it is " just and equitable " for the complaint to be considered out of time (SDA, s. 76(5), and RRA, s. 68(6)).

When the application has been made to the Tribunal, a Conciliation Officer from the Advisory Conciliation and

Arbitration Service will come on the scene with a view to promoting a settlement. The powers and duties of the Conciliation Officer are considered more fully in Chapter 24 (page 335, *post*).

If conciliation fails, the Tribunal hears the case and can make one of three orders—

(*a*) a declaration as to the rights of the parties in relation to the act complained of.

(*b*) an order requiring the employer to pay compensation up to a maximum sum, at the present time, of £5,200. The sum awarded can include compensation for injury to feelings.

(*c*) a recommendation that the employer takes specified action within a particular period for the purpose of obviating or reducing the adverse effect on the complainant.[1]

Employers should appreciate at the outset that the powers of the Tribunal are considerable. For example, the " recommendation " referred to could include a recommendation that the particular job should after all be offered to the applicant and if the employer refuses to do this " without reasonable justification " then the Tribunal can increase the compensation already awarded or make a compensation award (which it seems will now be restricted to the £5,200 limit)[1] or [2].

In the event of indirect discrimination, no award of damages can be made if the employer proves that the requirement or condition in question was not applied with the **intention** of treating the applicant unfavourably on the ground of sex or marital status. Thus, if the employer can show that he did not intend to discriminate, no damages will be awarded against him. This would seem to be a very important " defence " to a discrimination claim. It does, as indicated, only apply in a case of indirect discrimination.

---

[1] SDA, ss. 65 and 66; RRA, ss. 56 and 57.
[1] or [2] SDA, S. 65(3) and RRA, s. 56(4).

Section 66(4) of the SDA (s. 57(4) of the RRA) provides that
" for the avoidance of doubt " damages may include " **compensation for injury to feelings** ".   It is not certain how this
new concept will work in practice and, in particular, how
substantial an award will be for injury to feelings.   It is felt
that some awards may be quite significant.

In the case of *Cox v. Philips Industries Ltd.* (1976) ICR
138 a sum of £500 was awarded for emotional distress caused
by breach of an employment contract.   This case is referred
to in more detail on page 232.

Where the same circumstances give rise to a claim for
unfair dismissal **and** a claim under the SDA, the overall
aggregate compensation cannot exceed £5,200.   Similarly,
an employee cannot recover damages twice for the same head
of loss (Employment Protection Act 1975, s. 77).

Individuals can in certain limited cases (*e.g.* where the
case raises a question of principle) be assisted by the Commission (see paragraph 3 *below*) and this assistance can
include giving advice and arranging representation.[1]   The
Commission does not, however, have any special position
before the Tribunal.

2. **Criminal liability**

There is no criminal liability under the SDA or the RRA
for the actual discrimination itself.

An employer can, however, be prosecuted for knowingly
or recklessly making a misleading or false statement to
certain specified persons to the effect that a certain act or
omission or the publication of an advertisement is not
unlawful under the two Acts.   The specified persons are
limited to employment agencies or education authorities
(SDA, s. 15, and RRA, s. 14); publishers of advertisements
(SDA, s. 38, and RRA, s. 29); and other persons who would

---

[1] SDA, s. 75 and RRA, s. 66.

otherwise be held to have acted unlawfully by aiding the unlawful act but who have acted in reliance on the statement from the employer (SDA, s. 42, and RRA, s. 33).

The penalty for such a statement is a fine not exceeding £400.

In addition, in certain limited cases during a formal investigation by the Commission (see *below*), if a notice is served on a person requiring him to produce relevant information and that person wilfully alters, destroys or conceals any document he has been required to produce or if he knowingly or recklessly makes a false statement, he can be prosecuted and fined up to a maximum of £400.[1]

An employer may also be guilty of contempt of court and thus liable to be sent to prison if he refuses to obey an injunction ordered by the County Court (see pages 19/20, *below*).

Finally, section 70 of the RRA contains special provisions relating to offences committed by inciting racial hatred.

3. Action by the Commission

The SDA established an **Equal Opportunities Commission** to help to enforce the legislation and to promote equality of opportunity between the sexes generally. The EOC has a general responsibility for advising the Government on the working of the SDA and the Equal Pay Act 1970. It is also a principal source of information and advice for the general public. The EOC has discretion, where there are special considerations, to assist individuals who consider that they may have been discriminated again.

In a very similar way the Race Relations Act 1976 sets up a **Commission for Racial Equality** with the duties of working towards the elimination of discrimination, promoting equality of opportunity and good relations between different racial groups. The Commission for Racial Equality takes the place of the previous Race Relations Board.

---

[1] SDA, s. 59 and **RRA, s. 50.**

For the purposes of this chapter references to " the Commission " are intended to include both the Equal Opportunities Commission and the Commission for Racial Equality.

The Commission can take action against an employer under the following heads:—

(a) It can issue a **non-discrimination notice** to an employer requiring that employer to commit (or omit) certain acts which contravene the legislation or to supply information. Such a notice can only be issued in the course of a formal investigation. In addition, the Commission has to warn the employer of what it proposes to do and allow him 28 days in which to put forward representations. It does seem that a non-discrimination notice will be unlikely to arise in an individual complaint, but that it will be more relevant where there is a full enquiry by the Commission, for example, into specific areas of discrimination in a certain part of the country or at a very large company. It is not, therefore, proposed to consider this aspect of the matter in great detail in this book. The relevant provisions are contained in sections 67 to 70 of the SDA and sections 58 to 61 of the RRA.

An employer can appeal to an Industrial Tribunal against any requirement of a non-discrimination notice, but he must do so within six weeks of being served with the notice. The Tribunal has a wide discretion and it can either quash or amend the notice.

Once a notice becomes final the Commission can apply to the County Court for an order to enforce compliance if it has " reasonable cause to believe " that the employer will not comply with it. Failure without reasonable excuse to comply with the County Court order renders the person concerned liable to a fine of up to £10; it also gives the Commission the right to apply for an injunction (see *below*).

(b) The Commission can apply to the County Court for an **injunction** either where a non-discrimination notice has been served or where a Court or Tribunal has made a finding that the employer has committed an act of unlawful discrimination. In each case the Commission **may** (not must) apply for an injunction if they believe that, unless restrained, the employer is **likely to commit** another unlawful discriminatory act. Employers should note that the Commission have a period of five years (either from the finding against the employer or from the non-discrimination notice becoming final) in which to apply for an injunction. From a close consideration of the detailed provisions of the sections of the Acts it seems that it may in practice be necessary to have two or more adverse findings against an employer before the Commission can obtain an injunction; this is because the Commission has to show that the employer is " likely to " contravene one of the Acts unless restrained.

The Commission can also apply for an injunction if it appears that a person has published a discriminatory advertisement or instructed an employee or agent to discriminate or put pressure on someone else to discriminate unlawfully[1] and that person is likely to do further unlawful acts unless restrained.

If an injunction is granted by the Court and the employer does not obey it, then he may be in " contempt of court " and this could give rise to the employer being sent to prison.

(c) The Commission can also apply to an **Industrial Tribunal** for a finding that an employer has unlawfully discriminated against an individual.[2] The Tribunal can make an order declaring the rights of the parties and also an order that the employer should have taken certain specified action to obviate or reduce the adverse effect of the discrimination. The Tribunal

---

[1] SDA, s. 72 and RRA, s. 63.
[2] SDA, s. 73(1) and RRA, s. 64(1).

cannot, however, make an order for compensation in this case.

A similar application (for a decision whether an alleged contravention occurred) can be made to a Tribunal with regard to discriminatory advertisements, instructions to discriminate and pressure to discriminate. In respect of these matters only the Commission can take action—not the individual.

Avoiding the Pitfalls

The employer must obviously now take very great care in the manner in which he selects and employs his workers and staff.

Advertisements must not infringe the law either by way of sex discrimination or racial discrimination. The employer must make sure at the very outset that the advertisement is not discriminatory. He should not simply leave this to the newspaper or to the advertising agency. It is the employer who is primarily responsible. " Offensive " words must be avoided, *e.g.* " waiter " is now a discriminatory word. If there is any doubt, then it is better actually to include in the advertisement a specific reference to the fact that members of either sex can apply for the job. For example, " Hotel Manager (male or female) required ". We have seen that an employer cannot be prosecuted for a discriminatory advertisement, but various forms of action can be taken against him—under the SDA by the Equal Opportunities Commission and under the Race Relations Act by the Commission for Racial Equality. In addition, an applicant to a Tribunal who claims that there has been discrimination may well be helped in the proving of that claim if he can produce to the Tribunal the advertisement which in itself was discriminatory. Certainly, in the first reported SDA case[1] a non-discriminatory advertisement helped the employer to show that he had not discriminated against a male applicant for a job[2].

The employer must take care that his **recruitment policy** does not put him in breach of the law as to discrimination, *e.g.* by

---

[1] *McDonald v. Applied Art Glass Co. Ltd.* (1976) 1 RLR 130.
[2] See also *Brindley v. Tayside Health Board* [1976] IRLR 364.

approaching only a boys' school to offer vacancies to school leavers.

Job application forms (which are used by many employers) should be carefully framed so as to avoid any possible hint of discrimination. The same forms must be used for both men and women and for both single and married persons. Questions about race or nationality should be avoided. Dealing with applications over the telephone should be avoided—see again the first SDA reported case.[1]

Interview procedures must be laid down and applied by employers in a standard manner and without discrimination. It may help employers to have a form of " check list " for the personnel manager or other interviewer. This list should cover the usual questions that are put during such an interview. The same questions must, of course, be put to all applicants (whether male or female and whether coloured or not). To ask the young married woman who applies for a job as a personnel manager how long it is likely to be before she has children is likely to be discriminatory. If she does not get the job, she may then apply to an Industrial Tribunal. If at the end of an interview the applicant is told that the job is not being offered to her, it is better, from the legal point of view, to give reasons there and then, but if this is done great care must be taken. For example, if a woman applies for a job such as a storekeeper which in fact involves lifting heavy weights, the employer would be unwise simply to assume that the applicant is not suitable; he should treat the female applicant as an individual and see if she can in fact cope with the heavy weights.

The **short-listing** of applicants should also be treated with care. In the Tribunal case of *McDonald* referred to on page 21, the fact that men had short-listed for a particular job (previously performed by women) was held to indicate that the employers had not " closed their minds " to male applicants.

Keeping of Records. The " check list " referred to above should be retained by the employer, as should all other papers relating to each applicant for a job. Indeed, an employer

---

[1] *McDonald v. Applied Art Glass Co. Ltd.* (1976) 1 RLR 130.

would now be well advised to keep full records of each applicant for a particular job. These records will include a copy of the advertisement (if any), all correspondence, the " check list " referred to above, full notes of the interview and, finally, a note on the papers stating briefly the reason for not offering the job to that particular applicant, *e.g.* " Jane Smith not appointed because she does not have sufficient experience ". If a letter is sent to an unsuccessful applicant for a job, great care should be taken in the wording of the letter. If such a letter is sent it is better to specify the reason why that particular applicant has not been offered the job.

These records should be kept for at least 12 months. This may seem an unnecessary burden and expense to employers. Provided, however, that a proper procedure is set up, it should be very easy to follow and it could save that employer very considerable expense in the future. As we have seen, a " disappointed " applicant can apply to an Industrial Tribunal and can be awarded compensation up to £5,200. A very small amount of organisation on the lines referred to above could, therefore, be well worthwhile.

An applicant alleging discrimination (both under the SDA and the RRA) must lodge his application to the Tribunal within three months of the alleged discriminatory act. In a case where a person has applied unsuccessfully for a job and alleges that this was because of discrimination, the time will normally run from the date on which the employer makes and communicates his decision to appoint another person to that job.   It is, however, possible for the time limit to be extended— in particular if the applicant can convince the Tribunal that it is " just and equitable " to consider the complaint outside the three month period.[1] To be safe, therefore, the employer should keep all the relevant records for a period of at least 12 months—possible even a little longer.

The records referred to above will be **admissible in evidence** at a hearing before the Tribunal. Notes made at the time of (or immediately after) the interview can also be produced. They will be of very great value; they were made at the time

---

[1] SDA, s. 76(5) and RRA, s. 68(6).

the decision was taken. The hearing before the Tribunal will take place several months later; memories can become clouded with the passage of time and witnesses, under cross examination, can become uncertain. If the employer produces his notes showing clearly why that applicant was not appointed to the job, the Tribunal will attach very great weight indeed to that evidence. If there is a conflict of evidence between the applicant and the employer as to what took place, the written records may well provide the answer.

It is, of course, for the applicant to prove the discrimination. In many cases, however, it will be comparatively easy for the applicant to show sufficient preliminary evidence, *e.g.* " out of six applicants for the job, I was the only coloured person and yet I was the only person with full qualifications ". In that sort of situation, the burden of proof will then swing over to the employer and he will have to show that the reason for **not** offering the job to that particular person related to a ground other than race or sex, as the case may be.

Questionnaires for use prior to proceedings

The **SDA** does contain provisions in **section 74** under which a person who feels that he or she may have been discriminated against can send to the respondent a form of questionnaire. The respondent to be considered for our purposes is an employer although section 74 itself is of wider application. The purpose of the form is to help a person to decide whether or not to institute proceedings and, if he does so, to help him to formulate and present his case in the most effective manner. Regulations have been issued[1] setting out the form itself and these forms are now available from offices of the Department of Employment, the Equal Opportunities Commission and elsewhere. Employers must treat this form with very great caution. Although there is no direct " penalty " for not replying to the form, there is a very heavy sanction contained in **section 74(2)(b).** Under that section not only is the form admissible in evidence, but if the employer has deliberately omitted without reasonable excuse to reply within a reasonable period to

---

[1] The Sex Discrimination (Questions and Replies) Order 1975 (S.I. No. 2048).

the questions or if the replies are " evasive or equivocal " then the Tribunal may draw any inference it considers just and equitable including an inference that the employer committed an unlawful act.

Exactly similar provisions with regard to racial discrimination are now contained in **section 65** of the **RRA.**

The form of questionnaire will only be admissible in evidence if, where it is served before commencement of Tribunal proceedings, it was served within three months of the act complained of or, where a complaint has already been presented to a Tribunal, it is served within twenty one days of the date of presentation of the complaint to the Tribunal.[1] The 21 day limit can be extended with the consent of the Tribunal.

The forms of questionnaire and reply set out in the 1975 Order[2] have been set out in Appendix I (see page 350), together with the marginal notes from the Order.   It is anticipated that comparable forms will be issued under the Race Relations Act 1976.

It is not, however, obligatory for the standard form of questionnaire to be used. An " aggrieved person " may, therefore, make the approach simply by way of a letter.   The employer must, therefore, reply to any such approach very carefully.   His reply will be admissible in evidence; if he does not reply, that in itself can entitle the Tribunal to draw the inference that there was discrimination.

The employer should always keep a copy of his reply; if the reply is sent by post, it is advisable to use the recorded delivery service.

Employers' responsibility for managers and other employees

One of the practical problems for many employers is that although the " man at the top " (*e.g.* the managing director of a limited company or the office manager of a firm) may be very conscious that there should be no discrimination, this policy may not always be appreciated or properly carried out by the

---

[1] The Sex Discrimination (Questions and Replies) Order 1975, para. 5.
[2] The Sex Discrimination (Questions and Replies) Order 1975.

line managers, senior executives, foremen, etc., involved in the running of the business.

Can the employer, in those circumstances, be held liable for acts and omissions of those working for him?

On general legal principles this would normally be the case. In order to remove any doubt, however, the position is confirmed by the legislation.[1] The employer is liable for discrimination by his employees against another employee " in the course of their employment " and whether it was done with the employer's knowledge or approval or not. The employer is also liable for unlawful discrimination by his agent if the agent has authority expressed or implied from the circumstances.

Section 41(3) of the SDA (and similarly section 32(3) of the RRA) does, however, provide one very useful defence to the employer. If the employer can prove that he " took such steps as were reasonably practicable to prevent the employee from doing that act or from doing in the course of his employment acts of that description ", that will be a defence to any proceedings.

This is a most important provision and employers should consider it carefully. It would seem that a specific written instruction to all employees confirming that it is not the employer's policy to discriminate and reminding employees that they are not to do any act which might be discriminatory against a fellow employee either under the Sex Discrimination Act 1975 or the Race Relations Act 1976 could well afford a defence to that employer if subsequently proceedings were brought against him arising out of some discriminatory act on the part of another employee.

REHABILITATION OF OFFENDERS ACT 1974

Although it is not clear what sanctions (if any) arise if an employer is in breach of this Act, it is appropriate to consider it at this stage in view of the terms of section 4(3)(b), which provide that

---

[1] SDA, s. 41 and RRA, s. 32.

" a conviction which has become spent . . . or any failure to disclose a spent conviction . . . shall not be a proper ground for dismissing or **excluding a person from any office,** profession, occupation **or employment** or for prejudicing him in any way in any occupation or employment ".

The Rehabilitation of Offenders Act 1974 came into force on 1st July 1975, its purpose being to draw a veil over the " **spent conviction** " of a person who has become a rehabilitated member of society.   The Act applies where—

(a) a person is convicted of a criminal offence and

(b) is sentenced to a non-custodial sentence or to a custodial sentence of 30 months or less and

(c) a specified period (e.g. 10 years in the case of a sentence exceeding six months) has elapsed without a further conviction during that period.

Once the conviction is spent the convicted person becomes a " rehabilitated person " with the consequence that for legal purposes he is to be treated as not having committed the offence at all.

If an employer " excludes " an applicant from a particular job on the ground of a spent conviction, it is difficult to know what action that applicant can take even if he is able to prove the reason for being excluded.   The Common Law provides no remedy,[1] nor does the Rehabilitation of Offenders Act itself lay down any penalty or sanction.   It seems that the applicant will only have a cause of action if he can establish it under some other head e.g. sex discrimination or racial discrimination. The Act allows (s. 4(4)) the Secretary of State to modify its provision by regulation and this may possibly be done in the future to provide an " aggrieved person " with remedies similar to those under, say, the Race Relations Act 1976.

It should be noted that the Act also in effect provides that an applicant for a job need not disclose a spent conviction (s. 4(3)(a)) nor need he answer any questions put to him which in any way relate to that spent conviction (s. 4(2)).   Despite these provisions, an employer would be advised to try and

---

[1] See *Allen v. Flood* (1898) AC. 1 (and p. 3, *ante*).

ascertain (either by seeking references, credit ratings, fidelity guarantees or otherwise) whether an applicant for a job involving trust and responsibility does in fact have any convictions for dishonesty. The reason for this is that if after the commencement of the employment, the employer finds out about a previous conviction (which may be " spent ") he may have problems regarding the dismissal of the employee. Section 4(3)(*b*) (see *above*) provides that this shall not be a " proper ground " for dismissal. It is unlikely, therefore, that the employer would have a defence to proceedings by the employee under the Trade Union and Labour Relations Act 1974 alleging unfair dismissal (see page 290).

DISABLED PERSONS (EMPLOYMENT) ACT 1944

The final statute which should be considered is the Disabled Persons (Employment) Act 1944 which received the Royal Assent on 1st March 1944 and was amended by a further Act in 1958. The object of the Act was to make better provision for enabling handicapped persons to secure employment. The Act provides for a register of disabled persons and it then placed an obligation on every employer of 20 or more people to include a quota of registered disabled persons (s. 9). The Act provides for the ascertaining of the required quota. Since 1946 the quota has been fixed at 3 per cent.[1] An employer can apply for a permit (s. 11) absolving him from the provisions of the Act in relation to the employment of a particular person or persons.

The Act—unlike the more recent Sex Discrimination Act 1975 and Race Relations Act 1976—does not provide a direct remedy for the disabled person. It is, however, **an offence** under the Act for an employer who is subject to its provisions—

(*a*) to employ a person other than a registered disabled person if on taking on that person the employer's quota will be less than the designated quota under the Act (s. 9(2)).

(*b*) to discontinue the employment of a registered disabled person, unless he has reasonable cause for doing so, if

---

[1] Disabled Persons (Standard Percentage) Order 1946.

after such discontinuance the employer's quota will be less than the designated quota under the Act (s. 9(5)).

An employer found guilty of one of these offences is liable on summary conviction to a fine not exceeding £100 or to imprisonment for a term not exceeding three months or to both a fine and a term of imprisonment.

A prosecution can only be brought by or with the consent of the appropriate Minister and a prosecution under section 9(5) (see (b) above) cannot be instituted unless the matter has been referred to a district advisory committee (set up under the Act) and a certain procedure followed.

An employer can also be prosecuted if he does not keep certain records specified in section 14 of the Act.

For many years this Act has not been enforced. In 1972 there were said to be more than 35,000 companies who were not maintaining their quotas. Employers should, however, be mindful of their obligations under the Act, particularly as the T.U.C. was advocating in 1975 that the quota system should be more strictly enforced. The matter has also recently been under consideration by the Department of Employment, who are concerned that the percentage of unemployed on the disabled persons' register was considerably in excess of the national rate (12.1% compared with the national rate of 3.6% in June 1975).

PART II

THE EMPLOYMENT ITSELF

CHAPTER 2

THE CONTRACT OF EMPLOYMENT

The relationship of employer and employee is a contractual one and this is so whether or not there is a legal agreement in writing. The basis of the relationship is that the employee undertakes to do work for the employer and the employer agrees to pay wages.

The general principle is that an employer and an employee can agree the terms of the contract in whatever form they wish. There are, however, now a great number of statutory exceptions to that principle and these must be considered. The question of equal pay under the Equal Pay Act 1970 and the law relating to racial or sex discrimination will be dealt with in Chapters 3 and 4. It should also be remembered that, in very many cases, collective bargaining between Trade Unions and employers plays a very large part in defining and establishing the actual terms of employment.

In addition, the contract of employment can be affected by such things as Collective Agreements with a Trade Union, Works Rules, Cus om and Practice and various other matters.

The most important principle—for both employer and employee—is that, at the very outset of the relationship, the terms and conditions of the employment should be clearly defined. Much greater care should be taken by employers. If the terms remain vague and undefined, then at some time in the future the employer may find that he is in difficulties, *e.g.* if a matter reaches an Industrial Tribunal. The courts and Tribunals will not readily imply into a contract terms which were not clearly agreed at the outset.

[30]

THE TERMS OF EMPLOYMENT

Express Terms

It is not strictly necessary, from the legal point of view, for a contract of employment to be in writing (except a contract of apprenticeship and a contract under the Merchant Shipping Act 1970).

The employer should, however, beware of two factors:—

(a) under the Contracts of Employment Act 1972 an employer has to give to most of his employees a written statement setting out certain main terms of the contract (see page 36).

(b) if the terms are not recorded in writing, it could be very difficult to prove their existence at a later date.

Ideally, therefore, all the terms of a particular employment (including the statutory particulars) should be set out in writing and delivered to the employee. **The Code of Practice**[1] (originally issued under the Industrial Relations Act 1971 and subsequently affirmed by the Trade Union and Labour Relations Act 1974) provides in paragraph 62 that—

" apart from the statutory requirements, management should ensure that each employee is given information about:

(i) the requirements of his job and to whom he is directly responsible;

(ii) disciplinary rules and procedures and the types of circumstances which can lead to suspension or dismissal;

(iii) trade union arrangements;

(iv) opportunities for promotion and any training necessary to achieve it;

(v) social or welfare facilities;

(vi) fire prevention and safety and health rules;

(vii) any suggestion schemes ".

One of the " dangers " about the Contracts of Employment Act Statement, from the employer's point of view, is that the employer tends to consider only the statutory requirements. Far too often, he does not at the outset consider what other

---

[1] See also p. 302.

express terms should be included in the contract. If a problem arises later in the course of the employment it is then too late to introduce a new term into the contract.

By way of **example** only (and the list is not intended to be exhaustive) the employer should ask himself the following questions:—

(*a*) Will I require to call upon this employee to work overtime?

(*b*) Do I need a provision giving me the right to transfer the employee to another place of work?

(*c*) Is there to be transferability between particular jobs?

Unless there are specific provisions in the contract, then the employer will not be able to insist on performance of those terms. Thus if, for example, the employee refuses to work overtime and is then dismissed, it is more than likely that the dismissal will be unfair, as the employee would not be in breach of his contract in refusing to work overtime.[1]

One vital matter which must be dealt with is (as referred to above in paragraph 62 of the Code of Practice) the question of disciplinary rules. Since 1st June 1976[2] this has also become one of the statutory requirements under the Contracts of Employment Act 1972 and it will be dealt with under that heading (see page 39, *post*). In addition, a new draft Code with regard to Disciplinary Practice and Procedures has now been issued (see Appendix IV—page 364).

Implied Terms

Apart from the **express terms** of the contract, it is sometimes possible to **imply** certain terms. For example, an employee must exercise reasonable care and skill in carrying out his job; he must also serve the employer honestly and faithfully and he should not disclose to another his employer's trade secrets or misuse confidential information acquired by him during his employment.

---

[1] See, for example, *Graham v. Anthony Todd (Haulage) Ltd.* (1975) IRLR 45.

[2] Employment Protection Act 1975—Sch. 16, Part II, para. 5(*b*).

It is, however, as indicated above, dangerous to rely on implied terms. It is much safer for the employer to specify in writing the exact terms that are applicable.

The provisions of the Equal Pay Act 1970 (as amended) are dealt with on the basis that " an equality clause " shall be deemed to be included in a contract of employment. This will, however, be considered later (see Chapter 3, page 49, *post*).

Collective Agreements

It is now very common for there to be a Collective or Procedure Agreement between an employer and a Trade Union or on a national basis between an employers' organisation and one or more Trade Unions. Such Agreements may deal with the procedures for settling a dispute but in addition they often deal with matters affecting the individual's contract of employment.

The individual employee is not a party to such an agreement. Is he, therefore, bound by its terms? Many employers assume that he will be bound.

It is not, however, absolutely safe for an employer to assume that this is the case. The Collective Agreement can contain all manner of vital provisions relating to such things as holidays, time-keeping, discipline, etc.

It is obviously not practicable for every employee to sign the Collective Agreement. It is, however, very easy for a reference to the terms of the Collective Agreement to be made in the Contracts of Employment Act statement. If this is done and the Collective Agreement is made available to the employee in the course of his employment, then the terms of the Collective Agreement are effectively " written into " the contract.[1]

Employers should be advised to deal with the matter in this way. In the writer's experience, however, it is very seldom done.

If this is not done, the employer can be at risk, although he may be able in certain cases to establish either that the terms

---

[1] Contracts of Employment Act 1972, s. 4(5).

of the Collective Agreement have become implied into the individual's contract or that the Trade Union (or its officials) acted as the agent of its members for the purpose of making a contract on their behalf with a particular employer. Reliance on this agency principle is not, however, recommended.

It must also be remembered that under section 18 of the Trade Union and Labour Relations Act a collective agreement is conclusively presumed **not** to have been intended to be a legally enforceable contract unless it is in writing and contains a provision that the parties do intend it to be legally enforceable.

Works Rules

Many employers issue their employees with a book of rules, Staff Hand Book or other Terms and Conditions either at the commencement of employment or later. Sometimes, there are also Notices at the place of work, setting out certain rules and regulations. Very often these rules deal with disciplinary matters and with grievance and disciplinary procedures.

Are these rules a part of the individual's contract of employment?

It could be vital to the employer to establish that they are, *e.g.* if the employer is faced with a claim alleging unfair dismissal when the dismissal itself arose because of a breach of the rules.

Here again, the position can—and should—be dealt with quite simply. The Rules should either be referred to in the Contracts of Employment Act Statement or the employee should sign a simple acknowledgement to the effect that he has received a copy of the Rules and that he accepts them as part of his contract of employment. If this is done, the employer will have no problem.

If this is not done, all may not be lost as far as the employer is concerned. He may be able to show that the rules were drawn to the attention of the employee or otherwise displayed at the commencement of the employment and that the rules would be construed by the ordinary employee as terms and conditions of his contract of employment. Alternatively, the employer may be able to claim that the Works Rules were implied into the contract.

As indicated previously, however, an express reference to the Works Rules is the only safe way of dealing with this matter.

One of the other problems with regard to Works Rules is that not all of the rules are always contractual in nature. They may, for example, include a reference to canteen or social facilities, or they may be " only instructions to a man as to how he is to do his work ". For a detailed consideration of this aspect of the matter—see the judgement of Lord Denning M.R. in *Secretary of State for Employment v. ASLEF (No.* 2) (1972) ICR at page 51.

Statutory Rights

It has already been seen that Statute Law has in recent years become more and more involved in the relationship of employer and employee. In practice, it can now be said that various Acts of Parliament in effect imply certain terms or rights into most contracts of employment. In most cases, these rights are " compulsory "; it is not possible for the parties to contract out of them. It is not proposed to deal with these in detail at this stage; the more important matters will be dealt with later in this book and a summary in tabular form is set out in Appendix VI. They do, however, include:—

(1) The right not to be unfairly dismissed (see Chapter 19).

(2) The right not to be discriminated against on the ground of sex or marital status or on the grounds of race, colour, etc. (see Chapters 1 and 4).

(3) The right to receive a minimum period of notice of termination of employment (see Chapter 17 on Wrongful Dismissal).

(4) The right—as between men and women who are doing the same job or " like work "—to receive equal pay (see Chapter 3).

(5) A number of new rights introduced by the Employment Protection Act 1975 and dealt with in more detail in Part III of this book (Chapters 5 to 10). These include rights as to guarantee payments, certain maternity rights, rights as to Trade Union membership and activities and as to time off work for carrying out various duties.

THE CONTRACTS OF EMPLOYMENT ACT 1972

In 1963 the first Contracts of Employment Act came on to the statute book. In addition to providing for the first time minimum notice periods with regard to termination of an employee's contract (as to which see Chapter 17, page 228, *post*), the Act set out to compel employers to tell their employees more about the terms of their employment.

The 1963 Act was amended by subsequent legislation and the provisions were then consolidated in the Contracts of Employment Act 1972 which came into force on 27th July 1972. That Act will be referred to in this chapter as the CEA, and will include the amendments made to it by the Trade Union and Labour Relations Act 1974 and by the Employment Protection Act 1975[1] (to be referred to here as the EPA).

The required particulars

Section 4 of the CEA does **not** require **a written contract** to be given to an employee. It does, however, provide that an employer must give to an employee (with certain exceptions— see page 44) not later than thirteen weeks after the commencement of the employment **a written statement** identifying the parties, specifying the date when the employment began and stating whether employment with a previous employer counts as part of the employee's continuous employment and if so the date on which such continuous period began.

The statement must also give certain specified **particulars of the terms of the employment** as at a stated date not more than one week before the statement is given and a **note** of certain other matters (s. 4(2)).

---

[1] Employment Protection Act 1975—Sch. 16, Part II—which came into force on 1st June 1976 by virtue of the Employment Protection Act 1975 (Commencement No. 4) Order 1976.

It will be seen from the above that, strictly, the CEA deals with three sorts of information:—

(a) the names of the parties, the date of commencement and whether past employment counts for continuity (s. 4(1)).

(b) the particulars of certain specified " terms of employment " (paragraphs (a) to (f) of section 4(1)), and

(c) a " note " about disciplinary rules and disciplinary and grievance procedures.

Strictly, therefore, only the matters in (b) above relate to the actual terms of the employment. This can be of significance when there is a change in the terms of employment (s. 5) (and see page 42).

For practical purposes, however, all the " information " referred to in the CEA will be given or referred to in one statement or document. The employer may decide to use a standard printed form obtainable from stationers or he may prepare a form appropriate for his own employees. Indeed, a letter of appointment will suffice provided it contains all the required information as will a formal service agreement. The information can be summarised as follows:—

(1) **The names** of the employer and of the employee.

(2) **The date** when the employment began.

(3) Whether any **employment with a previous employer** counts as part of that employee's continuous period of employment and if so the date on which that previous employment began.

> This provision is one of the matters introduced by the EPA and it became effective certainly for new employees (see page 43, *ante*) on 1st June 1976. The period of " continuous employment " (defined in CEA Schedule 1) is important to an employee in many situations, *e.g.* calculating redundancy pay, ascertaining whether he or she has become entitled to various rights, such as the right not to be unfairly dismissed, the right to maternity pay, etc.[1] Not all past employments count for continuity purposes. They will count if, for example, the employee has worked

---

[1] See Appendix II. (page 352 *post*)

for " associated companies "[1] or if there has been a change of employer by virtue of transfer of a trade, business or undertaking.[2] A summary of the rules and definitions relating to "continuous employment" is set out in Appendix II (page 352).

(4) The scale or rate of **remuneration** or the method of calculating it.

(5) The **intervals** at which remuneration is paid (whether weekly, monthly or otherwise).

(6) Any terms and conditions relating to **hours of work** (including any terms relating to normal working hours).

As indicated previously (page 32), an employer should consider whether to include under this head any reference to overtime. If the employer wishes to have a right to call upon an employee to work overtime, he should specify this in the contract statement.

(7) Any terms and conditions relating to **holiday entitlement,** including public holidays and holiday pay and including sufficient information to enable an employee's entitlement to accrued holiday pay to be precisely calculated on the termination of his employment.

Under this head, the employer should specify what in fact is the holiday year for the purpose of the calculations, *e.g.* does the holiday year commence on 1st January or 1st April or some other date?

(8) Any terms and conditions relating to incapacity for work due to **sickness or injury,** including any provisions for sick pay.

It will be seen (page 279) that these terms and conditions can be of great relevance in deciding whether or not an employer has acted fairly in dismissing an employee who has been absent due to sickness or injury.

(9) Any terms and conditions relating to **pensions** and **pension schemes.** If there is no pension scheme the statement should say so.

---

[1] Para. 10 of 1st Sch. to CEA (as amended by EPA, Sch. 16, Part II, para. 19).
[2] Para. 9 of 1st Sch. to CEA.

(10) The length of **notice** which the employee is obliged to give and entitled to receive to determine his contract of employment.

> The statutory notice periods are dealt with in chapter 17 (page 228). An employee will be entitled to the statutory minimum period of notice even if a lesser period is referred to in the contract statement.

(11) **The title of the job** which the employee is employed to do.

> .Rather surprisingly, this item was not covered by the original legislation and has only been introduced since 1st June 1976 by paragraph 4(*b*) of Part II of the 16th Schedule to the EPA.
>
> What is required here is the title of the job—not a job description. This item should, however, be considered carefully by employers, as it could in certain circumstances be of great relevance. For example, it will be very relevant in redundancy cases when the issue before a Tribunal may be the need for less " work of a particular kind "; similarly in a claim under the Equal Pay Act 1970 the question of what is " like work " may well arise. In addition, the question of job flexibility and mobility may be affected by the reference to the job title.
>
> In all these circumstances, there seem to be very good reasons for making the job title reflect accurately the type of work the employee is required to do. There is no need to go into great detail, but a vague title may not be a proper title at all and in any event could cause problems.

In respect of the terms of employment set out above and numbered (4) to (11) inclusive the CEA does not say that every contract of employment must include these specified terms. It simply provides that if there are such terms then particulars of those terms must be given in writing to the employee and if there are no such terms about the specified matters then that fact must be stated (s. 4(3)).

(12) A note specifying **any disciplinary rules** applicable to the employee, or referring to a document which is reasonably accessible to the employee and which specifies such rules.

> Although a similar recommendation has been included in the Code of Practice paragraph 62(ii) (see page 31, *ante*) and paragraph 131 this provision only became part

of the law on 1st June 1976 when the EPA amendments came into force.

It is felt that this provision is of very great importance and requires careful attention by employers. For example, quite apart from the employer's obligation under the CEA to supply this information, it is a matter which will be very relevant if an employee is dismissed for misconduct. If the employer can show that there was a clear written disciplinary rule referring to dismissal in certain circumstances, then the employer is more likely to be able to prove to the Tribunal that he acted " fairly ".

Employers should—if they have not already done so—urgently consider drafting a set of disciplinary rules, which could also include references to such things as warnings (as to which see page 304) as well as the disciplinary procedures referred to under (13) below. The rules can then be referred to in the Contracts of Employment Act statement, although even then it is advisable that a copy should be given to (and if possible acknowledged by) each employee. Attention should also now be paid to the new Draft Code as to Disciplinary Practice and Procedures—see Appendix IV (page 364).

(13) A note specifying (by description or otherwise) **a person to whom the employee can apply if** he is **dissatisfied** with any disciplinary decision relating to him, the manner in which any such application should be made and, where there are **further steps** consequent upon such application, an explanation of those steps.

This may prove to be one of the most far-reaching changes introduced by the EPA. Employers now seem to be **compelled** to set up an **appeals procedure** at least to the extent of specifying a person to whom the employee can apply. It is not sufficient to say " There is no such person".

Employers should, therefore, set up a proper Appeals Procedure—see also in this respect paragraph 132 of the Code of Practice, which recommends a procedure in writing under which (*inter alia*) there is provision for—

" a right of appeal, wherever practicable, to a level of management not previously involved ". (See also the new Draft Code referred to in Appendix IV—page 364, *post.*)

(14) A note specifying (by description or otherwise) **a person to whom the employee can apply for** the purpose of seeking

redress of any grievance relating to his employment, the manner in which any such application should be made and, where there are **further steps** consequent upon such application, an explanation of those steps.

The " grievance procedure " provisions were first introduced into the law by the Industrial Relations Act 1971 and they have been confirmed by the subsequent legislation. The aim is to encourage employers to establish clear procedures. It will be noted that the actual name of the relevant person does not have to be given; the reference can be " by description ", *e.g.* " the Personnel Manager ".

Method of Time and communication

The above particulars must be in writing. " The written statement should be as comprehensive and easy to understand as possible ".[1]   They do not, however, have to be in one single document. It is possible to refer in the Contracts of Employment Act statement to some other " document which the employee has reasonable opportunities of reading in the course of his employment or which is made reasonably accessible to him in some other way ". (CEA, s. 4(5)).

This will certainly be done in the case of, for example, pension schemes and it will often be done with regard to Disciplinary Rules. The provisions of Collective Agreements and Works Rules should also be dealt with in this way (see page 33, *ante*).

A letter of appointment sent to an employee can be sufficient if all the required particulars are set out or referred to in it.

Similarly, if an employee is given a formal contract in writing (*e.g.* a Service Agreement), then the employer is relieved of his obligations under the CEA provided that—

(a) the contract contains all the specified particulars referred to in the CEA (number (1) to (11) *above*).

(b) the employee is given a copy of the contract or he can read it during the course of his employment or a copy is made reasonably accessible to him in some other way.

---

[1] The 1972 Code of Practice, para. 61.

(c) the employee is given (or has access to) a note of the particulars set out as numbers (12) to (14) above.[1]

It should again be stressed that the CEA particulars may not in themselves cover all the terms of the employment. If other matters are necessary, it is advisable to deal with them in the same document.

As to the question of **when to deliver** the particulars, the 1972 Act provides that this should be done not later than **thirteen weeks** after commencement of the employment. In practice, however, an employer has nothing to lose—and possibly a lot to gain—by delivering the required particulars right at the outset, *i.e.* either when confirming the offer of a job or on the very first day of employment. If this is done, then the main terms are immediately established (unless, of course, the employee objects to them). In addition, it will be complying with the general recommendations as to " Communication " contained in the Code of Practice.

It is good practice to prepare the necessary Statement for each employee in duplicate and to obtain his signature to one copy. There can then be absolutely no doubt at all in the future about establishing the terms of employment.

There is, however, no provision in the CEA regarding signature by the employee. Indeed, it has been held that an employee cannot be made to sign a copy of the statement.

Changes in terms of employment

Once the terms of employment are agreed, they cannot normally be changed by one party unless the other party agrees or unless there is some provision in the original terms giving a right to vary those terms.

If, however, the terms of employment are changed then—if the change relates to any of the terms of which written particulars must be given under the CEA (paragraphs (4) to (11) *above*)—then the changes in those terms must be communicated in writing to the employee within **one month** of the change (section 5 of the 1972 Act).

---

[1] CEA, s. 6.

In practice, the employer would be advised to deliver a copy of the amendments to the employee. If this is not done, the statement must be preserved and made accessible to the employee.

A failure on the part of the employer to inform the employee of the change under the CEA does not of itself nullify the change, provided that in all other respects the change in the terms of the employment was in order.

If the original Statement refers to another document (*e.g.* Collective Agreement) and the employer indicates at the outset that any changes in that other document will be entered up in the document itself, then there is no need to notify the employee of any change in the terms. They must, however, be duly entered up on the document within one month of the change.

Changes in the law

What is the position if the law relating to the required particulars under the CEA changes? In particular, what about the new requirements introduced by the Employment Protection Act 1975 on 1st June 1976 (see paragraphs (3), (11), (12) and (13) on pages 37 to 40).

There is no doubt that in the case of all employees (subject to the exceptions referred to below) who commence work after 1st June 1976 **all** the required particulars must be delivered.

In the case of employees who were already employed in their particular jobs on 1st June 1976, should their employers give a further statement as envisaged by section 5 of the CEA? Legally, they may not have to—although the requirement regarding establishment of a disciplinary appeal procedure appears to be mandatory. In practice, however, employers should up-date their Contracts of Employment Act statements and include in them the EPA amendments. Quite apart from the strict legal position, this would seem to be good industrial relations practice. There could, however, be problems in some areas. For example, an employer who now specifies disciplinary rules which were not part of the original terms of employment could be faced with resistance by his employees or their representatives, and indeed may not be entitled to vary the terms of the original contract.

Excluded categories of employees

The following employees are excluded from the provisions of the CEA and the employer is not, therefore, under an obligation to deliver the required particulars to them. There is, of course, nothing to stop the employer delivering a Statement of terms to these employees; indeed, in many situations, it may be advisable for the employer to do so. The employees referred to are:—

(1) **Certain part-time employees:** With effect from 1st February 1977 employees whose working hours are " normally less than 16 hours weekly " are not covered by the CEA (see section 4(7)). No written statement need be given to them.

The Employment Protection Act 1975 contains provisions (in Part II of Schedule 16) which reduce the definition of " part-time " to those who normally work 16 hours and, in certain cases, only 8 hours.

The following employees are now classed as " full-time " employees and are entitled to a Contracts of Employment Act statement:—

(a) employees whose contract of employment normally involves employment for 16 hours or more weekly.

(b) employees whose contract of employment normally involves employment for 16 hours or more weekly, but who then subsequently become governed by a contract normally involving 8 hours or more (but less than 16) shall nevertheless—for a period of 26 weeks—be treated as if they were still " 16 hour " employees.

(c) employees whose contract of employment normally involves employment for 8 hours or more (but less than 16) but who have been continuously employed for a period of 5 years.

The main practical effect of these changes is that part-time employees (who do not have the rights under the Contracts of Employment Act, nor rights as to unfair dismissal or redundancy pay) are as from 1st February 1977 defined as those who work less than 16 hours or, in the case of employees with 5 years' service, those who work between 8 and 16 hours per week. (See also Appendix II, pages 352 to 359 for a more detailed consideration of the definition).

Prior to 1st February 1977 the relevant period was 21 hours weekly.

(2) Where the employee is the **husband or wife** of the employer,
    The exception here is now more limited since 1st June 1976 when that part of the EPA came into force.[1]   Prior to that date the " close relative " exception extended to situations where the employer was the father, mother, husband, wife son or daughter.

(3) Registered **dock workers** except when engaged in work which is not dock work as defined by any scheme in force under the Dock Workers (Regulation of Employment) Act 1946.

(4) **Merchant seamen** or master of certain British ships or apprentices under the Merchant Shipping Act 1894.[2]

(5) The provisions of the CEA do not apply to employment during any period when the employee is engaged in work wholly or mainly **outside Great Britain** unless the employee ordinarily works in Great Britain and the work outside Great Britain is for the same employer.   The EPA contains power to extend protection to workers on installations in U.K. territorial waters and those working on the exploration of the seabed or exploitation of certain natural resources and this extension was brought into effect on 21st June 1976.

(6) Under an amendment introduced by the EPA with effect from 1st June 1976 the provisions of the 1972 Act do not

---

[1] CEA, s. 9(3); as amended by EPA, Sch. 16, Pt. II, para. 10(*b*).
[2] For detailed definition, see CEA, s. 9(2).

apply in the case of a person employed under a contract made in contemplation of a specific task which is **not** expected to last for **more than twelve weeks,** unless that employee has in fact been continuously employed for more than twelve weeks.

It will be appreciated, however, that an employee is in any event only entitled to a statement under the CEA after 13 weeks' employment (see page 42). This exclusion, therefore, is really only of relevance in relation to the CEA notice requirements (see page 228).

(7) **Crown servants.**

Sanctions

If an employer does not comply with his obligations under the Contracts of Employment Act, an employee can apply to an Industrial Tribunal and the Tribunal will determine and order what particulars ought to have been given under the Act. Similarly, where a statement has been given under the Act and a question arises as to the particulars which ought to have been given, then either the employer or the employee can refer the matter to a Tribunal.

An employee can apply to a Tribunal either during the course of his employment or within three months of its termination. The time limit here has been held to be a procedural matter and does not go the actual jurisdiction of the Tribunal.

There is now no criminal penalty imposed on an employer, although under the original 1963 Act an employer could be prosecuted and fined.

It should be noted that the Tribunal can only **declare** what particulars should have been delivered under the Act. It cannot then enforce those particulars against the employer. For example, it can declare what length of notice to terminate the employment should have been included in a statement under the Act; if, however, the employment has been terminated and insufficient notice has been given, the Tribunal cannot award to the employee the appropriate money in lieu of notice; in those circumstances, the Tribunal having declared the correct period of notice, the employee must take proceedings in the

High Court or County Court, as the case may be, to recover the money.

This does seem illogical and the Employment Protection Act 1975 now contains power in section 109 for the appropriate Minister to confer on Industrial Tribunals jurisdiction to deal with claims for damages for breach of a contract of employment, in particular where such a claim arises either on termination of employment or in circumstances which give rise to proceedings before an Industrial Tribunal. (See also page 238.)

CHAPTER 3

EQUAL PAY

We have now considered the position prior to the actual engagement of an employee and the terms of the employment itself.

It goes without saying that the most vital term of any employment is the actual wage or salary to be paid.

What restrictions or limitations (if any) are there on the wage to be paid to a particular employee?

Again, the principle at Common Law is that there is no restriction or limitation. But—as we have already noted in other spheres of the law—Statute Law comes " on the scene " and provides various important exceptions to the general rule.

The most important statute which must now be taken into account is the **Equal Pay Act 1970.**

Before dealing with that, however, it must be remembered that there can be other matters affecting the question of pay. In recent years there has been a series of Counter-Inflation Acts and White Papers which have restricted increases in wages and other benefits. In addition, in certain large industries, wages are agreed or fixed at a national level and the individual employer and employee may have very little say in the matter. Finally, even at local level, negotiations as to wages will often be carried out on behalf of the employees by their trade union representatives. In certain circumstances (for example where an employer refuses to recognise a trade union when recommended so to do by the ACAS or refuses to disclose certain information to a recognised trade union) an increase in wages can be imposed on an employer by the Central Arbitration Committee, regardless of whether he agrees to such increase (see Chapter 5).

THE EQUAL PAY ACT 1970

The Equal Pay Act, although passed in 1970, did not take effect until 29th December 1975. Parliament had allowed employers a period of about five years in which to move towards equal pay as between the sexes.

The 1970 Act has now been amended by the Sex Discrimination Act 1975 (which sets out in full the Act, as amended, in Part II of the 1st Schedule). For the purposes of this chapter the Equal Pay Act, as amended, will simply be referred to as " the Act ".

The Act applies equally to both men and women, although for the purposes of this chapter references will be to the female employee.

The equality clause

In every contract relating to employment in Great Britain there is now deemed to be an " equality clause "[1] i.e. a provision which relates to terms of employment and has the effect that where a woman is either employed on " like work " or on " work rated as equivalent " with that of a man in the same employment, then if any term of the contract of employment is or becomes less favourable to the woman that term shall be treated as modified so as not to be less favourable.

Similarly, if, in the above circumstances, the woman's contract does not include a term corresponding to a term in the man's contract, then her contract shall be treated as including such a term.

What does the Act cover ?

The Act deals with terms of a contract " whether concerned with pay or not ". Thus, quite apart from wage rates and salaries, it applies to such things as overtime pay, bonuses, shift work allowances, luncheon vouchers, sick pay schemes, health insurance and other fringe benefits, provided that they are terms of the contract of employment. It will also cover

---

[1] Equal Pay Act 1970, s. 1(1).

conditions of employment relating to hours of work, holidays and terms of notice.

The Act does not cover matters outside the contract of employment, but those matters may be covered by the Sex Discrimination Act 1975 (see Chapter 4, *post*).

Special treatment for maternity (*e.g.* paid leave) is excluded from the provisions of the Act and so are retirement ages. Employers can, therefore, still lay down different retirement ages for men and women. As far as pension schemes are concerned, they are not at present protected by the Act, although the position will change as from 1st April 1978. After that date it will be unlawful for employers to have different membership conditions for women.

An equality clause does not operate where specific statutes regulate or restrict the employment of women, *e.g.* restrictions as to working nights.

Who is entitled to the benefit of the Act ?

An employee does not have to have a qualifying period of employment to be entitled to the benefit of the Act nor does it matter how many hours per week the employee works. There is no exclusion for small firms.

All the employee has to show is that she is either doing " like work " to a man or that her job has been rated as being of " equivalent " value to that of a man.

It will be seen from this that for a woman to establish a claim she must be able to compare her work with a man doing similar work. If men are doing the same sort of work at the same establishment, then that will be sufficient. This can also be extended under the Act so that the comparison can be made with men doing the same sort of job at another place of work belonging to the same employer (or associated employers[1]) if there are the same terms and conditions of employment at both places of work. If, therefore, there are no men at the same

---

[1] Employers are treated as " associated " if one is a company of which the other has control or both are companies of which a third person has control (s. 1(6)).

place of work or at some " associated " works or if the terms and conditions vary from factory to factory, then the female employee will not have any rights under the Act. A woman doing the same job as another woman (but at a different rate of pay) cannot claim equality with that other woman under the Act.

What is " like work " ?

There is no full definition in the Act, but **section 1(4)** in effect provides that the work must be " **of the same or a broadly similar nature** " and that the differences in the work are " not of practical importance in relation to terms and conditions of employment ".

Regard must also be had to " the frequency or otherwise with which any such differences occur in practice as well as to the nature and extent of the differences ". Jobs with the same job title may involve differing responsibilities and hence not involve " like work ".

Thus, the jobs do not have to be identical. What matters is how big the differences are and how often they occur in practice.[1]

It seems that the onus of establishing " like work " is on the applicant and, if the matter reaches a Tribunal, it will be for the applicant to prove this in the first instance. This is contrary to most of the recent Employment Law legislation where the burden is normally put on the employer, *e.g.* the burden is on the employer to show that he has not " unfairly dismissed " an employee.

If an applicant to a Tribunal does manage to establish " like work ", then the employer may still be able to show that any difference in pay or conditions is genuinely due to a real or material difference other than the difference in sex. For example, an employer may pay more for " heavy " work (which is traditionally done by men); he may be able to establish that certain employees have higher skills or qualifications; or he may pay more to " long-service " employees.

---

[1] An industrial tribunal ought not to undertake too minute an examination, but should bring a broad judgement to bear (see EAT decision in *Capper Pass Ltd. v. Lawton* [1976] IRLR 366).

What is work of " equivalent value " ?

Work of equivalent value is defined in section 1(5) of the Act. In effect, it means that the woman's job has been rated the same as the man's job by virtue of a **job evaluation exercise.** The jobs must be given " an equal value, in terms of the demand made on a worker under various headings (for instance effort, skill, decision) on a study undertaken with a view to evaluating " the jobs to be done by all or any employees in an undertaking.

It has been said that there are a number of ways in which a job evaluation exercise can discriminate against women.[1]   In a normal job evaluation exercise points are awarded for different factors, *e.g.* manual dexterity, qualifications, experience, etc.   The awarding of actual points should be the same to both sexes, but there is nothing to stop certain factors being given a higher rating than other factors.   Thus manual dexterity or accuracy may be given a low rating and factors such as physical effort or strength could be given a high rating.

An employee claiming equal pay by virtue of work " of equivalent value " has to show—

(1) that her work has been rated as equivalent to a man's job under a job evaluation exercise or study.

(2) that the terms of her employment are not as favourable as his and

(3) that there is no genuine material difference between their cases (other than the difference in sex).

Thus, the job itself does not have to be the same—as in the case of " like work ".   The job must, however, have been rated as equivalent to a man's job under a job evaluation study.   In addition, the study itself must be a proper study, involving full discussions with the employees and/or their representatives (see, in this respect, paragraph (*h*) on page 58).

---

[1] See in particular " *Rights for Women* " by Patricia Hewitt.

The employee's remedies

An employee who feels that she is not receiving equal treatment under the Act can obviously approach her employer in the hope that it will be possible to settle the matter amicably.

In addition, the employee can approach the Equal Opportunities Commission (EOC) which has power to help individuals who have a complaint under the Act (or, of course, under the Sex Discrimination Act 1975). The EOC can give advice and can help by way of conciliation. The EOC may also help an employee with an application to an Industrial Tribunal, but it is thought that it will probably only do so if the case establishes or raises a matter of principle.

In any event, if the matter cannot be agreed, the employee can apply to an Industrial Tribunal.[1] Any such application under the Equal Pay Act must be made either during the employment or within six months of the termination of the employment. The Tribunal can declare the rights of the parties including in particular what is the proper entitlement of the employee under the " equality clause " and/or it can award damages or arrears of remuneration. The Tribunal cannot award any pay for the weeks prior to 29th December 1975 (on which date the right to equality of treatment came into existence) nor can it award back pay for more than two years prior to the date of commencement of proceedings. Subject to this, however, the Tribunal is not limited as to the amount of compensation it can award, e.g. it is not subject to the normal Tribunal limit (at present, in many matters, £5,200).

It should be noted that under section 2(1A) if a dispute arises as to an equality matter, the employer himself can—if he wishes—apply to an Industrial Tribunal for an order declaring the rights of the employer and of the employee in relation to the matter in question.

If in any proceedings before the ordinary courts an issue as to equality of treatment arises, the matter can be referred by the court to an Industrial Tribunal.

---

[1] See Chapter 24 as to a more detailed consideration of the Industrial Tribunals.

Central Arbitration Committee

The Act also provides for the CAC (prior to 1st February 1976 it was the Industrial Arbitration Board) to remove discrimination in collective agreements, employers' pay structures and statutory wages orders which have been referred to it. Such references cannot be made by the individual, but the Secretary of State for Employment or the employer can make a reference and, in the case of a collective agreement, a reference can also be made by the trade union which is a party to the Agreement.

Examples of decided cases under the Equal Pay Act

Statistics up to 31st May 1976 seem to confirm that the burden of proof on the applicant is a heavy one. It seems to be difficult in many cases to establish " like work " and, even when this hurdle is overcome the employer has often been able to show that the difference in pay was due to a genuine material difference (other than sex). Approximately 4,000 complaints were lodged under the Equal Pay Act up to 31st May 1976 and of the cases actually heard by that date only 18 women actually won their cases before an Industrial Tribunal. Admittedly, of the remainder, some were withdrawn and others were settled with the help of the Advisory Conciliation and Arbitration Service. The situation may change if and when cases reach the higher courts.

As in all aspects of employment law, each particular case does depend on its own facts and circumstances; it does seem that this is of even greater relevance in cases under the Equal Pay Act. References to decided cases should, therefore, be treated with very great care. Having said this, the first reported cases under the Act do show the way in which the Tribunals are interpreting the provisions of the Act.

The following case notes are, however, set out as examples only:—

(a) A woman paid £23 per week as an order clerk, collating orders and doing a small amount of stocktaking and packing, failed in her claim for equality with a man who was paid £29 per week and who worked full-time on packing books delivered to him after the orders had been collated. The Tribunal held that the work was **not work of the same or a broadly similar nature.** Indeed, the evidence of the female applicant that her work was "more skilled and more responsible" than that of the male employee seemed to go against her. The Tribunal stated that this factor did "to some extent impair her own case" as it tended to imply that her work was not "**like work**". (*Hopkinson v. EP Publishing Ltd.* (1976) IRLR 99.)

This seems to be a strange—but legally correct—outcome of the Act. The female employee must be able to show "like work". She will fail in her claim for equality if she does less important or responsible work; and it seems that she will also fail if her job is more important and responsible, even though she is paid less than a man who has a less responsible job.

(*b*) An unreported case which seems to stress the above point related to a community worker in Leicester who sought equal pay with a male colleague whom she had trained and whom she supervised, but who earned £400 a year more than she did. Her application was refused by an Industrial Tribunal because she had **more responsibility** than the man.[1]

It will be interesting to see whether this aspect of the law will be changed in the future.

(*c*) Two women employed as drill operators on an hourly rate of 71.3p per hour claimed equality with a male drill operator who was paid at the rate of £1.016 per hour. On the face of it, it seemed that all three, working alongside each other, were doing much the same sort of work. The Tribunal, however, found that the male employee had the ability to obtain the appropriate jig and drill and to set his own machine and that he was also able to sharpen and replace drills and carry out minor repairs thus relieving the charge-hand of responsibility. This

---

[1] On appeal the Employment Appeal Tribunal remitted this case to the Industrial Tribunal for further consideration—see *Waddington v. Leicester Council for Voluntary Service.* (*The Times,* December 17, 1976.)

was not the case with the women and their applications, therefore, failed. The difference in pay was " **genuinely due to a material difference other than the difference of sex** ". (*Brodie v. Startrite Engineering Co. Ltd.* (1976) IRLR 101.)

(*d*) In *Sharp and Lister v. Mogil Motors (Stirling) Ltd.* (1976) IRLR 132, Mrs. Sharp succeeded in her application for equal pay in a job entailing the supply of spare vehicle parts to the public and the compiling estimates, etc.; the Tribunal held that there was no genuine material difference justifying the men's higher rate of pay, despite their additional experience in the motor trade. In the same case, however, Mrs. Lister failed in her claim for equality because, although she and a male employee worked " as a team ", unloading and storing parts, there was a **genuine material difference** between his case and her's in that he acted as manager of the Tyre Department and Petrol Station for 4 or 5 weeks in a year when the manager was on holiday or off sick. Other than those additional duties, the work was of a broadly similar nature. In fact, in this case the Tribunal (without any power to make a formal order) suggested to the employers that they might in any event consider re-classifying Mrs. Lister in a higher grade for pay purposes. No formal order could be made because in the higher grade in question (which seemed most appropriate to the Tribunal) no men were employed and, therefore, there was no one with whom Mrs. Lister could claim equality.

(*e*) In *Peskett v. Robinsons (Woking) Ltd.* (1976) IRLR 134 a female buyer in the Tobacco Department of a store claimed equality with the buyer in the Men's Department. She argued that the duties and the job specification were basically the same. The Tribunal dismissed the application and found that there were substantial differences in the work, although the job title of " buyer " was the same. It was held that the responsibilities of the buyer in the Men's Department depended much more on experience and knowledge, *e.g.* as to which lines would be likely to sell and in which price bracket. The same experience was not necessary in the Tobacco Department, and mistakes there would not be as costly to the Company.

(*f*) A female application of 25 years standing was successful in the case of *Buckland v. Dowty Rotol Ltd.* (1976) IRLR 162, even though there were differences between what she did and what the men did. 18 people (14 men and 4 women) were employed as viewers, inspecting and examining various aero components, checking them for quality and then passing them to the senior foreman. The men were classed as " inspectors ". The employers contended that one material difference was that the men fixed their own approval stamps to the components whilst in the case of the applicant her work had to be counter-stamped by the foreman; in addition, the applicant did not work on certain machines, nor did she have to make certain technical calculations. Despite this—and on the evidence of the foreman that it was not in fact necessary to check the applicant's work—the Tribunal held that there was no material difference between the applicant's case and that of the inspectors as a whole. There was, however, a difference between the three grades of inspectors and the Tribunal ordered that the applicant be treated in the same way as an inspector in the middle grade.

An award was made whereby the applicant was to be paid at the middle grade rate (£53.65 per week basic) with effect from the implementation date of the Act—which the Tribunal treated as being effectively 1st January 1976.

(*g*) A case arising out of a **job evaluation exercise** produced a rather surprising result. In *Bedwell and others v. Hellerman Deutsch Ltd.* [1976] IRLR 98, women were employed as viewers and were responsible for inspecting components; they were classed as hourly paid workers and paid at a woman's rate. 8 men did similar work, but were on staff status and were called " inspectors ". There then followed a job evaluation exercise and the men and the women were placed in the same grade. A new grade rate was fixed and the women received an appropriate pay increase. In the case of the men, however, their previous staff status rate of pay was higher than the new grade rate. Faced with this dilemma, the employers decided to leave the 8 men at the higher rate, undertaking that all new male employees would be taken on at the same grade rate as the women. The women applied to a Tribunal and the Tribunal dismissed their claim, holding that the men's **previous** staff status amounted to a **genuine material difference** other than a difference in sex.

This may seem a controversial decision. Is the Tribunal saying that because men were paid more in the past, this justifies them being paid more even after 29th December 1975? With respect, one would have thought that this should not be correct.

Of course, the case depended on its own particular facts and there is no doubt that two factors which weighed heavily with the Tribunal were, firstly, that the employers were only implementing their policy with the existing 8 male employees and not with any new male employees and secondly, that—" those responsible for the Act could not have imagined that such a major change in industrial relations could be instantly achieved on 29th December 1975 without problems ".

(*h*) In several unreported cases involving allegations of work of " equivalent value ", Tribunals have refused to accept the job evaluation study as a valid base for the claim. In particular, if a study has been undertaken without involving the participation or views of the employees at all, it may be subsequently ignored. Even then, of course, the Tribunal can still consider the matter under the " like work " heading. This in fact happened in the Brodie case (see paragraph (*c*) above).

(*i*) In *Dugdale v. Kraft Foods Ltd.* [1976] IRLR 368 EAT held that the mere fact that men doing work of the same or a broadly similar nature as women were required to work night shifts and on Sundays did not in itself constitute a difference under section 1(4) and should, therefore, be disregarded.

CHAPTER 4

DISCRIMINATION DURING EMPLOY-MENT

We have already considered the matter of discrimination (under both the Sex Discrimination Act 1975 and the Race Relations Act 1976) in relation to the offer of employment or the withholding of an offer of employment.

We must now consider the position with regard to discrimination during the employment.

SEX DISCRIMINATION

Equality in the actual terms of a contract of employment has been dealt with in the preceding chapter (pages 48 to 58).

There can, however, be discrimination in non-contractual matters, *e.g.* training, promotion, benefits, etc. This will be covered by the Sex Discrimination Act 1975 (referred to in this chapter as the SDA). The SDA came into force on 29th December 1975 (the same commencement date as the Equal Pay Act 1970).

The **definition** of discrimination (direct and indirect) has already been considered and is set out on pages 4 to 6.

Similarly, the **exceptions** to the SDA provisions are set out on pages 7 to 11.

All those matters are equally applicable to the position during the employment.

Discrimination in terms of employment

Section 6(1) of the SDA deals with discrimination **prior to** the applicant accepting an offer of employment (see pages 4 to 11, *ante*).

After the applicant has accepted an offer of employment section 6(2)(*a*) of the SDA states that it is unlawful for the employer to discriminate—

"(*a*) in the way he affords her access to opportunities for **promotion, transfer or training,** or to any other **benefits, facilities or services,** or by refusing or deliberately omitting to afford her access to them."

It is also unlawful under section 6(2)(*b*) of the SDA to discriminate by **dismissing** an employee or subjecting her to any **other detriment.** The dismissal aspect of the matter will be dealt with in Chapters 19 to 22.

There are some rather complicated provisions in the SDA intended to cover the possible overlapping provisions of the SDA and the Equal Pay Act—see, in particular, sections 6(5), 6(6) and 8(5) of the SDA. The effect of these provisions is that, in general terms, matters regulated by a woman's contract of employment (*e.g.* pay and other contractual matters) are dealt with under the Equal Pay Act 1970. It has been said[1] that these provisions do leave " a gaping hole in the anti-discrimination legislation ". It is not, however, proposed in this book to embark upon a rather technical discussion as to inter-relation of the various sections of the two Statutes.

It is, however, interesting to note that whereas under the Equal Pay Act a woman to be successful has to establish that her work is comparable with a specified man in the same employment (see page 50) this is not the case under the SDA. The comparison under the SDA can be made with a hypothetical man.

Promotion, transfer and training

The employer (unless the matter falls within one of the exceptions referred to previously) must now take great care with regard to the selection of employees for training and with regard to opportunities for promotion or transfers to other jobs.

---

[1] " *Sex Discrimination* " by D. J. Walker (*published by Shaw & Sons Ltd.*), at p. 21.

As far as **promotion** is concerned, each employee (whether male or female or married or single) must be considered on his or her merits. The same opportunities must be offered to **all** employees. This will cover, for example, opportunities for broadening work experience, grading structures and advertising of promotion opportunities. It may be indirect discrimination to call for experience in a certain grade if such experience has not been required previously. Similarly, if an employer says that all applicants for a managerial post must go on a 3 months' residential course, this could be indirect discrimination because women (with home responsibilities) are less likely to be able to go on such a course; in that situation, the employer would have to prove that the 3 months' course was both justified and necessary.

If **transfer** opportunities are offered to one sex only, this will be direct discrimination. The employer must not assume that female employees will not be interested in a transfer, for example because it will involve longer working hours. The employer should " play safe " and offer the chance of a transfer to all employees.

It is also dangerous to forget that the SDA applies equally to men.[1] The same criteria must be applied to both sexes. Thus if the employer only calls upon the men to move to another part of the country and assume that it would be unfair to ask the women (with their family commitments) to move, then this may give rise to a complaint from the men. This could be " subjecting " the men to " any other detriment " under section 6(2)(*b*).

Equal opportunities for **training** must be offered. Statistics do show that female employees have fared extremely badly in the past in this particular area. Employers must now give their female employees the chance to attend such things as day-release courses, seminars, and management training courses. Again, the employer must **not** assume that female employees will not want or be able to attend such courses, even where, for example, the course is a residential one.

---

[1] SDA, s. 2(1).

Benefits, facilities and services

There must be " equal access " to all benefits, facilities and services. This covers a multitude of matters and will include, for example, such things as loans (whether for house purchase or other matters), free overalls, dress allowances, removal expenses, car and general expenses, club memberships, flexible working hours, etc.

In this sphere direct discrimination is more likely to arise than indirect discrimination. Employers should, therefore, review these matters carefully in relation to all their employees.

The provisions of the SDA relating to discrimination in respect of an employee's access to benefits, facilities or services do not apply if the employer is concerned with provision of those benefits, facilities or services to the public unless they are materially different or their provision is regulated by her contract of employment.[1]

Other detriment

What sort of **detrimental treatment** is unlawful under section 6(2)(*b*)?

This can include almost anything short of actual dismissal (which is dealt with on page 60).

If, therefore, a female employee is laid off or put on short time and this does not happen to one or more male employees, the employer must be able to show that there was a good reason for this action and that it did not relate to the sex of that particular employee.

Similarly, selection of employees for shift-work or for over-time must not be discriminatory, unless the matter is already allowed by some other statute, *e.g.* the Factories Act provisions forbidding night work for women.

In the case of *Morris v. Scott and Knowles* (1976) IRLR 238 a reduction in the hours of work of certain female employees from 40 to 30 hours per week, following implementation of the Equal Pay Act, was held to be unlawful discrimination; the

---

[1] SDA, s. 6(7).

female employees had been singled out and had suffered loss of pay and this treatment was clearly on grounds of their sex.

In selecting female employees for redundancy, the employer must not act in a discriminatory manner and should be able to show a good reason for such selection. If he cannot do so, the action may be unlawful and give rise to a claim under the SDA. This will be regardless of whether the selection was also " unfair " within the meaning of the Trade Union and Labour Relations Act 1974 (see page 293).

Sanctions

The sanctions imposed on an employer by the SDA have already been covered on pages 15 to 21.

They apply equally to discrimination under the SDA which arises during the course of the employment.

In particular, the employee can apply within three months from the date of the discriminatory act to an Industrial Tribunal. Compensation of up to £5,200 can be awarded. The awards that the Tribunal can make are dealt with on page 16. They include compensation for injury to feelings.

Victimisation

Section 4 of the SDA makes it unlawful for an employer (and other persons) to victimise another person (for example, another employee) because that person has—

(a) brought proceedings under the SDA or under the Equal Pay Act or

(b) given evidence or information in connection with any such proceedings or

(c) otherwise done anything under or by reference to the two Acts referred to or

(d) alleged that the employer has contravened either of the two Acts

or because the employer knows or suspects that the other person has done, or intends to do, any of those things.

Thus, if an employer tries to down-grade an employee or treat her detrimentally because she has, say, helped other female employees to stand up for their rights, that will be an unlawful act of discrimination and she will be able to take the matter to an Industrial Tribunal.

The victimisation section also covers persons other than the one against whom action may have been taken. For example, if after taking action against an employer in respect of discrimination, a person subsequently finds that other employers will not offer her a job, that also could be unlawful.

RACIAL DISCRIMINATION

Reference has already been made to the Race Relations Act 1976 (pages 11 to 15, *supra*). Everything set out in those pages (in particular the definitions and the exceptions to the 1976 Act) are equally applicable to questions of racial discrimination **during** the employment.

It has already been noted that the Race Relations Act 1976 is based almost entirely on the Sex Discrimination Act 1975. Leaving aside that each Act deals with a different type of discrimination, the wording of the relevant sections for employment matters is almost identical.

Thus section 4(2) of the Race Relations Act 1976 is almost identical to section 6(2) of the SDA. It provides that it is unlawful to discriminate against an employee—

(*a*) in the terms of employment which he affords him or

(*b*) in the way he affords him access to opportunities for promotion, transfer or training or to any other benefits, facilities or services, or by refusing or deliberately omitting to afford him access to them, or

(*c*) by dismissing him or subjecting him to any other detriment.

It is not proposed to deal further with racial discrimination, as all the comments made in the preceding pages relating to sex discrimination and the rights and remedies of the employee are equally applicable.

PRACTICAL IMPLICATIONS FOR EMPLOYERS

The practical position with regard to promotion, transfer and training and with regard to the provision of other benefits, facilities or services has been covered on pages 60 to 63.

As far as avoidance of discrimination during the employment is concerned, the employer **must** now take care that he is aware of the provisions of the Sex Discrimination Act 1975 and the Race Relations Act 1976. He should check and re-think his employment policies and procedures. As long as every comparable employee is treated the same way and is given equal treatment, there can be no problem. In particular, employees must be given equal opportunities.

Again, it is suggested that the **keeping of records** is now of vital importance (see page 22). If an employee is to be promoted, then all possible existing employees should be considered, and relevant details should be noted in the records of each individual, together with the ultimate reason for selection for promotion or otherwise.

Similar procedures should be adopted with regard to transfers and training. As indicated previously, an employer should never assume that an employee does not want to be considered for such things as promotion or transfer to another job or for training.

In addition to the record system, the **questionnaires** for use prior to proceedings under either Act must be dealt with very carefully indeed. This has been considered on page 24.

Finally, employers should review those of their employees who are in **positions of authority** and ensure that they are all fully aware of the provisions of the law relating to discrimination. Reference should be made to page 25, where this problem has already been considered. The employer will normally be responsible for the acts and omissions of those who work for him and he should, therefore, take every possible step to try and ensure that they do not commit unlawful acts. Consideration should be given to the issuing of a formal written notice or instruction on the lines suggested on page 26.

E

PART III

DURING THE EMPLOYMENT

THE OBLIGATIONS OF THE EMPLOYER AND THE RIGHTS OF THE EMPLOYEE

Having considered in the preceding chapters the relationship between employer and employee and the establishment of the terms of the contract of employment itself, what are the obligations of the employer and the rights of an employee **during** the term of the employment?

In the first instance, one must look at the actual terms of the contract (express or implied)—see pages 31 to 35, *ante*. Quite apart from such terms, there are now a considerable number of rights to which nearly all employees are entitled. These rights arise under various statutes and, in general, it is not possible to "contract out" of their provisions. It is proposed to consider these rights under separate headings in the following chapters. The rights can be summarised very briefly as follows, the qualifying period in each case being shown in brackets:—

1. The right to receive a statement under the Contracts of Employment Act 1972 (13 weeks).
2. A right to equal pay (none).
3. No discrimination on grounds of sex or marital status (none).
4. No discrimination on grounds of race, colour, etc. (none).
5. The right to receive an itemised pay statement (none).
6. A right to be a member of Trade Union and to become involved in Trade Union activities (none).

7. A right to have time off (with pay) for Trade Union officials (none).

8. A right to have time off for Trade Union Members (none).

9. A right to have time off for public duties (none).

10. A right in certain redundancy circumstances to have time off to look for work or for training (2 years).

11. Medical suspension pay (4 weeks).

12. Guarantee pay when no work available (4 weeks).

13. Maternity pay of up to 6 weeks (2 years).

14. Reinstatement in job after maternity leave (2 years).

15. Redundancy consultation and protective award (none).

16. A right to receive redundancy pay (2 years).

17. A right not to be unfairly dismissed (26 weeks, or none, if for Trade Union involvement).

18. A right to receive a written statement of reasons for dismissal (26 weeks).

19. A right to receive a minimum period of notice to terminate the employment (4 weeks).

20. Insolvency payment from the Redundancy Fund (none)

This formidable list must now be considered in more detail.

For ease of reference a simple form of chart dealing with the various employee rights has also been prepared and this is set out as Appendix VI (pages 372 to 382).

CHAPTER 5

THE EMPLOYER AND THE TRADE UNION

It is not the purpose of this book to deal with the historical development of the Trade Union movement nor is it intended to cover in detail the various aspects of the relationship between a Trade Union and its members and the Trade Union and the employer respectively.

There are, however, several vital matters involving Trade Unions which do directly affect the Law of Employment and these matters have now been crystallised by the recent legislation. They include the question of Union recognition, the principle of the Closed Shop and the problem of disclosure of information. These are practical matters which cannot be ignored by an employer and they must be considered. It is also appropriate to consider here the provisions of the EPA under which a union can claim an improvement in terms and conditions of employment by comparison with the general level of terms in the same trade or industry.

UNION RECOGNITION

An employer may be approached by an official of a Trade Union[1] with a request that the particular Union be recognised by the employer for the purpose of collective bargaining on behalf of its members.

Should the employer agree to " recognise " the Trade Union?

The answer to that question must depend on the circumstances of the particular case and on many other matters (some possibly political) which will not be considered here.

---

[1] For these purposes a Trade Union is assumed to be " an independent trade union ", *i.e.* a Trade Union which is not under the domination or control of an employer **and** which is not liable to interference by an employer (arising out of financial or other support) tending towards such control—Trade Union and Labour Relations Act 1974, s. 30(1), and Employment Protection Act 1975, s. 126(1).

An independent trade union must also obtain a certificate of independence from the Certification Officer under ss. 7 and 8 of the EPA.

One thing, however, is certain and that is that the employer who is approached in this way must think very carefully before reaching a decision. In particular, he should be aware of the fact that if he refuses recognition, then in certain circumstances (which we will now consider), an Order can be made imposing upon him certain terms and conditions relating to the contract of employment.

The 1972 Code of Practice (introduced under the Industrial Relations Act 1971 and still in force under the Trade Union and Labour Relations Act 1974) appears (without directly saying so) to recommend recognition of a Trade Union. The Code, it will be remembered, sets standards which reflect good industrial relations practice.

The Introduction to **the 1972 Code** stresses " the vital role of collective bargaining carried out in a reasonable and constructive manner between employers and strong representative trade unions ".

Paragraph 3 of that Code states that—" good industrial relations are the joint responsibility of management and of employees and trade unions representing them ".

But—the Code continues—" the primary responsibility " rests with management.

Where trade unions are recognised for negotiating purposes paragraph 4 of the Code lays down the obligations of management, which should—

" (i) maintain jointly with the trade unions effective arrangements for negotiation, consultation and communication, and for settling grievances and disputes;

(ii) take all reasonable steps to ensure that managers observe agreements and use agreed procedures;

(iii) make clear to employees that it welcomes their membership of an appropriate recognised union and their participation in the union's activities ".

A Trade Union seeking recognition will normally wish to be **" recognised "** for the purpose of **collective bargaining** on behalf of its members.

" **Collective bargaining** " means negotiations relating to or connected with one or more of the following matters:—

(a) terms and conditions (including also physical conditions) of employment

(b) engagement or termination or suspension of employment of one or more workers

(c) allocation of work or duties as between workers

(d) matters of discipline

(e) the membership or non-membership of a trade union

(f) facilities for trade union officials

(g) machinery for negotiation or consultation, including the actual recognition by the employer of a particular trade union.[1]

It will be noted that the strict definition of "collective bargaining " is limited to the above matters; thus, *e.g.* matters such as financial planning and investment policy are not included.

One of the aims of the Employment Protection Act 1975—as part of its overall aim to improve industrial relations—is to further recognition of independent trade unions. The provisions are contained in **sections 11 to 16 of the EPA** and these sections came into force on 1st February 1976, by virtue of the Employment Protection Act 1975 (Commencement No. 1) Order 1975.

The effect of these sections is that a recognition issue (defined as an issue arising from a request by a trade union for recognition by an employer for the purpose of collective bargaining) can be referred **by the trade union** to the Advisory, Conciliation and Arbitration Service (ACAS). The Act does **not** provide for the employer to refer a recognition issue to the ACAS (*e.g.* in an inter-union rivalry dispute) although the ACAS could still be asked to advise and conciliate.

The EPA emphasises the desirability of voluntary settlement.

The ACAS will look into the matter and **consult** all parties who may be affected. These parties may include other unions and, indeed, the TUC. The ACAS will **conciliate** and will try

---

[1] See Employment Protection Act 1975, s. 126(1), and Trade Union and Labour Relations Act 1974, s. 29(1).

and encourage a settlement. In the course of its enquiries the ACAS must ascertain the opinion of the employees affected by the matter; this can be done in any way, but it can be by way of a formal ballot. In the event of a ballot the voting must be secret and every employee must have an equal right and a fair opportunity of voting. The result of the ballot must be notified to the employer and to the union and the employer must notify the result to all employees who were entitled to vote. The ballot result is not binding on ACAS; failure to get a majority will not, therefore, be decisive. Under the recognition procedure established by the Industrial Relations Act 1971 (and abolished by the Trade Union and Labour Relations Act 1974) it was not unusual for a union with as little as 33% of the employees as members to be recommended for recognition by the then CIR (Commission on Industrial Relations). What is important is not the actual membership at the time of the ballot or enquiry, but the potential membership and support if recommendation is recommended. If the issue is not settled by conciliation—and the union has not withdrawn its application—the ACAS has to prepare a report setting out its findings, its advice and (if appropriate) its recommendation for recognition. The reasons for such recommendation must be stated and the employer and union concerned must be informed.

It is not at present known what criteria ACAS will apply. A new Code of Practice relating to recognition will be issued in due course under the EPA. This Code should help employers and unions to reach voluntary agreement. Before any new Code comes into force a draft must be published for consultation (section 6(3), EPA).

The first step in a recognition issue is for the parties themselves, *i.e.* the employer and the union claiming recognition, to seek to resolve the issue by their own efforts. ACAS can help in this matter, if necessary, but the assistance of ACAS is not meant to be a substitute for direct discussion between the parties.

Recognition questions sometimes involve very complex issues. On other occasions the issue can be quite simple. ACAS has various methods of assisting trade unions and employers who cannot reach an agreement on a recognition issue; these methods are as follows:—

(a) **Advice.**—ACAS can give free advice on the organisation of workers or of employers for the purpose of collective bargaining and on the recognition of trade unions by employers. ·

(b) **Conciliation.**—Where there is a dispute about recognition, ACAS may be invited to assist or it may offer assistance by conciliation to try to settle the matter. Its own officers may act or someone else may be appointed from outside the Service. Acceptance of assistance by the parties is an entirely voluntary matter.

(c) **Inquiry.**—Subject to consultation with all parties likely to be interested, ACAS may inquire into any recognition question and may publish its findings if, after full consultation with the parties concerned, it thinks it would be helpful to do so.

It is important to remember that the above services are available equally to employers and to trade unions. Having said this, ACAS will always take into account any existing procedures that are available to resolve the matter, including TUC procedures where appropriate. ACAS will not normally intervene unless these procedures have been fully used.

Since the introduction of sections 11 to 16 of the EPA—and prior to the issuing of the Code as to Trade Union Recognition —ACAS has proceeded with the examination of various recognition disputes and, over the period from 1st February 1976 to 30th November 1976 seven written reports were issued by ACAS, setting out its findings and recommendations in the particular cases under review.

It is clear from these reports that ACAS will consider each and every application on its merits. In many cases there will be a majority of employees supporting the application for recognition, but this is not essential for a recommendation of recognition. Actual union membership at the time of the ACAS inquiry is not as important as are the views and intentions of employees if a union was in fact recognised. Thus, it is quite likely that employees will be asked by ACAS whether they would join the particular union if it was recognised.

If recognition is recommended by the ACAS, it becomes operative within 14 days from the date on which the employer receives the report (or, in the case of a conditional recommendation within 14 days from notification of compliance with the conditions) and it remains operative until superseded by agreement or revoked by the ACAS (if circumstances change).

The ACAS must specify the employer and trade union concerned, the description of employees covered by recognition and the matters for and levels at which recognition is recommended. It should be noted that there is **no appeal** against an ACAS recommendation nor against its refusal to recommend recognition. An employer can, however, apply for the terms of a recommendation to be altered or revoked; if the application is solely by the employer he will normally have to show that re-consideration is necessary because circumstances have changed or further information has become available.

Once the recommendation is operative the employer effectively has two months in which to comply. This does not mean that final agreement has to be reached in that time; the employer must, however, take such action " as might reasonably be expected to be taken by an employer ready and willing to carry on such negotiations " as are envisaged by the ACAS recommendation. The test here is objective. If after two months there is no sign that the employer is acting in accordance with the recommendation, the union can again refer the matter to ACAS and claim that the employer had not complied with the recommendation. Again, the ACAS must try and settle the matter by conciliation. If, however, this fails the trade union **may** apply to the Central Arbitration Committee (CAC). (The CAC is a body set up under the EPA 1975, section 10, and, amongst other things, it takes the place of the old Industrial Arbitration Board).

The application to the CAC has to be in writing and must consist of—

(a) a complaint that the employer is not complying with the ACAS recommendation and

(b) a claim that in respect of one or more descriptions of employees covered by that recommendation their contracts should include the terms and conditions specified in the claim.

The CAC will not consider an application if it is substantially the same as a complaint on which it has ruled within the last 12 months.

The CAC will hear the complaint and make a declaration as to whether or not it finds the complaint " well founded ". If such a finding is made, the CAC may—after hearing the parties—make an award that, in respect of the employees specified in its declaration, the employer shall observe either the terms and conditions specified in the claim by the trade union or such other terms and conditions as the CAC considers appropriate.

Those terms and conditions then become effective as part of the contract of employment of those particular employees as from the date specified in the award.

The CAC cannot enforce recognition as such, but the practical outcome of the above provisions in fact will produce the result required by the union, *i.e.* certain specified terms and conditions will be " written " into the contract.

It will, therefore, be seen that in this way it is possible for certain terms of a contract of employment (*e.g.* a wage increase) to be imposed unilaterally upon and without the consent of the other party. Employers may well feel, in the light of this, that once they are satisfied that a reasonable proportion of their employees (or of a particular group of employees) are members of an independent trade union, then there is more to be gained than lost by recognising that trade union for collective bargaining purposes. An employer who grants recognition voluntarily may well have more control over the outcome of negotiations with the union that if he refuses recognition and leaves himself open to the above procedures.

DISCLOSURE OF INFORMATION

Disclosure under the Code of Practice

" Collective bargaining can be conducted responsibly only if management and unions have adequate information on the matters being negotiated "—paragraph 96 of the Code of Practice issued under the Industrial Relations Act 1971.

That Code goes on, in paragraph 97, to say that management should make available to trade unions at least " the information which is supplied to shareholders or published in annual reports ".

It will be appreciated that such matters as Accounts and Balance Sheets are in any event filed at the Companies Registry under the Companies Act 1948-67 and that such information can be readily obtained by any member of the public. In this context, it should be noted that there will probably be amendments to the Companies Act 1967 under which Company Reports will in future have to disclose much more information, *e.g.* statements of co-operative objectives, policy statements on industrial relations and related matters and various other items of general interest.

A new Code of Practice on Disclosure of Information for Collective Bargaining Purposes is issued under the Employment Protection Act 1975 and this now deals with the matter in rather more detail.

The question of disclosure has been put on a formal statutory basis by the Employment Protection Act 1975 and, in certain specified areas, by the Industry Act 1975.

Disclosure under the Employment Protection Act 1975

The relevant provisions of the Employment Protection Act 1975 are contained in sections 17 to 21. Those provisions come into force during 1977 after the new Code referred to above has been approved by Parliament.

The disclosure provisions of EPA are linked entirely to disclosure to the representatives of a **recognised independent trade union** (which includes a trade union recommended for recognition by the ACAS). There are no provisions regarding disclosure direct to an employee. There is still, therefore, no legal obligation on an employer to disclose information to his employees.

Under the EPA it will be the duty of every employer regardless of size (there is no exclusion for small firms) to disclose to the representatives of an independent trade union recognised by the employer all information in his possession which is both—

    (*a*) information without which the union would be to a material extent impeded in carrying out collective bargaining **and**

    (*b*) information which it would be in accordance with good industrial relations practice that he should disclose.

The disclosure only has to be made if the union requests the relevant information, and the employer can insist that such request shall be in writing.

The ACAS has to issue a Code of Practice, giving guidance as to the information which should be disclosed " in accordance with good industrial relations practice ".

A draft Code was issued as a Consultative Document during the summer of 1976 and this shows the sort of information that employers can be called upon to disclose. The Code becomes effective when approved by Parliament.

As with the Codes issued under other parts of Employment legislation, the Code does not impose legal obligations on an employer to disclose any specification of information. Failure to observe it does not by itself render anyone liable to proceedings. The Employment Protection Act does, however, provide that any relevant provisions of the Code must be taken into account in any proceedings before the Central Arbitration Committee (see *below*). Careful attention should, therefore, be paid to the contents of the Code.

The Code makes it clear that relevant information provided by employers can be an essential ingredient to good industrial relations and successful negotiations. Obviously, the types of information which will be relevant will vary. It is, therefore, impossible to compile a list of items of information which should be disclosed in all circumstances. The draft Code does, however, give some examples of the types of information which " could be relevant in certain collective bargaining situations ". They are as follows:—

(i) PAY: principles and structure of payment systems including grading criteria; earnings and hours analysed by either work-group, grade, plant, sex, department or company giving, where appropriate, distributions and make up of pay showing any additions to basic rate or salary; details of fringe benefits and non-wage labour costs.

(ii) CONDITIONS OF SERVICE: principal conditions of service; recruitment, redeployment, training, promotion policies, redundancy plans; proposed charges in work methods and materials; health, welfare and safety matters; job evaluation systems; appraisal systems; pensions scheme (including benefits, contributions, financial and administrative policy).

(iii) EMPLOYMENT: number employed analysed by grades, department, location, age; labour turnover; absenteeism; overtime and short time appropriately analysed; manning standards; proposed organisational or technical changes, available manpower plans.

(iv) PRODUCTIVITY: productivity data appropriately analysed; schedules and methods of work; savings from increased productivity; return on capital invested; market share of products and state of order book.

(v) FINANCIAL: relevant cost structures; gross and net profits; sources of earnings; assets; liabilities; allocation of profits; details of government financial assistance; transfer prices; loans to parent companies and interest charged.

The Code urges both employers and trade unions to consider entering into agreements (referred to as " **Information Agreements** ") with regard to the disclosure of information. Such agreements would set out the type of information that might be available, the form in which it is to be presented and when and to whom it is to be presented and when and to whom it should be given; arrangements for ensuring confidentiality should be agreed and a procedure laid down for resolving disputes relating to any issues associated with the disclosure of information.

The Code states that **management** should formulate a policy on disclosure of information for collective bargaining, the policy to be as open and helpful as possible in meeting trade union requirements unless these are genuine considered reasons for refusal. Information should be made available without unnecessary delay once a request has been made by an accredited union representative. The information should be presented in a form and style which is readily understood by its recipients.

Trade unions are recommended, by the Code, to identify in advance of negotiations the information they require for collective bargaining. "Misunderstandings can be avoided, costs reduced, and time saved, if requests state precisely all the information required and if they conform to an agreed procedure". A reasonable period of time should be allowed for employers to consider a request.

Trade unions are also asked to try and ensure that negotiators are equipped to understand and use information effectively. To this end consideration should be given to allowing union representatives who are employees to have time off to undergo training (as to which see page 101).

There are certain **restrictions** on the general duty to disclose. These are contained in **section 18** of the EPA and are, to a certain extent, amplified by the new Code. An employer is **not** obliged to disclose the following information:—

(a) information that would be against the interests of national security or that would contravene any statute

(b) information communicated to the employer in confidence and information relating specifically to an individual (unless that individual has consented to its disclosure).

(c) information that would cause substantial injury to the employer's business for reasons other than its effect on bargaining.

(d) information obtained by the employer for the purpose of any legal proceedings.

(e) information that would involve an amount of work or expenditure out of reasonable proportion to its value in the conduct of collective bargaining.

The reasons for refusing a request for information should always be explained and be capable of being substantiated by independent enquiry.

The EPA specifically states that an employer is not obliged to produce original documents for inspection or copying.

The Code throws some light on the situation where a request for information is refused because of the prospect of substantial injury to the employer's business.

Substantial injury may be claimed if, for example, certain customers would be lost to competitors, or suppliers would refuse to supply necessary materials, or the ability to raise funds to finance the company would be seriously impaired as a result of disclosing certain information. The burden of establishing a claim that disclosure of certain information would cause substantial injury lies with the employer.

Examples of types of information which in particular circumstances may be likely to cause substantial injury if disclosed outside the context of the negotiations are: cost information on individual products, research and development plans and projects, detailed analysis of proposed investment, marketing or pricing policies, and price quotas or the make-up of tender prices. Information which has to be made available publicly, for example under the Companies Acts, would not fall into this category.

Failure to disclose

What is the position if the employer refuses to disclose the required information? He cannot be prosecuted nor can he be taken to an Industrial Tribunal. There is, however, an indirect enforcement procedure very similar to the Union Recognition procedures referred to above (pages 72 to 74).

If the employer fails to disclose the required information the union can complain to the Central Arbitration Committee (CAC). The CAC will normally then order conciliation via the ACAS. If this fails, the CAC will then hear the complaint and will decide (giving reasons) whether the complaint is well founded. If it is, the CAC will declare a date by which the information must be disclosed.

If the employer still does not comply by the specified date, the union can make a further complaint to the CAC, who will then hold another hearing and make a further declaration stating whether it finds that complaint well-founded.

At this stage, if the complaint has been found to be well-founded, the union can put a claim to the CAC for improvements in the terms and conditions of employment (including, of course, wages) of certain employees. The CAC then has power to make an award on such a claim and such award then becomes a term of the individual employee's contract of employment.

Here again (as in the case of the Union Recognition provisions), although an employer cannot be forced to disclose the required information, the sanction against him is that, if he does not disclose, certain terms and conditions can be imposed upon him unilaterally and without his consent. In practice, therefore, the employer should disclose voluntarily and readily all information which is relevant to the negotiations in hand.

Discloure under the Industry Act 1975

The Industry Act 1975 came into force on 20th November 1975 and, although the Act is not really one which affects the relationship of employer and employee, it does contain provisions relating to the disclosure of information by certain employers. These provisions will probably not affect very many employers and they are, therefore, only summarised very briefly in this book.

The employers are in effect **limited** to large companies in important sectors of the economy. They must be engaged wholly or mainly in the manufacturing industry in the United Kingdom and must make a significant contribution to an industrial sector important to the economy or to a substantial part of it.

The information is to be used to form national economic policies and for consultations between Government, employers or workers on the prospects and outlook for a particular industrial sector.

The information or forecasts must be given first to the Industry or Agriculture Minister and only subsequently to trade union representatives. For these purposes, a union representative must be a union official or someone authorised by the union to carry on negotiations and the union must be an independent trade union with recognised negotiating status with the company. The information is specified in the Act (s. 29) and includes details of the persons normally employed, capital expenditure, fixed capital assets, any disposal or acquisition (actual or intended) of such assets, output and productivity, sales, exports, etc.

Under the Industry Act it is not only information as to the past which has to be given. Companies can now be asked to give forecasts for the future (for the next one, two or ten years) about such matters as numbers to be employed, expected capital expenditure, expenditure on research or development programmes and various other matters. Some companies have expressed fears that this information might get into the hands of competitors. The information and forecasts will normally have to be supplied to the union representatives. It is interesting to note that the Act does not provide that information given to the unions is to be treated by them as confidential.

There are very similar exclusions to those referred to above in the Employment Protection Act relating to sensitive and confidential information. If there is doubt about whether certain information should be disclosed, the matter can be referred—either by the employer or by the union—to a special advisory committee. That committee will then consider the matter and report back to the appropriate Minister and it will be the Minister who will make the final decision.

The Government has expressed the hope that information and forecasts will be given voluntarily but if this is not done there are procedures to obtain disclosure compulsorily. These procedures commence with a **preliminary notice** served on the company by the Minister asking for the information and threatening compulsion if necessary. This notice also requires the company within 14 days to inform authorised trade union representatives of the receipt of the preliminary notice and to give the Minister a list of those union representatives. If this is not done, the company and any responsible officer of the company can be prosecuted and fined up to £400.

If such a preliminary notice has been served, a statement to that effect must be laid before each House of Parliament. If the company still does not give the required information within 3 months of the notice, a **disclosure order** can be made compelling the company to disclose. Before such order is made the company and the trade union are given an opportunity to make representations. After the order, the Minister can serve notice on the company requiring the specified information to be provided within " such reasonable time as may be " stated in the notice. If the company remains in breach, it (and any responsible officer) can be fined up to £400.

It has been seen that the information or forecasts must initially be supplied to the Minister. When this is done, the company (and the union) can make representations about any information which should (or should not) be withheld from the Union. The Minister can then serve a notice on the company telling it to pass certain information on to the union representatives. Again, if this is not complied with, a fine of up to £400 can be levied.

If at any stage of the above procedures a statement is made which is false in a material particular and it is made either recklessly or knowing it to be false, then the Company or any director or responsible officer can be prosecuted and fined up to £400.

THE CLOSED SHOP

The Trade Union and Labour Relations Act 1974 restored the right of employers and trade unions to operate a closed shop, *i.e.* to make it a term of employment of each individual that he should be or become a member of a specified trade union. There were, however, various problems under the 1974 Act, which in parts was too rigid and elsewhere was a little vague.

A closed shop had been quite legal prior to the Industrial Relations Act 1971, but that Act made void any agreement relating to a pre-entry closed shop. Despite this, the closed shop did not die out in practice even whilst the 1971 Act was in force.

The position is now dealt with by the Trade Union and Labour Relations Act 1974, as amended by the Trade Union and Labour Relations (Amendment) Act 1976. The amendments under the latter Act came into force on 25th March 1976.

The law is based on the statutory definition of a **Union membership agreement** as contained in section 30(1) of the 1974 Act. That definition (with its 1976 Act amendments) is of such importance it is proposed to set it out verbatim, including the 1976 amendments—

" ' **Union Membership Agreement** ' means an agreement or arrangement which—

(*a*) is made by or on behalf of, or otherwise exists between, one or more independent trade unions[1] and one or more employers or employers' associations **and**

(*b*) relates to employees of an identifiable class[2] **and**

(*c*) has the effect **in practice** of requiring the employees for the time being of the class to which it relates (whether or not there is a condition to that effect in their contract of employment) to be or become a member of the union or one of the unions which is or are parties to the agreement or arrangement or of another specified independent trade union

---

[1]
[2] As to " independent trade union "—see footnote to p. 68.

and references in this definition to a trade union include references to a branch or section of a trade union; and a trade union is specified for the purposes of, or in relation to, a union membership agreement if it is specified in the agreement or is accepted by the parties to the agreement as being the equivalent of a union so specified ".

The statutes contain no direct provisions—other than the definition itself—relating to a union membership agreement. Whether or not such an agreement should be entered into is a matter for the particular employers and the trade union or unions involved. It is not the purpose of this book to express an opinion as to the desirability (or otherwise) of the closed shop. In practice, there are a great number of union membership agreements both in the public and the private sector.

It would seem that there has been a substantial increase in such agreements, particularly since the enactment of the 1976 Amendment Act referred to above.

Those involved in the negotiation of a union membership agreement should take into account such things as—

(a) which categories of employees are to be covered by the agreement and which are to be excluded.

(b) whether any particular other groups of employees are to be excluded, e.g. part-time workers or workers who have been employed since a date prior to a specified agreed date.

(c) what rights of appeal an employee will have if he is expelled or excluded from a union. In this respect, it should be remembered that under the present legislation a trade union member who is expelled or excluded from his union cannot now take the matter to an Industrial Tribunal. The T.U.C. has, however, set up a " closed shop court " to which a worker can apply once he has exhausted any appeals procedure that may be available to him within his own Union.

(d) provision for future changes which may affect the operation of the union membership agreement.

The importance of the union membership agreement lies in the fact that in general it will now be held to be fair to dismiss an employee on the grounds that he has failed or refused to become a member of an independent trade union where his employment is subject to a union membership agreement.[1] In most cases this will automatically be a fair dismissal (as to which see pages 267 to 268). The only exception now remaining is where an employee genuinely objects on grounds of religious belief to being a member of any trade union whatsoever. It is, of course, possible to exclude at the outset certain specified employees from the union membership agreement, e.g. casual employees or certain part-time employees.

It will, however, be noted that the vital words " **in practice** " are included in section 30(1)(c) (as amended). The existence of a union membership agreement is, therefore, not in itself sufficient. The question must be asked—is the agreement being operated in practice? If it is not, then a Tribunal may well find (as happened in the case of " *The Ferrybridge Six* "[2]) that the agreement has by implication been altered and that the dismissal of an employee who has refused to join a specified union is, therefore, unfair.

It will be seen from the definition that a union membership agreement does not have to be a formal agreement in writing— although very often this will be the case and, if the employer does agree to a closed shop, it is much better to put the matter on a formal basis. The definition also refers to " **an arrangement** " which " exists between " the parties.

The union which is a party to an agreement or arrangement as defined in the Act is obviously covered by it. What, however, is the position of the union which has members working at a particular establishment and which is not a party to a union membership agreement and is not accepted by the parties as a " **specified** " union ?

Under the TUALR, as originally enacted, members of such a union (which in practice would often be a smaller union)

---

1 See TUALR, 1st Sch., para. 6(5) (as amended) and see page 260.
2 *Sarvent and Others v. Central Electricity Generating Board* (1976) IRLR 66, and see p. 268.

were not protected. The Employment Protection Act 1975 has now (with effect from 1st February 1976) partly covered this situation by providing that a union shall be treated as specified for the purposes of a union membership agreement if the ACAS has recommended it for recognition under the EPA provisions as to recognition (see page 73) or if the union having applied for recognition has referred the recognition issue to ACAS and the issue has not been settled. Whether ACAS will in practice recommend the recognition of a " minority union " when a " shop union " strongly objects is, of course, another matter.

TERMS AND CONDITIONS OF EMPLOYMENT

Under section 8 of the Terms and Conditions of Employment Act 1959 an employee could have terms or conditions of employment brought up to the level of other employees where their terms and conditions were established by an " industry agreement " or award in the particular trade or industry concerned. This legislation was very seldom used and had, indeed, almost been forgotten.

Section 98 of the **Employment Protection Act 1975** repeals the 1959 legislation and introduces in its place provisions which are contained in the **11th Schedule** to the EPA. This part of the EPA came into force on 1st January 1977. The Secretary of State for Employment had indicated that its implementation depended on economic factors and on the capacity of the Central Arbitration Committee and the ACAS to deal with the increased work involved. Having said this, in the House of Commons the Secretary of State for Employment indicated that it was the view of the Government that this schedule would only be of limited effect. In practice, however, it seems that the provisions in the 11th Schedule could have far reaching consequences.

The basic principle is that a claim in writing can be submitted to the Advisory Conciliation and Arbitration Service (ACAS) that as respects any worker an employer is observing terms and conditions of employment either

(a) less favourable than the recognised terms and conditions or

(b) where (or so far as) there are no recognised terms and conditions, less favourable than the general level of terms and conditions.

It will be seen, therefore, that the matter can be dealt with under one of these two heads.

Recognised Terms and Conditions

This phrase is defined in paragraph 2(a) of the 11th Schedule and it means terms and conditions of workers in comparable employment in the trade or industry (or section thereof) in which the employer in question is engaged, which terms and conditions have been settled by an agreement or award made between an employers' association and an independent Trade Union which represents a substantial proportion of the employers and of the workers in the trade or industry concerned. The workers in respect of whom the claim is made must be workers of the description to which the agreement or award relates.

This part of the EPA does in fact replace section 8 of the Terms and Conditions of Employment Act 1959. It will be noted that there must here be an agreement or award between an employer's association and an independent Trade Union and that, in particular, the Trade Union must represent a substantial proportion of the workers in the particular trade or industry concerned. If these detailed provisions cannot be complied with in a particular case, paragraph 2(a) will not apply, but it may still be possible for the matter to be dealt with under the next head.

General level of Terms and Conditions

This phrase is defined in paragraph 2(b) of the 11th Schedule as the general level of terms and conditions observed for comparable workers by employers—

(a) in the trade or industry in which the employer in question is engaged in the district for which he is so engaged and

(b) whose circumstances are similar to those of the employer in question.

It will be seen that a claim can arise under this head even where there is no existing industry agreement. These provisions were not contained in the original 1959 Act. It will be possible here for a claim to be made by reference to the " general level " of terms and conditions which is observed for comparable workers by other employers in the same trade in the district. It appears that it will now be open for any worker in a particular industry where there is no formal agreement dealing with terms and conditions to have a claim presented by his trade union to the ACAS.

Claims may also arise under this heading with regard to a worker whose terms and conditions are covered by a wages council or a statutory joint industrial council.

Who can make the claim ?

This is another situation where the employee himself does not have any rights to make a direct claim. If the claim is made in respect of " recognised terms and conditions " then the claim can be made to the ACAS either by the employers' association or the independent Trade Union which is a party to the agreement or award which fixed the terms and conditions.

Where the claim relates to the " general level of terms and conditions " the claim can be presented to the ACAS either by an employers' association having members engaged in the trade or industry in the district to which the claim relates or by a Trade Union of which any worker concerned is a member. In this latter case, however, if the worker is of a description in respect of which the employer recognises one or more independent Trade Unions, the claim may be reported by the Trade Union only if it is that recognised Union or one of the recognised Unions. Thus, if there is a collective agreement between a Union and an employer and that agreement covers the terms and conditions relating to a particular worker, only the recognised Union can present a claim on behalf of that worker.

The claim in either case must be in writing and must contain such particulars as the ACAS may require.

The Advisory Conciliation and Arbitration Service

When a claim is reported to the ACAS it has to take any steps which seem to it expedient to settle the claim or to secure the use of appropriate machinery to do so. If the claim is not otherwise settled, it must be referred to the Central Arbitration Committee (CAC).

It will be seen that the ACAS has a wide scope to do everything possible to try and achieve a settlement.

The Central Arbitration Committee

When the claim is referred to the CAC it must hear and determine the claim. Paragraph 8 of the 11th Schedule makes it clear that the burden of proof is initially on the party making the particular claim to show either that there are recognised terms and conditions and what those terms and conditions are or to show what are the general level of terms and conditions. Presumably, in most cases, the claim will initially be made by a Trade Union. It will, therefore, be for the Trade Union to establish the matters referred to above.

If this is done, it seems that the burden of proof then " swings over " to the employer and it is provided that the employer must then satisfy the CAC that he is observing terms and conditions of employment not less favourable either than the recognised terms and conditions or than the general level of terms and conditions. In this respect, the employer is helped to a small extent by paragraph 9 which states that, in ascertaining the above matter, regard shall be had to the whole of the terms and conditions observed by the employer with regard to the particular worker to whom the claim relates. It would seem, therefore, that under this head an employer may be able to claim that, although in certain respects his terms and conditions are less favourable (*e.g.* a lower overtime rate) in other respects the terms are more favourable (*e.g.* longer holidays).

If the CAC finds the claim to be either wholly or partly well founded it will make an award that the employer shall observe either the recognised terms and conditions or the terms and conditions conforming to the general level. At the same time, the CAC must identify or specify—

(a) either the recognised terms and conditions or the terms and conditions conforming to the general level

(b) the description of employees in respect of which they are to be observed and

(c) the date from which they are to be observed, this being a date not earlier than the date on which the employer was first informed of the claim.

Once this stage has been reached any terms and conditions under the CAC award which the employer is required to observe in respect of particular employees then has effect as part of the contract of employment of any such employees as from the date specified in the award. Those terms and conditions can only be superseded or varied either by a subsequent award by the CAC or by a collective agreement between the employer and the particular Trade Union representing the employee or by express or implied agreement between the employee and the employer so far as that agreement effects an improvement in those terms and conditions.

Part II of Schedule 11 to the EPA also contains provisions under which a complaint can be made to the ACAS by an independent Trade Union where a worker has been paid at a lower rate of pay than is agreed in a collective agreement between a Union and an employers' association and the worker falls within the field of operation of a wages council, a statutory joint industrial council or the Agricultural Wages Board.

INDUCEMENT OF A BREACH OF CONTRACT

Although this is not a matter which directly affects the relationship of employer and employee, it should be mentioned at this stage in view of recent important changes in the law. Many strikes and other forms of industrial action in fact can involve inducing employees to break their employment contracts. In addition, picketing or boycotting can also involve inducing third parties (such as suppliers) to break a commercial contract with the employer.

Under the Trade Union and Labour Relations Act 1974 (s. 13), as amended by the Trade Union and Labour Relations (Amendment) Act 1976 (s. 3(2)), the position now is that any act done in contemplation or furtherance of a trade dispute is not actionable in tort on the ground only that it induces or threatens to induce the breach of any contract or interferes with or threatens or induces interference with the performance of any contract.

There have been many changes in the law on this topic since the Trade Disputes Act 1906. In particular, the Industrial Relations Act 1971 took away protection from the non-registered unions. The 1974 Act tried to restore the immunity of the trade union, but, due to an amendment to the 1974 Bill, the immunity under section 13(1) in fact only extended to the inducement of a breach of a contract of employment and it did not cover interference with such a contract. The 1976 Amendment Act has now closed those gaps. All contracts are now covered, whether they are contracts of employment or not. In addition, interference with a contract by any means short of actually breaking the contract is also protected.

The immunity from action in the above circumstances extends to trade unions and to any officials or members of the union.

It must, of course, be remembered that the immunity only extends to acts done in contemplation or furtherance of a " trade dispute ". This is defined at some length by section 29(1) of the 1974 Act; in the main, it will be a dispute between employees and workers (or between workers and workers) connected with terms and conditions of employment or the engagement or sacking of one or more workers or matters of discipline, trade union membership, facilities for trade union officials or various other matters affecting the employment.

There have over the years been very few cases of an employer having recourse to the law to take action in respect of industrial action which is adversely affecting his business. Such action can, of course, cause serious damage to a business, and in certain cases (*e.g.* picketing or boycotting) the employer may have little or no control over the cause of the dispute, *e.g.*

where the dispute is not directly with his own employees. In any event, since 25th March 1976 (when the 1976 Amendment Act came into force), such an employer will have no right of action against the persons concerned (or their union), assuming of course that the action is in fact in contemplation or further-ance of a trade dispute.

One recent example of the sort of problem that may arise with regard to inducement of a breach of contract is the case of *Camellia Tanker Ltd. S.A. v. International Transport Workers Federation and Nelson* (1976) IRLR 183 (being the report of the High Court findings) and 190 (being the report of the Court of Appeal decision). In that case the defendant Mr. Nelson was secretary of the Manchester Branch of the National Union of Seamen (which was affiliated to the Internationl Transport Workers Federation) (ITF). He acted as an ITF Inspector to check the seaworthiness and conditions of employment aboard vessels flying flags of convenience. The " Camellia " was a tanker flying the flag of Panama and berthed in the Manchester Ship Canal. A dispute arose between the owners of the tanker and the ITF concerning rates of pay and other matters. This resulted in some of the crew of the Camellia—in breach of their contracts of employment—refusing to sail the tanker. In support of this, the crew of certain of the dockyard tugs—also in breach of their contracts of employment with the tug owners —refused or indicated that they would refuse to assist in the moving the tanker; and in addition, the staff of the docks who operate the lock gates also refused—in breach of their con-tracts of employment with the dock authorities—to open the dock gates to allow the tanker to put to sea. This was obvi-ously a costly matter for the owners of the tanker and they applied for an interlocutory injunction to restrain Mr. Nelson and the ITF from inducing the various breaches of contract referred to above. It should be stressed that the hearing only related to the application for an interlocutory injunction. It was not a full hearing of the case. In the High Court Mr. Justice Templeman dismissed the application of the owners of the tanker and this was mainly based on the provisions of section 13 of the Trade Union and Labour Relations Act 1974 (referred to above). The Judge found that even if there was

inducement of breaches of various contracts of employment
the defendants were immune from liability by reason of section
13. He stressed that the section offered absolution from actions
in tort relating to an inducement or threatened inducement to
break a contract of employment where it was committed in
contemplation or furtherance of a trade dispute. The case
was heard in February 1976—prior to the passing of the 1976
Amendment Act—and at that point of time, as indicatd above,
the section only dealt with a breach of a contract of employment. The Judge held that there was a trade dispute within
the definition referred to above and that this was the case even
though none of the members of the crew of the Camellia were
members of the ITF. The Judge indicated that the definition
of a trade dispute was a wide definition and that the section
enabled the trade union to raise a dispute with an employer.
The owners of the tanker tried to avoid the immunity conferred
by the section by endeavouring to claim that the defendants
had committed the tort of intimidation or the tort of conspiracy. The Judge held that the immunity and liability
established by section 13 covered all torts, including the torts
of intimidation and conspiracy. The intention of the section
was to ensure that the absolution given to the tort of inducing
another person to break a contract should not be out-man-
oeuvred by calling the tort another name. If it were otherwise,
most strikes in this country would involve actionable tort.
Finally, the Judge stated that the absolution given by section
13 is not restricted to cases where the contract broken—or
induced or threatened to be broken—is a contract of employment with the employer involved in the trade dispute; in 1974
Parliament would no longer have contemplated that a trade
dispute within the Act would only involve the parties to the
dispute. In the circumstances, what Mr. Nelson had done
was in furtherance of a trade dispute and all he did was to
induce another person to break a contract of employment; he
was, therefore, absolved from liability by section 13. In addition, since trade unions are absolved from liability for action
in tort by virtue of section 14, no relief could be obtained
against ITF unless there was some breach of public duty and
unless in some way a breach of public duty was not covered
by the terms of section 14; the Judge held that there was no

breach of public duty and that, therefore, no relief could be obtained against ITF.

The matter was immediately taken by way of appeal to the Court of Appeal. That court confirmed the decision of the Judge with regard to ITF, holding that there was no breach of any statutory duty and that, therefore, no right lay against ITF. With regard to Mr. Nelson, however, the Court of Appeal dealt with the matter in a different way. They found that there was insufficient factual material before the court for the owners of the tanker to show " a good arguable case " or " a real prospect of succeeding " in establishing that any supposed breaches of contract had in fact been induced by Mr. Nelson. The court held that the word " induced " involved some " pressures, persuasion or procuration ". The court felt that no evidence of this had been given, although it was clear that Mr. Nelson desired that the tug men and the lock men should refuse to provide their services. The evidence before the court was, however, evidence of what was believed to have been done and not of what had been done by the defendants. It would not have been right or fair to allow an injunction on that basis. The Court of Appeal, therefore, still refused the application of the tanker owners, although on different grounds from Mr. Justice Templeman. The court, therefore, indicated that it was not necessary or proper to express any view as to the Judge's conclusions of law relating to the meaning and effect of the 1974 Act.

No great matters of principle are decided by the above case, but the facts and findings have been considered in some detail because the case is a good example of the sort of situation that may arise and which may then be covered by the legislation referred to above.

OTHER MATTERS

There are certain other matters arising out of the relationship between an employer and a trade union which affect the individual's terms and conditions of employment. In very many cases, the very terms and conditions themselves are negotiated by the union on behalf of its members. Collective

Agreements have been referred to previously (Chapter 2, page 33).

The trend of the more recent legislation is, in many cases, to give special rights and privileges to the trade union (particularly the " recognised " union) and in several cases these rights are not given to the individual employee at all. Some of these matters are considered elsewhere in this book, *e.g.* the redundancy consultations provisions of the EPA,[1] and the disclosure of information provisions referred to earlier in this chapter.

Another example is that under the **Health and Safety at Work etc. Act 1974** the Employment Secretary is empowered to make regulations about the selection of the safety representatives with whom employers will have to consult. That Act stated that those representatives would either be appointed by recognised trade unions or be elected by the employees. The Employment Protection Act 1975 (s. 116 and the 15th Schedule) now deletes " election by employees ", so that the appointment of safety representatives is now restricted to those appointed by recognised trade unions. This is effective as from 1st January 1976. One result of this is that if at a particular factory there are no union members at all, then it seems that the employees cannot insist on a Safety Committee being set up.

The individual member of a recognised trade union also has certain special rights (*e.g.* as to time off for involvement in union activities). These rights will be considered in the next chapter.

---

[1] See p. 193.

CHAPTER 6

THE EMPLOYEE AND THE TRADE UNION

An employee who is a member of a trade union has various rights arising out of such membership in relation to his employer.

These rights exist under statute law and they arise without the consent or agreement of the employer. For convenience, they are grouped together in this chapter, although they are not particularly linked to each other and they stem from more than one Act of Parliament.

TRADE UNION MEMBERSHIP AND ACTIVITIES

The provisions of the Industrial Relations Act 1971 under which it was clearly stated that every employee had a right either to be a member of a trade union or not to be a member were, of course, abolished by the Trade Union and Labour Relations Act 1974. The position was then for a time left rather " in limbo ", except for actual dismissal due to involvement in trade union activities.

The legal position with regard to membership of a trade union and involvement in union activities is now governed by **section 53 of the Employment Protection Act 1975** (EPA). That section came into force on 1st June 1976.[1]

Section 53(1) provides that an employee has the right not to have action (short of dismissal)[2] taken against him as an individual for the purpose of—

---

[1] See EPA 1975 (Commencement No. 4) Order 1976.
[2] As to which see p. 260, *ante.*

(*a*) preventing or deterring him from being or seeking to become a member of an independent trade union or penalising him from doing so; or

(*b*) preventing or deterring him from taking part in the activities of an independent trade union **at any appropriate time,** or penalising him from doing so; or

(*c*) compelling him to be or become a member of a trade union which is not independent.

" **Appropriate time** " is defined as time which either is **out- side** his working hours or is a time **within** his working hours at which, by arrangement or with the **consent** of the employer, it is permissible for him to take part in those activities.

" **Working hours** " means any time when, in accordance with his contract of employment, he is required to be at work.

The right to partake in union activities on the employers' premises will not apply, in situations where there is a union membership agreement,[1] to members of unions who are not specified in that agreement. It should be remembered that " specified " here has been extended to cover unions who are claiming recognition via the ACAS. With this one exception, it is not possible to contract out of the EPA provisions and any agreement to exclude or limit the operation of the Act is void (s. 118).

The above provisions protect the position of the employee who wishes to be a member of a trade union and/or to involve himself in trade union activities.

What of the employee who does **not** wish to join a union?

As far as dismissal is concerned, the position is dealt with on pages 262 and 268.

With regard to action short of dismissal, an employee who " **genuinely objects on grounds of religious belief** to being a member of **any** trade union whatsoever " has the right **not** to have such action taken against him by his employer for the purpose of compelling him to belong to a trade union (s. 53(6)).

---

1 As to which, see p. 83, *ante*.

Excluded categories of employees

The only employees who do not have the above rights with regard to Trade Union membership and activities are as follows:—

(1) employment where the employer is the husband or wife of the employee.

(2) employment as master or as a member of the crew of a fishing vessel where the employee is not remunerated otherwise than by a share in the profits or gross earnings of the vessel.

(3) employment where under his contract of employment the employee ordinarily works outside Great Britain. In this respect a person employed to work on board a ship registered in the United Kingdom is regarded as ordinarily working in Great Britain unless either his employment is wholly outside Great Britain or he is not ordinarily resident in Great Britain.

Sanctions

An employee who claims that action has been taken against him contrary to the above provisions can present a complaint **to an Industrial Tribunal** within three months of the date of the action about which he now complains. The time limit can be extended if it was not reasonably practicable[1] for the complaint to be lodged in time.

The onus is then placed firmly on the employer. He will have to show the real reason for the action taken against the employee and also that the reason was not because of the employee's trade union activities. It is no defence for the employer to show that he was forced to take the action by industrial action or threats of it from other employees or from a trade union. In those circumstances, an employer can find himself in a very difficult position.

One complete defence to a claim is to produce a certificate from a Minister of the Crown showing that the action was taken to safeguard national security.

---

[1] See p. 311, *ante.*

If the Tribunal finds the complaint justified, it can award compensation. The compensation will be the amount the Tribunal considers just and equitable, having regard to any loss sustained by the employee and also taking into account the infringement of his rights as referred to above.

The EPA does **not** limit the amount of compensation to the usual £5,200 ceiling. Other general compensation rules do, however, apply—the employee must do what he can to mitigate his loss and an award can be reduced if there is " contributory fault " on the part of the employee. Here again, pressure from outside parties (*e.g.* a trade union) is not a reason for reducing the compensation awarded.

The 1972 Code of Practice

The 1972 Code of Practice (issued under the Industrial Relations Act 1971) does not contain any firm direction or recommendation relating to union membership. This may be changed if and when the ACAS issue a new Code under the EPA.

The Code does, however, acknowledge the need for employers to have representatives to put forward their collective views to management and to safeguard their interests in consultation and negotiation (para. 99). It is also acknowledged that these representatives are very often employees who are accredited union representatives—referred to as " shop stewards ".

Paragraphs 116 and 117 then suggest the sort of facilities that should be afforded to shop stewards and these include

(i) time off from his job (as to which see also now page 101)

(ii) maintenance of earnings whilst carrying out union activities

and various other matters, *e.g.* use of a telephone.

TIME OFF FOR UNION MEMBERS

Section 58 of the Employment Protection Act 1975 provides that an employer must permit an employee who is a member of an appropriate trade union to take **time off** during working hours for the purpose of taking part in trade union activities. **This section is not yet in force.**

" Appropriate trade union " means an independent trade union which is recognised by the employer.

" Trade union activities " are any activities of an appropriate trade union of which the employee is a member and any activities in relation to which the employee is acting as a representative of such union. Obviously, attending union meetings will be covered as will collecting union dues and attending other meetings on behalf of the union.

These activities do not, however, include industrial action.

The vital question is, of course, how much time off is an employee to be allowed to take?

Section 58(3) provides that the time off must be " reasonable having regard to any relevant provisions of a Code of Practice issued by " the ACAS.

This section **will not come into force until** the Code of Practice referred to has been issued.   It is anticipated that the provisions will become effective during 1977.   The draft Code issued as a consultative document is summarised in Appendix V (see page 368).

The employee having time off under these provisions does **not** have to be **paid** by his employer during that time.   In practice, of course, many employers will continue to pay the employee.

Excluded categories of employees

The above rights do not apply to—

(1) Part-time workers, *i.e.* mainly those who work less than 16 hours weekly (but see page 353 for full details).

(2) employment where the employer is the husband or wife of the employee.

(3) employment as master or crew of a fishing vessel where remuneration is only by a share in the profits or earnings of the vessel.

(4) employees who under their contract ordinarily work outside Great Britain. This includes a person employed to work on board a ship registered in the U.K. unless either the employment is wholly outside Great Britain or the employee is not ordinarily resident in Great Britain.

Sanctions

If an employer refuses time off for an employee the employee can complain to an Industrial Tribunal within three months of the date of the refusal (or within such further period as the Tribunal considers reasonable where it was not reasonably practicable for the complaint to be presented in time). The Tribunal can make a declaration that the complaint was well-founded and can award compensation to the employee.

The amount of compensation must take into account the employer's default in failing to permit time off and it must also have regard to any loss sustained by the employee. The employee is under the usual duty to mitigate his loss.

It is difficult to see how employees will suffer any money-loss through infringement of the " time off " rights. It does seem, therefore, that the compensation awarded by tribunals may in effect be a " fine " on employers who are found to be in default. Here again, the provisions of the section cannot be excluded (even by agreement).

TIME OFF FOR UNION OFFICIALS

Section 57(1) of the Employment Protection Act 1975 provides that an employer must permit any employee of his who is an official (e.g. shop steward) of an independent trade union recognised by the employer to take time off during working hours for the purpose of enabling him—

(a) to carry out those duties of his as a union official which are concerned with industrial relations between the employer (or associated employer) and the employees or

(b) to undergo training in aspects of industrial relations which is—

(i) relevant to the carrying out of those duties and

(ii) approved by the Trades Union Congress or by the independent trade uion of which he is an official.

Excluded categories of employees are exactly the same as for union members (see *above*).

The **amount of time** is such as is reasonable having regard to the provisions of the Code to be issued by the ACAS. The Code will also give guidance as to the circumstances in which an official may have time off in respect of duties connected with industrial action.

As with time off for union members (page 100) the provisions of this section **will not come into force until** the Code is approved —probably during 1977.[1]

One major difference, however, between the time off provisions for union officials, as compared with that for ordinary union members, is that the union officials are **entitled to be paid** by the employer during the time taken off for the above purposes. The EPA contains detailed provisions relating to the calculation of the employee's remuneration so that he is no worse off by reason of having been allowed time off for his duties and/or training. Lost overtime can be taken into account in calculating any loss of remuneration.

" **Official** " is widely defined by section 30(1) of the Trade Union and Labour Relations Act 1974 and, in practice, it means not only an official duly elected by the union members but any person (whether an officer of the union or not) who is appointed in accordance with the rules of the union to be a representative.

A union will be treated as " recognised " for these purposes if there is an ACAS recommendation of recognition (see page 72).

Sanctions

An employee who is refused his rights as a union official to have time off can apply to an Industrial Tribunal within three months of the refusal (but subject to the usual extension of time if it was not reasonably practicable to apply sooner).

---

[1] For the Draft Code—see Appendix V (pp. 368-371).

The Tribunal can award compensation on the same basis as for the union member (page 101, *ante*). In the case of the union official, however, if the Tribunal finds that the employer has not paid the official properly in respect of his " time off ", the Tribunal can order that the necessary moneys shall be paid.

It is not possible to contract out of these provisions of the EPA.

UNFAIR DISMISSAL

The employee who is a member of an independent trade union is in many situations in a special position with regard to unfair dismissal.

This position will be covered in more detail in Chapter 20 (see pages 259 to 262, *post*), but, for the sake of completeness, it should be noted at this stage that:—

(i) Dismissal is automatically unfair if the reason was that the employee was, or proposed to become, a member of an independent trade union or that the employee had taken part in union activities or proposed to do so (Trade Union and Labour Relations Act 1974, 1st Sched., para. 6(4)).

(ii) The employee dismissed for the above " inadmissible reason " does not have to serve the initial qualifying period of twenty six weeks continuous employment.

(iii) An employee dismissed for an " inadmissible reason " can now with the help of his trade union apply quickly to an Industrial Tribunal for interim relief and obtain a protective award (Employment Protection Act 1975, ss. 78 to 80)—see pages 262 to 267.

CHAPTER 7

MATERNITY RIGHTS

Until the passing of the Employment Protection Act 1975 a female employee had no special position under the law. If she became pregnant, she had no right to return to her job, unless, of course, this was specifically written into her contract. If she was dismissed because of her pregnancy, the dismissal was not automatically unfair—although she may have been able to satisfy a Tribunal, on the normal rules, that the dismissal was in fact unfair in her particular case.

The EPA (ss. 34 to 52) has now introduced major changes into this aspect of the law and the female employee now has special rights with regard to—

1. Dismissal due to her pregnancy.
2. Maternity pay.
3. Re-instatement in her job.

It should be noted at the outset that these rights are applicable whether the female employee is married or single. Employers, however, can still discriminate against single women if they provide benefits over and above the EPA benefits (*e.g.* paid maternity leave for longer than six weeks); this is because the Sex Discrimination Act 1975 does not affect discrimination against single people on the grounds that they are unmarried.

Each of the above rights will now be considered in more detail.

DISMISSAL ON GROUNDS OF PREGNANCY

The general position with regard to unfair dismissal is dealt with in Chapters 19 to 23, *post*. It is proposed, however, to deal with this aspect of unfair dismissal in the present chapter.

The provisions of the EPA relating to dismissal on the ground of pregnancy came into force on 1st June 1976.

An employee will be **unfairly dismissed** if the reason or principal reason for her dismissal was that she was pregnant or was any other reason connected with her pregnancy except one of the following two reasons:—

(a) that at the date of her dismissal she was or would have been incapable, because of her pregnancy, of adequately doing the work she is employed to do; or

(b) that, because of her pregnancy, she could not continue to do that work without there being a contravention of some statute.[1]

The employer has more than one hurdle to surmount if he is to avoid being held to have unfairly dismissed a female employee who is pregnant.

If, of course, the employer can show that the real reason for the dismissal was not in any way connected with the pregnancy, he will have no problem.   If the Tribunal are satisfied as to this, the dismissal will be a " fair " one.

If the employer can show that because of her pregnancy the employee was incapable of doing her job, then he is over the first hurdle (s. 34(1)(a)).   That, however, is not in itself sufficient defence under the EPA provisions.

The employer still has to try and find another suitable job for the employee either with himself, his successor in the business or an associated employer.[2]

Offer of suitable alternative employment

Section 34(2) provides that even if the employer dismisses an employee for one of the reasons mentioned in paragraph (a) and (b) above, the dismissal will still be unfair unless, where there is a suitable available vacancy, he makes her an offer to engage her under a new contract of employment.

---

1 EPA, s. 34(1).
2 For definition, see p. 179.

The offer must be made **before or on** the date of termination of her employment. It seems, therefore, that an employer who dismisses a pregnant employee and then subsequently realises his obligations under the EPA, cannot retrieve the position by then offering her other employment.

To satisfy the terms of the Act the new contract of employment must comply with three conditions—

(a) it must take effect immediately on the ending of the previous job (or after an intervening week-end)[1];

(b) the work to be done must be both suitable in relation to the employee and appropriate for her to do in the circumstances; and

(c) the provisions of the new contract as to the capacity and place in which she is to be employed and as to the other terms and conditions of her employment must be not substantially less favourable to her than the corresponding provisions of her previous contract.[1]

If the matter reaches an Industrial Tribunal the onus will be on the employer to show one of the following " **defences** "—

(i) that the principal reason for the dismissal was not because of her pregnancy **or**

(ii) that the employee either could not or would not continue to do her job because of her pregnancy **and** that there was no suitable available vacancy for her in another job or

(iii) that the employee, because of her pregnancy, could not or would not continue to do her job **and** that the employer (or an associated employer) had offered to engage her under a new contract of employment complying with the above conditions, or

(iv) the defences under (ii) and (iii) will also be available if the reason for the dismissal was that the employee could not continue without there being a contravention of some statute.

---

[1] EPA, s. 34(3).

It will be seen, therefore, that the above provisions give the female employee the right to continue in either her own job or some other suitable job until her baby is due. She can, if she wishes, stay on even after the 11th week deadline which will be referred to under the Maternity Pay provisions.

The EPA is silent as to what happens if the employee refuses the offer of another suitable job. If, however, the new job complies with the conditions referred to, the employer will have a defence. Even if, however, the actual dismissal is a " fair " dismissal, the employee may still be entitled to maternity pay and to re-instatement in her job after the pregnancy.

The **remedy** of the female employee who feels that she has been unfairly dismissed under these provisions is to apply **to an Industrial Tribunal.** Subject to what has been stated above, the matter will then be treated like any other unfair dismissal application. The provisions relating to this are set out on pages 246 to 310. It should be remembered that the Tribunal now has power to order re-instatment or re-engagement.

One final point under this head is whether or not the female employee has to have been employed for the minimum **qualifying period** of twenty six weeks (TUALRA, 1st Sched., para. 10). It is arguable that because of the wording of section 34 EPA she does **not** have to be in the job for the 26 week period. The section states that " an employee **shall** be treated for the purposes of Schedule 1 to the 1974 Act as unfairly dismissed if . . . ". This seems to be mandatory.

No doubt the matter will be clarified in due course by a Tribunal decision. In the meantime, it is the view of the writer that it would be advisable for employers to assume that all female employees will have this right not to be dismissed on grounds of pregnancy, regardless of how long they have been empolyed. Having said this, it is noted that the Department of Employment booklet on " New rights for the expectant mother " indicates that the employee must have worked for at least six months.

As indicated at the outset, these provisions only relate to dismissals taking effect after 1st June 1976.

RIGHT TO MATERNITY PAY

The provisions of the Employment Protection Act 1975 (ss. 35 to 47) relating to maternity pay will come into force on 6th April 1977 (see the EPA Commencement Order No. 4).

Employers should, therefore, prepare now for the introduction of these rights.

The " qualifying period " under this head is two years (as for redundancy pay) and employees with less than two years' service will not have a right to receive maternity pay.

Excluded employees

The only employees who do not have rights with regard to maternity pay are as follows:—

(1) employment where the employer is the husband of the employee.

(2) employment as master or as a member of the crew of a fishing vessel where the employee is not remunerated otherwise than by a share in the profits or gross earnings of the vessel.

(3) employment where under her contract of employment the employee ordinarily works outside Great Britain. In this respect a person employed to work on board a ship registered in the United Kingdom is regarded as ordinarily working in Great Britain unless either her employment is wholly outside Great Britain or she is not ordinarily resident in Great Britain.

(4) " part-time " employees. Although this category is not specifically excluded by the EPA the requirement as to two years' continuous employment has the effect of excluding " part-time " employees (see definition in Appendix II, page 353, *post*).

Conditions of entitlement

An employee will only be entitled to maternity pay if she can comply with the following conditions:—

(*a*) She must continue to be employed (whether or not she is actually at work) until immediately before the beginning of the 11th week before the expected week of confinement;

(*b*) she must—at the beginning of that 11th week—have been continuously employed for a period of not less than two years; and

(*c*) she must inform her employer (in writing if he so requests) at least three weeks before her absence begins (or as soon as is reasonably practicable) that she will be (or is) absent from work wholly or partly because of pregnancy or confinement.

These conditions must be strictly complied with. In addition, if requested by the employer, the employee must produce for inspection a medical certificate stating the expected week of confinement.

Employers should note that under condition (*a*) the employee does not actually have to work until the 11th week. She may be on leave or absent with a proper sick-note without losing her rights.

The employer cannot avoid his responsibilities under this head by terminating the employment prior to the 11th week before the expected confinement (condition (*a*) above) and thereby restricting that employee's service to less than two years. If the employment is terminated for a reason falling within paragraphs (*a*) and (*b*) on page 105, *supra,* and the employee has not been re-engaged in accordance with the EPA provisions, then the employee can count the weeks between the dismissal date and the 11th week in order to establish the two year qualification period.

Even if the dismissal of the employee is held to be " fair ", she will still be entitled to maternity pay, provided that the necessary conditions are complied with.

If, of course, the employee **resigns** before the 11th week deadline, she loses her rights to maternity pay.

There is no limit in the EPA as to the number of times an employee can claim maternity pay, *i.e.* it can be claimed on each pregnancy during employment with the same (or an associated) employer. The employee, must, of course, still comply with the EPA conditions. She does not, however, have to " chalk up " another two year service period after the first maternity leave. The only requirement is that the employee should have worked for a two year period as at the 11th week before the expected confinement.

Amount of Maternity Pay

Put very simply, the amount of maternity pay is $6 \times 90\%$ of a week's pay, less National Insurance Maternity Allowance.

The starting base is a week's pay and detailed provisions with regard to this are contained in Part II of the 4th Schedule of the EPA. Normally, there will, of course, be no difficulty about calculating what is in fact one week's pay. The pay will be based on " normal working hours " and thus, for example, overtime will not be included unless it is obligatory on both sides both to provide and to work overtime. The maximum week's pay is in any event limited to £80. The full definition of a week's pay is set out in Appendix III (see page 361).

The week's pay is then reduced by one tenth, *i.e.* the maternity pay is nine tenths (9/10ths) of a week's pay.

Finally, that figure is reduced by the amount of maternity allowance provided by National Insurance[1] **whether or not** the employee in question is entitled to the whole or any part of that allowance. The National Insurance Maternity allowance varies from time to time; at present, for those paying the full stamp, it is £12.90 per week. In any event, it is the **full** amount of the allowance which is deducted, whether or not the employee will be entitled to receive the full allowance from the State.

The earnings related supplement will not be taken into account. It may, therefore, be possible for the employee, at least for the six week period, to obtain full pay made up of National Insurance Maternity Allowance + Earnings Related Supplement + Maternity Pay under EPA.

---

[1] Under Part I of Schedule 4 of the Social Security Act 1975.

Maternity pay accrues from day to day, Sunday being normally disregarded, thus giving a daily rate of 1/6th of the maternity pay.

An employee may have certain other rights as to remuneration under her contract of employment (*e.g.* there may be a company maternity benefit scheme); if this is so, those rights are still enforceable. The employer can, however, set those contractual payments against his liability under EPA to pay maternity pay. This would, not, however, apply in the case of discretionary or ex gratia payments made to an employee.

When is maternity pay due ?

Maternity pay has to be paid for a period of six weeks during which the employee is absent from work.

The employee is not entitled to receive any payment prior to the beginning of the 11th week before the expected confinement.

Normally, therefore, the employee will be paid for six weeks as from the 11th week prior to the expected confinement, provided that she is no longer in employment at that time.

An amendment to the relevant Commencement Order has now made it clear that the provisions relating to maternity pay only have effect where the first of the six weeks of absence begins on or after 6th April 1977.

It seems that there is nothing to stop an employer giving an employee her maternity pay entitlement in one lump sum when she leaves.

The employee who is unfairly dismissed will obtain her maternity pay (if entitled to it) as part of the compensation awarded by the Tribunal.

Sanctions

As with most of the other employee rights, an employee who feels she is entitled to maternity pay can, if it is not paid, apply to an Industrial Tribunal who can order the employer to pay any maternity pay which is due. Any such application must be made within three months from the last day of the six weeks period as calculated under EPA or within such further period as the Tribunal considers reasonable where it was not reasonably practicable for the complaint to be presented within the three month period.

Certain other sanctions do arise under the Maternity Pay Fund provisions.

The Maternity Pay Fund

There were some " last minute " amendments to the EPA which resulted in the setting up of a Maternity Pay Fund (see ss. 39 to 47). The Fund is set up on a very similar basis to the Redundancy Fund set up under the Redundancy Payments Act 1965.

As with the other maternity pay provisions, the Fund and any contributions to it will not be operative until 6th April 1977.

Contributions to the Fund will be paid by all employers who pay secondary Class 1 contributions, whether they employ women or not. This will mean an increase in those contributions, at present calculated.

The Maternity Pay Fund will make payments out of the Fund in two main sets of circumstances:—

(a) **a rebate** will be paid to the employer in respect of maternity pay paid to an employee under the provisions set out above. The " rebate " will in fact be a refund **in full** of the maternity pay (unlike the redundancy pay position where only a 50% rebate is paid).[1] The Secretary of State is responsible for paying eligible employers and he will make detailed Regulations as to the administration of the Fund. If the Secretary of State refuses to pay out to an employer, the employer can apply to an Industrial Tribunal within three months.

(b) **Maternity pay** may be paid direct from the Fund to the employee (without waiting for the decision of a Tribunal) if in fact maternity pay is due to the employee **and** has not been paid by the empoyer and—

---

[1] But see footnote to p. 187.

    (i) the employee has taken all reasonable steps (short of applying to a tribunal) to recover payments from the employer; **or**

    (ii) the employer is insolvent (*e.g.* if a company, it is wound up or has had a receiver appointed).

If the payment is paid to the employee, the Secretary of State (presumably through the Department of Employment) can recover from the employer and, in that event, if the employer's default was " without reasonable excuse ", the amount of the normal rebate can be reduced or withheld.

If an employee applies direct to the Secretary of State for a payment out of the Fund, the Secretary of State has power by notice in writing to call upon the employer to provide him with information and any relevant documents so that the employee's claim can be checked. If this does happen, the employer must supply the necessary information. If he refuses or wilfully neglects to do so, he can be prosecuted and fined up to £100; if the employer knowingly or recklessly makes a false statement, the fine can be up to £400.

All " disputes " relating to maternity pay and relating to payments out of the Fund (whether as between employer and employee, employer and Secretary of State or employee and Secretary of State) can be referred to and determined by an Industrial Tribunal.

THE RIGHT TO RETURN TO WORK

The third main right of a female employee who is pregnant is the right, in certain circumstances, to return to her job after she has had her baby.

These provisions are contained in sections 35 and 48 to 50 of the Employment Protection Act 1975 and they came into force on 1st June 1976 by virtue of the EPA Commencement Order No. 4.

As with maternity pay, only employees with at least two years' service have this right. The excluded categories are the same categories set out on page 108. We will now consider the matter in more detail.

Conditions of entitlement

An employee who is absent from work **wholly or partly** because of pregnancy or confinement is entitled to **return to work** provided that she complies with the three conditions set out on page 108 (paragraphs (*a*) to (*c*) (relating to the right to maternity pay) **and** provided also that when she informs her employer (under paragraph (*c*)) that she will be absent from work because of the baby she also informs her employer that she intends to return to work.

It will be remembered that this information must be given to the employer at least three weeks before the absence begins, unless that was not practicable, in which case the employer must be informed as soon as reasonably practicable. The employer can insist that the notification from the employee is in writing.

Thus, before an employee can think about getting her job back she must—

(*a*) remain employed until the 11th week before the expected confinement

(*b*) have two years' service with the employer by the time of the 11th week and

(*c*) tell the employer three weeks before she leaves that she is leaving because she is pregnant **and** that she wants to return to work with her employer.

As with maternity pay (see page 109) an employee complying with the above conditions has a right to return to work after her pregnancy, regardless of how many times over the years she has exercised this right.

The right to return

If the employee complies with the above conditions, then the employee can return to work with the employer (or his successor or an associated employer) at any time before the end of the period of **29 weeks** from the confinement.

Thus, the employee can have a total of 40 weeks' leave (11 weeks prior to the birth of the baby and 29 weeks after) and—

after 6th April 1977—she will get maternity pay for 6 of those weeks.

Section 49 of the EPA deals with how the right to return operates.   In the first instance, the employee must give to the employer at least one week's notice that she proposes to return. This notice does not have to be in writing.   The date of the proposed return is referred to as " the notified day of return ".

The employer then has a right to " put off " the employee's return for up to four weeks, but he must notify the employee of this, giving reasons and specifying a date of return within the four week period.   The EPA does not lay down any specified reasons; it simply states that the employer must give reasons.

Similarly, the **employee can postpone** her return for up to four weeks beyond the notified day of return—even if this takes the date beyond the 29 week period, but this can **only** be done **on medical grounds.**   The employee must, in these circumstances, give the employer a certificate from a doctor stating that she will be " incapable of work on the notified day of return ".   If the employee has not even given notice of the date that she is to return to work, then similarly the time for the giving of such notice can on provision of a medical certificate be extended by four weeks.

The right of the employee to postpone the date of her return on medical grounds can only be exercised **once.**

The legislation also provides for the situation where there is an interruption of work so that it is unreasonable to expect the employee to return.   In that event, the 29 week period can be extended.   The interruption may be due to industrial action or to some other reason.   If the employee has already informed the employer of the day of her return and there is then an interruption of work, she may return to work as soon as is reasonably practicable after the interruption ceases.   If the employee has not notified the day of her proposed return, she can return at any time within 14 days from the end of the interruption.

The job itself

What if the female employee's job is no longer available when she decides to return?

Initially, the right to return to work is a right to go back to " the job in which she was employed under the original contract of employment and on terms and conditions not less favourable than those which would have been applicable " if she had not been absent (EPA, s. 48 (1)).

The job is the work that the employee was employed to do under her original contract of employment.

As far as **terms and conditions** are concerned, she must be treated in exactly the same way if she had continuous employment, but leaving out the absence due to the pregnancy, *i.e.* the periods of employment prior to her absence are regarded as continuous with her employment after that absence. This will affect such things as seniority and pension rights.

In addition, for purposes of " continuity of employment " as defined in the contracts of Employment Act 1972 (which definition affects such things as entitlement to notice and redundancy pay), the absence due to the pregnancy does **not** break the continuity if the employee returns to work.[1] In this case, the " maternity leave " counts towards the number of weeks worked by that employee.

If an employee is entitled to return to work under these provisions, but it is not practicable by reason of redundancy for the employer to permit her return to return, then she will be entitled to a **redundancy payment** under the Redundancy Payments Act 1965,[2] **unless** the employer (or his successor or an associated employer) offers **alternative employment**. The alternative employment must be such that—

(*a*) the work itself is of a kind which is suitable to the employee and appropriate for her to do in the circumstances; and

---

[1] See EPA, Sch. 16, Pt. II, para. 17.
[2] As to which see p. 185, *ante*.

(b) the terms and conditions of the new job and the capacity of the employee and the place of work are not substantially less favourable than the original job (section 48(5)).

If the employer does not re-engage an employee who is entitled to return to work, then—unless there is a redundancy situation as referred to above—the employer will be deemed to have dismissed the employee. The employee can then claim that she was unfairly dismissed.

Thus, the only defence available to an employer to a claim by a female employee to return to work (assuming that she complies with all the necessary conditions) is that her original job has gone completely and no other suitable job exists.

Temporary replacements

It is **not** a defence to a claim to say that the employer had had to replace the pregnant employee with another person.

The EPA takes this matter further by providing some (but not complete) protection for the employer in relation to the **temporary replacement.** If the employer tells the " replacement " **in writing** at the very beginning of the employment that he or she will be dismissed on the return to work of another employee who is absent due to pregnancy or confinement, then, when the " replacement " is dismissed, the dismissal shall be regarded as having been for a " substantial reason " within the meaning of the Trade Union and Labour Relations Act 1974. As will be seen, however, in the chapters relating to unfair dismissal, this will only get the employer over the first hurdle of the defence. He must still show that he acted reasonably in dismissing the replacement.[1]

It must also, of course, be remembered that " the temporary replacement " will not normally have any rights at all as to unfair dismissal until he or she has been employed for 26 weeks.

Sanctions

If an employee is entitled to return to work under the EPA provisions and the employer does not comply with the law, the

---

[1] Paragraph 6(8) of Schedule to the TUARLA and p. 300, *ante.*

employee can apply to an Industrial Tribunal within the usual three month period.

The three month period will run from the date of the " notified day of return " and the employee will be treated as having been dismissed from that date (s. 50).

The normal **unfair dismissal** provisions then apply, the Tribunal having the right to re-instate the employee or to award compensation.[1]

If the employee's original job has disappeared because of **redundancy** and no suitable alternative employment (as referred to above) is offered, then the employee will be entitled to redundancy pay. Again, the " dismissal " will normally be the date of the " notified day of return " and the employee's period of continuous employment for the purpose of calculating the amount of redundancy will also run up to that date.

The employer—in a redundancy situation—may be able to show that in any event the female employee would genuinely have been made redundant during her absence, *i.e.* between the 11th week prior to the expected confinement and the notified day of return. If the employer can establish this, then the redundancy payment will only be calculated up to that date and **not** up to the notified day of return (EPA, 3rd Sched., para. 6). If an employer does find himself in such a situation, it is much better to inform the employee of her redundancy during her absence, rather than wait until she makes a claim under the EPA.

If an employee who is entitled to return to work under the above provisions is dismissed whilst on " maternity leave " (normally after the 11th week deadline) she still has the right to return to work under EPA, but she can also there and then apply to a Tribunal alleging unfair dismissal. If the Tribunal awards compensation, it must do so without regard to the employee's right to return to work. This will increase the compensation quite substantially. If, however, the employee does subsequently exercise her right to return to work, then

---

[1] As to which see pp. 315 to 332, *ante*.

she must, if her employer requests it, repay to that employer any compensation received (para. 4 of 3rd Schedule to EPA).

Is there any **sanction** imposed on **the employee** who indicates, prior to leaving her job, that she does intend to return to work after she has had her baby and then does not do so?

No saction is contained in the EPA, nor in practice is there anything that the employer can do to rescue the situation. Employers should, however, be aware of the position. In addition, they must take care to inform any " temporary replacements " of the true position (see page 117).

CONTRACTING OUT

Any provision in an agreement (or otherwise) which purports to exclude or limit the EPA maternity rights or tries to preclude an employee from bringing any proceedings is void (EPA, s. 118(1)).

CHAPTER 8

MEDICAL SUSPENSION PAY

One of the rights new to the law of employment and now contained in the **Employment Protection Act 1975 (ss. 29 to 33)** is the right for certain employees who are suspended because of some health or safety hazard to be paid for the whole or part of their absence.   This right is restricted to workers employed in certain processes involving potential health hazards.

These provisions of the EPA were brought into force on 1st June 1976.   Any attempt to contract out of the provisions will be void.

It must be made clear at the outset that firstly this is **not** a right to sickness pay and secondly it only applies in certain specified industries where an employee is exposed to " toxic " substances.

Conditions of entitlement

Before an employee can even qualify for these rights he must have been **employed** for at least **four weeks** ending with the last complete week before the suspension begins.

The suspension itself is at present fairly limited, although the Secretary of State has power to amend the provisions.

Only certain provisions will give rise to the entitlement to be paid and these are set out in the 2nd Schedule to the EPA. The 2nd Schedule at present sets out 15 different sets of Regulations which relate to certain occupations dealing, for example, with such things as paint, vitreous enamelling, lead smelting, certain chemicals, india rubber, radioactive substances, and other matters.   These provisions can be varied by the Secretary of State.

An employee who is **suspended** from work **by his employer** on medical grounds in consequence of any requirement imposed

under any of the provisions in the **2nd Schedule or** in consequence of any recommendation in any provision of **a code of
practice** (issued or approved under the Health and Safety at
Work etc. Act 1974) which is a provision specified in the 2nd
Schedule becomes entitled to be paid remuneration while he
is suspended for a period not exceeding 26 weeks.

Exclusions

Apart from having to satisfy the conditions referred to above,
the employee will **not** be entitled to be paid in the following
circumstances:—

(*a*) if he actually becomes **incapable of working** because of
ill-health or sickness. An employee seeking pay under
the Medical Suspension provisions must, therefore, be fit
and available for work and must only be prevented from
actually working by virtue of the provisions referred to
above. The EPA does **not** provide a form of sick pay,
although there seems to be a common misapprehension
that this is the case. The aim of the EPA provisions
under this head is in fact to try and prevent the employee
from becoming " sick ".

(*b*) if he is an employee under a fixed term contract **for 12
weeks or less** (or an employee for a specific task not
expected to last for more than 12 weeks) unless the
employee has in fact been employed for more than 12
weeks.

(*c*) if the employer offers to provide **suitable alternative work**
and the employee unreasonably refuses to do that work.

The offer of work does not have to be work which the
employee was originally employed to do. Each situation
must, therefore, be considered on its merits. The words
" suitable alternative work " and " unreasonably refuses " bear some resemblance to the provisions of the
Redundancy Payments Act 1965 relating to the " offer
of suitable employment "[1] and it is thought that the
EPA provisions will be interpreted in a very similar way.

---

[1] Redundancy Payments Act 1965, s. 2(4), and see p. 172.

(*d*) if the employee does not comply with **reasonable requirements** imposed by his employer with a view to ensuring that his services are available.

No guidance has yet been given as to the meaning of this provision. Presumably, however, an employer is entitled, once he has suspended an employee on medical grounds, to ask that employee to do everything possible to ensure that he will be in a position to return to his job in the future. This could include asking the employee not to take another during the 26 week (or lesser) period.

In addition to the above exclusions, the following categories of employees do **not** have rights to " medical suspension pay ":—

(1) employment where the employer is the husband or wife of the employee.

(2) registered dock workers unless wholly or mainly engaged in work which is not dock work as defined by any scheme for the time being in force under the Dock Workers (Regulation of Employment) Act 1946.

(3) employment as master or as a member of the crew of a fishing vessel where the employee is not remunerated otherwise than by a share in the profits or gross earnings of the vessel.

(4) employment where under his contract of employment the employee ordinarily works outside Great Britain. With regard to employment on board a ship registered in the United Kingdom, see page 108.

(5) employment under a contract for a fixed term of 12 weeks or less or employment under a contract made in contemplation of the performance of a specific task which is not expected to last for more than 12 weeks unless in either case the employee has in fact been continuously employed for a period of more than 12 weeks.

(6) " part-time " employees as defined for the purposes of " continuous employment " (see page 353).

The amount of pay

The amount to be paid under these provisions is one week's pay for each week of the suspension up to a maximum of 26 weeks. A part week will be reduced proportionately.

There are detailed provisions in Part II of Schedule 4 dealing with the calculation of " a week's pay " and the position as to such calculation is set out in Appendix III.[1] Basically, an employee must be paid all contractual pay entitlements.

It is provided that if the employee has a specific right under his contract to be paid during medical suspension, this right still subsists and any contractual payments so made can be set against the employer's obligations under the EPA provisions. Similarly, any statutory payments can be set against the employer's contractual obligations.

Dismissals

If an employee, instead of being suspended on the specified medical grounds, is dismissed, he will have the normal rights to claim unfair dismissal (as to which, see pages 246 to 256). It is felt that such a dismissal will normally be unfair. There is, in addition, one change to the " qualifying period " relating to an unfair dismissal claim—the rights of an employee to claim that a dismissal on the specified medical grounds is unfair will arise after he has been employed for only four weeks (not the usual TUALRA period of 26 weeks).

If the employer has to take on a temporary replacement whilst the original employee is suspended, the dismissal of the replacement when the original employee returns is dealt with in exactly the same way as under the Maternity replacement provisions.[2]

In other words, if the employer has informed the replacement **in writing** that he will be dismissed at the end of a medical suspension period and the employer does then dismiss him to allow the original employee to return, then this will be regarded

---

[1] See p. 360.
[2] See p. 117.

as " a substantial reason of a kind such as to justify the dismissal ".[1]

It must be remembered that even this provision will only get the employer over the first hurdle; the employer will still have to prove and show that he acted " reasonably ".[2]

Sanctions

If an employer does not pay the whole or any part of the medical suspension pay under these provisions, the employee can present a complaint to an Industrial Tribunal and the Tribunal can order the employer to pay to the employee the amount of remuneration pay.

There is no provision for payments of other " damages " or loss, but, on the other hand, there is no limit on the amount of the weekly pay. It is not, for example, restricted to £80 per week as in certain other areas (*e.g.* redundancy).

There is the usual Industrial Tribunal rule to the effect that the complaint to the Tribunal must be within three months or such further period as the Tribunal considers reasonable where it was not reasonably practicable for the complaint to be presented within the period.

For medical suspension pay claims, the three month period runs from the day or " any day " of the suspension (EPA, s. 32(2)). It would seem, therefore, that the matter will be dealt with on a day to day basis. Thus if, for example, an employee is suspended for six months (26 weeks) and then immediately lodges a claim with the Tribunal, he may only be awarded 3 months (13 weeks) pay—unless, of course, he can bring himself within the " not reasonably practicable " provisions.[3]

---

1 EPA, s. 33.
2 See para. 6(8) of 1st Sch. of the TUALRA and p. 297.
3 As to which see p. 300.

CHAPTER 9

ITEMISED PAY STATEMENT

Section 81 of the Employment Protection Act 1975 provides that every employee has the right to be given an **itemised pay statement.**

Many employers may be surprised that it should have been nceessary to give employees a statutory right to such a statement. It seems, however, that there are very many employees (including in particular part-time or casual employees or those working in very small businesses) who have not in the past been provided with a proper statement as to their pay and deductions. This provision comes into force on 6th April 1977, the Government having allowed employers time to prepare themselves for this change and also having indicated that it was convenient to introduce the new arrangements at the beginning of a tax year.

The right is given to the employee, regardless of his length of service.

The pay statement must be **in writing;** it must be given to the employee at the time at which the wages are paid (or before that time); and it must contain the following particulars:—

(a) the gross amount of the wages or salary.

(b) the amounts of any deductions (whether fixed or variable).

(c) the net amount of the wages or salary.

(d) if the pay is made up and paid in different ways, the amount and method of each part payment.

If certain deductions are fixed, these need not be itemised every time provided that the aggregate amount of the deductions (including that deduction) is given each time and provided also

[125]

that the employer has previously given to the employee in writing a **standing statement of fixed deductions** containing in respect of each deduction—

(*a*) the amount of the deduction;

(*b*) the intervals at which the deduction is made; and

(*c*) the purpose for which it is made.

This might arise, for example, with fixed contributions to a Superannuation or Pension Scheme.

Any amendment to a standing statement of fixed deductions can be made by notice in writing. In addition, the standing statement must be re-issued and confirmed (or amended) at least every twelve months; if this is not done, the standing statement will cease to be effective after twelve months from the date on which it was issued.

The Secretary of State has power (s. 83) to vary the above provisions.

Excluded categories of employees

The above rights (to an itemised pay statement) do not apply to—

(1) Part-time workers, *i.e.* mainly those who work less than 16 hours weekly (but see page 353 for full details).

(2) employment where the employer is the husband or wife of the employee.

(3) employment as master or crew of a fishing vessel where remuneration is only by a share in the profits or gross earnings of the vessel.

(4) employees whom under their contract ordinarily work outside Great Britain. This includes a person employed to work on board a ship registered in the U.K. unless either the employment is wholly outside Great Britain or the employee is not ordinarily resident in Great Britain.

(5) merchant seamen.

Sanctions

If an employee is not given the required pay statement, he can refer the matter to an Industrial Tribunal which can determine " what particulars ought to have been included in a statement so as to comply with " the EPA requirements (s. 84).

This covers the position where no pay statement at all is issued.

In addition, however, if a pay statement (or a standing statement of fixed deductions) is issued and a question arises as to the particulars which ought to have been included, then either the employer or the employee can refer the question to a Tribunal for a ruling.

In either of the above situations, the Tribunal has no power to deal with the accuracy of any amount stated in a pay statement (s. 84(3)).

A reference to a Tribunal can only be made either during the employment or within three months from the end of the employment. There is no provision in the Act to extend this three month period.

If the Tribunal finds either that no pay statement has been given or that the required particulars have not been given, it can—

(a) make a declaration to that effect, and

(b) where the Tribunal finds that unnotified deductions have been made from an employee's pay during the 13 weeks prior to the application to a Tribunal it can order the employer to pay the employee " a sum not exceeding the aggregate of the unnotified deductions " (s. 84(5)).

Under this latter provision, the Tribunal can make such an order even if the employer was quite entitled to make the deduction under the contract of employment. Thus, it would seem that the real " penalty " on an employer who does not provide a proper statement is that a Tribunal can make him repay to the employee certain deductions (up to a maximum of 13 weeks) which it was quite proper for the employer to make, *e.g.* National Insurance contributions, payments to an approved Pension Scheme and even presumably PAYE tax deductions.

Employers who do not already comply with these provisions should, therefore, make arrangements to do so immediately in readiness for the implementation of this part of the EPA on 6th April 1977; A very helpful booklet is issued by the Department of Employment.

Any agreement purporting to exclude these provisions will be void.

CHAPTER 10

TIME OFF FOR PUBLIC DUTIES

The final right to be considered in this section is the right for employees to have time off from their job to carry out certain specified " public duties ".

The detailed provisions are contained in **section 59 of the Employment Protection Act 1975** and they are not yet effective. It is anticipated that these provisions (along with the other " time off " provisions[1]) will come into force during 1977. When they are in force, it will not be possible to contract out of them.

Conditions

The provisions relating to time off for public duties apply to **all** employees regardless of their length of service. There is no exclusion for small firms, but part-time workers (see page 353, *below*) are excluded. The employee claiming this right does not have to be a member of a recognised trade union.

The **public duties** themselves are specified in the Act, although they can be modified by the Secretary of State. The provisions thus only apply where the employee is—

(*a*) a justice of the peace.

(*b*) a member of a local authority.

(*c*) a member of any statutory Tribunal.

(*d*) a member of a Regional Health Authority.

(*e*) a member of the managing or governing body of an educational establishment maintained by a local education authority.

(*f*) a member of a water authority.

---

[1] See pp. 99 and 103, *supra*.

Unless and until the Secretary of State makes some amendment to these provisions, these are the only public duties for which an employee can claim time off.

The Act does not provide for the employee to be paid in respect of time off for public duties (as is the case with time off for union officials). There is, therefore, no obligation on an employer to pay the employee whilst he is away from his job for the performance of the public duties. Whether an employer does in practice decide to maintain the employee's pay is a matter for the employer.

The time off

The time off is, of course, time off during the employee's working hours and must be for the purposes of carrying out any of the duties of his office. These duties include attending meetings of the appropriate body or of any related committee and they also include doing anything else which is required or approved by the body concerned for the purpose of discharging its functions.

The amount of time off and the occasions on which it can be taken are specified as those that are " **reasonable in all the circumstances** " having regard, in particular, to the following:—

(a) how much time off is required for the performance of the duties of the office or as a member of the body in question.

(b) how much time off the employee has already been allowed for carrying out trade union duties (see page 101, *above*) and for involvement in trade union activities (see page 99, *above*).

(c) the circumstances of the employer's business and the effect of the employee's absence on the running of that business (s. 59(4)).

It is not intended that a Code of Practice will be issued by the ACAS on this particular topic (as is the case with time off for trade union duties and activities—see pages 100 and 102).

The only guidelines are those set out above. These guidelines seem to maintain a reasonably fair balance between the employer and the employee. It will be noted that the effect of the absence on the employer's business is one of the factors to be taken into account. Thus if, for example, in a small business a vital employee wishes to have time off for certain public duties and if, at that time, his absence would seriously affect the business (*e.g.* during the busy pre-Christmas period in a shop), then it seems likely that the employer would not be unreasonable in refusing to allow that employee to have the time off.

In practice, it may often happen that an employee who is appointed to some public body will also be a keen union member and/or union official. One example of this, of course, is the lay member of an Industrial Tribunal who is selected from the T.U.C. approved panel of names. In that event, any time off that the employee has had for his union duties or activities will be taken into account. Employers should, therefore, keep records of all " time off " allowed. They should also verify that the time off is for a proper purpose.

For the time being, employers can only rely on the guidelines laid down in the Act. No doubt, when the provisions have been in force for some time, Tribunals will be in a position to give further guidance on matters which will come before them under this head.

Excluded categories of employees

The above rights relating to time off for public duties do not apply to—

(1) Part-time workers, *i.e.* mainly those who work less than 16 hours weekly (but see page 353 for full details).

(2) employment where the employer is the husband or wife of the employee.

(3) employment as master or crew of a fishing vessel where remuneration is only by a share in the profits or gross earnings of the vessel.

(4) employees who under their contract ordinarily work outside Great Britain. This includes a person employed to work on board a ship registered in the U.K. unless either

the employment is wholly outside Great Britain or the employee is not ordinarily resident in Great Britain.

(5) merchant seamen.

Sanctions

If an employer refuses to allow an employee to have time off for public duties, the employee can, if he wishes, present a complaint to an Industrial Tribunal.

The complaint must be presented within three months from the date of the refusal. If the complaint is not made within that period, the Tribunal will have no jurisdiction to deal with the matter unless it is satisfied that it was not reasonably practicable for the complaint to be presented within the three months, in which case the period can be extended as the Tribunal " considers reasonable " (s. 60(1)).

If the Tribunal finds in favour of the employee it will make a declaration that the complaint is well founded and it can also award compensation. The compensation will be such amount " as the Tribunal considers just and equitable in all the circumstances having regard to the employer's default in failing to permit time off . . . and to any loss sustained by the employee which is attributable to the matters complained of ".

It is difficult to assess how in fact a Tribunal will calculate compensation. The employee will not normally have suffered any financial loss. If this is the case, what amount will the Tribunal award? It seems possible that a Tribunal may only award a comparatively nominal sum, which will in effect be a form of penalty or " fine ". Here again, one can only await the decisions of the Tribunals.

PART IV

THE EMPLOYER IN A CHANGING BUSINESS

CHAPTER 11

LAY-OFF AND SHORT-TIME

Before redundancy itself is considered, what is the general position if an employer, during a period of recession or when there is a fall-off in work or orders, decides that he cannot continue to employ one or more employees on a full-time basis?

Can the employer tell the employee that there is no work available at present and that he will inform the employee when he should again report for work? Alternatively, can that employer say that he is only able to provide work for 4 days out of 5 and that he will, therefore, pay the employee accordingly? The first question raises the problem of " lay-off " and the second question the problem of " short-time ".

The answers to these questions are to be found partly in the general principles of the Common Law and partly in statute law.

In this section of the book (Chapters 11 to 14) the Redundancy Payments Act 1965 is referred to as RPA the Trade Union and Labour Relations Act 1974 as TUALRA and the Employment Protection Act 1975 as EPA.

LAY-OFF

" Lay-off " is not a strictly legal term, although it will be seen (page 143, *post*) that section 5(1) of the RPA does contain a form of definition for redundancy purposes.

[133]

The word as normally used by the businessman or worker simply means that no work is available at a particular time for a particular employee. In the legal sense, however, " lay-off " can cover two different situations—

(1) Dismissal

The first situation is where the employer in effect dismisses the employee, although there may be an understanding or even an agreement that the employee will be taken back when work is once again available. The dismissal here may be by way of notice or by virtue of some other legal reason such as frustration[1] (e.g. the factory is burned down and no work is possible).

If lay-off is by way of dismissal (and it should be stated that in practice this is not very common), then the employee can claim a full redundancy payment under the RPA, provided that he complies with the RPA requirements, in particular having been continuously employed for the necessary two year qualifying period.

The detailed provisions with regard to redundancy are considered in Chapter 13. The lay-off by way of dismissal is clearly a redundancy dismissal since the dismissal is attributable to the cessation or diminution of work of a particular kind.

In addition, the employee may also be entitled to apply to an Industrial Tribunal and claim that he was " unfairly dismissed "—as to which see pages 246 to 256, post.

If, despite the dismissal, the employee does not claim redundancy or unfair dismissal compensation and he is again taken on by his employer, he will have continuity of employment throughout the " laid off " period. That period will count towards his total period of " continuous employment ".[2] This could be the case even if the employee takes a temporary job elsewhere.

---

[1] See pp. 220 to 225, post.
[2] CEA, Sch. 1, para. 5(1)(b), and see Appendix II (p. 352).

There are special provisions in the RPA (ss. 5 to 7) relating to the rights of employees who are laid-off or put on short-time, but these are not applicable to the situation considered above where the employee is in fact dismissed.

(2) Suspension

The second situation is where the employer fails to provide the employee with work during the contract of employment.

This is a form of suspension of the relationship until work is once again available. There is no dismissal as such. It is thought that, although many employers do not concern themselves with the legal niceties of the distinction between dismissal and suspension, this will be the more common procedure in practice.

If the lay-off happens in this way, what are the rights of the employee against the employer?

The answer to this question must be considered under two heads—(*a*) at Common Law and (*b*) under the RPA.

(a) *At Common Law*

The general principle is that an employer only has a right to suspend an employee from his job if there is a right to do so under the contract of employment itself. Suspension cannot be imposed unilaterally by the employer.

In the first instance, therefore, the **terms of the contract** must be carefully considered. We have already seen (pages 31 and 32, *ante*) that the terms of a contract can be express or implied.

If there is an **express term** giving the employer a right to lay-off an employee because of lack of work, there will be no problem from the point of view of the employer (subject to the statutory provisions referred to below). Such a clause should be expressly incorporated in the contract of employment[1] and should be worded so as to cover all the anticipated problem areas, *e.g.* lack of business, shortage of materials or other supplies, bad weather conditions, etc.

---

[1] See p. 32, *ante*.

Very often, a **collective agreement** between an employer and a trade union will give the employer a right to lay-off employees. If this is the case, consideration should then be given as to whether or not the terms of the collective agreement have been properly incorporated into the individual's contract of employment.[1]

If there is no express term in the contract as to lay-off can such a term be **implied**? The question of implied terms generally has already been considered in Chapter 2 (page 32, *ante*). On some occasions a term can be implied from a collective agreement, even if that agreement is not specifically referred to in the individual's contract. It may also be possible to imply the term from **custom and practice**. The custom and practice must, however, be absolutely clear and beyond all doubt. It is very difficult to establish. An employer wishing to have the power to lay-off is much better advised to deal with the matter specifically in the contract.

There is very little decided case law throwing light on this matter. In one case[2] a firm of bookmakers tried to establish that there was an implied right to lay-off employees when horse racing was cancelled for a period due to bad weather and to a foot and mouth epidemic; the employers failed on the ground that the alleged custom was insufficiently known to employees and was too vague. A recent case in which a lay-off was held to be a repudiation of the contract by the employer, thus enabling the employee to a redundancy payment was *McCarthy v. Burroughs Machines Ltd.* [1975] ITR 46.

In theory, a right to lay off can be implied in other circumstances. It has been suggested[3] that this might arise in circumstances where it becomes for the time being physically impossible to carry on with the particular work, *e.g.* the burning down of a factory; a dangerous condition in a coalmine; a breakdown in machinery. Here again, however, there is very little authority and the position is, therefore, uncertain.

---

1 See p. 33, *ante*.
2 *Jones v. Harry Sherman Ltd.* [1969] ITR 63.
3 Grunfeld on the Law of Redundancy at p. 127.

It will be clear from the foregoing that it is much safer for the employers to be able to rely on an express term in the contract of employment. It is not safe to rely on an industrial custom or practice.

One thing is, however, clear. If there is not in fact any term (express or implied) giving the employer power to lay-off an employee, then if the employer does suspend the employee this will legally be a breach of contract by the employer. Such a breach will entitle the employee to treat himself as dismissed. It will in effect be a " constructive dismissal "[1] and will entitle the employee to claim a full redundancy payment under the RPA and also to claim that he has been unfairly dismissed within the meaning of the TUALRA. If this does happen, the employee will become entitled to the rights referred to in Chapters 13 and 19 respectively.

In practice, of course, many employees will not take such action. This may be for various reasons, but in particular they may well hope that the " fortunes " of the employer will soon improve and that they will then be able to return to work. This should not, however, be relied upon by employers. Many employers are still of the view that they automatically have a right to lay-off employees. As seen above, this is very often not the case and a claim can then be made by the employee to an Industrial Tribunal. This is quite separate from any rights an employee may have with regard to a " guarantee payment " as to which see page 149, *post*).

One final matter should be considered with regard to lay-off by way of suspension. What is the position if the employer **suspends** an employee **on full pay** ?

Admittedly, this is a very unlikely eventuality. It would— to say the least—be unusual for an employer, with a declining order book, to wish to suspend employees and yet still pay them in full.

In any event, the position normally will be that a suspension on full pay is not a breach of contract by the employer and will not give rise to any claim by the employee.

---

[1] RPA, s. 3(2)(*c*), and TUALRA, Sch. 1, para. 5(2)(*c*), and see p. 216, *ante*.

The general principle is that an employer is not under any obligation to provide work. As was said in a leading case in 1940—

> " A contract of employment does not necessarily, or perhaps normally, oblige the master to provide the servant with work. Provided I pay my cook her wages regularly, she cannot complain if I choose to take any or all of my meals out."[1]

Exceptions to this principle include apprentices, theatrical performers, and employees employed on a commission or piece-work basis.

Having said this, there is no doubt that the whole relationship of employer and employee has changed—even since 1940—and is no doubt still changing. There have in recent times been indications (in particular by the Court of Appeal in *Langston v. AUEW* [1974] ICR 180) that it is at least arguable that an employee has by implication a right to do his work—particularly when it is available. Lord Denning, M.R. in the Langston case refers to a skilled man taking a pride in his job and having " the satisfaction of a job well done ". Reference is made by his Lordship to paragraph 9 of the Code of Practice—

> " . . . management should recognise the employee's need to achieve a sense of satisfaction in his job and should provide for it so far as practicable."

The point did not, however, have to be decided by the Court of Appeal in the Langston Case.

More recently—in one of the very first cases heard by the Employment Appeal Tribunal—Mr. Justice Phillips seemed to indicate that nowadays the courts and tribunals might be more ready to find that there is an obligation on employers to provide work for the employee. In the case in question—*Breach v. Epsylon Industries Ltd.* [1976] IRLR 181—the employee was a Chief Engineer and from about the middle of 1974 the work upon which he was engaged was transferred to Canada and the employers' engineering activities in the U.K. had almost entirely ceased. By the autumn of 1974 the employee had no work left to do—at least in his capacity as Chief Engineer.

---

[1] Asquith, J., in *Collier v. Sunday Referee Publishing Co. Ltd.* [1940] 2 K.B. 647.

He was reluctant to resign lest he should lose his right to a redundancy payment. On the other hand, he felt that if he did nothing he would quickly get out of touch with the expertise required in his industry. Ultimately, he left the employment, informing the employers that their failure to provide him with work in his capacity as Chief Engineer was a repudiation of the contract by them and, that therefore, he had in effect been dismissed. He claimed a redundancy payment and this was refused by the Tribunal, mainly on the grounds that the employers were under no obligation to provide the employee with work (this being based on the general principle referred to above), and that the employers had not, therefore, repudiated the contract. On appeal, the Employment Appeal Tribunal considered whether there was a term implied in the contract of employment that suitable work should be provided for the employee. The Tribunal said that whilst the general principle referred to above was binding on it, the principle itself did envisage that there would be exceptions to the general rule. These would arise where it could be said that from the nature of the employment and the circumstances surrounding it there was an obligation to provide work. The Judge expressed the view that the general principle might nowadays be thought to be out of date and old fashioned and that this could lead to the consequence that at the present time a consideration of the facts of a particular case might more easily lead to the conclusion that the case will be one where there is an obligation to provide work. The Judge felt that the Industrial Tribunal might have erred in the manner in which it considered this general principle and the case was, therefore, sent back to the Industrial Tribunal to re-hear the case on this particular point. The Judge indicated that the Tribunal should take into account " the changed climate of opinion and outlook which is general since the Redundancy Payments Act 1965 and the change in industrial relations since 1971 ".

Here again, therefore, no definite finding was made by the Employment Appeal Tribunal.

It does, therefore, seem that this aspect of the law is changing in the light of social conditions and industrial relations. The general principle referred to above has not yet been overruled. It would seem, however, that Tribunals might now be prepared to find that the circumstances of a particular case do form an exception to the general rule. This will be particularly so in the case of more senior employees whose future career may become prejudiced if they are unable during their employment to carry out the job they were employed to do.

(b) The statutory provisions

Sections 5 to 7 of the RPA contain certain special provisions relating to employees who are laid off or put on short time.

These will be dealt with in detail after consideration has been given to the question of short-time.

SHORT-TIME

Again, there is no particular magic in the word " short-time ". It obviously arises where an employee is not employed and paid for a full normal working week. " Lay-off ", as we have seen, involves the loss of a whole week's wages.

The RPA definition is, however, rather stricter than this, section 5(2) dealing with the matter by reference to half a week's pay (see page 144, *post*).

Before dealing, however, with the special statutory provisions relating to short-time we must first deal with the Common Law position.

(a) Short-time at Common Law

Whether an employer has a right to put an employee on short-time will depend (as with a complete lay-off) on the terms of the contract of employment.

If the contract gives the employer such a right, then no complaint can be made by the employee.

If, on the other hand, an employer unilaterally puts an employee on shorter time than was originally agreed, then that will be a breach of contract and the employee can leave his job and claim that he has been dismissed. This is another example of constructive dismissal.[1] Arising out of such dismissal, the employee can then present a claim to an Industrial Tribunal and claim a redundancy payment and/or that he has been unfairly dismissed. Details of such claims are considered in later chapters.

The comments made earlier in this chapter relating to lay-off at Common Law apply equally to short-time.

As with a lay-off situation, an employee may decide not to take any action in respect of the short-time and his consequently reduced " pay packet ". He may hope that, all being well, the employer will be able to return to a full working week. There are, however, from the legal point of view, dangers in this for the employee.

If the employee " puts up " with the shorter working week and continues to work on that basis for some time, it may then be held that he has started to work under a new contract of employment. There will have been what is called " a consensual variation " in the terms of the original contract of employment. When that happens, the position will be that the employee will not be on short-time, but will in fact be working full time under a new contract.

A good example of this situation was the case of *Spelman v. George Garnham*[2] where the employee had worked a 36 hour week from 1949 until 1967; she was then ill for a few months and on her return to work was employed for afternoons only (a period of 17½ hours per week). The employee worked on that basis and then after a while left and claimed redundancy pay. The Divisional Court held that the employee had accepted a " new contract for the future, involving 17½ hours per week. Accordingly . . . she was never put on short-time at all ". The employee's claim failed.

It is not possible to be definite as to the length of time an employee must work under new terms (*e.g.* on short working hours) before those terms become part of a " new contract " (as in the Spelman Case). Everything will depend on the

---

1 RPA, s. 3(1)(*c*), and TUALRA, Sch. 1, para. 5(2)(*c*), and see p. 216.
2 [1968] ITR 370.

circumstances of the particular case. An employee is certainly entitled to " try out " the new terms and this will not bar him from treating the reduction in hours as a breach of contract, provided that he acts within a reasonable time. In view of the new " trial period " provisions[1] introduced into the RPA, it is felt that a period of up to four weeks will normally be quite reasonable. After four weeks, however, an employee may well be deemed to have accepted the new terms.

(b) Guaranteed Pay

An employee may have a right to receive his normal wage even though he has been put on short-time.

This can arise either by statute (the EPA Guarantee payments provisions) or under a guaranteed wage agreement.

These are matters of great importance and will be considered in Chapter 12.

(c) The Statutory Provisions

The RPA, as has already been mentioned, contains some special provisions giving an employee who is laid off or put on short-time within the meaning of the Act the right to claim a redundancy payment. These provisions will now be considered.

RIGHTS TO A REDUNDANCY PAYMENT BY REASON OF LAY-OFF OR SHORT-TIME

An employee is not entitled to redundancy pay simply because he has been laid-off or put on short-time.

In certain circumstances, however, the RPA varies this general principle. The relevant provisions are in sections 5 to 7 of the RPA.

The provisions relate both to the employee who is laid-off and the employee who is on short-time, but the definitions of lay-off and short-time are special definitions set down in the Act.

---

[1] As to which see p. 177, *below.*

Lay-Off

Section 5(1) of the RPA provides as follows:—

" Where an employee is employed under a contract on such terms and conditions that his remuneration thereunder depends upon his being provided by the employer with work of the kind which he is employed to do, he shall . . . be taken to be **laid-off** for any week in respect of which, by reason that the employer does not provide such work for him, he is not entitled to any remuneration under the contract ".

It will be seen from this definition that there appear to be two conditions applicable before the statutory provisions can apply—

(a) the contract of employment must give the employer an express or implied power to lay-off the employee without pay and

(b) the employee must have been laid off under such power and is not being paid.

It has already been seen (page 137, *above*) that if the employer has no right to lay off without pay and he nevertheless does so, the employee can treat the lay-off as a repudiation of contract, leave his job and claim redundancy. This situation, therefore, is not covered by the special sections 5 to 7 provisions.

In addition, where employees are laid off under a guaranteed week agreement and are receiving their full weekly wage under such an agreement, they will not qualify under section 5(1) because they are " entitled to . . . remuneration ". Nor, in those circumstances, will the employees be able to claim a breach of contract and thus a dismissal because the employers will have had power under the guaranteed week agreement to lay them off.

The question of whether the employer has an implied power to lay off an employee without pay has already been considered (page 136, *above*).

Short-time

Only certain specified short-time gives rise to the RPA rights to claim redundancy pay. The definition is contained in section 5(2) as follows:—

" Where by reason of a dimunition in the work provided for an employee by his employer (being work of a kind which under his contract the employee is employed to do) the employee's remuneration for any week is **less than half a week's pay** . . . he shall . . . be taken to be kept on short-time for that week ".

Here again there seem to be two main conditions before the statutory definition can arise—

(a) there must be a diminution of work, and

(b) the employee's earnings must drop to less than half a week's pay.

The definition does not, as for lay-off, require the employer to have a right under the contract to reduce the working week. Nevertheless, as has already been seen (page 140, *above*), if the employer has no contractual right to reduce an employee's remuneration, he will be in breach of contract if he attempts to do so.

The calculation of " half a week's pay " is rather complicated. The original RPA provisions in Schedule 2 to the Act have now been amended by the Employment Protection Act 1975 and Part II of Schedule 4 of that Act contain detailed rules as to calculation of **" a week's pay ".**[1]

If an employee's pay for employment in normal working hours does not vary with the amount of work done, the amount of a week's pay is the amount payable by the employer under the contract of employment.

It will be noted that under section 5(2) the short-time must reduce the remuneration to less than half the minimum remuneration payable under the contract of employment. This may have to be less than one half of the employee's normal pay, *e.g.* overtime will not be taken into account unless it is obligatory on both the employer to provide overtime and the employee to work it.

In cases where the contract does not lay down fixed " normal working hours " and the weekly pay can vary, then the EPA amendments in effect provide for the averaging out of an employee's remuneration over a 12 week period. From this point of view, employees with no " normal working hours "

---

[1] See Appendix III (pp. 360 to 363).

may find it easier to bring themselves within the section 5(2) definition. Their pay will be averaged out over a 12 week period, and one half of the average will then be taken for the purposes of the definition.

The right to a redundancy payment

Section 6 of the RPA is worded in the negative. Thus—

" An employee shall **not** be entitled to a redundancy payment by reason of his being laid off or kept on short-time unless he gives notice in writing to his employer indicating (in whatsoever terms) his intention to claim a redundancy payment in respect of lay-off or short-time . . . ".

The employee must, therefore, give such a notice in writing. That in itself, however, is not sufficient. The following **conditions** must be complied with:—

(*a*) the employee must have been laid off or kept on short-time either for at least **four consecutive weeks** (ending with the date of the notice or not more than four weeks before that date) or for a series of at least six weeks (of which not more than three were consecutive) within a period of thirteen weeks (the last of the six weeks ending as provided above).

The periods referred to can be a mixture of " laid-off " weeks and " short-time " weeks.

No account is taken of any week where the lay-off or short-time is wholly or mainly attributable to a strike or lock-out and this is the case whether the strike or lock-out is at the employee's place of work or not and— states section 7(3)—" whether it is in Great Britain or elsewhere ".

(*b*) the employee must give the required **notice of intention to claim** no earlier than the last of the four or six weeks referred to above but not later than four weeks from the last day of either of those periods.

(*c*) the employee must **terminate his contract of employment** by giving **one week's notice** (or such other minimum period of notice as may be required by his contract). Thus, the giving of the notice of intention to claim does not of itself terminate the contract. That is a separate matter. The notice may be given before the notice of intention to claim, or at the same time, or even after—provided that, in the latter case and assuming that the employer is not contesting the claim, it is given within four weeks of service of the notice of intention to claim. A longer period is allowed if the employer serves a counter-notice (see page 147, *post*).

Section 6(3)(*b*) of the RPA provides that if the employee is dismissed he will not be entitled to a redundancy payment " in pursuance of the notice of intention to claim ". This is, however, without prejudice to his right to claim redundancy pay in the normal way by virtue of the dismissal.

The conditions referred to above—and the various time limits contained in them—are strictly applied. There is no provision for extending the time limits or waiving any of the conditions. If, therefore, an employee does not comply with them, he will not be entitled to claim redundancy pay. If, however, he does comply, he will—subject to the remainder of this chapter—become entitled to a full redundancy payment.

Similarly, if an employee who is laid off or on short-time leaves his job and commences another one, he will lose his rights under the RPA provisions. If the employer was also entitled to lay him off or put him on short-time, there will not have been a breach of contract and the employee will not be able to claim he has been " dismissed ". Certain categories of employees do not in any event have rights to a redundancy payment and they are set out in Chapter 13 (pages 158 to 162, *post*).

If the employee does fall within the above provisions and he has complied with the various conditions, what steps should the employer take?

The position of the employer

If the employer takes **no steps** whatsoever and the employee has complied with all the conditions referred to above, then the employee will be entitled to a redundancy payment, provided only that he has the necessary two years' " continuous service " qualification which is necessary for general redundancy purposes.[1]

There is, however, one main **defence** that is available to an employer.

The defence is to show that " it was reasonably to be expected that the employee (if he continued to be employed by the same employer) would, not later than four weeks after " the date of service of the notice of intention to claim " enter upon a period of employment of not less than thirteen weeks during which he would not be laid off or kept on short-time for any week " (s. 6(4)).

This defence is, however, subject to one very strict condition and that is that the defence will only be applicable if the employer—within seven days of receiving the employee's notice of intention to claim—gives a **counter-notice** to the employee in writing indicating that he will contest the claim.

If the counter-notice is given and not withdrawn, then—unless, of course, the employee withdraws—the matter will be referred to an Industrial Tribunal. It will then be for the employer to establish his defence.

The defence, as we have seen, relates to a **reasonable expectation** of a return to full capacity. This will, of course, depend on the evidence. The burden of proof is on the employer. If the employer has actual evidence of future work, there should be no difficulty in establishing the defence. On the other hand, if by the time the matter reaches the Tribunal the employee has remained laid off or on short-time for the whole of the four week period referred to in section 6(4) then the Tribunal will be bound to find in favour of the employee. Section 7(1) lays down that in that event " it shall be conclusively presumed " that the employer's defence cannot succeed.

The work expected to be available must be work of the kind covered by the employee's contract before he was laid off or put on short-time. It is no defence to say that suitable alternative work will be available.

---

[1] See p., 158 *post*.

On the other hand, it is worthy of note that in the case of an employee either laid-off or on short-time, the employer does not under the section have to establish an expectation that the employee will return to full-time work. A return to part-time work would be sufficient provided that it gave the employee more than half a week's pay (see the section 5(2) definition on page 144).

If the matter reaches a Tribunal, after the employer has given a counter-notice, the employee does not have to give the required notice to terminate the contract immediately, although he can, of course, do so. He must, however, in any event give such notice within three weeks of the Tribunal notifying him of its decision.

Similarly, if the employer serves a counter-notice and then withdraws it by subsequent notice in writing, the employee (who will then have become automatically entitled to a redundancy payment) must give his notice to terminate no later than three weeks after service of the notice of withdrawal.

The actual amount of redundancy pay will be considered in Chapter 13 (page 185, *post*).

The position with regard to lay-off and short-time has been considered in some detail, as it is the experience of the writer that these important provisions despite having been introduced in 1965 are still not sufficiently known to those dealing with employment matters.

CHAPTER 12

GUARANTEED PAY

There is no basic legal principle providing for an employee to be paid when no work is available for him.

Guaranteed payment of wages can, however, arise—

(*a*) By agreement and/or

(*b*) By statute.

GUARANTEED PAY AGREEMENTS

Lay-off and short-time will only arise when the employer finds himself in a difficult situation, *e.g.* he does not have enough work available to employ all his staff on a full-time basis.

In an effort to avoid such difficulties many employers nowadays reach agreement with their employees (often via a trade union) under which the employers are given a right to lay off workers or put them on short time and the employees are guaranteed a certain minimum weekly wage. It is thought that about half of all manual workers in the United Kingdom are probably covered by guaranteed week agreements. Most of these agreements will form part of a Collective Agreement with a recognised trade union.

Each agreement will, of course, depend on its own particular terms. The following matters will normally be taken into account:—

(*a*) most guaranteed week agreements provide for payment of less than a full week's wages. Employees laid off under these agreements will, therefore, normally suffer a reduction in earnings.

(*b*) many guaranteed week agreements do not apply to new employees until they have been employed for a certain period. The most usual period seems to be four weeks.

(*c*) some agreements limit the number of weeks during which the agreed remuneration will be paid in a particular year.

(*d*) some agreements give the employer power to suspend the operation of the guarantee particularly in the event of strikes or other industrial action by the employees.

(*e*) in many agreements the employees are bound to undertake reasonable alternative work. Difficulties can then arise as to what is reasonable alternative work.

As indicated above, each agreement must be looked at individually. An employer who is about to enter into such an agreement must consider carefully the full implications of the agreement and should endeavour at the outset to provide solutions for any problems that might arise in the future.

If, as is likely, the agreement forms part of a Collective Agreement, it will only be enforceable by—and against—an individual employee if the terms of the Agreement are incorporated by reference into the terms of his employment (see page 33, *above*).

Most employees will now in any event be protected by the statutory rights contained in the Employment Protection Act 1975. It is quite likely that these rights will now be considered as the bare minima and that they will be used by trade unions as a starting point for negotiating improved agreements.

STATUTORY GUARANTEE PAYMENTS

The guarantee payment rights under the **Employment Protection Act 1975** are contained in **sections 22 to 28.** These sections came into force on 1st February 1977 by virtue of The Employment Protection Act 1975 (Commencement No. 6) Order 1976.

The right itself

In the first instance, the right to receive a guarantee payment will only arise in the case of an employee who has **four weeks' continuous service** with the employer, the four weeks ending with the last complete week before the " workless day ".

By referring to the employee being " continuously employed for a period of four weeks " the definition of " continuous employment " is introduced into the Act (as to which see Appendix II, page 352). In particular, this means that " part-time " workers (see page 353) will not have a right to a guarantee payment. Under the EPA " part-time " has become less than 16 hours a week or, after 5 years' service, less than 8 hours a week.

Other employees who will **not** have any rights to a guarantee payment are the husband or wife of the employee; registered dock workers; share fishermen; employees ordinarily working outside Great Britain (for full definition, see page 101); and employees on a fixed term contract of 12 weeks or less (or employment under a contract made in contemplation of the performance of a specific task which is not expected to last more than 12 weeks) unless in either case the employee has in fact been continuously employed for more than 12 weeks.

Subject to the above, **section 22(1)** provides that—

" Where an employee throughout a day during any part of which he would normally be required to work in accordance with his contract of employment is not provided with work by his employer by reason of—

(*a*) a diminution in the requirements of the employer's business for work of the kind which the employee is employed to do, or

(*b*) any other occurrence affecting the normal working of the employer's business in relation to work of the kind which the employee is employed to do

he shall . . . be entitled to be paid . . . a guaranteed payment ".

The day referred to (*i.e.* when no work or reduced work was provided) is known as a " workless day ".

The above section sets out the position reasonably clearly. It will be noted that the statutory right in effect only covers

" lay-off " and not " short-time ", *i.e.* the guarantee only arises in respect of **whole days** in which no work is provided. If work is provided for part of the day, no right to a guarantee payment will arise.   In addition, it must be a day during which the particular employee is bound under his contract to work (either the complete day or any part of it).   Thus, if, for example, no work is provided on a particular Saturday, a guarantee payment will only arise if the employee was bound under his contract to work Saturdays.

There are special provisions in section 22(2) to cover the position of nightworkers, *e.g.* if the bulk of their work is done before midnight all their work is treated as done on the first day.

Section 26(1) of the EPA specifically provides that the statutory rights do not affect any right of an employee to be paid under his contract of employment.   Thus, if the employer has no contractual right to lay-off the employee, it would seem that the employee can, despite his rights to receive guarantee pay, sue his employer for any wages due under his contract. Similarly, receipt of guarantee pay will not affect the employee's right to claim a redundancy payment under the special lay-off provisions of the Redundancy Payments Act 1965 (see page 177, *ante*).

The amount of the payment

The EPA provides in section 24 what seems, on the face of it, a complicated formula for working out the daily guarantee pay.   It should, however, be noted at the outset that the amount cannot exceed £6 per day.

Subject to this limitation, the daily rate should be worked out as follows:—

(*a*) take **one week's pay,** which is calculated as for redundancy pay—see Part II of the 4th Schedule to the EPA (summarised in Appendix III—page 361, *post*).   Normally, overtime will not be included—unless it is compulsory on both sides.

(*b*) calculate the number of **normal working hours** in a week— again, the 4th Schedule (Part I) to the EPA is relevant

(and see Appendix III—page 360, *post*).   If the normal
hours worked do not vary, the position is simple.   If the
hours vary, a twelve week average is taken; if the
employee has not worked twelve weeks, a fair average
will be worked out by reference to comparable employees.
If by any chance there are **no** normal working hours, then
there will be no guarantee payment.

(c) divide the week's pay by the normal or average working
hours; this gives you the " **guaranteed hourly rate** ".

(d) multiply the guaranteed hourly rate by the number of
normal working hours on the day in question (*i.e.* the
workless day).

(e) the final figure is then the amount of guarantee pay for
that day, provided that it is no more than £6.

If an employee is in receipt of guarantee pay, he will not be
entitled to Unemployment Benefit for that day.

Limitations on guarantee payments

As seen above, the amount per day cannot exceed £6.

Secondly, **section 25** of the EPA limits the number of days
in respect of which a guarantee payment can be made.

Put very shortly, the limitation is a payment of up to five
days per quarter in each of the three month periods commencing on 1st February, 1st May, 1st August and 1st November in each year.

These limits (which at present seem comparatively modest)
can be varied from time to time by the Secretary of State.

The number of days in respect of which a guarantee payment
can be claimed are defined as the number of days (not exceeding
five) on which the employee normally works in a week under
his contract of employment.   Here again, if the number varies,
an average over a twelve week period is taken.

Where the right is lost

An employee will **not be entitled** to a guarantee payment in
respect of a workless day in the following circumstances:—

(*a*) if the failure to provide him with work occurs in consequence of a **trade dispute** involving any employee of the employer or of an associated employer.

This is quite a wide exclusion and covers employees who are laid off because of a strike, a go-slow or a work to rule. The trade dispute need not be confined to the particular place of work of the employee; it could extend to a dispute in an associated company. In view of this, some employees may find themselves laid off and yet be unable to claim a guarantee payment, even though they had not been in any way at fault.

(*b*) if the employer offers to provide **alternative work** for the day in question and the work is **suitable in all the circumstances** and the employee has **unreasonably refused** that offer.

The work offered does not have to be work which the employee was bound to do under his contract of employment.

Each case will be looked at on its merits and decisions of Tribunals will no doubt be awaited with interest when this part of the EPA comes into force. It is felt that the test of " suitability " will be less strict than it is for redundancy purposes.

It seems that an employer will be able, when offering the alternative work, to impose reasonable conditions.

(*c*) if the employee does not comply with **reasonable requirements** imposed by his employer with a view to **ensuring that his services are available.**

Guarantee Agreements

The statutory rights are not intended to take away the rights of an employee under a guaranteed week agreement. Payments under a collective or other agreement can be set against the statutory payments by the employer and *vice versa*.

Section 28 of the EPA contains provisions under which parties to a Collective Agreement which gives guarantee payments at least as beneficial as the EPA rights can apply to the

Minister and seek an Order exempting them from the statutory provisions.   This Exemption Order will only be granted if the guaranteed week agreement gives the employees a right to arbitration by an independent referee or a right to complain to an Industrial Tribunal in the event of a dispute.

It is not anticipated that the Exemption Order procedure will be used very much in practice.   Except for this procedure, it is not possible to contract out of the provisions of the EPA relating to guarantee payments.

Sanctions

If an employer does not pay the statutory guarantee pay, then the employee can apply to an Industrial Tribunal, which can order the employer to pay " the amount of guarantee payment which it finds is due to him " (s. 27(3)).

The application to the Tribunal must be presented within three months from the " workless day " in respect of which the claim is made.   There are the usual provisions regarding a possible extension of the three month period, *i.e.* where it was not " reasonably practicable " for the complaint to be presented within the three months.

The original Employment Protection Bill contained provisions under which additional penalties were imposed on an employer if he did not within a specified period tell the employee of his guarantee pay rights.   These provisions were, however, struck out and they are **not** now in the Act.

CHAPTER 13

REDUNDANCY

The law of Redundancy is a complete topic in itself. This chapter will attempt only to summarise the law and to deal with the practical implications for employers, particularly in the light of the Redundancy Payments Act 1965 (RPA) as amended by the recent provisions of the Employment Protection Act 1975 (EPA).

Redundancy arises when an employee loses his job because the business closes down or moves to another area or because the needs for that employee to carry out his particular work cease or diminish.

Until 1965 an employee in a redundancy situation was not entitled to any special payment because of his redundancy. Provided that he was given the correct amount of notice to terminate his employment or money in lieu of notice, there was no further legal obligation imposed on the employer. Employers could, of course, enter into voluntary agreements under which a form of redundancy payment might be made.

In 1965 the RPA was passed and this put an obligation on an employer to make special payments (based on the length of service of the employee) to employees who were dismissed by reason of redundancy or who were in certain circumstances (dealt with in Chapter 11) laid-off or kept on short-time. The RPA provisions became effective on 6th December 1965.

The Act was intended to achieve two main objectives—one was to reduce any resistance there might be to industrial re-organisation and to facilitate mobility of labour; the other objective was to compensate the employee for the loss of the " property in his job " or, as has been stated by Lord

Denning, M.R. the loss of some " accrued right in his job ".[1] The compensation is for what the employee has actually lost and not his future loss; the compensation is based on a statutory figure according to the years of service of the employee and is simply worked out on an arithmetical basis (see page 185).

The RPA has been amended from time to time by subsequent legislation, including in particular the TUALRA and the EPA. The amendments made by the latter Act were brought into effect on 1st June 1976 (see EPA Commencement Order No. 4).

THE BASIC PRINCIPLE OF REDUNDANCY

Section 1(1) RPA provides—

" Where . . . an employee who has been continuously employed for the requisite period—

(a) is dismissed by reason of redundancy or

(b) is laid-off or kept on short-time to the extent specified in . . . this Act . . . then . . . the employer shall be liable to pay to him a sum (. . . referred to as " a redundancy payment ") calculated in accordance with Schedule 1 to this Act and Schedule 4 to the Employment Protection Act 1975 ".

It is necessary to consider the various parts of this principle in more detail. The lay-off and short-time provisions have already been considered in Chapter 11.

WHO IS PROTECTED BY THE ACT ?

The benefits under the RPA only arise in the case of " an employee ".

Under section 25(1) " employee " means an individual who has entered into or works under a contract with an employer. The contract can be express or implied, oral or in writing and a contract of apprenticeship is included. The contract can be " for manual labour, clerical work or otherwise ".

---

[1] *Lloyd v. Brassey* [1969] ITR 100.

The RPA provisions do not, therefore, apply to the self-employed, nor do they apply to genuine independent agents or contractors. There can be a thin dividing line on occasions between a " full " employee in the legal sense and an independent agent. This will not, however, arise a very great deal in practice. If it does, the main test will be whether and to what extent the employer can control not only **what** the employee does but also **how** he does it. If this control does exist, then the relationship is that of employer and employee. A relevant (but not necessarily conclusive) factor can also be the type of stamp purchased by the " employee " under the National Insurance Acts, and also whether or not he is assessed to income tax under Schedule D as a self-employed person.[1]

Company directors can sometimes come within this " grey area ". A director of a public company who holds a minority of shares in that company will be an employee. If, however, a director has full control of a company either because of his shareholding (which may be effectively 100%) or because he is the only executive director on the board, he may not be classed as an employee. This will particularly be the case where there is a " one man " company, the director owning virtually all the shares. Each case will, of course, depend on its own particular facts.

Apart from persons who may not be employees at all in the legal sense, certain specific employees are excluded from the provisions of the RPA.

Excluded employees

The following employees are **not protected** by the RPA and will not be entitled to any redundancy payment:—

(a) **Employees who do not have two years' " continuous employment "**: The question of continuous employment is dealt with in Appendix II (page 352, *post*). The two years' service must have been acquired by the time of the actual dismissal.

---

[1] By way of example, see the Court of Appeal decision in *Ferguson v. John Dawson & Partners (Contractors) Ltd.* [1976] IRLR 346 (a contractor " on the lump " nevertheless held to be an " employee ").

In much of the employment legislation since 1965 a shorter " qualifying period " has been used, *e.g.* a period of 26 weeks in respect of unfair dismissal.

The two year period is, however, still applicable for redundancy purposes and there are not at present any proposals to reduce this period.

The RPA provides that a person's employment shall, unless the contrary is proved, be presumed to have been continuous and this applies even if there has been more than one employer.

An employee who is dismissed because of redundancy during his first two years will, therefore, have no claim to a redundancy payment. He may, of course, be able to claim that his dismissal due to redundancy was " unfair " if he has been employed for at least 26 weeks.[1]

(*b*) **Certain part-time employees:** The exclusion here arises by virtue of the definition of " continuous employment " (see Appendix II, at page 352).

An employee whose contract requires less than 16 hours to be worked in a week will not qualify for a redundancy payment (nor for various other rights, including unfair dismissal).

These provisions were amended by the EPA and came into force on 1st February 1977.

In some cases even a period of 8 hours per week will be sufficient, *e.g.* where the employee has five years' service.

This matter is covered in more detail in Appendix II (pages 352 to 359) (and see also page 44).

Prior to 1st February 1977 the relevant period was 21 hours weekly.

(*c*) **Employees** who are at the date of their dismissal **over the age of 65** (in the case of **men**) and **over the age of 60** (in the case of **women**).

(*d*) **Employees** who are **under the age of 18** are **not** covered by the RPA provisions mainly because the statutory

---

[1] See p. 290, *post.*

formula for working out the amount of a redundancy
payment excludes " any week which began before the
employee attained the age of eighteen " (paragraph 1 of
the 1st Schedule to the RPA).

The effect of this exclusion coupled with the two year
qualifying period (paragraph (*a*) *above*) is that in practice
an employee who has not attained the age of 20 at the
time of his dismissal will not have any right to a
redundancy payment.

(*e*) **Certain employees who are contracted out of the Act:**
Normally, an individual cannot contract out of the
provisions of the Act, but there is one exception to this.

" An employee under a contract of employment for
a fixed term of two years or more . . . is not entitled to a
redundancy payment in respect of **the expiry of that term
without its being renewed,** if before the term so expires he
has agreed in writing to exclude any right to a redundancy
payment in that event ". (RPA, s. 15(2)).

In practice, this may arise where a senior employee
is given a Service Agreement for two years or more.
The term must be a **fixed term** and the Agreement must be
in writing. It has now been held by the Court of Appeal
that a contract for a stated period which is determinable
in the meantime by either party giving to the other a
specified period of notice (*e.g.* three months) is not a
contract for a fixed term.[1] The exclusion will only
apply on the expiry of the term of years; it will not apply
if the employee is dismissed during the period of the
term.

The other form of " contracting out " can arise where
there is a **collective agreement** which contains redundancy
provisions at least as satisfactory as the statutory provisions and the Minister makes an exemption order
excluding the provisions of the RPA. The exemption
order will have to be made by a formal statutory order.

(*f*) **Crown servants** do not have the benefit of the RPA
provisions and, thus, civil servants are **excluded.** So are
National Health Service employees and **holders of certain
public offices.**

---

[1] *BBC v. Ioannou* [1975] ICR 267.

(g) **Registered dock workers** are not covered by the RPA scheme, as they have their own scheme outside the Act.

(h) **Share fishermen** are excluded, *i.e.* fishermen who are remunerated " by a share in the profits of gross earnings of the vessel " (RPA, s. 16(2)). Certain **merchant seamen** are also now excluded from the RPA provisions, those seamen being covered by a special scheme.

(i) The RPA does not apply where **the employer is the husband or wife** of the employee. It seems that for the exclusion to apply the spouse must be the sole employer. Thus, where the husband was one of two partners who carried on business and they employed the wife, the wife was entitled to a redundancy payment.[1] It will be noted that the RPA has never extended this particular exemption to other close relatives.

(j) **Domestic servants** are normally covered by the RPA provisions, the private household being (for these purposes) classed as a business (RPA, s. 19(1)).

This is, however, **not** the case where the **domestic servant is a close relative** of the employer and is employed in a private household. Such employees do not have the benefit of the RPA provisions. For the " close relative " exclusion to apply the employer must be the father, mother, grandfather, grandmother, stepfather, stepmother, son, daughter, grandson, granddaughter, stepson, stepdaughter, brother, sister, half-brother or half-sister of the employee.

This " close relative " exclusion only, however, applies to domestic servants in a private household—**not** to other employees, *e.g.* in a shop.

(k) An employee is **not entitled** to a redundancy payment if on the termination of his employment he is **outside Great Britain** " unless under his contract of employment he ordinarily worked in Great Britain " (RPA, s. 17(1)).

Similarly an employee who normally works outside Great Britain will not be entitled to a redundancy pay-

---

[1] *Bernstein v. Bernstein Brothers* [1969] ITR 106.

ment unless on the termination date he is in Great Britain in accordance with instructions given to him by his employer.[1]

Whether a particular employee " ordinarily works " in Great Britain will depend on the facts of each particular case.

It will be noted that the employment outside Great Britain exclusion referred to above differs in its wording from that contained in the Contracts of Employment Act 1972 (see page 45, *above*) and also from that contained in the Trade Union and Labour Relations Act 1974 (see page 251, *below*).

Employees of an overseas Government are also excluded from the Act even though they may work in this country.

(*l*) In certain circumstances an **offer of alternative employment** to an employee will exclude his right to a redundancy payment. This will be considered in more detail on pages 172 to 179 (*below*).

The Secretary of State has an overall power to alter any of the above exclusions, to exclude other employees or to widen the scope of those affected by the RPA. This power can only be exercised by formal statutory instrument.

In particular, the EPA gave power to the Secretary of State for Employment to extend the RPA rights to workers on installations in U.K. territorial waters or to employees working on the exploration of the seabed or the exploitation of its natural resources in designated areas of the Continental Shelf. This power has now been exericsed with effect from 21st June 1976.

Conditions

Having considered the categories of employees who may be entitled to a redundancy payment, what are the conditions which must be met before that payment becomes due?

The main conditions referred to in section 1(1) (see page 157, *above*) are—

---

[1] For a consideration of this matter, see the EAT decision (11 Nov. 1976) in *Costain Civil Engineering Ltd. v. Draycott* (1976) *The Times*, November 12, 1976.

(1) the employee must have been continuously employed for two years.

(2) the employee must be dismissed.

(3) the dismissal must be by reason of redundancy.

DISMISSAL

Before an employee can become entitled to a redundancy payment he must be dismissed. Dismissal for these purposes has a statutory definition.[1] Problems can, however, arise. The definition and a detailed consideration of " dismissal " is dealt with in Chapter 16 (pages 212 to 225).[1]

Dismissal includes the non-renewal of a fixed term contract and it also includes " constructive dismissal ", *i.e.* where the employee becomes entitled in certain circumstances to terminate his own employment because of the employer's conduct.

Matters such as resignation, termination by mutual consent and termination under the legal doctrine of frustration are all considered in Chapter 16.

It is important to note at this stage that if a claim for a redundancy payment is contested by the employer and the matter reaches a Tribunal, the first **burden of proof** is placed on the employee and he must establish that he has been dismissed. If he cannot do this, his claim will fail at the very first hurdle. There is no presumption—either in the RPA or elsewhere—that when a contract of employment has been terminated, it is because the employee has been dismissed.

Once the employee is over that hurdle, there is then, as we shall see (page 164, *below*), a presumption that the dismissal was by reason of redundancy.

WHAT IS REDUNDANCY ?

The word " redundancy " is often misused and misunderstood by employers. On occasions, it seems to be used by employers simply to indicate that they no longer wish to

---

[1] The definition is now contained in RPA, s. 3(2), which was introduced by the EPA 1975 (Sched. 16, Part I, para. 3).

employ a particular person in their business, regardless of whether or not there is in fact a falling off of work.

Employers should take care to confine references to redundancy simply to redundancy as defined in the RPA.

It will be remembered that the employee who claims a redundancy payment must have been dismissed " by reason of redundancy ".

Section 1(2) defines this further by stating that—

" An employee who is dismissed shall be taken to be dismissed by reason of redundancy if the dismissal is attributed wholly or mainly to—

(a) the fact that his employer has ceased or intends to cease, to carry on the business for the purposes of which the employee was employed by him or has ceased, or intends to cease, to carry on that business in the place where the employee was so employed, or

(b) the fact that the requirements of that business for employees to carry out work of a particular kind, or for employees to carry out work of a particular kind in the place where he was so employed, have ceased or diminished or are expected to cease or diminish ".

In view of the above, the obvious must be stated, namely, only if the reason for the dismissal is redundancy will the employee be entitled to a redundancy payment.

How then is this proved?

Proof of redundancy

It has already been seen that the burden of proving the actual dismissal lies on the employee himself. In many—indeed most—cases this will not constitute a problem.

Once this has been established—or admitted by the employer—the RPA then provides that, unless the contrary is proved, the employee shall be presumed to have been dismissed by reason of redundancy (RPA, s. 9(2)(b).

In other words, the pendulum swings across in favour of the employee. The employer has to show that the reason for the dismissal related to some other factor (e.g. misconduct). If he cannot show this, then the pendulum does not swing back, the presumption of redundancy will remain and the employee will be entitled to a redundancy payment.

If the matter reaches a Tribunal, the employer must show that, on the balance of probabilities, the dismissal was not due to redundancy. If the evidence is evenly balanced, then, again, the pendulum will stay in favour of the employee and he will be successful.

The actual reason given by the employer at the time of dismissal is not of itself conclusive. The Tribunal will try and ascertain the real reason.[1] Now that the provisions of the EPA (s. 70) relating to the provision, on request, of a written statement of the reasons for dismissal, are in force, such statement will no doubt be taken into account by Tribunals.[2]

Employers must, therefore, be prepared for this when they are dismissing an employee for any reason at a time when business is declining. If it is not their intention to replace that employee, but to absorb his work elsewhere, then they well may have very great difficulty in resisting a claim for a redundancy payment even if redundancy as such was not in their minds at the time of the dismissal. In that sort of situation, the evidence of the reason for the dismissal must be very clear indeed if the employer wishes to avoid a redundancy payment.

Conversely, where an employee is dismissed and then replaced, this in itself will go a long way towards establishing that the dismissal was not due to redundancy.

It must be appreciated that very often an application to a Tribunal will claim not only unfair dismissal but also a right to a redundancy payment. In that event, the case will normally proceed as one entity, with the Tribunal hearing all the evidence relating to both claims.

Occasions can, of course, arise where there may be more than one reason behind the dismissal. The RPA, as seen

---

[1] See, for example, *Abernethy v. Mott, Haye and Anderson* [1974] ICR 323 (referred to on p. 273).
[2] See Chapter 18, pp. 241 to 243.

above, provides that the dismissal should be attributable **wholly or mainly** to redundancy.

Thus, dismissal does not have to be solely due to redundancy. Nor, at the other end of the scale, is it sufficient if redundancy is only one contributory factor. The Tribunal will look for **the main cause.** If the employer can show that this was some cause other than redundancy, the employee's claim will fail. If he cannot do so then the claim will be successful.

Some possible non-redundancy causes will be considered later in this chapter.

TYPES OF REDUNDANCY

The definition of redundancy referred to above really covers three situations—

(1) Cessation of the business

(2) Moving the place of the business.

(3) Where the business no longer requires the same number of employees.

These categories will now be considered.

Cessation of the business

There should be no difficulty about the situation where a business closes down completely. If the cessation is in effect only a temporary closure or lay-off, then the employee may still be entitled to a redundancy payment under the special provisions dealt with in Chapter 11.

Section 1(1) of the RPA also refers to the situation where an employer " intends to cease " carrying on the business. It must, however, be remembered that there must be an actual dismissal before an entitlement to a redundancy payment arises. Thus a warning of an impending redundancy at some time in the future is not a dismissal; if an employee acts on such warning by leaving and then getting another job, he will not be entitled to a redundancy payment because he will not have been dismissed.[1]

---

[1] See, for example, *Morton Sundour Fabrics v. Shaw* [1967] ITR 84.

The " business " referred to is, strictly, limited to that part of the business in which the employee was employed. Thus, even if the complete undertaking of an employer has not closed down, there will be redundancy if the employer ceases to carry on that part of the business in which the particular employee worked.

Moving the place of business

Redundancy can—and often does—arise where an employer closes down a business in one particular place and then transfers that business elsewhere. In these circumstances, can the employees claim redundancy pay?

The answer to this question will mainly depend on the terms of the original contract of employment.

The vital words in this respect in the Act are—" **the place where the employee was so employed** ". If the employer ceases to carry on business at the place where the employee was employed under his contract, then it is probable that the employee will have a claim.

Even here, however, there can be problems in deciding what is the place of employment. It has been clearly established that the place of work for these purposes is not only the place where the employee actually physically works at the relevant time but also any other place at which the employer may call upon the employee to work under his contract of employment.

If, therefore, the contract gives the employer the right to transfer employees from one factory in a particular town to another, then the closing down of the factory where the employee in fact works is not a cessation of business for redundancy purposes. Similarly, if the terms of the contract of employment give the employees a right to require their staff to work at any of their establishments in Great Britain and an employee refuses such a transfer when the establishment where he works closes down, then he will not be entitled to a redundancy payment. This was the situation in *U.K. Atomic Energy Authority v. Claydon* [1974] ICR 128 where the NIRC held that " the place where he was so employed " meant the place where under his contract of employment he could be required to work—in that case the employer's establishments as a whole—and that since accordingly there was work available for him, the employee was not dismissed by reason of redundancy.

If, of course, the employer does not in the contract have such a right of transfer, then (subject to the question of a possible offer of suitable alternative employment—as to which see page 172) only the actual place of work of the employee is relevant and there will be redundancy.[1]

Employers should, therefore, consider this factor right at the outset of the employment and, if necessary, include an appropriate provision in the contract of employment (see page 32, *above*).

If such a right is included in a collective agreement or in works rules, then, as noted previously (page 33), care should be taken to ensure that those terms are written into the individual's contract.

In certain circumstances or industries, it may be possible to imply a custom or right to move an employee to another place of work within a particular area.

In a recent case (*Rowbotham v. Arthur Lee & Sons Ltd.* [1975] ICR 109) the appeal Court (O'Connor, J.) allowed an appeal from an Industrial Tribunal which had held that the place of employment in that case was " the industrial complex of Sheffield ", thus enabling the employers to call upon employees to move from one factory to another. The learned judge found that this provision was not in the written terms of employment and that there was no evidence from which it could be implied.

In *Times Newspapers Ltd. v. Bartlett* [1976] ITR 106 the Employment Appeal Tribunal said that—" one would have thought an employee cannot refuse justifiably to continue to work for his employers merely because the employers move the office to a new building down the street. But when it comes to moving to a different town or to a different quarter

---

[1] See *O'Brien v. Associated Fire Alarms Ltd.* [1968] ITR 182, and, more recently, *Maher v. Fram Gerrard Ltd.* [1974] ICR 31.

of the same town, or even a few miles away in the same town, different considerations may apply ".

These decisions highlight the fact that it is not safe for an employer to rely simply upon an implied right or custom; it is much better to try and cover the position in writing in the contract of employment itself.

Reduction in work

The third category of redundancy arises when the requirement for employees to carry out work of a particular kind has ceased or diminished or is expected so to do. It will also be redundancy if the requirements of the business for employees to carry out work of a particular kind **in the place** where the employee was employed have ceased or diminshed.

Under this head, therefore, two main situations are covered—

(*a*) where the **number of employees** required to carry out work of a particular kind is **reduced,** or is expected to reduce, and the particular employee is then dismissed, **or**

(*b*) where the **work itself ceases** or **diminishes** (either permanently or temporarily), so that fewer employees are needed and the particular employee is then dismissed.

It must be remembered, however, that the vital question is whether the dismissal is wholly or mainly attributable to one of the above situations.

This will be the case where, for example, the work is absorbed by other employees. This can arise after re-organisation of a business or, very often, after a company take-over. Similarly, one consequence of a productivity agreement can be a reduction in the number of employees who work at a particular plant, their work being absorbed by the remaining staff.

The introduction of new systems or modern plant and machinery may also give rise to a reduction in the work-force and, if that does happen, there will be a clear case of redundancy.

If an employee is dismissed and then the employers arrange to have that employee's work done by outside contractors, the employee will be entitled to a redundancy payment. This has even been held to be the case where the " employee " after his dismissal still continues to do the work but does so as a " freelance " or self-employed person.

It must, of course, now be remembered that an employee who is made redundant may also be able to claim that he was unfairly dismissed within the meaning of the TUALRA. Many employers still do not seem to be aware of this. Although redundancy is one of the " defences " to an unfair dismissal claim, this is not by itself sufficient. The employers must still act fairly and reasonably both with regard to the actual selection for redundancy and in giving as much advance warning as possible of the impending redundancy. This will be considered in Chapters 21 and 22 relating to Unfair Dismissal.

The EPA also now contains detailed provisions as to the procedure for handling redundancies and these are dealt with in the next chapter (pages 191 to 204).

NON-REDUNDANCY REASONS FOR DISMISSAL

As indicated previously, it will be for the employer, who is resisting an application for a redundancy payment, to show that the **main** reason for the dismissal did **not** relate to redundancy, as already defined.

If the employer, soon after the dismissal, takes on another employee to do the same work, then the employer will be well on the way to establishing that the dismissal was not due to redundancy. Evidence of such replacement should be enough to swing the pendulum over in favour of the employer and the burden of proving the redundancy will then fall back on the employee.

Very often, the new employee only takes over **part** of the original employee's work. If this is the case, it will tend to confirm a redundancy situation.

If, of course, the real reason for the dismissal is established as some form of misconduct, the employee will not be entitled to a redundancy payment. Misconduct will include all the " problems " which are considered in Chapter 21 (see pages 282 to 290), *e.g.* bad timekeeping, disobedience to orders, incompetence, gross misconduct, etc.

Similarly, if an employee becomes incapable of meeting the developing demands of his job, dismissal for that reason will not be due to redundancy. If he is incompetent and lacking in ability and is dismissed because of this, he will not be able to recover redundancy pay. If an employee is dismissed because he causes upset and ill-feeling at his place of work again that will not be redundancy. In all these situations, the employee may, of course, still be able to claim that he was unfairly dismissed.

If an employer seeks to alter the existing terms and conditions of employment to less beneficial terms and the employee, being unwilling to accept the new terms, leaves, then, although this will be deemed to be a " dismissal " it will not—despite the presumption referred to above—be taken to be a dismissal " by reason of redundancy " (see *Chapman v. Goonvean & Rostowrack China Clay Co. Ltd.* [1973] ICR 310—where, during a trade recession, the employer discontinued the free transport service previously provided for certain employees).

Similarly a change in the hours of working (to achieve greater efficiency) will not constitute a change in the particular kind of work carried out by the employees and a dismissal of those employees because of their refusal to work the new hours will not be a dismissal due to redundancy.[1]

It is interesting to note that section 2(2) of the RPA specifically provides that an employee dismissed for conduct which justifies summary dismissal will not be entitled to a redundancy payment. As already noted, an employee will in any event not be entitled to redundancy pay if the main reason for the

---

[1] In *Lesney Products & Co. Ltd. v. Nolan* (20/10/76) the Court of Appeal held that re-organisation by employers of their work force and of the work being done so as to improve efficiency (including a reduction in overtime) did not of itself create a redundancy situation.

dismissal was not due to redundancy. It is not, therefore, clear as to why a specific provision was included in section 2(2).

This particular provision did, however, recently come under review by the Employment Appeal Tribunal in a case (*Simmons v. Hoover Ltd.* [1976] IRLR 266) where the employee was dismissed due to redundancy whilst he was on strike. It was held that participation in a strike entitled the employers " to terminate his contract of employment without notice by reason of his conduct " and that he was, therefore, not entitled to a redundancy payment.

OFFER OF ALTERNATIVE EMPLOYMENT

The RPA has since its inception contained provisions (in s. 2) under which an employer can offer either to renew the employee's contract or to give him alternative employment. If such offer is accepted, the need for redundancy, is obviated. If the employee refuses that offer, the question will arise as to whether or not he can then claim a redundancy payment. This will depend on how **suitable** the offer of employment was and how **reasonable** the employee was in refusing it. In certain circumstances, such an offer will bar the employee's right to a redundancy payment.

Substantial changes have been made to the original RPA provisions by the EPA—Part I of Schedule 16. Those changes came into force on 1st June 1976 and the law must now be considered in the light of those changes.

The offer

If an employer makes an offer (whether in writing or not) to an employee **to renew** his contract of employment or to **re-engage** him under a new contract of employment, and the employee refuses that offer, the employee will **not** be entitled to a redundancy payment by reason of his dismissal, provided that the following four conditions are complied with—

(*a*) the offer must be made **before** the ending of the original employment:

(*b*) the new contract of employment must **take effect** either **immediately** on the ending of the original employment or within four weeks thereafter;

(*c*) the employee's refusal must be **unreasonable;** and

(*d*) **either** the provisions of the contract as renewed, or of the new contract, as to the capacity and place in which he would be employed, and as to the other terms and conditions of his employment would not differ from the corresponding provisions of the previous contract **or** the first mentioned provisions would differ (wholly or in part) from those corresponding provisions, but the offer constitutes an offer of **suitable employment** in relation to the employee.

The above provisions are the effect of section 2(3) and 2(5) of the RPA (as introduced by the EPA, Schedule 16, Part I, paragraph 2).

The EPA also introduces, in cases where the offer of employment is accepted but the **terms and conditions** of the new contract **differ** from the corresponding provisions of the original contract, the concept of **a trial period.**

If an employee's contract of employment is re-newed or he is re-engaged in the circumstances referred to above, then the employee is not regarded as having been dismissed by reason of the ending of his employment under the previous contract. In addition, if the " new contract " differs as to the capacity and place of work and as to the other terms and conditions of employment, there is **a trial period** in relation to the new contract. The trial period will be dealt with in more detail later in this chapter.

It will have been seen from the above that the legal position will differ according to whether an employee refuses or accepts an offer of further or new employment. Those two situations must now be considered.

Refusal of offer of new employment

If an employer is unable due to redundancy to continue to employ a person in a particular job, then if that employer wishes to use the defence of " offer of alternative employment " he will only be able to do so if he can establish the four conditions referred to above.

The burden of proof here will be on the employer. If he cannot establish all four conditions, the employee will be entitled to a redundancy payment.

The offer of employment must, of course, be made by the employer, but this will include " an associated employer "[1] and also the new owner of a business if the business has been transferred.[2]

The offer itself must be clear and specific. It need **not** legally be **in writing,** although prior to 1st June 1976 this was the case where the offer was of a job on different terms and conditions of employment. This particular amendment to the law has caused some surprise, as it is felt that it has removed a provision which was really for the benefit of the employee. Having said this, it is always advisable for the employer to make the offer in writing; the position will then be clear and it will be much easier for the employer to show that he has complied with the conditions referred to above.

Where the offer of new employment does **not differ** from the original employment, the position should not give rise to any difficulties. If there is a dispute and the matter reaches a Tribunal, the Tribunal will compare the terms of the two jobs and, in particular, will look at the job itself, the place of work and the other terms and conditions of the job. Obviously, the latter will include such things as pay, holidays, and any " fringe benefits " that may arise under the contract. If the terms of the new job do not differ from the original job, then it is very likely that the employee's refusal of the new job will be held to be unreasonable and the employee will not then be entitled to a redundancy payment.

The main problems arise under this head when the new job is in fact on different terms and conditions. In that case, the offer must, as we have seen, be one of " suitable employment in relation to the employee ".

What is " suitable employment " ?

As in all employment law cases, each matter depends on its own particular facts and circumstances. Any reported deci-

---

[1] See note to p. 50 as to the meaning of " associated employer ".
[2] See p. 179 as to the transfer of a business.

sions are therefore, only really applicable to their own particular facts.   Tied in with the question of " suitable employment ", there is also the question of whether a refusal of an
offer of a new job is " unreasonable ".

It will be appreciated that these two matters can, and often
do, overlap.

As far as **" suitable employment "** is concerned attention
should be directed to such things as **pay** and fringe benefits
and, of course, the place of work itself.   It will be remembered
(see page 167, *above*) that the contract of employment may give
the employer a right to transfer the employee to another plant
or factory and that, in that case, there will not have been any
change at all in the " contractual **place of work** ".   Apart from
this situation, however, a change in the place of work has been
held in some cases not to be " suitable employment ";   the
Tribunal will consider whether the employee has to move house
in order to do the new job and, even if this is not the case,
such things as the time and expense of travelling to the new
job and its affect on the employee's home life will be taken
into account.

If the new job will have an adverse effect on the **health** of
the employee, this will be a relevant factor, as will the question
of whether the employee will lose **status** in the new job.

The question of **status** seems to crop up more and more in
practice.   Very often, an employer is quite prepared to continue to pay the employee at the same rate, but he cannot or
does not wish to allow the employee to continue in the same
job as far as responsibility and managerial authority are concerned.   Here again, each case must be considered on its own
particular facts.   Tribunals do now seem to take into account
the fact that an employer is entitled to organise and run his
own business, whilst, of course, balancing this with his obligation to be fair to his employees.   In recent times, Tribunals
have also taken into account the general economic position
either of the country as a whole or in a particular industry or
area.   Situations can arise where for economic reasons an
employer is faced with either dismissing an employee completely or offering that employee a job with lower status.   In

that sort of case, the offer of a new job may well be held to be " suitable ". The employee here is, of course, now protected by the " trial period " provisions of the EPA (see page 177, *below*).

When considering whether **refusal** of an offer on different terms is **unreasonable**, similar factors to those affecting the suitability of the offer are taken into account. They will include such matters as **pay, travelling time** and the expense of travelling and changes in **status.** In some cases, the **domestic circumstances** of the employee have justified the refusal of the new job, *e.g.* if the new job would involve moving away from an area and thus disturbing school arrangements and possibly even the marriage itself.

In *Thomas Wragg & Sons v. Wood* [1976] IRLR 145 the Appeal Tribunal held that an employee's refusal of an offer of alternative employment was not unreasonable due to the fact that the offer came within 24 hours of the expiration of his notice at a time when he had already committed himself to a new job and when he feared future unemployment in a contracting industry.

Acceptance of offer of new employment

(1) *On the same terms and conditions*

If an employee accepts the offer of a new job **on the same terms** as the original job, there are the following consequences:

(*a*) he is regarded as not having been dismissed at all (RPA, s. 3(3), as amended).

(*b*) no " trial period " arises.

(*c*) he is not entitled to a redundancy payment.

(*d*) he has continuity of employment throughout the period of the original job and his new job.

The position referred to above will only arise if the conditions numbered (*a*) and (*b*) on page 172 relating to the offer of employment are complied with. In particular, it will be noted that the new employment can now commence up to four weeks from the ending of the original employment without the employee being treated as having been dismissed. The offer must, however, have been made before the ending of the original employment.

(2) *On different terms and conditions*

As indicated previously, the EPA has introduced into this aspect of the law special provisions where an employee accepts an offer of new employment on different terms and conditions. These provisions (which are dealt with as amendments to the RPA) came into force on 1st June 1976. They relate to what is now known as the " trial period ".

The Trial Period

If an employee accepts an offer of new employment and that offer has been made before the end of the previous employment and the re-engagement is to take effect within four weeks thereafter, then, if the provisions of the new contract **differ** (wholly or in part) from the corresponding provisions of the previous contract " there **shall** be a trial period in relation to the contract as renewed ". (RPA, s. 3(5), as amended.)

The provisions of the contract which differ from the original contract must relate either to the capacity of the employee or to the place in which he is employed or to the other terms and conditions of his employment.

It is important to note that the trial period comes into effect automatically. There is no need for any agreement between the parties. The operative word in the section referred to above is " shall ", *i.e.* there **shall** be a trial period.

The **trial period** will normally be for four weeks from the time when the employee starts work under the new contract. The four week period cannot be reduced, but it can be extended for the specific purpose of re-training the employee for new work provided that—

(*a*) any agreement to extend the period is entered into between the employer and the employee (or his representative) before the employee starts work under his new contract

(*b*) such agreement is in writing

(c) such agreement specifies the date of the end of the trial period; and

(d) such agreement specifies the terms and conditions of employment which will apply after the end of that period.

If there is no agreement dealing with the four matters referred to above, then the trial period will automatically last for four weeks.

If **during the trial period the employee terminates** the contract—for whatever reason—then he will be treated as having been dismissed on the date on which his original employment ended and his entitlement to redundancy pay will depend on the normal factors referred to in section 2 of the RPA relating to an offer of suitable employment (see page 172, *above*).

These provisions will enable an employee to " try out " a new job for a period of up to four weeks. If the employee continues in the job after that period, he will be deemed to have accepted it and there will be no claim to redundancy pay arising out of the loss of the original job. If during the four week period the employee decides that he does not wish to continue in the new job, he will have lost nothing. He can put an end to the new contract and he is then " back to square one ", *i.e.* he is treated as having been dismissed from his original job and the Tribunal will then have to consider whether the offer of the new job was " suitable " and whether the employee was " unreasonable " in refusing that offer.

If during the trial period **the employer dismisses** the employee, then if the dismissal is for a reason connected with or arising out of the change to the new terms of employment, the employee is again treated as being dismissed on termination of his original employment and his entitlement to redundancy pay will be dealt with on the basis referred to above.

If the reason for the dismissal by the employer is not connected with the new job, then that is a different matter and that dismissal (*e.g.* for gross misconduct) will be looked at and considered on its merits.

The six month time limit (see page 183, *below*) in respect of claims to an Industrial Tribunal will run, in the circumstances, referred to above, from the date of termination of the trial period, rather than from the date of termination of the original employment.

TRANSFER OF BUSINESS

Employers who are acquiring or taking over an existing business should bear in mind that the employees they continue to employ will normally have **continuity of service.** If at some future date those employees are made redundant they will be entitled to a redundancy payment based on the whole of their service, including the years prior to the acquisition or takeover. The purchaser of a business may well, therefore, wish to take into account this " contingent liability " when agreeing the terms of acquisition.

Conversely, the seller of a business should ensure that the purchaser will take over all his liabilities with regard to redundancy.   In order to remove all doubts, the seller should include in the contract for sale a clause to the effect that the purchaser will continue to employ all the employees on the same terms and conditions of employment and will make an offer to them accordingly and that in any event the purchaser will indemnify the seller against any claim that may arise for redundancy.

No great problem arises on the change of **partners** in a firm, nor with regard to a transfer between **associated employers,** *i.e.* where one employer is a company of which the other (directly or indirectly) has control, or if both are companies of which a third person (directly or indirectly) has control (RPA, s. 48(4), as amended).

If an individual employer **dies,** the employee will not be treated as dismissed if the contract is renewed or he is re-engaged by a personal representative of the employer within eight weeks of the latter's death (see paragraphs 3 and 4 of Part I of Schedule 4 to RPA as amended).

Section 13 of the RPA contains provisions relating to the **change of ownership** of a business.   The gist of these provisions is that if there is a change in the ownership of a business and the " new owner " offers employment to the employees of that business, then that offer is treated as is any other offer of " alternative employment " (see pages 172 to 179, *above*). If the offer is an offer of a job on the same terms and conditions, then the employee will not normally be entitled to a redundancy payment.

In addition, if there has been a genuine transfer of a " trade or business or an undertaking " there will be continuity of employment for that particular employee.[1]

There can, however, be difficulties and problems with regard to the meaning of " a business ".

Section 25(1) of the RPA states that **a business** " includes a trade or profession and includes any activity carried on by a body of persons, whether corporate or incorporate ".

There is, however, no proper definition of a " business ".

A business can include many factors—premises, goodwill, stock, fixtures and fittings, employees, capital, etc.

Goodwill has, in many cases, been the decisive factor. If goodwill is included in the sale, it is likely that there will be a transfer of the business.

The position was well summed up in the case of *Kenmir Ltd. v. Frizzell* [1968] ITR 159—

" In deciding whether a transaction amounted to the transfer of a business regard must be had to its substance rather than its form, and consideration must be given to the whole of the circumstances. . . . In the end the vital consideration is whether the effect of the transaction was to put the transferee in possession of a going concern the activities of which he could carry on without interruption ".

Normally if there is only a **transfer of assets,** this will not be a transfer of a business and there will be no continuity for redundancy purposes. This can work a little unfairly on employees who may think that, on a transfer of, say, a factory, they have continuity of employment.

---

1 See CEA, Sched. 1, para. 9(2), and p. 358, *below*.

A very good example of the distinction between the sale or transfer of a business and the sale of the assets of a business was the case of *Woodhouse v. Peter Brotherhood Ltd.* [1972] ICR 186. The employees in that case had worked for more than 20 years at a factory near Nottingham; they were dismissed for redundancy and claimed redundancy pay. The employers were only repared to admit liability based on six years' service, *i.e.* six years from the date on which those employers acquired the factory. After the transfer of the factory the employees had worked at the same machines but on different products. On the sale of the factory the original employers had transferred their business to Manchester. There had been no sale or transfer of goodwill or of the business name, there had been no transfer of customers or the benefit of contracts and no restriction on competition. It was ultimately held by the Court of Appeal that there was no transfer of business from the original employers but only a transfer of its physical assets and that, because of this, the employees were only entitled to redundancy payments on the basis of their service since the date that they commenced employment with the new employers.

It will be seen from the above that such a situation can work in some cases unfairly in relation to the employees. In the *Peter Brotherhood* case, for example, the employees simply carried on work at the same factory and on the same machines. There was no " break " in their employment (other than in the legal sense). They simply thought that the Company had been "taken over ". The result of the decision was that those employees lost their entitlement in respect of their first fourteen years' service.

The employee may, of course, be lucky—or well-advised—and apply for a redundancy payment to his original employers who have sold out. In that event, if the sale was, for example, only a sale of the factory premises, plant and machinery, then the employee will be entitled to a redundancy payment—even though working on the same machine, in the same factory and under the same terms of employment (see *Crompton v. Truly Fair (International) Ltd.* [1975] ICR 359).

Under the Contracts of Employment Act 1972, as amended by the EPA (see page 37, *above*) the written particulars delivered to employees must now include details of any **previous employment** which the employer thinks will count for continuity purposes and the date when continuity began must also be stated. This provision may help some employees to avoid the worst consequences of the sort of case referred to above. In particular, it may alert the employee to the fact that he does not have continuity of employment and that he should, therefore, claim against the original employer.

From the employers' point of view, the most important thing is that if an employer is buying or selling either a business or premises at which a business is carried out, then he should consider carefully the position of any employees who are already working there. Having done this, it will be much better to have the matter specifically agreed in the contract for the sale or purchase.

The position, therefore, is that if there is a transfer of a business and the employees accept an offer of employment from the new owners, then those employees will have continuity of employment and they will not have any claim for redundancy against their original employers.

If, however, the employees do not accept the offer from the new owners, then whether those employees will have a claim against their original employers will be governed by the principles (already considered on pages 172 to 179, *above*) relating to whether or not the offer was one of " suitable employment " and whether the employees' refusal was " unreasonable ".

Finally, quite apart from the strict redundancy law position, if the new employer promises the employee that his employment (including all his employment with a previous employer) will be treated as continuous, he may be estopped from denying that it is in fact continous (see *Evenden v. Guildford City Association Football Club Ltd.* [1975] ICR 367).

CLAIMS FOR REDUNDANCY PAYMENTS

In the majority of cases of redundancy, the position will be clear and the employer will at the outset calculate the amount of redundancy pay due to the employee and inform him accordingly. This information must be in writing, indicating how the payment has been calculated. Failure to do this (without reasonable excuse) can render the employer liable to be prosecuted and fined.[1]

If an employer does not provide a proper statement, the employee can demand such a statement within a specified period, being not less than one week. The employee's demand must be also in writing. Here again, failure on the part of the employer to comply can result in a prosecution and fine.

Standard forms for completion by the parties are provided under the Redundancy Payments Act 1965 and these forms should be used.

Situations will, however, arise where the employer says that he is not under any obligation at all to make a redundancy payment, e.g. because the dismissal was not due to redundancy or because an offer of suitable alternative employment was made. In that event—if the matter cannot be agreed by the parties—the question can be referred by the employee to an Industrial Tribunal.

There is, however, a **time limit** in respect of all applications to an Industrial Tribunal—in redundancy cases, this will normally be six months from the date of dismissal.

The RPA, however, goes further than that and specifically states in section 21 that an employee shall **not** be entitled to a redundancy payment unless **within six months** from the date of the dismissal,[2] one of the following four events has happened—

(a) the payment has been agreed and paid, or

---

[1] Section 18, RPA.
[2] Strictly the section refers to six months from " the relevant date ", this phrase being defined at length in s. 3(9) of the RPA (as now amended); for all practical purposes, however, the " relevant date " is the date of termination of the contract of employment.

(*b*) the employee has made a claim for the payment by notice in writing to the employer, or

(*c*) the matter has been referred to an Industrial Tribunal under the RPA or

(*d*) a complaint alleging unfair dismissal has been lodged with the Industrial Tribunal under the TUALRA.

This six month time limit has also now been in effect extended by an amendment introduced—with effect from 1st June 1976—by paragraph 9 of Part I to Schedule 16 of the EPA. This amendment provides that the Tribunal can still deal with an application for a redundancy payment during a **further six month period** (*i.e.* six months immediately following the original six month period) provided that it appears to the Tribunal to be **just and equitable** that the employee should receive a redundancy payment having regard to the reason shown by the employee for failing to take the necessary steps within the original six month period and also having regard to " all the other relevant circumstances ".

It is not clear how this amendment will be interpreted by the Tribunals. It is, however, interesting to note that the employee here does not have to establish that it was " not reasonably practicable " for him to take the necessary action within the required period (which is, of course, the requirement under the TUALRA and with regard to most of the EPA rights). It would seem, therefore, that Tribunals may well be a little more lenient in interpreting these provisions and that, in many cases, employees may in practice have a period of twelve months in which to lodge a claim.

In the case of the *Bentley Engineering Company Ltd. v. Crown* [1976] ICR 225 (as to which see also page 356) the Employment Appeal Tribunal also held that if paragraphs (*a*) or (*b*) above have been complied with within the six month period then this " preserves " the applicant's rights and he can claim a redundancy payment from a Tribunal even outside that period, *e.g.* 2 years after his dismissal, as in that case.

THE AMOUNT OF THE REDUNDANCY PAYMENT

Calculation of an employee's entitlement to redundancy pay will normally be a simple matter. It is not a question of assessing compensation as for, say, unfair dismissal.

The amount of the payment is based primarily upon the length of continuous employment (as to which see Appendix II, page 352). Schedule 1 of the RPA provides that an employee is entitled to receive a payment based on the following principles—

(a) for each year of employment between the ages of 18 and 21—half a week's pay

(b) for each year of employment between the ages of 22 and 40—one week's pay

(c) for each year of employment between the age of 41 and 64 (in the case of a man) and 59 (in the case of a woman)—one and a half week's pay

(d) employment for longer than 20 years is not taken into account.

(e) the maximum of pay at present taken into account is £80 per week.[1]

In the year prior to normal retirement age (60 for women and 65 for men) there is provision for scaling down on a monthly basis.

Thus, the **maximum redundancy payment** that any employee can at present receive is **£2,400,** *i.e.* 20 years service for a man over 41 throughout that period with a weekly wage of at least £80 will give $20 \times 1\frac{1}{2} \times £80 = £2,400$.

Redundancy payments are not subject to tax.[2]

The weekly maximum figure can be altered from time to time by Statutory Order. Indeed, originally, the RPA maximum was £40 and this was increased to £80 in 1974.[1]

The relevant date for calculating the " week's wages " is normally the date on which the employment would have ter-

---

[1] Calculation of Redundancy Payments Order 1974 (S.I. No. 1327).
[2] Income and Corporation Taxes Act 1970, s. 412(1).

minated had proper notice been given under the CEA (as to which see page 228), whether or not such notice was in fact given. In effect, therefore, the redundancy payment is based on final earnings.

As so often in legal matters, it is the simple point which turns out to be the most difficult[1] Under this head, one problem can be—what is a " week's pay "?

" A week's pay " is now—since 1st June 1976—calculated in accordance with the provisions of Part II of Schedule 4 to the EPA (summarised in Appendix III, page 360).

Normally, a week's pay will be the amount of remuneration paid to an employee under his Contract of Employment during a particular week. If the number of " **normal working hours** " varies from week to week or if there are no normal working hours, then the Schedule contains provisions under which an average over a twelve week period is calculated. The detailed provisions of this Schedule are dealt with in Appendix III.

As far as the amount of a week's wage is concerned, it must be remembered that only moneys due under the contract of employment will be taken into account. Thus, **overtime pay** will only be taken into account if it was obligatory under the contract both for the employer to provide overtime **and** for the employee to work overtime.[1] The overtime must be obligatory on both sides. If it is not, it will not form part of the " normal working hours ". Even if it is customary for an employee to work overtime and even if he has done so for many years, the overtime earnings will not be taken into account unless the employer was legally obliged under the contract to provide overtime or payment in lieu. Similarly, if the contract gives the employer a right to call upon the employee to work overtime as and when required, but does not include an obligation on the employer to provide such overtime, then the overtime earnings are ignored in calculating a " week's pay ".[2]

Lest this should be felt to be unfair, Lord Denning, M.R. did point out in the *Tarmac* case[1] that there were two advan-

---

[1] *Tarmac Roadstone Holdings Ltd. v. Peacock* [1973] ICR 273.
[2] *Gascol Conversions Ltd. v. Mercer* [1974] ICR 420.

tages to the employees whose " normal working hours " were only (as in that case) 40 hours per week. One was that all work done over and above the 40 hours was paid for at overtime rates; the other was that the men could take industrial action—*e.g.* by barring overtime—without being in breach of their contracts of employment.

Other factors sometimes considered in relation to " a week's pay " are **bonuses and commission** (which **will** be included if the payment is a regular guaranteed payment), **travelling and other expenses** (which will **not** be taken into account **unless** the expenses represent a profit to the employee) and **payments in kind,** *e.g.* provision of company car, free board and lodging, etc. (which are **not** taken into account). **Tips and gratuities** will also be excluded, although where a service charge was distributed amongst all the employees on a proportion basis (the " tronc " system) the employee's share was added to his basic wage when calculating his total remuneration.[1]

Some employers do, of course, enter into agreements with their employees or with a trade union representing those employees, under which they may agree to pay more than the statutory redundancy payments or to make redundancy payments in circumstances which are not covered by the RPA provisions. If this is done, then everything will depend on the meaning and interpretation of the agreement itself.

THE EMPLOYER'S REBATE

Having made a redundancy payment, an employer is entitled to claim a rebate from the Department of Employment provided that he complies with certain conditions.

The rebate is 50 per cent. of the actual payment made by the employer under the RPA.[2] If the employer, by agreement, pays more than the statutory amount, he cannot claim any rebate on the additional payment.

The rebate is paid out of the **Redundancy Fund,** which is made up from employers' National Insurance contributions.

---

[1] *Tzoukka v. Potomac Restaurants Ltd.* [1968] ITR 260.
[2] There is a proposal that the rebate will be reduced to 40% during 1977.

In the event of any dispute involving the Fund, the Secretary of State can become a party to any proceedings before an Industrial Tribunal.

The conditions with which an employer must comply before he can obtain a rebate are contained in the Redundancy Payments Rebates Regulations 1965 (as amended). They may be summarised as follows:—

(1) A claim for a rebate must be accompanied by a **receipt** signed by the employee in respect of the payment made to him.

(2) The employer will only get a rebate if he was **legally liable** under the RPA provisions to make the payment. Thus the " kind " employer who makes a redundancy payment even though, for example, an employee had not been employed for two years, will not be entitled to a rebate.

(3) The employer must also have paid the **correct amount.** If the employer takes into account in calculating a week's pay factors which are not strictly relevant (*e.g.* overtime, free board and lodging), then the rebate will not be paid in respect of those factors.

(4) The employer must make his claim to the Department of Employment **before** the end of **six months** from the date on which he made the payment to the employee. The claim must be in writing and must specify the date on which the employment terminated and show how the amount has been calculated. In practice, special forms are issued by the Department of Employment and the claim will be submitted on that form.

(5) The employer must give **prior written notice** to the local **Employment Exchange** that a claim for a rebate may arise by virtue of the ending of an employee's contract. This provision is obviously included in the hope that it will be possible to obtain other employment for the redundant employee. The notice must include full details of the employee, his tax reference and National Insurance number, his date of birth, his period of employment, his

normal " week's pay ", and the anticipated date of and
reason for his dismissal.

The Regulations contained detailed provisions as to when the
above notification has to be given—ranging from 14 days prior
to the anticipated termination date (in the case of fewer than
10 employees about to be dismissed for redundancy) to 21 days
prior to the anticipated termination date (in the case of the
dismissal of 10 or more employees within a period of 6 days).
These provisions have now to a large extent been overtaken by
the more detailed provisions of the EPA relating to Consultation (see Chapter 14).

In the event of an employer not giving the required notice
under this head, or indeed under the EPA consultation provisions (see page 200) the Secretary of State can reduce the amount
of the rebate by such proportion (not exceeding 10% of the
total rebate) as appears to be appropriate in the circumstances.
This can only be done if the failure on the part of the employer
appears to be " without reasonable excuse ".

If the Secretary of State refuses to allow to an employer the
whole or any part of the redundancy rebate, the employer can
appeal to an Industrial Tribunal.   The decision of the Tribunal
will be final in the case of matters arising under condition
number (5) (*above*); in other matters there will be an appeal
on a point of law.

CONTRACTING OUT

An employer and an employee **cannot** (with only two exceptions) agree that the terms of the RPA will not apply to them.
This is expressly forbidden by the Act.   Any agreement to
" contract out " of the terms of the Act is unenforceable.

The two exceptions are:—

(1) Where there is a **fixed term contract for two years** or
    more and the employee has agreed in writing before
    expiration of the term that he will not be entitled to a

redundancy payment in respect of the expiry of such term without its being renewed.[1]

This has been considered previously (see page 160).

(2) Where the Minister makes an order exempting certain employees from the protection of the RPA provisions. This can be done where there is a **collective agreement** which makes provision for payments to employees in the event of their redundancy and **both** parties to the agreement apply to the Minister for an exemption order. The agreement will presumably contain provisions at least as beneficial as the statutory provisions and it must provide for access to an industrial tribunal for the settlement of any disputes arising out of the collective agreement.[2]

---

[1] RPA, s. 15.
[2] Section 11, RPA.

CHAPTER 14

REDUNDANCY CONSULTATION

Consultation with employees or their representatives was not envisaged in the original redundancy legislation in 1965.

The only statutory provision at that time in any way relating to advance notice or warning of redundancy was that referred to in Chapter 13 (see page 188) under which the employer was obliged to notify the Department of Employment about certain anticipated redundancies.

In more recent years the position has changed and we must now first consider the recommendations of the Code of Practice and then look at the detailed provisions of the Employment Protection Act 1975 (EPA).

THE CODE OF PRACTICE

Reference has already been made to the Code of Practice (see page 31, *above*) originally issued under the Industrial Relations Act 1971.

The importance of the Code is that, quite apart from laying down guide lines and recommending certain minimum standards, its provisions can be—and indeed are—taken into account by an Industrial Tribunal if these provisions are relevant to any question under consideration by that Tribunal. The Code itself is, of course, admissible in evidence.

In a redundancy matter this becomes of vital importance when one considers the interlocking and, at times, overlapping provisions of the Trade Union and Labour Relations Act 1974 relating to unfair dismissal. If an employee is made redundant, it is still possible for that employee to allege that he was "unfairly dismissed" and to recover compensation under that head.

What then are the relevant provisions of the Code of Practice?

Paragraphs 40 to 46 deal generally with the Status and Security of Employees. By far the most important provision is paragraph 46 which states as follows:—

" **46.** If redundancy becomes necessary, management in consultation, as appropriate, with employees or their representatives, should:

(i) give as much warning as practicable to the employees concerned and to the Department of Employment:

(ii) consider introducing schemes for voluntary redundancy, retirement, transfer to other establishments within the undertaking, and a phased rundown of employment:

(iii) establish which employees are to be made redundant and the order of discharge:

(iv) offer help to employees in finding other work in co-operation, where appropriate, with the Department of Employment, and allow them reasonable time off for the purpose:

(v) decide how and when to make the facts public, ensuring that no announcement is made before the employees and their representatives and trade unions have been informed."

It will be seen from the above that employers must give " **as much warning as practicable** " to employees who are to be made redundant. Failure to do this will not prejudice the employer's right to a rebate from the Redundancy Fund. It could, however, mean that the dismissal will be " unfair " thereby enabling the employee to recover compensation (see page 290). Employers should, therefore, be mindful of the provisions of paragraph 46 of the Code. The employer who, for example, immediately after a takeover of a company, moves in and instantly and without warning reduces the work-force, is today very much at risk.

The obligations of the employer have, of course, now been increased and put on a statutory basis. The new obligations are, however, in addition to the provisions contained in the Code of Practice. It seems that the ACAS do not at present intend to issue a new Code—presumably because of the specific statutory provisions now in the EPA.

CONSULTATION UNDER THE EMPLOYMENT PRO-TECTION ACT 1975

The statutory provisions relating to Consultation and Procedure for handling redundancies are contained in **sections 99 to 107** of the Employment Protection Act 1975. These provisions came into force on 8th March 1976.

The duty to consult

The first point to note is that under the EPA provisions the duty to consult is only with **representatives of a recognised trade union.**[1] It is not strictly necessary to consult with the employees themselves (which is, of course, the case under the Code of Practice—see *above*).

Section 99(1) states—

" An employer proposing to dismiss as redundant an employee of a description of which an independent trade union is recognised by him **shall** consult representatives of that trade union in accordance with the following provisions of this section."

The consultation required by the above section " shall begin **at the earliest opportunity** " (s. 99(3)).

These provisions apply regardless of the number of employees to be made redundant. Thus, they are applicable even if only one employee is to be made redundant. As indicated at the outset, however, the provisions will only apply in the case of employees who are part of the class of employees in respect of which there is union recognition. The employee himself does not have to be a member of that union, but he must be one of a group of employees in respect of whom the employer has recognised a trade union.

If no union is recognised, the employer is not bound by the consultation provisions of the EPA. He should, however, observe the Code of Practice referred to above.

Larger scale redundancies

When it is proposed to dismiss at one establishment—

(1) 100 or more employees within a period of 90 days or less, or

---

[1] " Recognised " includes the situation where the ACAS has recommended recognition—see p. 73, *above*, and EPA, s. 106(1).

(2) 10 or more employees within a period of 30 days or less

then—

(a) consultations must take place at least 90 days (in the first case) or 60 days (in the second case) respectively before the first dismissal takes effect **and**

(b) the employer must notify the Secretary of State in writing of such proposed redundancies within the same time period as above and give a copy of such notification to the trade union representatives.

It is provided that if consultation has already begun in respect of the proposed dismissal of certain employees due to redundancy, those employees are not taken into account when determining whether or not there are 100 or more (or 10 or more) employees about to be dismissed.

Section 99(5) provides some details of the actual consultation. The employer must disclose in writing to the union representatives—

(a) the reasons for his proposals

(b) the numbers and descriptions of employees whom it is proposed to dismiss as redundant

(c) the total number of employees of any such description employed at the establishment in question

(d) the proposed method of selecting the employees who may be dismissed and

(e) the proposed method of carrying out the dismissals, with regard to any agreed procedure, including the period over which the dismissals are to take effect.

These details should, of course, be disclosed at least 90 days (in the case of 100 or more employees to be made redundant) or 60 days (in the case of 10 or more employees) before the first dismissal takes effect.

In the intervening period, the union can put forward its views and suggestions. If it does so, the employer is under an obligation (s. 99(7)) to consider them and to reply to them.

If the employer rejects the union's representations, he must state his reasons for so doing.

The only " defence " an employer has to these requirements is if there are " **special circumstances** which render it not reasonably practicable " for the employer to comply with the above requirements. Even then the employer must take " all such steps towards compliance " as are " **reasonably practicable** in those circumstances " (s. 99(8)).

At present, there are virtually no guide lines as to what will be " special circumstances ". It is thought that the defence might be available in industries such as the construction and ship-building industries where it can be very difficult to give advance warning of large-scale redundancies. In addition, it would seem that where a company is insolvent or is in great financial difficulties, that could be held to be " special circumstances ". One example here would be where a receiver of a business is appointed and he immediately makes part of the work-force redundant in order to reduce overheads and in an effort to avoid liquidation.

Some of the first Tribunal decisions with regard to " special circumstances " indicate that Tribunals may well find in favour of employers where, for example, the employers lose a major contract or customer without any advance warning at all. The Tribunal will first ascertain the circumstances, then decide whether they are " special " and then ask two questions—

(*a*) did those circumstances (and not any other factor) make full consultation not reasonably practicable? and

(*b*) did the employer do as much as was reasonably practicable to comply under the circumstances? "

The consultations must take place before the first dismissal " takes effect ". It does seem, therefore, that an employer can actually issue dismissal notices either before or during consultation provided that none of the dismissals actually take effect during the minimum consultation period. If this is done, employers could well save a considerable amount of time; the notice period and the consultation period could then run concurrently. This is confirmed by the booklet on

" Procedure for handling redundancies " issued by the Department of Employment.

Notification to Secretary of State

As indicated above, it is also the duty of an employer to notify the Secretary of State (*i.e.* for these purposes the Department of Employment) in writing of his proposal to make redundant either

    (*a*) 100 or more employees at one establishment within a period of 90 days or less or

    (*b*) 10 or more employees at one establishment within a period of 30 days or less.

The notification must be 90 days or 60 days respectively before the first dismissal takes effect.

If a trade union is recognised in respect of these employees, a copy of the notice to the Department of Employment must be given to the union representatives.

The notice itself must be in the form prescribed by the Secretary of State and, if union consultation is necessary under the Act, it must identify the union concerned and the date when consultations began.

The Secretary of State has power to demand further information from the employer.

Again, the only " defence " open to the employer is that of special circumstances making it not reasonably practicable for him to comply (see *above*).

Excluded Employees

The above-mentioned duties to consult with the trade union representatives and to notify the Secretary of State **do not apply** if the employees to be made redundant fall into any of the following categories:—

    (1) merchant seamen.

    (2) registered dock workers unless wholly or mainly engaged in work which is not dock work as defined by any scheme for the time being in force under the Dock Workers (Regulation of Employment) Act 1946.

(3) employment as master or as a member of the crew of a fishing vessel where the employee is not remunerated otherwise than by a share in the profits or gross earnings of the vessel.

(4) employment where under his contract of employment the employee ordinarily works outside Great Britain. With regard to employment on board a ship registered in the United Kingdom, see page 98.

(5) employment under a contract for a fixed term of 12 weeks or less or employment under a contract made in contemplation of the performance of a specific task which is not expected to last for more than 12 weeks unless in either case the employee has in fact been continuously employed for a period of more than 12 weeks.

Sanctions—the protective award

If an employer does not comply with his duty to consult, then the trade union (meaning an independent trade union recognised by the employer in respect of that description of employee) can present a complaint to an Industrial Tribunal.[1]

Again, it is **not the individual** employee but the trade union who has the right to lodge the complaint. The claim will be that an employer has dismissed employees as redundant or is proposing to do so and that he has not complied with the statutory requirements as to consultation.

If this is done, the burden of proof is firmly placed on the employer (s. 101(2)). Unless the employer can show that he has complied with **all** his obligations as to disclosure, then his only defence is to show that—

(a) there were **special circumstances** which rendered it not reasonably practicable for him to comply with the statutory requirements **and**

(b) that he took all such steps towards compliance as were **reasonably practicable** in those circumstances.

If the tribunal finds such a complaint well-founded it **will** make a declaration to that effect and it **may** also make a protective award.

---

[1] See *Amalgamated Union of Engineering Workers v. Sefton Engineering Co. Ltd.* [1976] IRLR 318.

The **protective award** is a new concept in the Law of Employment. **Sections 101 and 102** contain detailed provisions relating to such an award. The effect of those provisions is as follows:—

(1) the award is made in respect of descriptions of employees who have been dismissed, or whom it is proposed to dismiss, due to redundancy.

(2) the award is that the employer shall pay remuneration for a **protected period.**

(3) the **protected period** will begin either with the date on which the first dismissal takes effect or the date of the award (whichever is earlier) and will continue until such time as the Tribunal thinks " just and equitable in all the circumstances having regard to the seriousness of the employer's default ", but the maximum protected period will be—

(a) in a 100 or more employees case, 90 days

(b) in a 10 or more employees case, 60 days

(c) in any other case, 28 days.

(4) the amount of remuneration is based on " a week's pay ", as for general redundancy purposes (see EPA, Sched. 4, Pt. II, and Appendix III, page 360, *post*). The employee, will thus receive a week's pay for each week falling within the protected period. Any payments made by the employer either under the contract or by way of damages for breach of contract in respect of any part of the protected period can be taken into account in the award and *vice versa.*

(5) The Tribunal can only consider a complaint under these provisions if it was lodged either before the proposed dismissal took effect or within three months from the date on which the dismissal did take effect. If the Tribunal is satisfied that it was not reasonably practicable to lodge the complaint within the three month period, it can deal with a complaint out of time.

So far, the provisions relating to a protective award have only dealt with the award itself arising out of a trade union making an application to an Industrial Tribunal.

What is the position of the individual employee?

If an **individual employee** is one of the employees of the
" description " referred to in a protective award, he is entitled
to be paid remuneration for the protected period specified in
the award.

The rate of remuneration is a week's pay (as previously
defined) for each week of the protected period or proportionately for any period less than a week.

An award will not be made to an employee in respect of a
period during which his employment continued unless he would
have been entitled to be paid either under his contract or under
the Contracts of Employment Act 1972.

If during the protected period the employee is fairly dismissed by his employer for a reason other than redundancy or
the employee unreasonably terminates his own employment,
he loses his right to remuneration under a protective award.

If the employer offers alternative employment to the employee
to take effect either before or during the protected period, then
this offer is treated in exactly the same way as is the offer of
new employment in a normal redundancy situation (see pages
172 to 179, *above*).   Thus, if the employee unreasonably refuses
the offer, he will not be entitled to any remuneration under a
protective award in respect of any period during which he would
have been employed had he accepted the offer.   Similarly, if
the employee accepts an offer of suitable employment but on
different terms and conditions, then a four weeks' trial period
takes effect with the consequences referred to previously (page
177).

If **the individual employee** is covered by a protective award
and is not paid by his employer, the employee himself can
apply to an Industrial Tribunal which, if it finds the complaint
well-founded, **must** order the employer to pay the amount of
remuneration due.   The application must be within three
months from the day in respect of which it is claimed that
remuneration under a protective award is due.   There is the
usual power to extend this period where it was not practicable
to present the complaint sooner.

Sanctions—the Secretary of State

One " penalty " by which the legislation hopes to ensure that employers will observe the consultation provisions is the protective award, which has now been considered. That award, however, only arises out of a failure to consult with trade union representatives.

What is the position if the employer fails in his obligations to notify the Secretary of State of the proposed redundancies? (see page 196, *above*).

There are two possible consequences of such a failure—

(1) the employer's **entitlement to a rebate** from the Redundancy Fund (see page 187, *above*) **can be reduced** by such amount (not exceeding one tenth) as appears appropriate in the circumstances.

If such a reduction is made, the employer can appeal to an Industrial Tribunal within three months of the date the Secretary of State's decision is communicated to him or within such further period as is reasonable where it was not reasonably practicable for the appeal to be presented earlier.

Employers should, however, think carefully about such an appeal. The Tribunal has a wide discretion—it can allow the appeal completely or in part, it can refuse the appeal and it can even increase the reduction of the rebate.

The decision of the Tribunal is binding upon the Secretary of State.

There can be no reduction of a rebate if criminal proceedings have been instituted under the next heading arising out of the same " failure " on the part of the employer.

(2) the employer can be **prosecuted** and on a summary conviction **fined up to £400.** The prosecution can only be instituted by or with the consent of the Secretary of State.

There can be no prosecution (in respect of the same " failure " to comply) if the employer has already suffered a reduction in rebate. There is provision for a certificate to be issued by or on behalf of the Secretary of State confirming that no such reduction has been made and such certificate is conclusive evidence on that point.

Collective Agreements

Section 107 of the EPA gives power to the Secretary of State to make an **exemption order** where there is in force a collective agreement containing provisions **at least as favourable** as the EPA provisions relating to the arrangements for handling redundancies or for providing alternative employment. Any application to the Secretary of State under this head must be by all the parties to the agreement.

The agreement must contain a provision allowing an employee in the event of a dispute to refer the matter either to an Industrial Tribunal or to an independent referee or arbitrator.

Contracting Out

Other than in relation to collective agreements referred to above, it is **not possible to contract out** of the EPA provisions relating to the handling of redundancies. Any agreement to exclude or limit the operation of the EPA provisions or to preclude any person from presenting a complaint to a Tribunal, is void (EPA, s. 118).

TIME OFF TO LOOK FOR WORK

Although not strictly part of the consultation provisions of the EPA, it seems logical to consider here the new rights of an employee to have time off to look for another job or to arrange for re-training.

As we have seen (page 192, *above*) there is a reference to " reasonable time off " being allowed in paragraph 46(iv) of the Code of Practice.

More formal rights are, however, contained in section 61 of the EPA which came into force on 1st June 1976.

Conditions

Before an employee becomes entitled to time off, the following conditions must be satisfied—

(1) he must have been given **notice of dismissal** by reason of redundancy

(2) he must have been in **continuous employment for two years** on the date on which the notice is due to expire or the date on which it would expire if it was the minimum period of notice laid down under the Contracts of Employment Act 1972.

The terms

The time off itself is simply specified as " **reasonable time off** during the employee's working hours in order to look for new employment **or** make arrangements for training for future employment " (s. 61(1)).

The EPA does not envisage (as it does for time off for union officials or union members—see page 100, *above*) the issuing by the ACAS of a Code of Practice as to what is " reasonable ". In view, however, of the Tribunal's limit to award only two days' pay, it seems that an employer will not be expected to allow more than two days off during the notice period.

The section does, however, specifically state that an employee who has time off under this head is entitled to be paid for the period of his absence at the appropriate hourly rate.

The rate is based on " a week's pay " (see page 361, *below*).

It should be noted that on the strict wording of section 61 time off does **not** have to be allowed for the **actual re-training** itself, *e.g.* attending a course of training. It is only the making of **arrangements** for training which is covered. This will include making enquiries about courses, attending interviews and enrolling.

Actual notice of dismissal must have been given—it should be noted that a warning about possible future redundancies is not a formal notice of dismissal.

Finally, the section only applies if the dismissal is because of redundancy.

Sanctions

The right to time off is, of course, the right of the individual employee—it is not linked to employees who are covered by a recognised trade union.

If, therefore, an employer **unreasonably** refuses to allow an employee to have time off, then section 61(7) provides that such employee will be entitled to be paid an amount equal to the remuneration he would have received had he been allowed the time off.

If necessary, the employee can apply to an Industrial Tribunal and the Tribunal has power to make a declaration as to the position and to order the employer to pay remuneration to the employee. The remuneration cannot exceed, in respect of the notice period of the employee, **two-fifths of a week's pay** of that employee.

There is the usual limitation that any application to a Tribunal must be lodged within three months from the day on which it is alleged that time off should have been allowed or within such further period as the Tribunal considers reasonable where it was not reasonably practicable for the complaint to be presented within the three month period.

It would seem from the above that the award of up to two-fifths of a week's pay is in effect a " fine " on the employer. The employee who is not allowed time off to look for work and who is still employed during the notice period will not have lost any remuneration as he will still have been paid by his employer. He will, however, if time off has been unreasonably refused, be entitled to claim further remuneration (in effect double pay) for a period of up to two days.

If, on the other hand, an employee is given time off and is still paid during that time under his contract, then such payment can be set against any liability there may be under section 61 of the EPA.

The converse will also apply—remuneration under section 61 being set against any contractual liability of the employer.

Excluded categories

The following classes of employees **do not** have the EPA rights to " reasonable time off ":—

(1) employment where the employer is the husband or wife of the employee.

(2) registered dock workers unless wholly or mainly engaged in work which is not dock work as defined by any scheme for the time being in force under the Dock Workers (Regulation of Employment) Act 1946.

(3) employment as master or as a member of the crew of a fishing vessel where the employee is not remunerated otherwise than by a share in the profits or gross earnings of the vessel.

(4) employment where under his contract of employment the employee ordinarily works outside Great Britain. With regard to employment on board a ship registered in the United Kingdom, see page 98.

(5) merchant seamen.

(6) " part-time " employees. Although this category is not specifically excluded by the EPA, the exclusion arises by virtue of the necessity for the employee to have been in " continuous employment " for two years (see Appendix II as to " continuous employment ").

CHAPTER 15

THE INSOLVENCY OF THE EMPLOYER

It has already been seen that an employee has today a great number of statutory rights arising out of his employment. These rights are summarised on pages 66 and 67, and in Appendix VI, page 372, *post*.

A situation may, however, arise where these rights can become of little practical value if the employer becomes insolvent and is unable to pay.

Until recently the employee in such a situation was very much " at risk ". **The Redundancy Payments Act 1965** has always contained provisions (in particular in **section 32**) whereby an employee can apply direct to the Department of Employment for a payment to him from the Redundancy Fund where he is entitled to a redundancy payment and the employer has not paid him and is insolvent. This provision is also extended to cover the position where the employee has taken all reasonable steps (other than legal proceedings) to recover from the employer and the employer has refused or failed to pay.

These provisions, however, only relate to an employee's entitlement to redundancy pay. There was until 20th April 1976 no similar provision relating to such things as unfair dismissal compensation, money in lieu of notice, accrued holiday pay, etc.

The problem was summarised by the Consultative Document issued by the Department of Employment prior to the publication of the Employment Protection Act—

" In recent years some 30,000 to 40,000 employees a year have been involved in such situations (*i.e.* not receiving arrears of wages, accrued holiday pay, etc. when an employer becomes insolvent) with claims of this kind probably totalling about £4m. Even where employees are able to recover some of what is owing to them, the process can sometimes take years."

The aim of the **Employment Protection Act 1975** was, therefore, to try and safeguard (within certain limits) employees where their employer becomes insolvent. This aim is carried out by **sections 63 to 69** of that Act and those sections came into force on 20th April 1976.

Priority of Debts

Under the general law relating to liquidation and bankruptcy —as contained in the Bankruptcy Act 1914 and the Companies Act 1948—certain debts have preferential status, *i.e.* they are paid out first and in preference to general trade and other creditors. They include such things as income tax, rates and National Insurance contributions.

As far as employment law is concerned, the following matters have for some years had preferential status—

(1) **arrears of wages** for up to four months before the commencement of the winding up or the date of the receiving order but in any event not exceeding £200. Any claim in excess of £200 will rank as an ordinary debt along with other unsecured debts.[1]

(2) all accrued **holiday pay** becoming payable on termination of employment before or by the effect of the winding up.

(3) **unpaid pension contributions** for up to four months prior to the winding up.

Section 63 of the EPA now provides that certain other " amounts " shall be treated for the above purposes as if they were " wages payable by the employer to the employee in respect of the period for which " they were payable. The amounts so specified are those relating to

(*a*) a guarantee payment (page 150, *above*).

(*b*) remuneration on suspension on medical grounds (page 123, *above*).

(*c*) any payment for time off for carrying out trade union duties (page 101) or to look for work when under notice due to redundancy (page 202).

(*d*) remuneration under a protective award (page 199).

---

[1] The Insolvency Act 1976 (which is expected to come into force before the end of 1977) increases this limit from £200 to £800.

Payments in respect of these four matters thus have the same priority as do wages under the Bankruptcy Act 1914 and the Companies Act 1948. This means that, for priority purposes, the £200 limit will apply.[1]

It will shortly be seen that, despite this limit for priority purposes, an employee may in certain circumstances be able to recover direct from the Redundancy Fund a sum in excess of £200.

The employee's rights on insolvency

The EPA has now introduced provisions under which employees will, on the insolvency of their employer, have rights to claim against the Redundancy Fund similar to those referred to on page 205 in relation to redundancy itself.

Before the rights themselves are considered, what is insolvency for these purposes?

An employer will be taken to be **insolvent** if—

(a) he becomes bankrupt or makes a composition or arrangement with his creditors or a receiving order is made against him, or

(b) he has died and an order is made under the Bankruptcy Act 1914 to administer his estate according to the law of bankruptcy; or

(c) where the employer is a company, a winding up order is made or a resolution for voluntary winding up is passed or a receiver or manager is appointed or possession is taken of company property by debenture holders under a floating charge (EPA, s. 69(1)).

If an employer is insolvent, then an employee can apply in writing to the Secretary of State (in practice the Department of Employment) and claim certain specified monies that are owing to him.

---

[1] The Insolvency Act 1976 (which is expected to come into force before the end of 1977) increases this limit from £200 to £800.

The specified monies are as follows:—

(a) **arrears of pay** not exceeding in aggregate eight weeks' pay. " Arrears of Pay " here will include the four types of payment (guarantee pay, protective award, etc.) referred to on page 206 (arising under section 63(2) of the EPA).

(b) any amount which the employer is liable to pay in respect of **notice to terminate** the employee's contract under the Contracts of Employment Act 1972 (as to which, see page 228). It will be seen in Chapter 17 (page 228) that the maximum period here could be twelve weeks. Under this head credit must be given for any remuneration or social security benefit received.

(c) **holiday pay,** not exceeding six weeks in all, to which the employee became entitled during the twelve month period immediately prior to the " relevant date " (see *below*).

(d) any basic award for **compensation** for unfair dismissal (see page 322). The present maximum basic award is £2,400.

(e) any reasonable sum by way of reimbursement of the whole or part of any fee or premium paid by an **apprentice or articled clerk.**

(f) certain unpaid " relevant contributions " to an **occupational pension scheme.** Detailed provisions are contained in section 65 of the EPA relating to pension schemes. The request for payment under this head can only be made by " persons competent to act " which will normally mean the trustees of the pension scheme and not the employee himself. " Relevant contributions " are contributions which an employer should have paid either on his own account or, having deducted monies from the employee's wages, on behalf of an employee. The maximum limit is the balance of unpaid contributions due from the employer as at the date of insolvency and payable in respect of the preceding **twelve month** period **or** the amount certified by an actuary as necessary to meet the liabilities of the scheme on dissolution **or** an amount equal to 10% of the employee's earnings during the twelve month period, whichever is the least.   There is also an overriding proviso, in respect of unpaid contributions on behalf of an employee, that the sum paid cannot exceed the amount deducted from the employee during the twelve month period.

Where any of the above monies are related to time, the **maximum** amount payable cannot exceed **£80** in respect of any **one week.** This limit can be varied by the Secretary of State by statutory order.   The £80 per week limit will, therefore, apply in the cases referred to in paragraphs (*a*), (*b*) and (*c*) *above.*

Before the Secretary of State can authorise a payment from the Redundancy Fund, he must be satisfied as to two matters—

(*a*) that the employer concerned has become **insolvent** (as defined above) **and**

(*b*) that on " the relevant date " the employee was **entitled** to be paid the whole or part of any of the debts referred to under (*a*) to (*e*) above or that there were unpaid relevant contributions under (*f*) above.

If these two conditions are established to the satisfaction of the Secretary of State, he **must** pay to the employee out of the Redundancy Fund the amount to which the employee is entitled.

" **Relevant date** " here means **either** the date on which the employer became **insolvent** or the date of **termination** of the employment, whichever is the later.   The monies must, therefore, be due and owing on the later of one of those dates.

When an employee makes an application to the Secretary of State under these provisions, the Secretary of State must obtain a statement from the liquidator, receiver or other " relevant officer " of the amount of the debt owing and unpaid. The Secretary of State has power (s. 68) by notice in writing to call upon the employer to provide information and to produce documents and records; failure to comply with such a notice can lead to a prosecution and a fine of up to £100.   If an employer makes a false statement knowingly or recklessly the fine can be up to £400.

If a payment is made to an employee from the Redundancy Fund, the Secretary of State then " steps into the shoes " of the employee, *i.e.* he has the same rights and remedies against the employer that the employee had. He will also have the same priority rights as referred to on page 206 *above*, but these may, of course, be limited (*e.g.* to £200, in the case of arrears of wages). Thus, the Fund will not always be able to make full recovery of the payments it makes to employees.

The remedies of the employee

If an employee applies to the Secretary of State for a payment under the above provisions and such payment is refused (either in whole or part), the employee can apply to an Industrial Tribunal. If the Tribunal finds that the payment should have been made, it will make a declaration to that effect.

An application to a Tribunal must be made within three months of the date of communication of the decision of the Secretary of State or, if that is not reasonably practicable, within such further period as is reasonable.

Excluded categories

The employee's rights referred to above in respect of the insolvency of the employer **do not apply** to the following categories of employees:—

(1) employment where the employer is the husband or wife of the employee.

(2) registered dock workers unless wholly or mainly engaged in work which is not dock work as defined by any scheme for the time being in force under the Dock Workers (Regulation of Employment) Act 1946.

(3) employment as master or as a member of the crew of a fishing vessel where the employee is not remunerated otherwise than by a share in the profits or gross earnings of the vessel.

(4) employment where under his contract of employment the employee ordinarily works outside Great Britain. With regard to employment on board a ship registered in the United Kingdom, see page 98.

(5) merchant seamen.

PART V

TERMINATION OF EMPLOYMENT

CHAPTER 16

DISMISSAL

Before dealing with the principles relating to wrongful dismissal and unfair dismissal, consideration must first be given to a much more basic problem—what is dismissal?

In many cases the position will be quite clear, *e.g.* the employer will have terminated the employment of the employee either by giving him notice or by paying money in lieu of notice. Other situations can, however, arise where the position is not clear cut. These must be considered.

It will be appreciated that an employee only has a right to a claim arising out of the ending of his employment if he has been dismissed. In particular, this applies to a claim for a redundancy payment and also to a claim alleging unfair dismissal.

Statutory Definition

There is now a common statutory definition both for redundancy and unfair dismissal purposes.

The definition is contained in section 3(2) of The Redundancy Payments Act 1965 (this being a new section introduced into the RPA with effect from 1st June 1976 by paragraph 3 of Part I of Schedule 16 to the Employment Protection Act 1975) and in paragraph 5(2) of the 1st Schedule to The Trade Union and Labour Relations Act 1974 (TUALRA).

Under these provisions an employee is to be treated as **dismissed** by his employer in any one of the following circumstances—

(a) where the contract under which he is employed by the employer is terminated by the employer, whether it is so terminated by notice or without notice, **or**

(b) where under that contract he is employed for a fixed term and the term expires without being renewed under the same contract, **or**

(c) where the employee terminates that contract, with or without notice, in circumstances such that he is entitled to terminate it without notice by reason of the employer's conduct.

If there is a dismissal under one of the above heads, then **" the effective date of termination "** is as follows[1]—

(a) in relation to an employee whose contract of employment is terminated by notice . . . the date on which that notice expires;

(b) in relation to an employee whose contract of employment is terminated without notice . . . the date on which the termination takes effect; and

(c) in relation to an employee who is employed under a contract for a fixed term, where that term expires without being renewed under the same contract . . . the date on which that term expires.

For trial period and redundancy purposes (see page 178, *above*) there is a special definition of the effective date of termination to cover the position where the employee leaves the new or " trial " job and is deemed to have been dismissed from his original job.

Each one of the above types of dismissal will now be considered before we look at the various situations which may not give rise to a dismissal at all.

Termination with or without notice

This normally is where there is no doubt about what has happened. The employee is " sacked ".

---

1 See RPA, s. 3(9) (as amended) and TUALRA, Sched. 1, para. 5(5).

If **notice is given** to the employee, the employment is at an end when the notice expires. The correct amount of notice will be either that contained in the contract or the notice laid down by the Contracts of Employment Act 1972 (as to which, see page 228).

Even if the correct amount of notice is not given, the contract will still come to an end when the notice expires. The employee may, of course, still have a claim in respect of the balance of the notice period (see page 231). An employer cannot, however, by giving less than the statutory notice prevent an employee from establishing his qualifying period of " continuous employment ", *e.g.* by sacking without notice an employee with 25 weeks' service, thereby preventing the employee from " chalking up " his qualifying 26 weeks. This will not work. It has been prevented by a provision in the Employment Protection Act 1975 (effective from 1st June 1976). The effect of this provision is that where the statutory notice would, if duly given, expire on a date later than the effective date of termination, that later date shall be treated as the effective date of termination in relation to the dismissal.[1]

Employers should, if they do intend to dismiss an employee, be careful to make clear exactly what is intended. If the date of termination is not clear and cannot be inferred from all the circumstances, there may not legally be a dismissal at all. Thus, an **advance warning** about possible future dismissal is **not sufficient** *e.g.* where the employee is told that the factory may be closing down and that he might look for another job.[2] Each case will, of course, depend on its own particular facts, but an employee who is given advance warning of a closure and who then leaves may lose his entitlement to redundancy pay and/or unfair dismissal compensation. Having said this, the employee may in certain situations be able to claim he has been " constructively dismissed ", *i.e.* that the conduct of the employer has forced him to leave (see page 216).

---

[1] See RPA, s. 3(1), as amended, and TUALRA, Sched. 1, para. 5(6), as amended.

[2] *Morton Sundour Fabrics Ltd. v. Shaw* [1967] ITR 84.

As far as **redundancy** is concerned section 4 of the RPA contains special provisions relating to the position where an employee is **given notice** to terminate his contract and he then finds another job. That employee can then during what will normally be the statutory notice period (see page 228) give **in writing** a form of notice to the employer to bring the employment to an end at an earlier date. If this is done, there will still be a " **dismissal** " which will be effective on the date on which the employee's notice expires. The employer can, however, give a counter-notice in writing requiring the employee to continue in his job and stating that, unless the employee does so, the employer will contest the employee's claim to redundancy pay.

If an employee is dismissed **without notice,** he may have a right to claim that the dismissal is wrongful (see page 226), but whether or not such a right exists, the employment itself comes to an end when the employee is actually dismissed.

The intention of the employer may be relevant here and Tribunals, from time to time, have had to consider whether particular words used by an employer did constitute a dismissal. Very often this will arise where there is a " row " between the employer and the employee and in the " heat of the moment " bad language is used. Here again, employers should avoid all doubt by making the position absolutely clear.

Where money **in lieu of notice** is paid, the contract of employment will normally be at an end when the money is paid and not at the expiration of the notice period to which the money relates. During that period a person is not employed by his employer and the money he receives is in effect damages for breach of contract.[1]

Where an employer gives notice to an employee, the employer has legally no right to withdraw the notice. If he attempts to do so, it is entirely up to the employee whether or not he wishes to allow the notice to be withdrawn or not.

---

[1] *Dixon v. Stenor Ltd.* [1973] ICR 157.

Non-renewal of a fixed-term contract.

This is defined as a " dismissal ". For a contract to be for a fixed term it must be for a set period of time, so that " the parties are bound for the term stated in the agreement, and unable to determine it by notice on either side ".[1] It cannot be a term which can be " unfixed by notice ".

It is not uncommon for employers to enter into a service agreement with an employee for, say, twelve months or more and at the same time to provide that the agreement can be determined at any time by either party giving to the other three months' notice. It is now clear that this is not a fixed term contract.

It will be remembered that fixed term contracts are of particular importance under both redundancy and unfair dismissal legislation because it is possible to contract out of those rights in the case of a fixed term contract in writing for two years or more where the dismissal arises simply by virtue of the expiration of the term.

Constructive dismissal

The statutory definition referred to under paragraph (c) on page 213 gives the employee a right to terminate his own contract and still be able to claim that he has been dismissed where the circumstances are such " that he is entitled to terminate it without notice by reason of the employer's conduct ".

This has become known as " **constructive dismissal** ". It is of vital importance to the law relating to unfair dismissal. An increasing number of cases of constructive dismissal are now coming before Industrial Tribunals. One of the big problems here for the employer is that because he has not deliberately " sacked " the employee in the ordinary sense of the word, he may find it very difficult to prove to the Tribunal one of the specified reasons for the dismissal (see page 271). If he cannot do this, then the dismissal will automatically be unfair regardless of whether the employer acted " reasonably ".

---

[1] *BBC v. Ioannou* [1975] ICR 267, per Lord Denning, M.R., at p. 272.

Employers should, therefore, be very careful of their own conduct in relation to an employee.

Having said this, what are the circumstances which would entitle an employee to terminate his own contract with justification? What **conduct of the employer** can give rise to constructive dismissal?

It cannot be stressed too strongly that each case must depend on its own particular facts and circumstances. The principle is that if an employer makes a substantial change in the terms of the employment so that he becomes guilty of a fundamental breach of the contract, then the employee is entitled to treat that breach as a repudiation of the contract by the employer and leave. If he does so, there will have been a " dismissal ".

The starting base, therefore, is to consider the terms and conditions of the contract—express, implied, statutory, collective agreements, works rules, etc. (see pages 31 to 41). As stressed in Chapter 2, it is most important that the employer should right at the commencement of the employment consider what are to be the detailed terms of that employment. Wherever possible, these terms should be incorporated in the Contracts of Employment Act statement. For example, if those terms do not give the employer a right to change the place of work and he insists on doing so, then a dismissal of an employee who refuses to move to the new place of work will normally be unfair and, indeed, that employee might—when threatened with a proposed change in his place of work—be able to leave before he is actually sacked and then claim " constructive dismissal ".

This is one example of a change in the terms of employment giving rise to a finding of constructive dismissal. Other examples include changes in the pay structure resulting in lower wages; offers of alternative employment with a substantial reduction in either status, wages or fringe benefits; suspension without pay where the contract does not expressly allow it; asking an employee to do work he was not employed to do; substantial changes to a shift system resulting in either loss of pay or great inconvenience to the employee; imposing lay-off and short-time working where this is not allowed by the terms of the employment. A recent case involving a claim of constructive dismissal has already been considered on page 138.[1]

The Tribunals will take into account all the circumstances of a particular case. Contracts of employment cannot always be fixed and rigid in their terms. Employees are entitled to issue reasonable orders to an employee. Changes in shift systems and pay structures are often necessary in the interests of the business and, if this can be established (*e.g.* in times of economic uncertainties), an employee's refusal to agree to changed terms may be held to be unreasonable. This arose in several cases during the three-day week imposed by the Government in the winter of 1973-1974.

Some Tribunals also seem to have extended the law relating to constructive dismissal and have, in certain cases, found in favour of the employee even where there has been no formal breach of the contract on the part of the employer. In particular, this has arisen where there has been a series of acts by an employer which have lead up to the employee finally leaving, *e.g.* victimisation of an employee by his foreman.[2] If this trend is followed, it seems that a series of acts, none of which in themselves amount to a breach by the employer, can cumulatively amount to a breach.

In *Gilbert v. Goldstone Ltd.* [1976] IRLR 257 the Employment Appeal Tribunal said that when considering a case of constructive dismissal the test should be what is reasonable in the circumstances, having regard to equity and the substantial merits of the case. The Tribunal must take into account all the factors which ultimately lead a man to say—" I cannot work. I must go ".

One of the problems in some constructive dismissal cases arises where an employee, faced with either leaving his job because of a breach by the employer or staying on and trying out the new terms of employment, decides to do the latter.

We have already seen (page 177) that, as far as redundancy is concerned, employees now have a " trial period " of four

---

[1] *Breach v. Epsylon Industries Ltd.* [1976] IRLR 181.
[2] *Fanshaw v. Robinsons & Sons Ltd.* [1975] IRLR 165.

weeks. Even where there is no redundancy situation, an employee is entitled to try out new terms that are offered to him provided that he makes it absolutely clear that either it is only a trial or that he is working " under protest ".[1] If this is not done, the employee may be held to have accepted the new terms, e.g. by working at a different factory. In the past, a trial period has been allowed for up to six months. It is felt, however, that it is now most unlikely that an employee will be allowed to " try out " the new terms for longer than four weeks (by analogy with the statutory " trial period " introduced into the Redundancy payments Act 1965).

Resignations

An employee who resigns from his employment cannot then claim that he has been dismissed. The resignation must, however, be a genuine " unforced " resignation. See, for example, the case of *Cox v. Philips Industries Ltd.* [1976] ICR 138 referred to on page 232.

On occasions an employer will say to an employee—" If you resign today I will give you six months' pay; if you do not accept this, I will dismiss you and you will only be entitled to one month's pay in lieu of notice ". If this is done and the employee does " resign " it will be a forced resignation; the employee can then apply to a Tribunal and claim that he has been unfairly dismissed. This will be so even though he has received the six months' pay (unless the settlement was negotiated via the Conciliation Officer—see page 255). If an employer places his employee in a position where he has no option but to tender his notice, this will be a dismissal.

One form of " resignation " that will still be classed as a dismissal for unfair dismissal purposes is where an employee, who has been given notice, leaves during the notice period. The employee in that situation must, during the notice period, inform the employer of his intention to terminate the contract at an earlier date than that specified in the notice. If he does this, he will still be taken to have been dismissed. The noti-

---

[1] *Marriott v. Oxford & District Co-operative Society Ltd.* [1969] ITR 377.

fication from the employee does not—since 1st June 1976—have to be in writing.[1]

An employee will be deemed to have **resigned** if he " so conducts himself as to lead a reasonable employer to believe that the employee has terminated the contract of employment ", *e.g.* where the employee was off sick and never contacted his employer.

The distinction here can, however, be a very fine one. Absence due to illness will be considered in more detail at a later stage (see pages 278 and 281).

The Tribunals and higher courts also tend not to support the employer who says to an employee—" If you do not do such and such (*e.g.* return to normal working), you will be deemed to have terminated your own employment ". Some support for this form of ultimatum does, however, seem to have been forthcoming from the Court of Appeal in the NPA/NGA dispute which culminated in *Chappell v. Times Newspapers Ltd.* [1975] ICR 145.

If, of course, the termination of the employment is by the **mutual consent** of the parties, this will not be a dismissal. Again, there must be a genuine " unforced " consent, *e.g.* where the employee agrees to become self-employed; or where an immigrant actually signed a letter, before going to his home country on holiday, that if he did not return by a specified date, his contract of employment would be at an end. On the other hand, an agreement to bring forward the actual date of dismissal, after notice has been given, will not make the dismissal itself ineffective.

Dismissal by operation of law

Dismissal can also arise by virtue of certain events which may be outside the control of the parties.

Redundancy

Section 22(1) of the RPA provides that where in accordance with any enactment or rule of law any act on the part of an

---

[1] TUALRA, Sched. 1, para. 5(3), as amended by EPA, Sched. 16, Pt. III, paras. 8 and 9 (but see p. 215 as to the position under RPA).

employer operates so as to terminate the contract that act shall be treated as a termination of the contract by the employer.

There are three situations of this kind and these are as follows:—

(1) **The death of the employer** will in itself terminate the employment. Having said this, the employee may in practice continue to work in the same job and, if he does so, the RPA provisions relating to suitable alternative employment, trial period, etc. (see pages 172 to 179) will apply.

(2) **The dissolution of a partnership** may terminate the employment, but this will not always be the case. In any event, the employee will normally continue to be employed on the same terms and conditions and will not, therefore, have any claim.

(3) **Liquidation and receivership** give rise to differing problems.

In the case of a **Receiver,** an appointment by the court automatically operates as a discharge of the company's employees and a similar position will arise if a receiver and manager is appointed by and acts on behalf of the debenture holders. If, however, a receiver is appointed by debenture holders but acts only on behalf of the company, that appointment does not automatically terminate the contracts of employment.

If a company goes into **liquidation,** then an order for compulsory winding up will automatically constitute a dismissal, but this will not be the case if there is a voluntary winding up.

Frustration

The doctrine of frustration in the general law of contract can, in some instances, be relevant to the relationship of employer and employee.

Frustration will arise where some unforeseen event makes the carrying out of the contract impossible or makes what has to be done under the contract completely different from what the parties originally intended.

If this happens, then the contract may come to an end, regardless of the intention of the parties and indeed sometimes without even their knowledge.

In the employment field this **may** arise where an employee becomes physically incapable of performing his contract of employment or if further performance of the contract becomes unlawful. If this does arise and the whole contract becomes " frustrated ", the contract will then be at an end. Legally, there will have been no dismissal and thus no rights relating to redundancy pay and/or unfair dismissal will arise.

In particular, cases have arisen under this head with regard to **imprisonment** and **ill-health.**

(1) **Imprisonment.** A sentence of imprisonment imposed on an employee will obviously prevent him from carrying out his duties under his contract of employment. Even though this " disability " is to a certain extent self-induced, it has been held to be a frustration of the contract. In *Hare v. Murphy Brothers Ltd.* [1975] ICR 603, the Court of Appeal held that a sentence of 12 months' imprisonment imposed on an employee for unlawful wounding in an incident not connected with his work terminated the contract of employment at the date of the conviction; it was an event which made it impossible for the applicant to continue to do his job; it was an event which frustrated the contract; accordingly the employee had no right to claim compensation for unfair dismissal.

The above decision seems to represent the common sense of the situation. It was obviously impossible for the employee to do his job. There may, however, be exceptional cases when this would not apply, *e.g.* when a man gets a very short sentence, such as three weeks for failing to pay maintenance monies due to his wife.

It will be appreciated that consideration of imprisonment under this head is a different matter to the situation where a criminal conviction is treated as " conduct " for the purpose of establishing an actual reason for the dismissal (see page 286).   Under the frustration heading, there is no dismissal at all.

(2) **Prolonged illness.**   Absence due to illness or injury may give rise to a reason entitling the employer to terminate a contract of employment (see page 278).   In unfair dismissal cases, the reason will relate to the " capability " of the employee for performing the work which he was employed to do.

In some cases, however, it is **possible** that the illness may be permanent or may be so prolonged that the contract will become **frustrated.**   It is very difficult to establish frustration by virtue of absence due to ill-health or incapacity and the burden of proving this will be on the employer.   There are very few reported cases of unfair dismissal where frustration has been established. Each case will depend on its own particular facts and circumstances.   Normally, of course, the employer will not rely solely on the doctrine of frustration; he will put forward the absence due to ill-health as a reason for the dismissal and will give proper notice to the employee. This is probably the safest course for an employer to adopt.

Some helpful guide lines as to the doctrine of frustration in relation to absence due to illness have, however, been laid down in the case of *Marshall v. Harland & Wolff Ltd.* [1972] ICR 101. In that case the employee was absent from work for 18 months prior to his dismissal because of illness.   He received no wages during his absence;   there was no medical evidence as to the likely duration of his incapacity.   The employers decided to close down their shipyard and accordingly gave the employee four weeks' notice of dismissal.   The employee claimed a redundancy payment.   On the facts of the particular case the National Industrial Relations Court held (reversing the decision of the Industrial Tribunal) that the relationship of employer and employee had not been terminated by frustration.

Sir John Donaldson stated that the test of whether the contract had been frustrated sounded more difficult than it really was. A tribunal, he said, should ask itself the following question—

> " Was the employee's incapacity, looked at before the purported dismissal, of such a nature, or did it appear likely to continue for such a period, that further performance of his obligations in the future would either be impossible or would be a thing radically different from that undertaken by him and agreed to be accepted by the employer under the agreed terms of his employment? ".

In considering the answer to this question, the Tribunal should take into account:—

(a) **the terms** of the contract, including the provisions as to sickness pay. If the contract provides for sick pay, the contract will not be frustrated if the employee is likely to return to work during the sick pay period.

(b) **how long** the employment was likely to last in the absence of sickness. A short-term employment is more likely to be frustrated than a long term job.

(c) **the nature of the employment.** If the employee occupies a key position, it is more likely that the contract will become frustrated.

(d) **the nature of the illness** or injury and how long it has already continued and the prospects of recovery. The greater the incapacity and the longer the absence, the more likely it will be that the relationship has been destroyed.

(e) **the period of past employment.** " A relationship which is of long standing is not so easily destroyed as one which has but a short history ".[1]

As indicated above, it is very difficult to satisfy the Tribunal that a contract has been frustrated even when the above principles are applied. Thus, in *Hebden v. Forsey & Son* [1973] ICR 607, an absence of nearly two years was held not to have frustrated the contract where there was a chance of a recovery if the employee had a further eye operation.

---

[1] *Marshall v. Harland & Wolff Ltd.* [1972] ICR, per Sir John Donaldson, at p. 105.

In practice, it seems that it will only really be possible to establish that the relationship of employer and employee has ended in cases where it is clear that there is little or no prospect of recovery from a particular illness or injury.

It must, however, be stressed that in this chapter we have only considered the doctrine of frustration and not the question of whether an employer can fairly dismiss an employee on the ground of ill-health or disability; that aspect of the matter will be considered in Chapter 21 (see page 278).

CHAPTER 17

WRONGFUL DISMISSAL

Since the introduction of the then new concept of "unfair dismissal" in 1972, there seems to have been a great deal of confusion about the meanings of "wrongful dismissal" and "unfair dismissal". Indeed, a great number of people seem to think that the phrases cover one and the same thing. This is not strictly the case.

"**Unfair dismissal**" is a special statutory right now enshrined in the Trade Union and Labour Relations Act 1974. It is the right for an employee (with a few exceptions) not to be unfairly dismissed. It depends on the strict wording of the statute and will be considered in detail in Chapters 19 to 23.

"**Wrongful dismissal**" is not governed by statute and arises where a contract of employment is terminated by an employer without giving proper notice to the employee and where the employee has not been guilty of conduct justifying his summary dismissal.

Before we consider what conduct justifies instant dismissal, we must look at the question of termination by proper notice.

Termination by notice

The general principle is that either party to a contract of employment can bring it to an end by giving notice to the other. Once notice is given it cannot be withdrawn unilaterally.

If, of course, the contract is for a fixed period then the employment cannot be lawfully terminated before the end of that period. Any such termination will be a breach of the contract and will give rise to a claim for damages (see page 231).

[226]

The length of the notice required to bring a contract of employment to an end can—and should—be expressly agreed between the parties. A wise employer will always do this. The length of notice is in any event one of the particulars which should be included in the Contracts of Employment Act statement (see page 39). Notice can normally be given on any day of the week—it does not have to be on a Friday.

If no period of notice is specifically agreed, then the law has for many years required that " **reasonable notice** " should be given. This requirement is quite separate from the statutory minimum period of notice now laid down in the Contracts of Employment legislation.

What is " reasonable notice " will depend on many factors, including the seniority of the job itself, the length of service, the rate of pay, the method and frequency (*e.g.* weekly or monthly) of pay and all other circumstances. The responsibility of a particular job and the skill and qualifications of the employee will also be relevant.

The " reasonable notice " provisions at Common Law are applicable equally both to employer and employee. In the absence of agreement to the contrary, therefore, an employee in respect of whom three months' notice would be " reasonable notice " must himself normally give that period of notice to the employer if he wishes to terminate his contract.

It is not proposed to deal with the respective amounts of notice which have over the years been held by the courts to be " reasonable " in certain circumstances and in relation to various categories of jobs.

In the vast majority of cases today the matter is either governed expressly by the terms of the contract or by the statutory minimum periods of notice.

The statutory minimum periods of notice

Until the Contracts of Employment Act 1963 was passed the only legal requirement regarding notice—in the absence of express provision in the contract—was the rule referred to above regarding " reasonable notice ".

The 1963 Act laid down minimum periods of notice based upon the length of service of an employee. These periods have been amended on more than one occasion and the law is now governed by the Contracts of Employment Act 1972, as varied and amended by the Employment Protection Act 1975 (Part II, Schedule 16). The EPA amendments came into force on 1st June 1976 by virtue of Commencement Order No. 4. The law now stated is, therefore, the law in force as from 1st June 1976, *i.e.* the under-mentioned provisions as to notice apply to notice given on or after 1st June 1976.

The statutory rights now arise after an employee has been continuously employed[1] for only four weeks. After that the notice required to be given **by an employer** to terminate a contract of employment—

(*a*) shall be not less than **one week's notice** if his period of continuous employment is more than four weeks but **less than two years;**

(*b*) shall be not less than **one week's notice for each year** of continuous employment if his period of employment is two years or more but less than twelve years; and

(*c*) shall be not less than **twelve weeks'** notice if his period of continuous employment is **twelve years** or more.

The statutory minimum period of **notice from employee** to employer is not linked to his years of service and is still, after four weeks' employment, **only one week.** Employers who have vital and important senior employees working for them may, therefore, consider including in the terms of the employment a longer period of notice to be given by those employees. Whether and to what extent this will be enforceable in practice is another matter (see page 235).

Certain employees are **not entitled** to the provisions of the Contracts of Employment Act relating to notice—these categories are as set out in Chapter 2, page 44, except that the husband/wife exclusion does not apply under this head.

---

[1] See Appendix II, p. 352, *post.*

The parties cannot contract out of the statutory provisions—
" any provision for shorter notice in any contract of employment . . . shall have effect subject to the foregoing " provisions
(CEA, s. 1(3)).

Having said this, there is nothing to prevent an employee
waiving his right to receive notice on a particular occasion as
and when this arises—although it is difficult to imagine circumstances when an employee would wish to do this.

Section 1(3) also provides that the section does not prevent
either party " from accepting a **payment in lieu of notice** ".

It has already been seen (page 214) that where notice to
terminate is given, the contract terminates on the expiration of
such notice.

Finally, section 1(6) of the CEA states that the statutory
provisions do " not effect the right of either party to treat the
contract as terminable without notice by reason of such **conduct**
by the other party as would have enabled him so to treat it
before the passing of " the Act.

What conduct, therefore, justifies summary dismissal?

Conduct justifying summary dismissal

It is extremely difficult to define the sort of conduct on the
part of an employee which will entitle the employer to " sack "
that employee immediately and without notice.   Similar problems arise in relation to a definition of " gross misconduct ",
which becomes of particular relevance in the light of the Code
of Practice (para. 133) and the law of unfair dismissal (see
page 304).

There is no proper single definition by the higher courts.   In
addition, this aspect of the law is constantly changing along
with social and other attitudes.   The new legal principles
relating to " unfair dismissal " seem now to be having their
effect on the general law.

An excellent recent example of the more recent trend is the
Court of Appeal case of *Wilson v. Racher* [1974] ICR 428, where
the employee (a head gardener) was successful in his claim for

wrongful dismissal despite the fact that he lost his temper with his employer and used " obscene and deplorable language " in the presence of the employer's wife and family.

Lord Justice Edmund Davies in that case said—

> " There is no rule of thumb to determine what misconduct on the part of a servant justifies summary termination of his contract "—

and subsequently—

> " Reported decisions provide useful, but only general guides, each case turning upon its own facts. Many of the decisions which are customarily cited in these cases date from the last century and may be wholly out of accord with current social conditions. What would be today regarded as almost an attitude of Czar-serf, which is to be found in some of the older cases where a dismissed employee failed to recover damages would, I venture to think, be decided differently today. We have by now come to realise that a contract of service imposes upon the parties a duty of mutual respect."

In view of the above, it is not proposed to cite a series of different cases, each one depending on its own particular facts. It is, however, apparent that the conduct must relate to a serious matter and must be a breach of one of the main terms of the contract. Theft, dishonesty and other criminal activities in the course of the employment will normally justify instant dismissal. Wilful damage to the employer's property and violence either in relation to the employer or fellow-employees will also normally constitute gross misconduct. Disobedience to lawful and reasonable orders may justify instant dismissal, but this will not always be the case. All the surrounding circumstances must be considered. Bad language is nowadays less likely to be held to be gross misconduct (see *Wilson v. Racher* referred to above).

Single acts of misconduct, unless exceptional (*e.g.* embezzlement), are less likely to give the employer a right to terminate without notice than a whole series of acts and omissions. The consequences of the misconduct (*e.g.* gross negligence involving substantial losses) can be relevant, but are by no means conclusive.

If an employee has been guilty of conduct justifying instant dismissal and this is known to the employer, the employer must decide within a reasonable time whether he wishes to dismiss the employee. If he does not do this within a reasonable time (which will depend on all the circumstances), he may be deemed to have waived his right to terminate the employment.

Remedies for wrongful dismissal

If an employee feels that he has been dismissed without proper notice (which will, of course, include instant dismissal without justification) he will be entitled to claim **damages** for the breach of the terms of his contract.

At Common Law the courts have for many years refused to grant **injunctions** or to order **specific performance** of a contract of employment. To do this, it was once said, would " turn contracts of service into contracts of slavery ".[1]

This principle was recently upheld and applied by the Court of Appeal in *Chappell v. Times Newspapers Ltd.* [1975] ICR 145, where it was held that no ground had been shown for not applying the general rule that the court would not grant an injunction or make an order for specific performance to force an employer or an employee to continue a contract of service once the relationship of mutual confidence had been destroyed.

The basis of this principle is that damages are an adequate remedy.

Despite the above, in recent years an injunction has on one occasion been ordered to restrain an employer from dismissing an employee without proper notice.[2] Doubts have, however, subsequently been cast on this particular decision (which was a majority decision of the Court of Appeal). It has been referred to as a " highly exceptional case " and as being of " unusual, if not unique, character ".[3] The uniqueness of the case was that if the particular contract of employment could be

---

1 *De Francesco v. Barnum* (1890) 43Ch.D. per 165, Foy, L.J.
2 *Hill v. C. A. Parsons & Co. Ltd.* [1972] Ch. 305.
3 Sir John Donaldson in *Sanders v. Ernest A. Neale Ltd.* [1974] ICR 565 (approved by Stephenson, L.J. in *Chappell v. Times Newspapers Ltd.* at p. 176).

" extended " by virtue of the injunction it would then still have been in existence when the unfair dismissal provisions of the Industrial Relations Act 1971 came into force on 28th February 1972. It is suggested, therefore, that for all practical purposes it can be assumed that the employee's only remedy is to sue for damages.

Re-instatement or re-engagement can, of course, arise with the consent of the employer. In addition, the Industrial Tribunals now have wide powers to order re-instatement or re-engagement in a case of unfair dismissal (see page 315).

The employee's loss

The measure of damages is governed by the general legal principles relating to compensation, *i.e.* the employee is entitled to recover his loss arising out of the breach of contract. Normally, this will be limited to the remuneration he would have received had he been given proper notice to terminate his contract.

In calculating the employee's loss, the court will also take into account his loss of any " fringe benefits " for the period in question, *e.g.* contributions to a pension scheme, provision of a car, or free board and lodging, etc. No damages are recoverable for hurt feelings or for the manner of the dismissal or for loss of reputation (except, *e.g.* in the case of an actor).

In the case of *Cox v. Philips Industries Ltd.* [1976] ICR 138, however, damages of £500 were awarded for the vexation, frustration and distress suffered by an employee who had been wrongfully dismissed in 1965 (*i.e.* well prior to the introduction of the unfair dismissal provisions). This case did, of course, turn on its own particular facts, one of which was that the employee, having in 1963 received an attractive offer of a job from a rival company, was persuaded by his employers to stay with them in a better position, with greater responsibility and with future increases in salary; subsequently, his employers removed him without notice to a position of less responsibility, where his duties were vague; he became depressed, anxious, frustrated and ill; and ultimately he was " induced " to sign a letter of resignation. The Court (Lawson, J.) held that there was a dismissal and that the employee, having received the correct amount of notice under his contract, was not entitled to any damages for wrongful dismissal. The learned judge did, however, hold that the employers were in breach of contract by relegating the employee to a position of lesser responsibility. Could damages be awarded for this? The judge held that they could—

" I can see no reason in principle why, if a situation arises which within the contemplation of the parties would have given rise to vexation, distress and general disappointment and frustration, the person who is injured by a contractual breach should not be compensated in damages for that breach. Doing the best I can, because money can never really make up for mental distress and vexation—this is a common problem of course in personal injury cases—I think the right sum to award the plaintiff under that head is the sum of £500 ".

The employee must **mitigate** his loss, *i.e.* in particular, he must try as hard as he can to get another job. If he does not do so, the court will make an appropriate deduction. Sometimes, the employers themselves are able to offer other employment to the employee at a reduced salary. This may be taken into account by the court, although in a recent case the fact that the employee refused an offer of a lower-grade job at about £1,800 per annum when as works manager he had been earning approximately £3,000 per annum was held not to be a failure to mitigate his loss.[1]

Employers should be prepared here to provide evidence to the court as to the availability of suitable jobs in a particular area. If the employee does get another job during the period of his notice, then any wages he earns will be deducted from the compensation to be paid by the employer. The employee must give credit for anything he earned or could have earned during the notice period. The aim of the law here is simply to compensate the employee for what he has lost. It is not intended that he should be better off financially than if his employment had continued.

If the court awards damages it will also make **deductions in** respect of the following matters:—

---

1 *Basnett v. J. & A. Jackson Ltd.* [1976] ICR 63.

(1) any monies received by the employee whilst out of work by way of unemployment benefit.

(2) his normal National Insurance contributions as if the money had in fact been paid as wages.

(3) income tax in respect of loss of wages up to £5,000, the tax being the amount the employee would have had to pay if he had received the money as his normal remuneration. Any amount in excess of £5,000 can be paid without deduction as this is taxable in the hands of the recipient.

There has been much argument about whether **redundancy pay** received by an employee should be deducted in assessing his loss. Despite one decision[1] to the effect that it should be deducted, the better view seems to be that **no deduction** should be made for redundancy pay.[2 and 3] It also now seems clear that **supplementary benefit** received by the employee will **not be deductible**,[3] because there is an element of discretion as to whether or not this benefit will be paid in a particular case.

The above factors should also be taken into account if a **settlement** is being negotiated between an employer and an employee. This will often arise where employers wish to terminate a senior employee's service agreement before it expires. If that is the case and there is a substantial amount of time still unexpired under the agreement, the employer is also entitled to make a proportionate deduction to allow for the " accelerated payment ", *i.e.* the employee will be receiving his salary in one lump sum instead of having it spread over a period of several months (or even years).

In the event of such a settlement being negotiated, the employer should obtain a proper signed receipt from the employee confirming that he has accepted the agreed sum of money " in full and final settlement of all claims that I may have arising out of the termination of my employment ". Such a receipt will then bar the employee from bringing court pro-

---

[1] *Stocks v. Magna Merchants Ltd.* [1973] ICR 530.
[2] *Yorks Engineering v. Burnham* [1974] ICR 77.
[3] *Basnett v. J. & A. Jackson Ltd.* [1976] ICR 63 (a very full review of all relevant cases by Crichton, J.).

ceedings against the employer in respect of his **wrongful** dismissal. It will **not,** however, prevent the employee from lodging a complaint with an Industrial Tribunal and alleging **unfair** dismissal; that problem is considered in Chapter 19 (page 255).

The employer's claim

It is perhaps appropriate here to consider the position where an employee wrongfully terminates his contract of employment.

If an employee does not give the correct amount of notice (either under his contract or under the statutory provisions) to his employer to bring the contract to an end, he is himself in breach of the contract. The principle then is just the same as in a case where an employee has been wrongfully dismissed, *i.e.* the " innocent party " (in this case, the employer) can sue the employee and recover what he has lost. The employer is entitled to damages to compensate him for the loss which flows naturally from the breach or which was reasonably foreseeable as likely to arise from the breach.

So much for the theory. In practice, however, the employer must be able to **prove** his loss; he must be able to show that because one of his employees left without giving proper notice, his business either lost money or did not make as much money as it otherwise would have done. In the vast majority of cases, this will be extremely difficult—probably impossible— to prove. Exceptional cases may arise where the employer will be able to prove a loss, *e.g.* where a temporary replacement has to be taken on at an additional cost.

In addition to the problem of proving a loss, the employer should also take into account his relationship with the continuing employees (and possibly their trade union representatives) and also the fact that in most cases litigation against the employee will be expensive, time-consuming and possibly, in the end, abortive.

For all these reasons, there are very few reported cases dealing with claims by employers against an employee. In practice, employers are advised that there is little to be gained by bringing such proceedings—and, indeed, much to be lost.

As far as **strikes** are concerned it will be remembered that an employee who terminates his employment will only be in breach of his contract if he does not give the correct notice to bring the contract to an end. The notice under the Contracts of Employment Act provisions is only one week and, in many cases, this will not have been increased by the contract itself. If, therefore, an employee—or a group of employees—gives proper notice and then goes on strike, there will not normally be a breach of the contract. This does, however, depend on the form of " strike notice " which is given—the form can vary enormously.

If, of course, the strike or other industrial action is in furtherance of a trade dispute, there will in any event be the restrictions on liability and proceedings contained in the Trade Union and Labour Relations Act 1974 (see page 91).

The employee's claim

Any claim in respect of wrongful dismissal must at present be brought in the ordinary courts—County Court (where the maximum compensation that can at present be awarded is £1,000) or High Court (where there is no limit on the amount that can be awarded).

It is not the purpose of this book to deal with the way in which proceedings are brought and defended in the County Court and High Court.

The only time limit imposed on the employee is that any such proceedings must be brought within six years of the breach of contract.[1] Having said this, if an employee did delay for a substantial period of time, there is no doubt that the matter would not be very kindly received by the judge; in addition, there are provisions in the Court Rules whereby a claim can be " struck out " for want of prosecution.

An employee cannot at present lodge a claim for wrongful dismissal with an Industrial Tribunal. The Industrial Tribunal can, however, be relevant to the wrongful dismissal situation under two heads:—

---

[1] Limitation Act 1939, s. 2(1) (as amended by the Law Reform (Limitation of Actions etc.) Act 1954).

(1) If the employee has not been given a statement of the **required particulars** under the **Contracts of Employment Act 1972,** he can apply to a Tribunal and ask the Tribunal to make an order declaring what those particulars are or should have been. It will be recalled that one of the required particulars is " the length of notice which the employee is . . . entitled to receive to determine his contract of employment ". If, therefore, it is not clear what notice the employee should have received, he can apply to the Tribunal and it will make an order.

The order of the Tribunal will only state what the terms of the contract should have been with regard to notice. The Tribunal cannot in fact award a sum of money to the employee in lieu of such notice. Thus, the employee—armed with an order from the Tribunal that he was entitled to, say, four weeks' notice—then has to commence separate proceedings in the County Court or High Court, unless, of course, the employer then pays up " quietly ".

The Tribunals interpret their limited powers here very strictly. In one case the Tribunal felt that the only order that it could make, as to the required Contracts of Employment Act particulars, was that the employee was entitled to " reasonable notice ".[1] It was then left to the employee to take that issue further before the ordinary courts.

The employee can apply to a Tribunal either during his employment or within three months from the date on which it ceased.

The above restrictions on what a Tribunal can do are obviously unsatisfactory, particularly when in many cases an employer and employee are in any event appearing before a Tribunal which is dealing generally with the termination of the employment. In the light of this, one can only hope that the provisions referred to under the next heading will soon be implemented.

---

[1] *Cuthbertson v. A.M.L. Distributions* [1975] IRLR 228.

(2) **Section 109 of the Employment Protection Act 1975** gives power to the appropriate Minister to make an Order giving Industrial Tribunals power to deal with claims for damages for breach of contract or for other monies due arising out of termination of an employee's employment. This would include a wrongful dismissal claim. It would not include a claim for damages in respect of personal injuries or death.

The above section is **not yet in force.** One reason for this is that the Government has been concerned about the work load of Tribunals, which has increased substantially in recent times.

It would seem that in the first instance an Order might be made giving Tribunals the power to deal with claims for breach of contract where these are associated with an application to a Tribunal in another matter, *e.g.* redundancy or unfair dismissal.

Inter-relationship of Wrongful Dismissal and Unfair Dismissal

Unfair dismissal is considered in detail in Chapters 19 to 23.

The Trade Union and Labour Relations Act 1974 makes no specific reference to an employee's claim for wrongful dismissal. The two matters are separate and distinct. Indeed, in the early days of unfair dismissal cases, it was stated by the National Industrial Relations Court—

" In our judgement, the common law rules and authorities on wrongful dismissal are irrelevant ".[1]

Failure to give the correct amount of notice under the contract (*i.e.* wrongful dismissal) does not necessarily make the dismissal an unfair dismissal—see, for example, *Treganowan v. Robert Knee & Co. Ltd.* [1975] ICR 405, where it was held that the summary dismissal of an employee (due to a personality clash between the employee and her colleagues for which she was to blame) was held to be a fair dismissal, despite the fact that the employee probably did have the basis for a successful

---

[1] Per Sir John Donaldson in *Norton Tool Co. Ltd. v. Tewson* [1972] ICR 504.

action for wrongful dismissal. The lack of notice may, however, be a factor in deciding whether or not the employer acted reasonably (see page 300).

Having said this, and leaving aside the powers of an Industrial Tribunal to order re-instatement or re-engagement, the basic principles as to assessment of compensation are very much the same with regard to both wrongful and unfair dismissal. The aim is to compensate the employee for the loss he has suffered. An employee cannot, therefore, recover two lots of damages for the same loss. The question of compensation for unfair dismissal is considered in Chapter 23.

In practice, since 1972 the majority of claims for compensation for dismissal will, in the first instance at any rate, be brought before the Industrial Tribunal. The procedures are informal, speedy and comparatively cheap. Even where an employee's claim is likely to exceed the statutory maximum (£5,200 compensation award + basic compensation of up to £2,400—see pages 321 to 332), that employee may well decide to have a " trial run " before an Industrial Tribunal, in view of the advantages just referred to. If he does this and is awarded compensation, that compensation will have to be taken into account in any proceedings he brings for wrongful dismissal.

In general, it seems that the only employees who will now take proceedings for wrongful dismissal in the ordinary courts are—

(a) employees who belong to one of the classes excluded from the unfair dismissal provisions (see page 247).

(b) employees whose loss is likely to exceed the statutory maximum (see pages 321 to 332).

It seems, however, that if proceedings before an Industrial Tribunal for unfair dismissal are pending at the same time as High Court proceedings for wrongful dismissal, the Tribunal may decide to " stand over " the unfair dismissal application pending a conclusion of the High Court proceedings (see *Jacobs v. Norsalka Ltd.*—Employment Appeal Tribunal—5.7.76).

CHAPTER 18

REASONS AND REFERENCES

Before considering the detailed provisions relating to unfair dismissal, it is proposed to deal briefly with two matters which invariably arise when an employee is dismissed—

(1) Does the employer have to give a reason for the dismissal?

(2) Should the employer give the employee a reference?

These matters are relevant in claims for both wrongful and unfair dismissal.

THE REASON FOR THE DISMISSAL

At Common Law

The general legal principle—apart from the Employment Protection Act 1975—is that the employer is not bound to give any reason at all for dismissing an employee.

The employer may have to give a certain amount of notice, but he does not have to tell the employee the reason for the dismissal. It may, of course, be wise—and, indeed, fair—for an employer to give the reason, but at Common Law the employer can, so to speak, " sit back " and wait for the employee to sue him. It will then be for the employer to plead in those proceedings the actual reason for the dismissal and to show that it is a sufficient defence to the claim for wrongful dismissal.

One consequence of this rule is that if an employer dismisses an employee in circumstances which would constitute wrongful dismissal and then subsequently finds out something which in fact would have justified the employee's instant dismissal, that will be a defence to the employee's claim. This principle— which is quite contrary to the unfair dismissal rule—(see page 272) was established in *Boston Deep Sea Fishing v. Ansell* (1888)

39 Ch.D. 339, and has been approved on several occasions in more recent years.

The Statutory Position

In **redundancy** matters there is a presumption that a dismissal is due to redundancy unless the employer can show to the contrary (see page 164).

In an **unfair dismissal** claim, the burden is also upon the employer to show both the reason for the dismissal and that it was one of the reasons specified in paragraph 6(2) or 6(1)(*b*) of the 1st Schedule to the Trade Union and Labour Relations Act 1974 (see page 257).

The effect of these provisions has in practice meant that the employer has in recent years felt it both necessary and advisable to inform the employee at the time of the dismissal of the actual reason or reasons for such dismissal.

An employer who does not even tell the employee the reason why he is dismissing him is unlikely to have acted fairly and reasonably. This position is confirmed by the provisions of the Code of Practice—in particular paragraph 133 (see page 304); see also the new Code under the EPA (Appendix IV, page 364, *post*).

The above provisions do not, however, actually state that the employer must give to the employee the reason for his dismissal. This is now changed in most cases by the provisions of the Employment Protection Act 1975.

The right to a written statement of reasons for dismissal

Section 70 of the EPA deals with the present legal position and it came into force on 1st June 1976 by virtue of Commencement Order No. 4.

The section provides that any employee who has been " **continuously employed** " for a period of **26 weeks** ending with the last complete week prior to the date of termination of his employment **can request** from his employer a written statement giving particulars of the **reasons** for his dismissal.

Before the employee can request such a written statement he must have been given notice to terminate his employment **or** his contract must have been terminated without notice **or** a fixed term contract must have expired without being renewed.

If the request is made, the employer must supply the written statement within 14 days from the request.   The request itself does not have to be in writing.   If the employer does not supply the statement of reasons, the employee can apply to an Industrial Tribunal on the ground either that the employer **unreasonably refused** to provide a written statement of reasons **or** that the reasons given were **inadequate or untrue.**

If the Tribunal finds that the complaint is well-founded—

" (*a*) it **may** make a declaration as to what it finds the employer's reasons were for dismissing the employee **and**

(*b*) it **shall** make an award that the employer pay to the employee a sum equal to the amount of two weeks' pay ". (Section 70(4).)

A week's pay is defined in the normal way in Part II of Schedule 4 to the EPA (see Appendix III, page 360, *post*). There is, however, no limit in the amount of the pay.   The compensation under the section will be payable whether or not the dismissal is found by the Tribunal to be an unfair dismissal.   It will be noted that if the Tribunal finds in favour of the employee it is bound to award two weeks' pay.

The Tribunal's power to make a declaration as to the true reasons for the dismissal can be of great value to the employee. It could affect other claims he may have (*e.g.* redundancy; unfair dismissal) and it may also be relevant in relation to his entitlement to unemployment benefit (*e.g.* he may be barred from entitlement if he is dismissed due to misconduct).

The written statement itself will be admissible in any proceedings, *e.g.* in a claim alleging unfair dismissal.

The **time limit** for an application by an employee to the Tribunal is the same as for unfair dismissal—normally three months from the date of termination (see page 311).   There appears to be no limit as to the time within which an employee must make his request to the employer, although in effect, because of the above provisions, this would have to be done no later than 14 days prior to the end of the three month period.

It will be noted from the above that the employee **has to ask** for the statement of reasons. There is no legal obligation on the employer to do anything unless and until he is asked. If the employer is not asked there is no need for him to give the reasons for the dismissal—although the matters referred to above on page 241 should be taken into account.

In view of those matters, it is felt that employers should in practice in every case give to an employee the reasons for his dismissal.

Excluded categories of employees

The following employees **do not have the EPA right** to a written statement of reasons for dismissal:—

(1) Part-time workers, *i.e.* mainly those who work less than 16 hours weekly (but see Appendix II, page 353, for full details). This exclusion arises by virtue of the necessity of having 26 weeks' continuous employment.

(2) employment where the employer is the husband or wife of the employee.

(3) employment as master or crew of a fishing vessel where remuneration is only by a share in the profits or gross earnings of the vessel.

(4) employees who under their contract ordinarily work outside Great Britain. This includes a person employed to work on board a ship registered in the U.K. unless either the employment is wholly outside Great Britain or the employee is not ordinarily resident in Great Britain.

(5) registered dock workers unless wholly or mainly engaged in work which is not dock work as defined by any scheme for the time being in force under the Dock Workers (Regulation of Employment) Act 1946.

REFERENCES

An employer is not under any legal obligation—either at Common Law or by statute—to provide a reference for an employee.

Different employers have different policies with regard to this matter.

The various statutory rights now given to employees have not affected the general principle.

If an employee asks for a reference and this is refused, this may be a factor which a Tribunal will in practice take into account in deciding whether an employer in dismissing an employee acted reasonably (see page 310). Whether strictly, a Tribunal can take this into account under paragraph 6(8) of Schedule 1 to the Trade Union and Labour Relations Act 1974 is doubtful. There is no doubt, however, that if an employer can tell the Tribunal in an unfair dismissal hearing that a reasonable reference has been supplied, this will certainly help the employer's case. At the very least, it will affect the amount of compensation that may be ordered.

Having said this, great care should be taken in the wording of a " general " reference which is then handed to an employee. A reference in " glowing terms " in respect of an employee who has been dismissed for alleged lack of ability will do the employer's case no good at all! It is amazing how often in practice this does happen.

Quite apart from these matters, care should be taken to ensure that the wording of a reference is not misleading or false. If it is false, not only may the employee himself have a right of action in defamation (subject to the employer's possible defence of qualified privilege) but also the new employer may have a right of action against the employer who gave the false reference.[1]

In view of all these problems, employers may begin to shrink from giving references at all. Perhaps, the best course to adopt is for employers **not** to hand to the employee a " blanket "

---

[1] See *Hedley Byrne v. Heller* [1964] A.C. 465.

or " general " reference (*e.g.* headed " To whom it may concern "), but to indicate to the employee that they will be quite
happy to deal with any applications for a reference which may
be sent to them by prospective employers.   In this way, the
employer will have been fair to the employee and, at the same
time, will avoid some of the risks referred to above.

CHAPTER 19

UNFAIR DISMISSAL—
THE RIGHTS OF THE EMPLOYEE

On 28th February 1972 there came into being a new and, from the legal point of view, revolutionary concept—the right of an employee not to be unfairly dismissed.

Until that date the fairness or unfairness of a dismissal was irrelevant. An employer could at any time and without having to have any reason whatsoever bring a contract of employment to an end by giving the correct amount of notice (see Chapter 17) or by paying money in lieu of notice. If this was done, no further enquiry or investigation could be made, even if the reason for the dismissal was completely without logic or foundation. The employee could not recover any compensation or other payment except his entitlement to notice or money in lieu and except (after 1965) his entitlement to redundancy pay if he was dismissed because of redundancy.

All this was changed by the Industrial Relations Act 1971 which came into force on the date referred to above. That Act was, of course, abolished by the Trade Union and Labour Relations Act 1974 (TUALRA), the main part of which came into force on 16th September 1974.

The TUALRA in fact right at the outset (s. 1(2)) re-enacted nearly all the provisions of the Industrial Relations Act 1971 relating to unfair dismissal. It had been found that those provisions had worked reasonably well over the period since 1972. They were, therefore, re-enacted with a few changes (*e.g.* the qualifying period was reduced from 104 weeks to 26 weeks).

The basic law relating to unfair dismissal, is, therefore, now contained in Schedule 1 to the TUALRA. References in the following chapters to numbered paragraphs are to those paragraphs in Schedule 1 to the TUALRA.

Finally, there have been amendments to the unfair dismissal provisions by the Employment Protection Act 1975 (EPA). Those amendments are set out in Part III of Schedule 16 to the EPA and they came into force on 1st June 1976 by virtue of The Employment Protection Act 1975 (Commencement No. 4) Order 1976. Most of the amendments deal with the numbered paragraphs in Schedule 1 to the TUALRA and, for the purposes of the following chapters, it will be assumed that they have been " written into " those paragraphs.

The right not to be unfairly dismissed

In every employment (except certain excluded employments) " every employee shall have the right not to be unfairly dismissed by his employer " (para. 4(1)).

The right is thus stated clearly and concisely. Later provisions deal with what is fair and unfair. First, however, we must consider the employments which are **not protected.**

Although **Crown employees** are not protected by the Redundancy Payments Act 1965 or the Contract of Employment Act 1972 there is a specific provision in paragraph 33 which gives Crown employees the right not to be unfairly dismissed. National Health Service employees, however, are specifically excluded.

Excluded categories of employees

(1) *Persons who are not employees*

Although not strictly an excluded category, it must be remembered that the right not to be unfairly dismissed does not apply to persons who are not employees. An employee is defined as " an individual who has entered into or works under (or, where the employment has ceased, worked under) a contract of employment, otherwise than in police service " (TUALRA, s. 39(1)).

A contract of employment means " a contract of service or of apprenticeship, whether it is express or implied and (if it is express) whether it is oral or in writing " (TUALRA, s. 30(1)).

Thus the self-employed are excluded as are most partners and some company directors. This problem has already been considered in relation to redundancy—see page 158.

(2) *Employees who have not been continuously employed[1] for 26 weeks ending with the effective date of termination*

The " qualifying period " was reduced to 26 weeks with effect from 16th March 1975. Originally, it had been two years and for the period between 16th September 1974 and 16th March 1975 it was 52 weeks.

In practice, all employers should now have internal procedures established under which they **review** the performance of each new employee during his first 26 weeks. If the employer then forms the view that the particular employee is not suitable for the job, he can dismiss him during that period and the employee will not normally have any rights with regard to unfair dismissal. Nor, it will be remembered, will that employee have a right to demand a statement in writing of the reasons for his dismissal (see page 241). The employee will, of course, be entitled to proper notice to terminate the contract (see page 228).

The employer who wishes to avail himself of this situation should not, however, leave the matter until " the last minute ", *e.g.* until the 25th week. In the first instance, an amendment introduced by the EPA has added a new paragraph 5(6) to the 1st Schedule, the effect of which is that where an employee is not given his statutory minimum period of notice (see page 228) he will be deemed to have been dismissed on the date on which such notice would have expired, had it been given. Secondly, it will in any event be possible for the employee to count the whole of his final week of employment as a full week even though he was dismissed during that week.[1] This was confirmed by a recent decision of the Employment Appeal Tribunal which held that an employee could take into account

---

[1] See Appendix II, p. 352, *post*, as to the meaning of " continuous employment ".

the whole of the week in which his employment started and the whole of the week in which his employment was terminated—see *Coulson v. City of London Polytechnic* [1976] ITR 121.

There is one exception to the 26 week qualifying rule and that is where the reason for the dismissal was an " inadmissible reason " (see page 259), *e.g.* because the employee had taken part in trade union activities. In that case all employees have rights as to unfair dismissal regardless of their length of service.

(3) Certain " part-time " employees

Any employment under a contract which normally involves employment for less than 16 hours weekly is excluded from the unfair dismissal provisions.

This is brought about by virtue of the definition of " continuous employment " (see Appendix II, pages 352 to 359).

The legal position with regard to " part-time " employees changed on 1st February 1977 by virtue of the EPA amendments which were made effective on that date. Prior to 1st February 1977 employment for less than 21 hours weekly was excluded.

This matter is dealt with in more detail in Appendix II (page 353). It should, however, be noted here that the following employees are deemed to be " 16 hour " employees:—

    (*a*) employees whose contract of employment normally involves employment for 16 hours or more weekly but who then become governed by a contract normally involving employment for 8 hours or more. (Only 26 weeks of such " reduced " service counts for the purpose of calculating a period of " continuous employment ".)

    (*b*) employees whose contract of employment normally involves employment for 8 hours or more (but less than 16) but who have been continuously employed for a period of 5 years.

It is anticipated that the introduction of these amendments will substantially increase the work-load of Tribunals—one estimate of the additional applications being in the region of 1,400 per annum.

(4) *Where the employer is the husband or wife of the employee*
This exclusion needs no comment.

Originally paragraph 9(1)(*b*) also excluded " close relatives " as defined. The " close relatives " part of the exclusion has, however, been removed by the EPA with effect from 1st June 1976. The exclusion is, therefore, now limited only to situations where the employer is the spouse of the employee. If, of course, the employer is a limited company, an employee will have unfair dismissal rights even though all the shares in the company are owned by the employee's husband.

(5) *Employees who on or before the dismissal date have reached the normal retiring age* for employees in their position or who, if male have attained 65 or, if female have attained the age of 60.

Under this head, the employee can, however, still claim unfair dismissal if the dismissal was for an " inadmissible reason " (see page 259). If the employee can establish that dismissal was due to an inadmissible reason, then he can claim unfair dismissal regardless of his age.

" Normal retiring age " is not the same as " pensionable age ", although they do very often coincide. The Tribunal will look at the practice in the particular employment and assess what is " normal ". Very often " normal retiring age " will be the same as pensionable age; if this is the case employees will not lose their rights regarding unfair dismissal until they reach the age of 65 (men) or 60 (women).[1]

Despite the above provisions, the Employment Appeal Tribunal held in the case of *Barrel Plating and Phosphating Co. Ltd. v. Danks* [1976] ITR 148 that an Industrial Tribunal when

---

[1] See, for example, *Ord v. Maidstone & District Hospital Management Committee* [1974] ICR 369 (where there was held to be no " normal retiring age " at all).

considering the amount of compensation for unfair dismissal to be awarded to a woman employee of 59 could take into account two years' loss of earnings including a period after her 60th birthday, even though had she been dismissed at the age of 60 she would have had no right whatsoever to claim compensation for unfair dismissal.

There is no lower age limit for employees wishing to claim unfair dismissal; they must, of course, have the minimum period of 26 weeks' continuous service.

(6) *An employee who under his contract of employment " ordinarily works outside Great Britain "* has no unfair dismissal rights. (This differs slightly from the redundancy position—see page 161).

The Tribunal will ultimately have to decide whether a person " ordinarily works outside Great Britain ". It will depend on the actual terms of the contract and on the facts in each particular case.

An employee based in this country and who is sent abroad on a short-term contract will probably not lose his rights. On the other hand an air-line employee who for over two years had been based in London but who had been out of the country for just over half of that period was held to be ordinarily working outside Great Britain.[1]

The Employment Appeal Tribunal has also now held that even though an employee may ordinarily work in Great Britain, he may also " ordinarily work outside Great Britain " as well. In the case in question (*Portec (U.K.) Ltd. v. Mogenson* [1976] ICR 396) a managing director with responsibility for European sales had a place of work both in Paris and in Wales; in 1973/74 he worked 83 days inside and 87 days outside Great Britain and in 1974/75 he worked 78 days inside and 132 days outside Great Britain. Although the Industrial Tribunal awarded maximum compensation of £5,200, the Employment Appeal Tribunal reversed the finding and held that the employee when he worked in Paris was " ordinarily working outside Great

---

[1] *Maulik v. Air India* [1974] ICR 528.

Britain " and, therefore, the Tribunal had no jurisdiction to
hear the claim.

This decision could be of great relevance to certain classes
of employee, such as overseas salesmen oil company executives
and " trouble-shooters ".   As Mr. Justice Bristow indicated—
" their pattern of employment may be that their work outside
Great Britain is their ordinary work and any work they do
inside is extraordinary ".[1]

There are special provisions relating to persons employed
to work on a ship registered in the United Kingdom (excluding
Northern Ireland);   they will be regarded as " ordinarily
working " in Great Britain unless their employment is wholly
outside Great Britain or they are not ordinarily resident in
Great Britain.

These special provisions only relate to persons employed to
work on board a ship.   Thus, work on an oil rig was not
covered by those provisions and, as such work is wholly outside Great Britain, employees did not originally have unfair
dismissal rights.   The EPA did, however, give the Secretary of
State power to extend protection to workers on installations
in U.K. territorial waters or to those working on the exploration of the seabed or the exploitation of its natural resources in
designated areas of the Continental Shelf and this power was
exercised with effect from 21st June 1976.

(7) *Registered dock workers* are excluded unless they are wholly
or mainly engaged in work which is not dock work as defined
by any Scheme for the time being in force under the Dock
Workers (Regulation of Employment) Act 1946.

(8) *Fishermen* (both masters and crew members) whose
remuneration is solely from a share in the earnings of a fishing
vessel are not covered by the unfair dismissal provisions.

(9) *Police* are excluded from the definition of " employee "
(see page 247).

The Secretary of State has power to add to or vary the above
excluded classes of employment.   This power can only be

---

1 This decision was approved in *Wilson v. Maynard Shipbuilding Consultants
AB* [1976] IRLR 384, when EAT commented that this part of TUALRA should
possibly be amended.

exercised by statutory instrument after a draft order has been approved by both Houses of Parliament.

Under the original unfair dismissal legislation " small firms " (*i.e.* where there were less than 4 employees who had been continuously employed for at least 13 weeks) were excluded. Thus employees of those firms had no rights with regard to unfair dismissal. This exclusion was, however, removed by the Employment Protection Act 1975 with effect from 1st October 1976. Now, therefore, even if a person is the sole employee of a firm he has the right not to be unfairly dismissed.

Finally, although not strictly " excluded categories " of employees, it is possible that certain other employees will not have the right to claim unfair dismissal because they have been, so to speak, " contracted out " of the Act. These employees will now be considered.

Contracting out

In common with most of the other employment legislation, an employer and an employee cannot normally contract out of the unfair dismissal provisions.

Any provision in an agreement will be **void** in so far as it purports—

(*a*) to exclude or limit the operation of any provision of the TUALRA or

(*b*) to preclude any person from presenting a complaint to or bringing any proceedings before an Industrial Tribunal (para. 32(1)).

The TUALRA does, however, provide certain exceptions to this general rule and in these situations (but no others) it is possible to contract out of the Act:—

(1) **In a fixed term contract** (not being a contract of apprenticeship) for a term **of more than 2 years** entered into **before 28th February 1972** the employee will have no right to claim unfair dismissal where the " dismissal " consists only of that contract expiring and not being renewed. Under section 34(6) of the EPA the unfair dismissal rights on the grounds of an employee's pregnancy are also excluded in such fixed term contracts

provided that the contract was made before 1st June
1976 (*i.e.* the date on which the section 34 rights came
into force).

(2) **A fixed term contract for two years or more** can include
a provision whereby the employee agrees in writing to
exclude any claim he may have for unfair dismissal where
the dismissal consists only of the expiry of that term
without its being renewed.

The provision excluding the employee's rights need
not be in the contract itself, provided that the employee
agrees in writing to such an exclusion clause **before** the
term expires.

It has already been seen (page 160) that if either party
can terminate a contract for a period of years by giving
notice during that period, the contract will not be for
" a fixed term ".

The case of *B.B.C.* v. *Ioannou* [1975] ICR 267 was
also decided (in favour of the employee) on the ground
that the renewal of the employee's contract (which had
originally been for more than 2 years) in 1972 for " a
further year " was not a contract for two years or more,
even though the employee had worked for the B.B.C.
for six years.

Some employers may well wish to consider including
an exclusion clause on the lines referred to above in a
Service Agreement with a director or other senior
employee. Rights to a redundancy payment can similarly be excluded (see page 160). It must, however, be
remembered that the exclusion only relates to the situation where the service agreement **expires** and is not
renewed. It will not cover the position where the
employer dismisses the employee during the term, nor
will it cover cases of constructive dismissal (as to which
see page 229).

(3) **Dismissal procedure agreements** between an employer and
a trade union may exclude the statutory unfair dismissal
rights. This is, however, unlikely to arise very often in
practice. Such an agreement will only be effective for

these purposes if, on the application of all the parties to the agreement, the Secretary of State makes an Order under paragraph 13. The Secretary of State must be satisfied as to various matters set out in paragraph 13(2) including that proper procedures are contained in the agreement giving employees unfair dismissal rights which are at least as beneficial as the statutory rights. In addition there must be a right to arbitration or adjudication by an independent referee or tribunal.

As far as is known, no order relating to a dismissal procedure agreement has yet been made under the above provisions.

(4) **Settlements** of unfair dismissal claims **made via a Conciliation Officer** are valid and binding even though part of the settlement is that the " employee " will refrain from presenting or continuing with an application to the Tribunal.

This exception will be considered at a later stage (see page 335).

In the meantime, however, it should be noted that a settlement made by an employer direct with an employee under which the employer pays a sum of money to the employee and the employee agrees not to take any action in respect of his dismissal, does **not** prevent the employee from taking the matter to a Tribunal. Such a settlement will be caught by paragraph 32(1)(*b*) above and will be classed as an agreement which is void because it precludes the employee from bringing proceedings before an Industrial Tribunal. The moral, therefore,—at least for the employer—is to use the services of the Conciliation Officer (see page 335).

(5) The restriction on contracting out does not apply in the case of a **union membership agreement** (as to which see page 83). Presumably, the intention of the legislation here is to cover the situation where under a union membership agreement an employee is required to become a member of a particular trade union and he refuses to join that union. If that employee is then

dismissed, the dismissal will normally be a fair dismissal (see page 85).

Dismissal

It was noted at the beginning of this chapter that the right of employees (other than those excluded for the reasons referred to above) is the right not to be unfairly dismissed.

It is, therefore, stating the obvious—but it must be done—to say that no rights arise unless there has been a dismissal.

If an employee genuinely resigns or leaves of his own accord, he will not have been dismissed.

The definition of " dismissal " and a consideration of the problems and borderline situations that can arise have been considered in Chapter 16.

CHAPTER 20

UNFAIR DISMISSAL—
WHEN IS A DISMISSAL UNFAIR ?

We have seen in the preceding chapter that most employees have the right not to be unfairly dismissed.

What then is unfair dismissal? And who has to prove the unfairness—the employer or the employee?

Burden of Proof

At the outset, as we have seen, there must be a **dismissal**. Although this is not stated specifically in the TUALRA it is in fact for the **employee to prove** that he has been dismissed. If he cannot do so, he will not have any claim at all. What is and what is not dismissal has been considered in Chapter 16.

One practical result of this principle is that if, when the matter reaches a Tribunal, the dismissal is not admitted, the employee will be called upon to present his case first to the Tribunal. If, however, the dismissal itself is not in dispute, the employer will have to put his case first.

Once dismissal is established or admitted, the burden of proof is placed clearly and firmly on the employer. Stated very shortly, the employer must show that the dismissal was not unfair. If he cannot do this, the Tribunal will find in favour of the employee.

How can the employer show that a dismissal was not unfair?

In most cases, the employer has to get over three hurdles—
(1) he has to show what was **the reason** (or, if there was more than one, the principal reason) for the dismissal;
(2) he has to show that the reason was one of five **specified** reasons (see *below*); and

[257]

L

(3) he has to satisfy the Tribunal that in the circumstances (having regard to equity and the substantial merits of the case) he **acted reasonably** in treating the reason as a sufficient reason for dismissing the employee.

The **specified reasons** laid down in the TUALRA (Sched. 1, paras. 6(1)(*b*) and 6(2)) are as follows, viz. the reason was one which—

(*a*) related to the **capability** or qualifications of the employee for performing work of the kind which he was employed by the employer to do, or

(*b*) related to the **conduct** of the employee, or

(*c*) was that the employee was **redundant** or

(*d*) was that the employee could not continue to work in the position which he held without **contravention** (either on his part or on that of his employer) **of a duty or restriction** imposed by or under an enactment, or

(*e*) was some **other substantial reason** of a kind such as to justify the dismissal of an employee holding the position which that employee held.

Only these five reasons are " acceptable " as far as the law is concerned. If the reason for the dismissal is not shown by the employer to be one of those reasons, then the employee is bound to be successful in his claim.

Even then, it must be remembered, the employer has, in most cases, to get over the third hurdle, *i.e.* he has to satisfy the Tribunal that he acted reasonably.

The specified reasons will be dealt with in detail in Chapter 21 and the question of reasonableness in Chapter 22.

In the meantime, it will have been noted that reference is made above to the employer having to get over three hurdles " in most cases ". The reason for this is that the TUALRA lays down certain special rules with regard to particular situations where a dismissal may, because of those rules, be **automatically** fair or unfair. In those cases not all of the three " hurdles " referred to above may be relevant. In particular,

in these special situations, the employer will **not** have to show that he acted reasonably.

Automatic Unfair Dismissal

To a certain extent the word " automatic " in this context is a misnomer because certain matters will still have to be proved by the employee. Once, however, those matters are proved, the Tribunal will not go on to consider whether the employer acted reasonably—it will automatically find in favour of the employee. This will arise in the following four situations:—

(1) If the employer **fails** completely to **establish one of the specified reasons** (see *above*).

(2) If the employee is **selected for redundancy in contravention of a customary arrangement or agreed procedure** and there were no special reasons justifying a departure from that arrangement or procedure (this will be considered in detail in Chapter 21—see page 292).

(3) If the employee is **selected for redundancy** and the reason for the selection was an **" inadmissible reason "**, *e.g.* because of his trade union involvement (see *below*) (this aspect of selection for redundancy will also be dealt with in Chapter 21).

(4) If the employee is **dismissed** for an **" inadmissible reason "**.

Inadmissible reasons—the statutory definition

So that the position may be absolutely clear with regard to the inadmissible reasons, it is proposed to set out in full the provisions of paragraphs 6(4) to 6(6) inclusive of Schedule 1 to the TUALRA. The importance of this is increased by the fact that these paragraphs have now been amended in certain vital respects by both the Employment Protection Act 1975 (paras. 11 and 12 of Part III of Schedule 16) and by the Trade Union and Labour Relations (Amendment) Act 1976 (sections 1(*e*) and 3(5)).

The relevant sub-paragraphs of paragraph 6 (including all amendments) now read as follows:—

" (4) For the purposes of this Schedule the dismissal of an employee shall be regarded as having been **unfair** if the reason for it (or, if more than one, the principal reason) was that the employee—

(a) was, or proposed to become, a member of an independent trade union;

(b) had taken, or proposed to take, part at any appropriate time in the activities of an independent trade union; or

(c) had refused, or proposed to refuse, to become or remain a member of a trade union which was not an independent trade union.

(4A) In sub-paragraph (4) above ' appropriate time ' in relation to an employee taking part in the activities of a trade union, means time which either—

(a) is outside his working hours or

(b) is a time within his working hours at which, in accordance with arrangements agreed with or consent given by his employer, it is permissible for him to take part in those activities;

and in this sub-paragraph ' working hours ' in relation to an employee, means any time when, in accordance with his contract of employment, he is required to be at work.

(5) Dismissal of an employee by an employer shall be regarded as **fair** for the purposes of this Schedule if—

(a) it is the practice, in accordance with a union membership agreement, for employees for the time being of the same class as the dismissed employee to belong to a specified independent trade union, or to one of a number of specified independent trade unions; and

(b) the reason for the dismissal was that the employee was not a member of the specified union or one of the specified unions, or had refused or proposed to refuse to become or remain a member of that union or one of those unions

unless the employee genuinely objects on grounds of religious belief to being a member of any trade union whatsoever in which case the dismissal shall be regarded as unfair.

(5A) For the purposes of sub-paragraph (5) above a union shall be treated as specified for the purposes of or in relation to a union membership agreement (in a case where it would not otherwise be so treated) if—

(a) the Service has made a recommendation for recognition covering the employee in question which is operative within the meaning of section 15 of the Employment Protection Act 1975; or

(b) the union has referred a recognition issue (within the meaning of that Act) covering that employee to the Advisory, Conciliation and Arbitration Service under section 11 of that Act and the Service has not declined to proceed on the reference under section 12 of that Act, the union has not withdrawn the reference, or from the reference, and the issue has not been settled or reported on under that section.

(6) any reason by virtue of which a dismissal is to be regarded as unfair in consequence of sub-paragraph (4) or (5) above is hereafter in this Schedule referred to as an **inadmissible reason.**"

Inadmissible reasons in practice

If an employee is dismissed and he feels that the dismissal is due to an inadmissible reason, the burden of proof will be on the employee to show that that was in fact the reason for the dismissal. In practice, this has proved to be very difficult for the employee to do. Very few employees have so far been successful in establishing such a claim. There seem to be various problems for the employee under this head, some of which are as follows:—

(a) It is often possible for the employer to show another reason for the dismissal, e.g. misconduct or lack of capability. If there is more than one reason, the Tribunal will look at what was the **principal reason.** Thus, an employee who is dismissed for misconduct but who also happens to be a " troublemaker " will not succeed in a claim alleging dismissal for his involvement in union activities if the employer can show that the principal reason for the dismissal was the employee's general misconduct.

(b) trade union " **activities** " seem to be strictly and narrowly interpreted by the Tribunals. Such " activities " are not defined in the TUALRA. Tribunals have held in particular cases that pressing for worker participation was not taking part in union activities, nor was unofficial action over a wages claim, nor was taking action to get an employee moved to another department.

(c) the definition of " **appropriate time** " which was introduced as paragraph 6(4A) by the EPA on 1st January 1976 is still quite a narrow definition. It is limited to activities in an employee's own time, unless the employer agrees to such activities taking place during working hours. Thus, an employee who is dismissed for organising an unofficial union meeting on works premises during working hours without the consent of his employer will not have been dismissed for an " inadmissible reason ".

(d) In the original paragraph 6(5) of Schedule 1 an employee could object to being a member of a trade union " on any reasonable grounds ". Those words were deleted by the TUALRA (Amendment) Act 1976 which came into force on 25th March 1976. Now if an employee is covered by a union membership agreement he can only refuse to join the union if he " **genuinely objects on grounds of religious belief** to being a member of any trade union whatsoever ".

(e) the detailed provisions of the legislation relating to the closed shop principle in general and a union membership agreement in particular have been considered in Chapter 5 (see page 83, *ante*). It is apparent that the definition of a union membership agreement will be strictly interpreted—see, for example, the case of " the Ferrybridge Six " referred to on page 85.

Interim Relief for Employees

The Employment Protection Act 1975 introduced some further provisions to " bolster up " the rights of an employee dismissed for trade union involvement. These rights were introduced into the Bill at a comparatively late stage of its passage through Parliament.

The relevant provisions are contained in sections 78 to 80 and they came into force on 1st June 1976. The aim is to enable employees to get a speedy hearing by the Tribunal which can then order re-employment or suspension on full pay until the case is heard in detail.

In order to obtain the benefit of these provisions the employee must be able to comply with or satisfy the following conditions:—

(1) the employee must have been dismissed or have received notice to terminate his employment.

(2) the employee must have presented a complaint to an Industrial Tribunal claiming unfair dismissal.

(3) the claim to the Tribunal must be on the ground that the reason (or principal reason) for the dismissal was that the employee—

    (a) was, or proposed to become, a member of a particular trade union, or

    (b) had taken, or proposed to take, part at any appropriate time in the activities of a particular trade union of which he was or proposed to become a member.

(4) the employee must then apply to the Tribunal for an order for interim relief within seven days from the effective date of termination of his employment. Presumably, in view of the very tight time limit imposed, this application can in practice be made at the same time as the main complaint is lodged.

(5) within the same seven day period there must also be presented to the Tribunal a certificate in writing signed by an authorised union official stating that on the date of dismissal—

    (a) the employee was or had proposed to become a member of the union **and**

    (b) there appear to be reasonable grounds for supposing that the reason for the dismissal was as alleged in the complaint

    (i.e. one of the reasons in (3) above).[1]

A document purporting to be a certificate signed by an authorised union official will be taken to be such a certificate unless the contrary is proved.

It will be seen from the above that not only must an employee move very quickly indeed, but also he will only be able to

---

[1] For a very full consideration of the conditions relating to Interim Relief, see *Farmeary v. Veterinary Drug Co. Ltd.* [1976] IRLR 322.

apply for interim relief if he can get the appropriate certificate from his trade union.

The Tribunal itself, on receipt of such an application, is bound to deal with the matter as quickly as possible.   Adjournments can only be granted where there are " special circumstances ".   Nevertheless, the employer has to be notified of the date and place of the hearing of the matter and has to be given a copy of the application at least seven days before the date of the hearing.

At the hearing itself (which can be before only one Tribunal member) and subsequently the Tribunal will in effect deal with the matter in four stages—

Stage 1.   The Tribunal will hear the application and any reply by the employer and will then have to decide whether it is **likely** that, after the full hearing of the unfair dismissal application itself, it will find both that the employee was unfairly dismissed **and** that the reason (or principal reason) for the dismissal was a " union reason " (as specified in paragraph (3) on page 263).

In other words, the employee will have to establish that he has a *prima facie* case.   If he cannot do so, that will be an end of the interim application.   The main application alleging unfair dismissal will, of course, proceed in the usual way and there will subsequently be a full hearing.   The employee may still succeed at the full hearing, even though he fails in his application for interim relief.

Stage 2.   If the Tribunal finds that the employee has established a *prima facie* case as referred to above, it will announce its findings and then explain to both parties (only, it seems, if they are present) what are the powers of the Tribunal with regard to interim relief.   Having done this, the Tribunal must then ask the employer (again, only if he is present) whether he is willing, pending the determination or settlement of the complaint, either—

(*a*) to re-instate the employee, *i.e.* treat the employee in all respects as if he had not been dismissed; or

(*b*) if not, to re-engage him in another job on terms and conditions not less favourable than those which would have been applicable to him if he had not been dismissed.

If the employer states that he is willing to **re-instate** the employee, the Tribunal will make an order to that effect. Again, this is only an interim order, *i.e.* it will come to an end when the full hearing takes place and a final decision is made.

If the employer is only prepared to **re-engage** the employee in another job, he must specify the terms and conditions. As seen above, they must be " not less favourable "—in particular, this means that, as regards seniority, pension rights and other similar rights, the periods of employment both prior to and after the dismissal shall be regarded as continuous.

If the employee accepts the new job on those terms and conditions, the Tribunal will make an order accordingly.

If the employee does not wish to accept the job on those terms and conditions, the Tribunal must decide whether or not the employee's refusal is reasonable. If it finds that the refusal is not reasonable, then no order will be made in favour of the employee. If the Tribunal finds that the employee's refusal is reasonable, it will make an order for the continuation of his contract of employment (see *below*).

Finally, at this stage, the Tribunal will make an **order for continuation** of the employee's contract of employment if the employer fails to attend the hearing before the Tribunal or if he states that he is unwilling either to re-instate or re-engage the employee as indicated above.

Stage 3. An Order for the continuation of a contract of employment when made by the Tribunal will—

(a) order that the contract of employment (whether terminated or not at that stage) shall continue in force until the determination or settlement of the employee's claim alleging unfair dismissal and

(b) specify the amount which is to be paid to the employee by way of pay for each normal pay period falling between the dismissal date and the final determination of the employee's claim.

The amount of pay under this head is not limited either in amount or by the definition of a week's pay (referred to elsewhere—in particular Appendix III). Pay here will be the full remuneration which that employee could have been expected to earn.

Any payment made by the employer to the employee under his contract or by way of damages for breach of contract can be set against the employer's liability referred to above and *vice versa*. Similarly, any lump sum paid to the employee in lieu of wages will be taken into account.

The continuation order will preserve for the employee his seniority, pension rights and other similar matters. It will also give him continuity of employment. The EPA does **not** provide that the employee has to work during the term of a continuation order.

Stage 4. Once an interim order has been made by the Tribunal either the employer or the employee can —at any time prior to final determination of the employee's claim—apply again to the Tribunal and ask for the order to be **revoked or varied** on the ground of " a relevant change of circumstances since the making of the order ".

Very little light has to date been thrown on what will be a " relevant change of circumstances ". Presumably, however, an employer's insolvency or financial problems giving rise to a pressing need to make employees redundant would be " relevant ".

If the employer does not comply with the terms of an interim order, the employee can go back to the Tribunal who will make one of the following orders:—

(a) If the employer has not complied with a reinstatement order, the Tribunal will make an order for the continuation of the employee's contract of employment (as under Stage 3 *above*) **and** will also order the employer to pay such compensation as the Tribunal considers just and equitable having regard to the infringement of the employee's rights under the interim order and to any loss suffered by the employee because of the non-compliance.

(b) If the employer has not complied with a continuation order under Stage 3, then if the non-compliance consists of a failure to pay remuneration, the Tribunal will determine the amount owing and make an order accordingly; if the non-compliance relates to matters other than pay, the Tribunal will award such compensation as it considers just and equitable having regard to any loss suffered by the employee because of the non-compliance.

Dismissal which is Automatically Fair

Earlier in this chapter consideration was given to certain special situations where a dismissal will be automatically unfair without any reference being made to the " reasonableness " of the dismissal.

Conversely, the law provides for certain situations where a dismissal will automatically be **fair.** These are as follows:—

(1) Dismissal of an employee for refusing to join a specified trade union where there is a practice in accordance with a union membership agreement for similar employees to belong to a specified trade union (see paragraph 6(5) of Schedule 1 set out in full on page 260). This is the **closed shop dismissal.** The TUALRA provides in paragraph 6(5) that such a dismissal " shall be regarded as fair ".

The terms of the paragraph must, however, be examined carefully. Thus, for example—

(a) it is not sufficient for there simply to be a union membership agreement; it must in addition be **the practice,** in accordance with such an agreement, for employees of the same class as the dismissed employee to belong to the union. This, it will be recalled, was where the employers failed in the " Ferrybridge Six " case—the union membership agreement in that case was not being applied in practice and there were various employees who were not union members.[1]

(b) the definition of a **" specified independent trade union "** has now been widened by paragraph 6(5A) and it includes a Union which has applied to ACAS for recognition (see Chapter 5, page 68, *ante*). Thus, the employer may be wrong in **only** considering a union which is a party to the union membership agreement.

(c) if the employee can establish that he has a genuine religious objection to joining any trade union at all, the dismissal will still be unfair. Decisions as to what is a " genuine religious objection " are awaited with interest.

---

[1] *Sarvent & Others v. Central Electricity Generating Board* [1976] IRLR 66.

(2) Certain **strike dismissals** are automatically fair. The provisions relating to this are now contained in paragraph 7 of Schedule 1 (this being a new paragraph introduced by the EPA with effect from 1st June 1976).

The effect of paragraph 7(2) is that if an employee is dismissed whilst he is taking part in a strike or other industrial action the Tribunal cannot even begin to determine whether the dismissal was fair or unfair unless the dismissed employee can show **either** that one or more other employees who took part in the strike or other action have not been dismissed **or** that one or more such employees have been offered re-engagement and that the employee concerned has not been offered re-engagement.

In other words, if **all** employees who take part in a strike or other industrial action are dismissed (or not re-engaged) those dismissals will automatically be **fair** dismissals.

One recent example of a " borderline " situation is the case of *Thompson & Others v. Eaton Ltd.* [1976] ICR 336 where the employees, who disagreed with the installation methods for certain new machines proposed by their employers, stood around the machines so as to prevent their employers from testing them. The dismissal was held to be fair (despite the fact that management had been " obtuse " and had handled the situation badly) because the principal reason for the dismissal was that the employees were taking part in industrial action and all employees had been dismissed.

On the other hand the dismissal in *Stock v. Frank Jones (Tipton) Ltd.* [1976] ITR 63 was held to be unfair because prior to the dismissal of the employee (whilst on strike) two other employees who had also been on strike returned to work for the employers; the dismissal was unfair because the other employees had been on strike but had not been dismissed.

The position where only certain individuals who have been on strike are selected for dismissal or not re-engaged is dealt with in the normal way, *i.e.* the employer must show one of the five specified reasons and must act reasonably.

(3) Dismissals **during a lock-out** are dealt with in exactly the same way as strike dismissals, *i.e.* a dismissal will automatically be fair unless the employee can show that other employees who were " locked out " have not been dismissed or have been re-engaged.

Here again, therefore, if **all** are dismissed, the dismissals will be fair.

If during a lock-out not all the employees are selected for dismissal or re-engaged, that may be an unfair dismissal—the normal test (see *above*) will apply.

(4) If a dismissal takes place for the purpose of safeguarding **national security,** it will automatically be a fair dismissal. The Tribunal must dismiss the complaint (para. 18(1)).

A Certificate signed by or on behalf of a Minister of the Crown certifying that action specified in the Certificate was taken for the purpose of safeguarding national security will be conclusive evidence of that fact.

CHAPTER 21

UNFAIR DISMISSAL—
THE REASON FOR THE DISMISSAL

At the beginning of the previous chapter, it was stressed that once a dismissal has been established, it is for the employer to show that the dismissal was due to one of five specified reasons (see page 258) and that the employer had acted reasonably.

Only proof of one of the five specified reasons will suffice to enable the employer to get over that hurdle. If the employer is unable to satisfy the Tribunal on this point, the Tribunal will find in favour of the employee. It will not need to go on and decide whether the employer acted reasonably.

What then are the specified reasons ?

Stated very shortly they are—

1. Capability or qualifications.
2. Conduct.
3. Redundancy.
4. Breach of statutory duty or restriction.
5. Some other substantial reason.

Each of these reasons must now be examined in rather more detail.

Before doing this, however, a reference should be made to the various decisions that have been made in recent years by Industrial Tribunals and the higher courts. There are now several thousand Tribunal decisions. Each case depends on its own particular facts and circumstances and all references to decided cases must be treated in this light. In this sphere of the law it is not possible to generalise about particular circumstances. For example, there may be one case where dismissal because of an absence for two months due to ill health was held to be a fair dismissal and another case where dismissal due to an absence of over two years gave rise to a finding of unfair dismissal.   Any comments made in this and the following chapter should, therefore, be read with the above caveat in mind.   In the main, case references relating to unfair dismissal matters are only to cases which involved matters of principle and which, therefore, normally reached the higher courts.

em
writ

It is
must b
other wo
the Tribu
the employ
whether the
with reference
the moment of d

This principle
where after a dismissal the employer ~~must o..~ ~~...~~ (*e.g.* embezzlement or other dishonesty) which would have justified an instant dismissal of the employee had the employer been in possession of those facts at the time.   Thus, in *Devis & Sons Ltd. v. Atkins* [1976] ICLR 428, the High Court (on appeal from an Industrial Tribunal) refused to allow evidence relating to the employee's conduct (taking " secret commissions " for himself) which had only come to the employers' knowledge after the dismissal.   The dismissal was found to be unfair.[2]   It

---

[1] Per Sir John Donaldson in *Earl v. Slater & Wheeler (Airlyne) Ltd.* [1972] ICR at p. 514

[2] Decision upheld by the Court of Appeal on 1/11/76, but leave to appeal to House of Lords granted on 10/12/76.

was also held that in view of the wording of the TUALRA provisions, the common law principle (see page 240) under which misconduct discovered after the dismissal can be a defence to an action for wrongful dismissal, could not be applied to a complaint of unfair dismissal.

Evidence acquired after a dismissal can, however, affect the amount of **compensation** that may be ordered and may even be relevant after the Tribunal decision itself (see page 346). Evidence may also be introduced to prove the accuracy or otherwise of evidence given in relation to matters prior to the dismissal, e.g. where an employee was dismissed for being drunk on duty, evidence of later drunkenness may be admissible in order to establish the accuracy of the evidence as to the earlier drunkenness.

A good example of this last point is the recent case of *Da Costa v. Optolis* [1976] IRLR 178 where the employee was dismissed for not keeping the firm's books properly; as a result of subsequent investigations he was charged with various criminal offences relating to the irregularities which had been revealed; he was acquitted of the criminal charges, and claimed unfair dismissal. The Appeal Tribunal (confirming that the dismissal was fair) said that the subsequently acquired evidence was admissible because the irregularities of which the employers were ignorant at the time of dismissal were similar in character to other irregularities which formed the basis on which the decision to dismiss was reached.

In the Court of Appeal case of *Abernethy v. Mott, Hay & Anderson* [1974] ICR 323 a distinction was drawn between the above principle (relating to the introduction of later acquired evidence) and the position where employers simply attached the wrong " legal label " to a particular set of facts. Thus, although the employers were wrong in law in telling the employee that his dismissal was due to redundancy, the wrong legal label did not matter so long as there was a set of facts (in that case refusal to work away from head office) which the tribunal could find was the principal reason for the dismissal.

We must now consider the five specified reasons. In doing so, it must be remembered that at this stage we are only dealing with the first two hurdles, *i.e.* establishing the reason for the dismissal and that it was one of the five specified reasons. There is still the other major hurdle of reasonableness (see Chapter 22). Very often an employer will have no problem in establishing the reason itself, but the dismissal will still be held to be unfair because the employer did not act reasonably. This must be borne in mind throughout the remainder of this chapter.

1. CAPABILITY OR QUALIFICATIONS

Definitions

The reference to this first specified reason is in paragraph 6(2)(*a*) of the First Schedule—" a reason which . . . related to the capability or qualifications of the employee for performing work of the kind which he was employed by the employer to do ".

By virtue of paragraph 6(9) of the Schedule—" **capability** " means capability assessed by reference to **skill, aptitude, health** or any **other physical or mental quality;**

" **qualifications** " means any degree, diploma or other academic, technical or professional qualification relevant to the position which the employee held.

The above definitions need no further comment. Their practical implications should, however, be considered.

The employee " on trial " or " on probation "

What is the position where right at the outset of the employment an employee is taken on specifically " on probation " or " on trial " for a limited period?

This in itself will not avoid the unfair dismissal provisions. Employers of certain staff may, however, like to consider the desirability of using such a procedure. If this is done, it will be much easier for the employer subsequently to satisfy the burden of proof imposed upon him—particularly the burden of showing under paragraph 6(8) that he acted reasonably. Employees do not in any event acquire their unfair dismissal rights until they have been employed for 26 weeks. In some jobs, however, this may not be a sufficient period to assess an employee's ability. In certain cases, therefore, employers may be able to justify a probationary period of longer than six months. Thus, in *Blackman v. Post Office* [1974] ICR 151 failure to pass an aptitude test was held to be a reason for dismissal relating to capability where the employee had been recruited in 1968 " on trial " with a view to subsequently gaining a permanent position by passing the aptitude test; the employee had failed the test three times and was dismissed in 1973; the dismissal was held not to be unfair.

As already indicated, the use of a probationary period from the employer's point of view will mainly be of value when the test of reasonableness is applied by the Tribunal. A probationary employee knows that he is on trial and that he must establish his suitability for the post. At the same time, the employer on his side must give the employee a proper opportunity to prove himself.[1]

(a) Skill or aptitude

The first part of the definition of capability refers to skill and aptitude. In other words—

" Is the employee in question doing his job properly? "

The skill and aptitude is, by paragraph 6(2)(*a*), only linked to " work of the kind which he was employed . . . to do ".

Some cases may arise where an employee is guilty of gross negligence which may involve the employer in serious financial loss or damage. In that event, the employer will on occasions be entitled to dismiss the employee summarily.

In the main, however, lack of skill will not have such serious consequences. In the normal case, the employer must, first of all, be able to prove the lack of skill and, secondly, he must be able to show that the employee was told of his shortcomings, given a chance to improve and, ultimately, warned that if he did not improve within a reasonable time he would be dismissed. A formal warning may not, however, always be necessary in the case of senior staff (see page 305).

---

[1] See, for example, *Hamblin v. London Borough of Ealing* [1975] IRLR 354.

One principle which is common to a great number of the reported decisions is that the longer an employee has been with a firm the more difficult it will be for the employer to say at a later date that the employee was not doing his job properly.

Employers who **take-over** a company and its employees and who wish to make the company more efficient (which often entails changing old-established methods of working) must be particularly careful that the existing employees are given a chance to adjust. Employers may have to provide facilities for the re-training of those employees whose jobs change drastically.

It seems that annual " **job appraisals** " if properly operated, can be very relevant here, both as a discipline and as a means of enabling the employer to review on a regular basis an employee's performance. If over a period of time it is made clear to the employee that his performance is not satisfactory, then it is more likely that the employer will be able to show that a subsequent dismissal was a fair dismissal.

Wage reviews will also fit into this pattern. The time of a wage review is the time when the employer should take stock of how efficiently each employee is doing his job. Quite often, it seems, an employer dismisses a man because his work is not satisfactory and is then faced—very often at the Tribunal itself—with the fact that only a short time prior to the dismissal that same employee was given a substantial wage increase. Sometimes, the wage increase is accompanied by a letter congratulating and thanking the employee for all his good work during the preceding year. Needless, to say, this sort of thing can be fatal to the employer's case if the matter reaches a Tribunal.

Similarly, **references** should not be made too " glowing " in the case of an employee dismissed for lack of skill or aptitude (see page 244 as to references).

The **actual proof** of the lack of ability can be difficult.

In addition to the matters referred to above, **job specifications** may be useful to employers; it should be possible to show by reference to a " job spec." whether the employee has done all that was asked of him. Evidence from persons outside the business will have great weight attached to it by the Tribunal, *e.g.* if a customer of the business is prepared to say that a particular employee was inefficient.

If an employee is **promoted** to another job and it does not " work out ", employers must give that employee every possible help, in terms of assistance, re-training and allowing that employee to achieve a satisfactory level of performance. If, after all this, it becomes apparent that the employee is just not fitted for the new job, the employee should be given a chance to go back to his old job or to another suitable job within the organisation.

Similarly, if new techniques or systems are introduced into a business the employees must be given every chance to adjust to the new techniques, including, where necessary, opportunities for re-training.

(*b*) Qualifications

" Qualifications " are widely defined (see page 274).

There have, however, been very few cases where an employee has been dismissed for lack of qualifications.

One of the few reported cases (*Blackman v. Post Office* [1974] ICR 151) has been referred to on page 275.

If an employer wishes an employee to have particular qualifications and is really only interested in employing that person on a permanent basis if he has those qualifications, he should make this clear at the outset. The employer should then take on the particular employee, as it were, " on probation ", until he has acquired the necessary qualifications. If the employee does not acquire the qualifications within the specified period, then his dismissal will normally not be unfair (as in the Blackman case).

If **during** the employment the employer decides that an employee should have a particular qualification, this is much more difficult. Unless the employer can show that such qualification is absolutely necessary and that only with such qualification can the employee do his original job properly, then it is likely that any dismissal for failing to acquire such qualification will be unfair.

It will be remembered that the qualifications must, under the paragraph 6(2)(*a*) definition, relate to " work of the kind which " the employee was employed to do.

It has been held that " trustworthiness " does not fall within the meaning of " qualifications "—see *Singh v. London Country Bus Services Ltd.* [1976] IRLR 176—although it may be classed as " conduct ".

(*c*) Health and sickness

The definition of " capability " in paragraph 6(9)(*a*) also refers to " **health or any other physical or mental quality** ".

In practice, there are probably more problems and queries raised by employers under this head than any other.

The question is asked—" My works foreman has been off sick for two months; we cannot do without him any longer; can I dismiss him? "

Again, a simple question to which it is difficult to give a simple and straightforward reply. Another common problem is where the employee is not absent for any one long period, but has a whole series of short absences.

It has already been seen (pages 223 to 225) that certain prolonged absences due to incapacity or serious illness may be such that the contract of employment automatically comes to an end, *i.e.* it is " frustrated " in the legal sense. This will not give rise to a dismissal at all. In practice, however, this will be very difficult to establish.

It is impossible under this head to generalise. If there is any general rule, it is that employers should act fairly in every sense of the word and should not be too hasty in dismissing an employee because of his absence due to ill health. Again, the longer an employee has worked for his employer, the fairer that employer must be.

In most cases, it will not be too difficult to establish ill-health or sickness as the actual reason for dismissal; the main problems will arise in showing that the employer acted reasonably (see Chapter 22).

The **Code of Practice** is relevant, stating in **paragraph 40** that—

" as far as is consistent with operational efficiency and the success of the undertaking management should . . . provide stable employment, including reasonable job security for employees absent through sickness or other causes beyond their control."

Paragraph 41 also recommends the provision of **sick pay schemes.**

There is no doubt that the **terms of the actual contract** of employment are relevant. If the contract provides for payment of wages (either in full or in part) for a specified period whilst an employee is away from work due to sickness, it will normally be unfair to dismiss that employee during such period. On the other hand, if the contract makes it clear that after absence for a specified period of time the employer reserves the right to dismiss the employee, it will be much easier, after that period has elapsed, for the employer to show that the dismissal was fair. It is, therefore, suggested that these factors should be borne in mind by employers when preparing contracts of employment or the required statement under the Contracts of Employment Act 1972. It will be remembered that any terms and conditions relating to incapacity for work due to sickness or injury must be included in the required CEA particulars (see page 38).

It does seem that in practice Tribunals tend to take into account the various tests laid down in the case of *Marshall v. Harland & Wolff Ltd.* [1972] ICR 101, when they are deciding whether a " sickness dismissal " is unfair. That case was considered in Chapter 16 (see page 223). More recently, however, in *Tan v. Berry Bros. & Rudd* [1974] ICR 586 the NIRC pointed out that the *Marshall v. Harland & Wolff Ltd.* principles **only** related to the discharge of a contract by frustration and not to termination by notice.

Certainly, the impossibility of future performance of the contract (which was the main factor in the *Marshall* case) will

not be conclusive in the normal dismissal due to illness situation. It does, however, seem that the five principles referred
to in that case (see page 224, *above*) will be very relevant
indeed.

Thus, the Tribunal will take into account a whole miscellany
of **factors** including—the terms of the contract; the length of
service of the employee; the type of illness and the prospects
of recovery; whether the employee holds a vital and key
position; and, of course, the interests of the business itself.

An employer faced with an absence due to sickness or injury
should himself take all those factors into account. He should
investigate the matter thoroughly and then get in touch with
the employee. The employee should, at this stage, in effect
be given a **warning**. Obviously, this is not a warning in the
sense of a warning for misconduct. The employee should,
however, be given an opportunity to show that he is—or
expects to be—fit for work by a particular date. If the employer can no longer do without that particular employee, he
should " warn " the employee that unless he can return to
work by a given date, there will be no alternative but to dismiss
him.

Medical evidence will be a relevant factor. It will, however,
only be relevant as at the date of dismissal. The prospects of
the employee becoming fit for return to work at a later date
can only be viewed as at the dismissal date. On occasions there
may be conflicting medical evidence—the employee's " panel
doctor " may say he is fit to return to work, the company's
doctor may say the opposite. Normally, the employer can
rely on his own medical evidence—particularly as the company
doctor will probably be more aware of the requirements and
problems of the particular job. In cases of doubt, however,
employers should consider referring the matter to an independent specialist or consultant.

Tribunals will take into account the **interests of the business**
of the employers. The absent employee may occupy a very
key position and may have to be replaced. Certain businesses
are exceptionally busy at particular times of the year, *e.g.* the
pre-Christmas period in many retail shops. A firm of builders

or an engineering company may be carrying out a contract which contains severe penalty clauses in the event of delays. Replacement of an absent employee by a temporary or " agency hired " person may be very expensive. At all times, however, the employer must try and strike a balance between the interests of the business on the one hand and treating an employee fairly and reasonably on the other hand.

In the event of an employee not being completely unfit to work, but being unable to do his own particular job, employers should consider whether they can find **alternative work** for that employee. This will be particularly relevant with larger employers. The employee might be able to do a lighter job, even though this would be at a lower rate of pay. Failure to consider such a possibility may make the dismissal unfair. Having said this, it has now been made clear in *Merseyside & North Wales Electricity Board v. Taylor* [1975] ICR 185 that an employer does not have to create a special job for an employee however long-serving he may have been.

The definition of " capability " also includes a reference to **" any other physical or mental quality "**. The position here will in general be as set out above. " Mental quality " may include personality defects or incompatability (either with customers or with fellow-employees): the tendency, however, has been to deal with that sort of case under the heading of " some other substantial reason " (see page 298).

(d) Pregnancy

Although not referred to specifically in the TUALRA provisions, pregnancy should be referred to here both under the " capability " heading of the TUALRA and under the new EPA provisions.

It is now unlikely that the capability provisions will be of any particular relevance in view of the fact that section 34 of the EPA came into force on 1st June 1976.

This section which provides that it is (subject to certain exceptions) unfair to dismiss an employee because she is pregnant has been dealt with in Chapter 7 (see page 105, *ante*).

2. CONDUCT

Paragraph 6(2)(b) simply refers to the reason for the dismissal as being a reason which is " **related to the conduct of the employee** ".

There is no statutory definition of conduct. The word can be said to cover " a multitude of sins ". Any form of misconduct will, therefore, be considered under this head. It must, of course, still be remembered that this is not the only hurdle for the employer. It may not be too difficult for him to establish some form of misconduct; he must, however, still show that he acted reasonably (see Chapter 22).

The conduct is not necessarily linked to the employee's actual work; it may arise out of working hours altogether. There must, however, be some relationship between the employee's conduct and his contract of employment.

Conduct can cover such things as theft or dishonesty, bad language, disobeying orders, bad time-keeping, absenteeism, drunkenness, violence, and breach of the terms of the employment. Again, each decided case will depend on its own particulars, facts and circumstances.

(a) Disobedience to instructions

A refusal by an employee to carry out instructions from his employer may give rise to his dismissal. If it does, the refusal by the employee may be sufficient misconduct for the purposes of the employer's first two hurdles in defending an unfair dismissal claim.

In considering this matter the starting point should be the **terms of the contract** itself. If the refusal is clearly contrary to the terms of the contract. then the employer will be over the first hurdle. If the refusal does not give rise to a breach of the contract, then any dismissal will normally be unfair. It is very difficult indeed to dismiss fairly a person who refuses to do something which he is not obliged to do under his contract. Thus, dismissal of an employee because he refused to work **overtime,** when he was not under the terms of his employment obliged to work overtime, will normally be unfair. Similarly, if the contract contains no provisions giving the employer a right to ask the employee to work at a different place of work, a refusal to move will not be unreasonable and any dismissal for that reason is likely to be unfair. In any event, an employer wishing to move an employee to another place of work should always take into account all relevant factors including the health and age of the employee and his domestic circumstances.

Thus, the vital factor is the contract of employment itself. An employer should, as suggested previously (see pages 31 and 32), take this into account when agreeing the terms of the employment before it commences.

There is an **implied term** in every contract of employment that employees will obey all reasonable and lawful orders relating to the job they do. Disobedience to such orders will not normally in itself justify instant dismissal. Whether the dismissal will be held to be unfair will depend in particular on the employee's previous record and whether he had had any warnings about previous misconduct (see page 304). An employee cannot be called upon to do anything unlawful, *e.g.* falsification of records.

Disobeying rules laid down for the **safety** of the work-place and those who work there will be a serious matter and could constitute gross misconduct justifying instant dismissal.

On occasions employers wish to **change the terms of the employment,** *e.g.* changing the shift system, the normal working hours, the pay structure, etc. This will ultimately entail asking the employees to agree to a change in the terms of their employment. Sometimes the employer will not ask—he will assume that the changes can lawfully be made.

This sort of situation seems now to crop up more often—particularly at times when general economic conditions are not very buoyant.

We have already seen that if the changes result in a lay-off, short-time or loss of jobs, employees are protected by the redundancy provisions (see Chapters 11 to 14). In addition, if employers insist on a change in the terms when they are not entitled to do so, the employee may be able to leave and to treat the matter as one of " constructive dismissal " (see page 216).

If the employee refuses to accept the new terms, then a dismissal will probably be unfair. On accasions, however, changes which are in the interests of the business and which are effected mainly to keep the business in existence and to preserve jobs for the employees may be accepted by a Tribunal as reasonable; if this is so, dismissal of an employee who refuses to accept such changes may be fair. This is also likely to be the case if the changes have been discussed, negotiated and ultimately agreed with a trade union representing the employees and the vast majority of the employees accept the changes.

(b) Lack of co-operation

Lack of co-operation can cover many things such as a refusal to work overtime (referred to on page 282), working to rule, a " go-slow ", persistent lateness, absenteeism, and even simple " bloody-mindedness ". Selection for dismissal of some (but not all) employees who are on strike will also come under this heading (see also page 269).

In all these cases, it is unlikely that the conduct in itself will justify instant dismissal and the question of " reasonableness " (see Chapter 22) is, therefore, vital.

Here again, the main considerations will be whether the employee is in breach of his contract of employment and whether he has previously been given warnings about his contract.

The question of the **work to rule** or " go-slow " was reviewed by the Court of Appeal in *Secretary of State for Employment v. ASLEF (No.* 2) [1972] ICR 19 (the case which arose out of the railway unions' work to rule in 1972). In that case, the court held that working to rule could constitute a breach of contract because an employee must not wilfully obstruct his employer's business. To quote Lord Denning, M.R.—

" Now I quite agree that a man is not bound positively to do more for his employer than his contract requires. He can withdraw his goodwill if he pleases. But what he must not do is wilfully to obstruct the employer as he goes about his business ".

There will be an implied term in every contract of employment that the employee will serve the employer faithfully within the requirement of the contract and will not (as in the *ASLEF* case) disrupt the efficient running of the system in which he is employed.

Bad time keeping or persistent **lateness** can give rise to dismissal of an employee after proper warnings. The warning must be a warning in the true sense of the word (see page 306). **Absence without leave** and without reasonable excuse (*e.g.* doctor's certificate) will be dealt with in the same way, as will the failure of an employee to come back from holiday on the agreed date. In all these cases, proper warnings are absolutely vital and without such warnings a dismissal could well be unfair despite the conduct of the employee, *i.e.* the employer will fail at the final hurdle because he will not be able to prove that he acted reasonably.

Disloyalty may also be dealt with under this head, *e.g.* where the employee during his employment also works for or assists a rival or competitor of the employer. The terms of the contract will be relevant and an employer who is concerned about this aspect of the matter should prepare specific terms for the contract, so that the position will be in no doubt.

It has been held that the fact that an employee simply seeks employment with a competitor is not sufficient reason for dismissing him, unless there are grounds for supposing that he was doing so in order to abuse his confidential position with his present employer (*Harris & Russell Ltd. v. Slingsby* [1973] ICR 454).

(c) Dishonesty

In many cases dishonesty arising during the employment itself and connected with the employee's work will constitute **gross misconduct** and will justify instant dismissal without notice or money in lieu. The dismissal will also normally be held to be a fair dismissal.

Dishonesty can cover **stealing** (either from the employer or from fellow employees) embezzlement and fraud and also such things as **clocking in offences** (either in relation to the employee's

own clock card or to the cards of fellow employees) and
" fiddling " time sheets and expenses.

If the employee is convicted of a criminal offence arising from
or related to his actual job, this will in practice put the matter
beyond all doubt, *i.e.* dismissal will normally be fair. As
indicated above, however, the " fairness " of the dismissal will
be considered in the light of the facts known to the employer
at the actual date of dismissal (see page 272). Normally, any
criminal prosecution will not have taken place at that time.

If the conviction relates to an offence which took place
outside working hours and which did not directly relate to the
employer's property or business, the employer will have
greater difficulty in establishing a fair reason for the dismissal.
Ideally, the employer should make it clear in the terms of the
employment that such a conviction (although arising " off-
duty ") will lead to a dismissal. If, however, this is not done
the employer will be able to justify the dismissal if he can show
that the reputation of the business would be adversely affected
by the conviction, *e.g.* the re-action of customers to the fact
that an employee had been convicted of an offence involving
dishonesty. This in itself, will, of course, depend on the nature
of the business and also the actual job of the employee.

It is interesting to note that specific reference to " criminal
offences " outside employment is made in the draft Code of
Practice relating to Disciplinary Practice and Procedures issued
under the Employment Protection Act 1975 (see Appendix IV
at page 364, *post*). The draft Code states that such criminal
offences should not be treated as automatic reasons for dismissal, regardless of whether the offence has any relevance to
the duties of the individual as an employee. The Code suggests
that the main consideration should be whether the offence is
one that makes the individual unsuitable for his type of work
or unacceptable to other employees. Even then, employers
should consider whether alternative jobs are available which
would be suitable for the employee.

The draft Code also states that employees should not normally be dismissed simply because a charge against them is
pending or because they are absent through having been

remanded in custody. If these provisions of the draft Code are in due course approved by Parliament and brought into force, employers will have to act even more carefully in these situations.

In a recent Employment Appeal Tribunal case dismissal of a bus driver after he had been convicted (and given a suspended sentence) of theft of a Building Society book was, in the particular circumstances, held to be fair (*Singh v. London Country Bus Services Ltd.* [1976] IRLR 176).

One of the real practical problems for employers under this head relates to the situation where they are " convinced " that something dishonest is going on but they cannot prove it. Can they fairly dismiss an employee where they only have suspicions of the dishonesty?

The answer to this is that—even without proper proof—the dismissal can still be fair provided that the employer acts fairly and reasonably. In particular the employer must investigate the whole matter thoroughly, interview all relevant witnesses and give the employee every possible opportunity to explain the position: if a formal written procedure is laid down, this must be followed " to the letter ". If, after a thorough investigation such as is referred to above, the employer honestly and reasonably forms the view that the employee is guilty of the alleged conduct or offence, then the dismissal will normally be a fair dismissal.

Even if an employee is acquitted of a criminal charge (relating to the same circumstances which gave rise to the dismissal) the dismissal can still be fair. The criminal court is concerned with whether the offence has been proved beyond reasonable doubt, whilst the Tribunal is merely concerned with the question of whether the employer had proved that grounds existed on which he could properly dismiss the employee (see *Da Costa v. Optolis* [1976] IRLR 178).

When a suspected " offence " first comes to the knowledge of the employer, he should not over-react, *e.g.* by instantly dismissing the employee without investigating the matter and without hearing the employee's explanation. One possible

" half-way " house for the employer in this situation is to
suspend the employee whilst the matter is investigated in depth.
This in itself could at a later date even help the employer to
convince the Tribunal that he acted reasonably. Suspension
must, however, be on full pay unless the terms of the employment specifically allow the employer to suspend an employee
without pay (see page 217). If an employee is suspended
without pay and there is no authority for the employer to do
this, then the employee may be able to treat this as " constructive dismissal " (see page 216).

It will be appreciated that if the suspension is to last until
a criminal trial has taken place the employee could be away
from work for a period of several months.

Even if a dismissal due to alleged dishonesty is ultimately
held to be unfair, the Tribunal is entitled (see page 327) to take
into account the conduct of the employee and this could reduce
substantially any award of compensation that might be made
in his favour.

(d) Violence, swearing and drinking

This rather " unusual " heading covers various " activities ".
which seem, from time to time, to cause problems for employers—and, indeed, for Tribunals!

In all three cases, the terms of employment or Works Rules
will be relevant, as will the length of service and previous
record of the employee.

Violence either against the employer himself or against a
fellow-employee will normally constitute gross misconduct.
All the circumstances must, however, be taken into account.
Again, there must be a full investigation of any particular
incident, the employee being given every opportunity to put
forward his version of what took place.

It is nowadays very difficult to be definite about whether
bad language will justify a dismissal. In very many cases it
will not. There is no doubt that the outlook of the courts has
changed in recent years (see page 229). Tribunals accept that
in a great number of jobs and places of work " robust "

language is an accepted fact. All factors must be taken into account, including the nature of the employment, whether the language was grossly offensive to a normal person, where and to whom the words were used, etc. In general, an employer should think very carefully before dismissing an employee simply because of the use of bad language.

Drunkenness whilst at work will be misconduct and could amount to gross misconduct, particularly where it may affect the safety of other employees or where company property could be endangered. Again, company rules will be relevant, *e.g.* there may be a specific embargo on any employee bringing alcoholic drink onto the works premises. A reputation for— or indeed evidence of—drunkenness outside normal working hours will not normally justify dismissal, unless it is likely to affect the reputation of the business itself.

(e) " Off-duty " Conduct

The effect of " off-duty " conduct on the contract of employment has been touched on under the previous headings. In general, a dismissal because of conduct whilst away from work will not justify dismissal unless it affects the business of the employer or the ability of the employee to do his job or unless it was made clear in the company's rules that such conduct would give rise to a dismissal. Other relevant factors will be the actual job and status of the employee concerned and whether the conduct might affect the reputation or integrity of the employer.

Taking all these factors into account, Tribunals have reached different decisions on different sets of circumstances. Examples include convictions for indecency and incest, drug offences, and driving convictions (as to which see page 286 also page 297).

It is unlikely that off-duty conduct not leading to a criminal conviction will justify dismissal. Conduct causing disharmony with fellow-employees may, however, be sufficient although this is probably better dealt with under the heading of " some other substantial reason " (see page 298).

It must also be remembered that a term of imprisonment (regardless of the type of offence) may give rise to " frustra-

M

tion " of the contract and, if so, the employee will have no unfair dismissal rights (see page 222).

Finally, employers should remember that discovery during employment of an employee's criminal conviction prior to commencement of the employment itself will not of itself be a proper ground for dismissing that employee—see the Rehabilitation of Offenders Act 1974 (page 26, *above*).

3. REDUNDANCY

One of the five specified reasons which is acceptable is where the reason (or, if there was more than one, the principal reason) for the dismissal " was that the employee was **redundant** " (para. 6(2)(c)).

Paragraph 6(9)(c) also states that—

" any reference to redundancy or to being redundant shall be construed as a reference to the existence of one or other of the facts specified in paragraphs (a) and (b) of section 1(2) of the Redundancy Payments Act 1965 ".

Those facts are set out on page 164.

It seems that there are still a great number of employers who think that if an employee is made redundant and receives a redundancy payment, then that is the end of the matter as far as the employer is concerned and that no action can lie for unfair dismissal. Their view is that redundancy is a complete defence to a claim for unfair dismissal.

This is not the case. Redundancy may be a defence and it will get the employer over the first two hurdles. There is still, however, the final hurdle.

Dismissal due to redundancy can still be an unfair dismissal in one of three situations—

(a) if the selection for redundancy was due to an inadmissible reason.

(b) if the selection for redundancy was in contravention of a customary arrangement or agreed procedure.

(c) if the employer did not act reasonably.

In the first instance, therefore, the employer must show that there was a redundancy situation and that the main reason for the dismissal was the redundancy of the employee. If the employer cannot show this, he will fail at the first hurdle and the dismissal will be unfair.

It should be noted that for an employee to be able to claim under this head he does not necessarily have to have actually received a redundancy payment. For example, he need only have been employed for the unfair dismissal qualifying period of 26 weeks—not for the redundancy qualifying period of two years.

(a) Selection for redundancy due to an inadmissible reason

The definition of an " inadmissible reason " has been covered in Chapter 20 (pages 259 to 262). It will normally relate to an employee's trade union " involvement ". Such a dismissal will be automatically unfair (see page 259).

It will be for the employee to show that:—

(1) the reason or principal reason for the dismissal was his redundancy.

(2) the circumstances applied equally to one or more other employees in the same undertaking who held positions similar to that held by him.

(3) those other employees were not dismissed by the employer and

(4) the reason (or principal reason) for his selection was an " inadmissible reason ".

The employee has to establish **all** four of the above requirements. The burden on the employee is a substantial one. It will be very difficult indeed for him to prove his claim under this head unless the employer has been quite blatant in his manner of selecting a well-known union-involved " troublemaker " for redundancy. As indicated previously (see page 261) the employer will very often be able to put forward some other reason (e.g. misconduct) as the real reason for the dismissal.

If the employee does fail under this head, he may still be successful under one of the following two heads.

(b) Selection for redundancy in contravention of a customary arrangement or agreed procedure

This is another example of automatic unfair dismissal (see page 259).

If this can be established, the employer will not be able to show that he acted reasonably; the dismissal will automatically be held to be unfair.

As for the preceding head of claim, special provisions are contained in paragraph 6(7) of Schedule 1.

The employee must satisfy the first three conditions (1), (2) and (3)—referred to above. **In addition,** he must show that—

" he was selected for redundancy **in contravention of a customary arrangement or agreed procedure** relating to redundancy and there were **no special reasons** justifying a departure from that arrangement or procedure in his case ".

Here again, it is not too easy to prove a customary arrangement or agreed procedure—although, in many cases, the burden on the employee is not as heavy as it is for establishing an " inadmissible reason ".

An **agreed procedure** will be a specific agreement relating to redundancies; it will normally be made between the employer and a recognised trade union; it does not have to be in writing, but almost invariably it will be. The agreed procedure could well be contained in a Collective Agreement entered into between management and trade union.

A **customary arrangement** is less precise than an agreed procedure. It will be a question of fact for the Tribunal to decide in each particular case. It will not be sufficient simply to show that a previous redundancy has taken place in a particular manner.

In practice, the claim is often made that the customary arrangement is " Last in, first out " or, as it is often referred to, " LIFO ". There is no doubt that this is very common in many industries. There is also no doubt that in considering the " reasonableness " of a particular redundancy (see the next heading) a Tribunal will attach great weight to the length of service of the particular employee.

Having said this, the LIFO principle is not automatically accepted by the Tribunals as a customary arrangement. There must be some evidence that LIFO was in fact the customary arrangement. As stated by the NIRC in *Bessenden Properties Ltd. v. Corness* [1974] 9 ITR 128, the customary arrangement must be " something which is so well known, so certain and so clear as to amount in effect to an implied " agreed procedure ", as contrasted with the express " agreed procedure " which is the alternative contemplated by the paragraph ".

This interpretation of the paragraph has in fact made it quite difficult for an employee to prove a customary arrangement or agreed procedure unless he is able to produce evidence either in writing or from a trade union representative of an agreement reached with the employers.

Even if there is an arrangement or procedure the employer will have a defence if he can show " **special reasons** " justifying a departure from it. The burden of proof will be on the employer; there have to be very good reasons indeed for not following the customary arrangement or agreed procedure.

If there is an arrangement or procedure and it is not followed, then the dismissal will be unfair.

(c) Where dismissal for redundancy is unreasonable

The unreasonableness of dismissal for one of the specified terms is considered in Chapter 22. The redundancy aspect of the matter will, however, be dealt with here.

Paragraph 6(8) of Schedule 1 provides that—" the determination of the question whether the dismissal was fair or unfair, having regard to the reason shown by the employer, shall depend on whether the employer can satisfy the tribunal that in the circumstances (having regard to equity and the substantial merits of the case) he **acted reasonably** in treating it as a sufficient reason for dismissing the employee ".

In other words—did the employer act reasonably?

It will be noted that the burden of proof is on the employer to show that he acted reasonably; if he cannot prove this, the dismissal will be held to be unfair.

From the various cases now heard by Tribunals it is apparent that unfairness can arise either in deciding to make a particular employee redundant or in the way in which the redundancy is carried out or both.

As far as the actual **decision** is concerned, employers have to balance the interests of their business on the one hand and being fair with their employees on the other hand. Tribunals will pay great attention to the interests of the business and will not normally question the right of an employer in a declining business to make people redundant. When, however, it comes to selecting the actual individual for redundancy, it is a different matter.

The employer must then take into account all factors. Even if the LIFO principle does not strictly apply, the employer must take into account the length of service of each employee. Normally, the selection of a long-serving employee for redundancy when other more junior employees (with no better records or qualifications) are retained will make it very difficult for the employer to show that he has acted " reasonably ".

The employer must be prepared to reveal to the Tribunal how he reached the decision to select a particular employee for redundancy. If he can show that he took all factors into account—e.g. length of service, the needs of the business, the age and qualifications of the various employees, their respective records in terms of work, discipline, etc.—then there is more chance of being able to establish a " fair dismissal ".

If the " candidates " for redundancy are almost indistinguishably evenly matched then provided the employers have applied their mind to the problem and have acted from genuine motives and with proper notice, the employers cannot be said to have acted unreasonably in choosing one employee for redundancy in preference to another. The Tribunal's function as an " industrial jury " is not to decide what they would have done had they been the management (see *Grundy* (*Teddington*) *Ltd. v. Willis* [1976] IRLR 118).

Pressure from other employees and/or from any unions involved at the particular undertaking must be ignored by the employer and cannot be taken into account by the Tribunal.

If management handles a redundancy problem by meeting with **union representatives** and if after discussions and negotiations a formula for the redundancies is worked out, it is most unlikely that any dismissals for redundancy in accordance with that formula will be unfair.

In view of the Employment Protection Act provisions relating to consultation regarding redundancies (see pages 193 to 201), it seems likely that there will now be an even greater tendency for employers to consult and agree with the union concerned the details of any proposed redundancies and the ultimate selection of which employees are in fact to the made redundant.

Selection for redundancy on the grounds of sex or race will also be unfair.

As far as the **manner of carrying out** redundancies is concerned, the provisions of the Code of Practice relating to redundancy are very relevant indeed. These were considered in Chapter 14 (see in particular pages 191 to 192). The consultation provisions of the EPA will also now be a vital factor. The " protective award " (see page 197) will, of course, be of great benefit to employees.

Thus, even though the actual selection of an employee for redundancy may have been quite reasonable, his dismissal could well be unfair if he was not given as much warning as practicable (para. 46 of the Code). Normally, if an employee is made redundant and at the same time is only given his minimum statutory notice to terminate his employment, this will be unfair. There should be some preliminary warning prior to and quite apart from the statutory notice.

It has been suggested that the preliminary warning might be dispensed with in exceptional cases where " a premature

announcement of redundancy may shake confidence in the
product and excessively long notice of intention to dismiss upon
grounds of redundancy may be very damaging to morale " (per
Sir John Donaldson in *Clarkson Ltd. v. Short* [1973] ICR 191).
The " exceptional circumstances " were, however, stressed in
that case and it is in any event felt that the whole situation
has now been changed by the EPA consultation provisions.

One of the most important decided cases in this field is
Vokes Ltd. v. Bear [1973] ICR 1 where it was held that it was
unreasonable to dismiss an employee for redundancy without
first trying to find him suitable alternative employment within
the group of companies of which the employer was part.

This will be of particular importance in the case of the
larger employers who are part of a group of companies or who
have more than one establishment or place of work. Such
employers must take steps to ensure whether or not the
employee can be fitted in elsewhere, and must be prepared to
give evidence accordingly to the Tribunal. Failure to do this
can result in a finding of unfair dismissal.

In discharging this obligation it is the responsibility of the
employers when making an offer of alternative employment to
give the employee sufficient information upon which he can
make a realistic decision whether to take the job and stay, or
whether to reject it and leave. The amount of information
will, of course, depend on the circumstances, but the financial
prospects of the new job will be of particular importance. The
fact that the employee does not press for such information will
not absolve the employers (see *Modern Injection Moulds Ltd.
v. Price* [1976] IRLR 172).

4. BREACH OF A STATUTORY DUTY OR RESTRICTION

The fourth of the specified reasons in paragraph 6(2) of
Schedule 1 is where " the employee could not continue to work
in the position which he held without contravention (either on
his part or that of his employer) of a duty or restriction imposed
by or under an enactment ".

Very few cases have arisen under this head. The employer must, of course, still act " reasonably ".

The main example covered by this reason is where an employee is **disqualified from driving** and cannot, therefore, continue to drive as part of his job.

If he is dismissed because of this, the reason will obviously come under this heading.

In deciding whether the employer has acted reasonably the Tribunal will take into account whether driving was the sole or main part of the employee's job, whether the job could still be done without the employee driving a car, whether an alternative job could be offered to the employee and the number of years the employee had worked for the firm.

Another possible problem area under this heading would arise where an employee from abroad failed to obtain a work permit or became involved in a breach of the immigration laws. In the event of dismissing such an employee, care would, however, have to be taken not to offend the provisions of the Race Relations legislation.

5. SOME OTHER SUBSTANTIAL REASON

Paragraph 6(1)(*b*) of Schedule 1 provides that the final reason which the employer can show in order to establish that a dismissal was fair is—

" some other substantial reason of a kind such as to justify the dismissal of an employee holding the position which that employee held ".

This is a general " sweeping up " provision. The TUALRA gives no other guidance or definition and, indeed, it would perhaps be both impossible and undesirable to do this.

Tribunals vary as to how they " categorise " a particular set of circumstances, *e.g.* some Tribunals will deal with the " incompatible " employee under the " conduct " heading, whilst others look at the matter under this heading.

Employers defending an application to a Tribunal may find it useful, in cases of doubt, to plead " some other substantial reason " as an alternative reason for the dismissal, *e.g.* as an alternative to conduct or capability.

The " other substantial reason " need only be a reason which **could** justify dismissal and **not** one which **does** justify the dismissal.[1] Showing some other substantial reason will only get the employer over the first hurdles; he will still have to show that he acted reasonably.

Some light was thrown on the meaning and interpretation of the phrase in *R.S. Components Ltd. v. Irwin* [1973] ICR 535, where the NIRC said that the phrase " some other substantial reason " should not be construed *eiusdem generis* with the other four specified reasons, *i.e.* it did not have to be linked with or arise from one or more of those four reasons. Parliament had not intended to produce an exhaustive category of reasons justifying the dismissal of an employee. Sir John Brightman giving the judgement of the court said—

> " There are not only legal, but also practical, objections to a narrow construction of " some other reason " ".

Applying this principle in practice, the following matters have been dealt with as " some other substantial reason "—

(a) where an employee causes disruption and **disharmony** because other employees find it impossible to work with him. Thus, **incompatability** can be a reason for dismissal, although the employer must first do everything he can (short of dismissal) to rectify the position. Cases here cover such situations as the domestic worker causing upset in an old people's home[2]; and the female employee causing disharmony by boasting to her fellow employees of her " sexual exploits " with a much younger man.[3]

(b) where an employee breaks the terms of his contract (express or implied) regarding his loyalty to his employer. This might be referred to as a matter of **commercial security.**

Examples here are misuse of trade secrets, working part-time for a competitor, persuading fellow employees

---

1 *Mercia Rubber Mouldings Ltd. v. Lingwood* [1974] ICR 256.
2 *Gorfin v. Distressed Gentlefolks Aid Association* [1973] IRLR 290.
3 *Treganowan v. Robert Knee* [1975] ICR 405.

to join a rival firm, or having an interest in another business which might damage either the employer's business or his repuation and standing.

The *Irwin* case (referred to above) related to the refusal of an employee to sign an undertaking not to solicit his employers' customers for a 12 month period after the end of his employment; such refusal was held to be " some other substantial reason ".

Tribunals may also treat these matters under the general heading of " Conduct " (see page 283).

(c) The interests and requirements of the business of the employer might become " some other substantial reason justifying the dismissal ".   An employer may, due to **economic necessity,** have to make savings in various spheres and this may in itself involve changing certain terms of the employment, *e.g.* changing the shift system, making duties and hours more flexible, withdrawing free transport to and from work.   It is impossible, however, to generalise.   There is a very thin dividing line indeed between the situation referred to above (which may justify dismissal) and the position where an employee refuses to do something which he is not contractually bound to do (see page 283).   Each case depends on its own particular facts and circumstances.

Two factors in particular will help an employer to establish the above reason.   One is if he can show that the changes in the terms of the employment will genuinely help the business to survive from an economic point of view; the other is if the changes are negotiated and agreed with the union or unions recognised by the employer in relation to his business, and then accepted by the vast majority of the work-force.

CHAPTER 22

UNFAIR DISMISSAL—
DID THE EMPLOYER ACT REASONABLY ?

We have seen that—except in the case of "automatic" unfairness (see page 259)—the burden of proof is on the employer to show not only that the reason for the dismissal was one of the five specified reasons considered in the preceding chapter, but also that the employer acted reasonably.

Various aspects of such "reasonableness" have already been considered in the preceding chapter.

There is no doubt that this factor is in practice the most important of all in a dismissal situation. Normally, it is comparatively easy to establish one of the five reasons. In the vast majority of cases, however, when the case reaches an Industrial Tribunal, the main problem is—did the employer act reasonably?

The exact wording of paragraph 6(8) of Schedule 1 to the TUALRA should be repeated—

" . . . the determination of the question whether the dismissal was fair or unfair, having regard to the reason shown by the employer, shall depend on whether the employer can satisfy the tribunal that in the circumstances (having regard to equity and the substantial merits of the case) he acted reasonably in treating it as a sufficient reason for dismissing the employee ".

The paragraph makes it quite clear that the onus is on the employer. It is **not** for the employee to prove that the employer acted unreasonably; it is for the employer himself to prove that he acted reasonably.

Although in considering this topic constant reference has been made to the various hurdles to be surmounted by an employer, in practice the evidence before the Tribunal will

[300]

normally cover all aspects of the matter at one and the same time. Here again, whether the employer acted reasonably will be judged in the light of the circumstances known to the employer at the time of the dismissal. Evidence acquired or action taken subsequent to the dismissal will not be relevant to the issue of whether the employer acted reasonably (see page 272).

The question of whether the employer acted reasonably can arise at two different stages. First, was the decision itself to dismiss the employee **a reasonable decision**? Secondly, once the decision was taken, was it carried out **in a reasonable manner**?

The reasonableness of the decision itself has in the main been covered in the preceding chapter. It has been seen that the interests of the business and its commercial viability are now matters which the Tribunal will take into account and that discussions and agreements with trade unions as to such things as redundancies and changes in the method of running the business are major factors.

Under the reasonableness heading it should be remembered that the test is as set out above. Thus, it is possible for an employer to be in breach of contract and yet still to be held to have acted reasonably (see page 238). This will, as always, depend on the circumstances of the particular case.

The Tribunal will, of course, only consider the reasonableness of the dismissal once the specified reason has been proved— unless the case is one where the dismissal is automatically unfair (see page 259). A very good example of this arises in the **constructive dismissal** cases (see page 216). In those cases the employer has not " sacked " the employee in the ordinary sense of the word, although he has been guilty of conduct entitling the employee to terminate his own employment. Because of this, in nearly all constructive dismissal cases, the employer's defence before the Tribunal will be that he did not dismiss the employee. If, therefore, the Tribunal ultimately holds that there was legally a " dismissal ", then it is more than likely that the dismissal will be held to be unfair purely and simply because the employer has not put forward any specified reason for the dismissal. The Tribunal will not, therefore, have to consider the reasonableness of the matter.

In considering whether or not an employer has acted reasonably in dismissing an employee, one of the most relevant matters is the Code of Practice.

The Code of Practice

The first Code of Practice (referred to in this chapter as " the 1972 Code ") was issued with the authority of Parliament under the Industrial Relations Act 1971 and it came into effect on 28th February 1972.

Although the Industrial Relations Act was, of course, abolished by the TUALRA, those parts relating to the Code of Practice were re-enacted (TUALRA, Sched. 1, Pt. I).

Paragraph 1(2) of Schedule 1 provides that the 1972 Code " shall remain in effect . . . unless and until revised ".

If the Code is revised the Secretary of State has to consult with the TUC and the CBI and take into account their views and advice. The Code stresses that those who " manage undertakings " should " accept the primary responsibility for the promotion of good industrial relations ".

The Employment Protection Act 1975 (s. 6(1)) also lays down that the ACAS " may issue Codes of Practice containing such practical guidance as the Service thinks fit for the purpose of promoting the improvement of industrial relations ".

Although not specifically referred to in the EPA, a new draft Code relating to Disciplinary Practice and Procedures has now been published for consultation. Details of this draft Code are considered on page 364 (Appendix IV).

As far as Tribunal proceedings are concerned, the relevance of the Code is made very clear by paragraph 3 of Schedule 1 to the TUALRA—

" A failure on the part of any person to observe any provision of a code of practice . . . shall not of itself render him liable to any proceedings; but in any proceedings before an Industrial Tribunal under this Act—

(a) any such code of practice shall be admissible in evidence, and

(b) any provision of such a code of practice which appears to the tribunal to be relevant to any question arising in the proceedings shall be taken into account by the tribunal in determining that question ".

A similar provision is contained in section 6(11) of the EPA. The 1972 Code (obtainable from HMSO) consists of 28 pages and has 133 numbered paragraphs. It is compulsory reading for all employers!

The Code is divided into various sections covering such things as employment policies; communication and consultation; collective bargaining; employee representation; grievance, disputes and disciplinary procedures.

Various aspects of the Code have already been touched on in earlier chapters—see, for example, pages 31, 70, 75 and 192.

Parts of the Code have, of course, now been considerably strengthened and to a certain extent overtaken by the provisions of the EPA, e.g. the redundancy consultation provisions, the rights as to written reasons for dismissal, and the revealing of disciplinary rules as now required under the Contracts of Employment Act.

For unfair dismissal purposes, the relevant paragraphs of the 1972 Code are those numbered 130 to 133. Because of their importance, it is proposed to set these paragraphs out verbatim.

They are as follows:—
" **Disciplinary Procedures.**
130. Management should ensure that fair and effective arrangements exist for dealing with disciplinary matters. These should be agreed with employee representatives or trade unions concerned and should provide for full and speedy consideration by management of all the relevant facts. There should be a formal procedure except in very small establishments where there is close personal contact between the employer and his employees.

131. Management should make known to each employee:
  i its disciplinary rules and the agreed procedure;
  ii the type of circumstances which can lead to suspension or dismissal.

132. The procedure should be in writing and should:

i specify who has the authority to take various forms of disciplinary action, and ensure that supervisors do not have the power to dismiss without reference to more senior management;

ii give the employee the opportunity to state his case and the right to be accompanied by his employee representative;

iii provide for a right of appeal, wherever practicable, to a level of management not previously involved;

iv provide for independent arbitration if the parties to the procedure wish it.

133. Where there has been misconduct, the disciplinary action to be taken will depend on the circumstances, including the nature of the misconduct. But normally the procedure should operate as follows:

i the first step should be an oral warning or, in the case of more serious misconduct, a written warning setting out the circumstances;

ii no employee should be dismissed for a first breach of discipline except in the case of gross misconduct;

iii action on any further misconduct, for example, final warning, suspension without pay or dismissal, should be recorded in writing;

iv details of any disciplinary action should be given in writing to the employee and, if he so wishes, to his employee representative;

v no disciplinary action should be taken against a shop steward until the circumstances of the case have been discussed with a full-time official of the union concerned ".

The above provisions are still not as well known amongst empoyers as they should be. Far too often employers are still learning about the Code the hard way, *i.e.* when a Tribunal decision goes against them. The relevant provisions of the new draft Code that is to replace these paragraphs are set out in Appendix IV (page 364, *post*).

Warnings

Perhaps, the most important part of the Code relates to warnings. Unless an employee is guilty of gross misconduct (as to which see page 229), it will in effect be unfair to dismiss him for a first " offence "—whether it relates to conduct, capability or any other reason.

Employers should, therefore, have a **proper disciplinary procedure,** conforming with the Code of Practice. In the event of misconduct, the first warning may be oral. It is, however, suggested that even the first warning should be confirmed in writing; if this is done, then there should be no difficulty at all in the future about proving the warning. A final warning should always be in writing. Under the new Code it seems that greater attention should be given to suspending an employee as a stage in the disciplinary procedure (see page 366).

The Code does not state **how many warnings** should be given, except that it envisages there being at least two (including the final written warning). If there is a detailed procedure laid down and agreed with a trade union, this will very often provide for at least three warnings before an actual dismissal. If nothing specific is agreed, then each case must be looked at on its merits and all factors taken into account. Those factors will include the length of service of the employee, his previous record, the nature of the " offence ", the period of time since any previous warning and the needs and requirements of the business itself.

It seems that the need for a proper warning may not be as vital in the case of senior employees. " Those employed in **senior management** may by the nature of their jobs be fully aware of what is required of them and fully capable of judging for themselves whether they are achieving that requirement. In such circumstances, the need for warning and an opportunity for improvement is much less apparent " (per Sir John Donaldson in *James v. Waltham Holy Cross U.D.C.* [1973] ICR at p. 404).

Any formal procedure should make it clear **how long a warning will last,** *i.e.* when it will become " spent " and the " slate wiped clean ". If nothing is specifically agreed, then, once again, all the circumstances must be taken into account, including in particular the nature of the conduct which gave rise to the warning. Subject to these factors, it is felt that certainly after a lapse of twelve months a warning will have become " spent ". The Draft Code issued under the EPA (summarised in Appendix IV—page 367, *post*) states that breaches of disciplinary

rules " should be removed from an employee's record after an
appropriate period of satisfactory conduct ".

It is important that the warning should be a **real warning.**
It must be made clear to the employee that if there is another
breach of discipline, he will be dismissed. Exhortations such
as—" We must all pull together " or " Let's pull our socks up "
or " If this happens again, I don't know what will happen "—
are not sufficient. The " kind " employer can fall into a trap
here. In certain circumstances the employer or senior manager
may " wrap up " the warning to such an extent that the real
meaning of the words becomes far from clear. This can be
dangerous. For example, in *Scottish C.W.S. Ltd.* v. *Lloyd*
[1973] ICR 137 an area manager had been sent letters criticising
his work, but at no time was he specifically warned that if the
sales in his area did not improve, he would be dismissed; the
dismissal was held to be unfair. It is vital that, at the end of
the interview, the employee should be left in no doubt that if
he is again guilty of misconduct, he is going to be dismissed.
This is another reason why ideally the " warning " should be
confirmed in writing.

Although paragraph 133 refers only to misconduct, it was
established at an early date that the system of warnings is
equally applicable to cases of dismissal due to **lack of capability.** As stated by Sir John Donaldson in *James* v. *Waltham
Holy Cross U.D.C.* [1973] ICR at p. 404—

> " An employer should be very slow to dismiss upon the ground
> that the employee is incapable of performing the work which he
> is employed to do, without first telling the employee of the
> respects in which he is failing to do his job adequately, warning
> him of the possibility or likelihood of dismissal on this ground,
> and giving him an opportunity of improving his performance ".

Will a breach of the Code make the dismissal unfair ?

A breach of the Code will be taken into account by the
Tribunal when it reaches its decision (see page 302).

Thus, a breach of the Code will often be fatal to the employer's case. In one of the earlier cases involving this aspect
of the law the NIRC held that a dismissal was unfair simply

because the employers did not give the employee a chance to give an explanation of his conduct (see para. 132(ii) of the Code).[1] This principle was upheld by the Employment Appeal Tribunal in *Budgen & Co. v. Thomas* [1976] IRLR 174 where dismissal of a shop assistant, who had signed a " confession " after interview by the firm's security officer, was held to be unfair because she was never interviewed by her actual employers and given an opportunity to explain her conduct. Lack of a proper warning will also often make the dismissal unfair (see, for example, the *Scottish C.W.S. Ltd. v. Lloyd* case referred to above).

It should also be remembered that there may be breaches of other parts of the Code which similarly could make a dismissal unfair, *e.g.* paragraph 46 relating to warnings of redundancy (see page 192); paragraph 40(i) relating to sickness (see page 279).

In some cases, however, a dismissal has been held to be fair despite a breach of the provisions of the Code. Perhaps, the " leading " statement here was made by Sir Hugh Griffiths in *Lewis Shops Group v. Wiggins* [1973] ICR 335. In that case the manageress of a dress shop had been dismissed summarily after warnings about her standards of work; the Tribunal held that, although the employers had established a valid reason (capability), the dismissal was unfair because the employee had not, in accordance with the Code, been given an opportunity to state her case. On appeal, the NIRC allowed the appeal and stated that although the Code was an important factor to be taken into account in every case, its significance would vary according to the circumstances of each individual case. In that case, they held, the employee knew exactly where she stood; there had been complaints about her work and she knew that, if it did not improve, she would be dismissed; observance of the Code would not have made any difference to the position; in other words, whatever she had

---

[1] *Earl v. Slater & Wheeler (Airlyne) Ltd.* [1972] ICR 508 (in fact, the employee did not receive any compensation at all in this case because the " unfairness " had caused him no loss).

said the employers would not have changed their decision to
dismiss her.[1]

In a subsequent case (*Lowndes v. Specialist Heavy Engineering Ltd.* [1976] IRLR 246) the Employment Appeal Tribunal
held that an unfair procedure did not always and of necessity
render a dismissal unfair. For example, the fact that an
employee was not given an opportunity to answer a complaint
would not make the dismissal unfair if it was " wildly unlikely "
that an explanation would have been given.

It is felt that, despite the principle stated in the above cases,
this is dangerous ground for an employer to tread. Indeed,
Sir John Donaldson in the *Earl v. Slater & Wheeler (Airlyne)
Ltd.* case said that—" This must be a very rare situation ".
Every effort should be made to follow the Code. If a formal
procedure is laid down, that procedure should be followed to
the letter. If there is no formal procedure, then, prior to a
dismissal, management should interview the employee, allowing him to be accompanied by his union representative. Care
should be taken in that interview to state the facts as known
to the employer and then to ask the employee for his comments.
This should be done even though the employer has in fact
already made his mind up that the employee is going to be
dismissed. Management should then listen carefully to everything that the employee has to say and, finally, having done
this, should give its decision.

It seems that if the employer investigates a matter thoroughly
and fairly and then reaches a decision based on that investigation, the Tribunal will not normally interfere with the decision
of the employer—see *St. Anne's Board Mill Ltd. v. Brien* [1973]
ICR 444 where the employers were faced with " two wholly
irreconcilable bodies of evidence " as to who was responsible
for cutting through a live electric cable; the employers, after
a full investigation, formed a *bona fide* view as to who was to
blame and in those circumstances were held not to have
acted unreasonably, even though the Tribunal itself might
have reached a different view.

---

[1] A similar case is *Dunning Ltd. v. Jacomb* [1973] ICR 448.

Reasons for the decision—and indeed for the dismissal itself—should be given. An employee (with 26 weeks' service) can in any event now demand a statement in writing of the reasons (see page 241), but the point has always in effect been covered by the Code itself (para. 133(iv)).

An **appeals procedure** is recommended by the Code and must also now be referred to in the Contracts of Employment Act statement (see page 40).

Even in quite **small establishments** the principles of conduct laid down in the Code should be observed. The reference in paragraph 130 only excludes " **very** small establishments " from the necessity to set up formal procedures. The new draft Code (see Appendix IV) contains no such exclusion.

Reasonableness and other factors

There are, of course, many other factors quite apart from the Code of Practice which may be taken into account by a Tribunal when it has to decide whether or not an employer has acted reasonably in dismissing an employee.

One factor is whether the employee could have been transferred to **other employment** with the same employer. This will, as we have seen, be of particular relevance in a redundancy situation (see page 296) and it may also arise in a sickness or injury case.

Length of service has already been mentioned on several occasions. If the employee has been employed for a long period of time, then whether the dismissal is due to conduct, capability or any other reason, that service is a vital factor. As stated previously, the longer an employee has been employed, the more difficult it will be to dismiss him fairly.

Another factor can be referred to as **consistency**. This is particularly relevant with regard to disciplinary rules. For example, it is no use having a rule that all employees who are found off the company premises during their shift will be dismissed, if in fact employees often leave the premises—to the knowledge of management—and are not dismissed. If there are rules, they must be applied—otherwise the employers will be presumed to have decided to waive the rules.

Consistency will also be relevant in the manner in which the rules are applied, *e.g.* if five men are found off the company premises and only one is dismissed, it is likely that such dismissal will be unfair.

Reference has already been made (see page 276) to **wage reviews** and employees' **references.** These can also be considered under the " consistency " heading. An employer who has just given a substantial wage or salary increase to an employee will be in some difficulty in establishing that the employee was " useless " at his job.

All employees should be given a chance to prove themselves in their job. Thus the **timing** of a dismissal can be relevant. A salesman must be given a reasonable amount of time to achieve his targets. If an employee is moved to a different job—or if the method or technique of working changes—he must be given time to adapt to the changed circumstances; in addition, he may need additional training and/or supervision. Lack of such help and consideration might make a subsequent dismissal unfair.

A final reference should be made to the situation where there is a **recognised trade union** which is active in a particular establishment. If this is the case, then even if there is no formal procedure agreement, it is likely—and indeed desirable—that the union representatives should be involved in all meetings and discussions prior to the taking of disciplinary action. If this is done, then this will certainly help the employer to show that he acted reasonably. It will obviously not be conclusive, but it is certainly a relevant factor.

In this chapter, reference has been made to a few decided cases. There are now hundreds of reported cases—and thousands of Tribunal decisions—dealing with this part of the topic. The preceding pages are, therefore, to be treated only as guidelines based on the main established principles. It cannot be stressed too strongly that the answer to each particular problem facing an employer will depend on **all** the facts and circumstances relating to the particular employee, the nature of the business, the reason for the dismissal and the general relationship of the employer and the employee.

CHAPTER 23

UNFAIR DISMISSAL—
THE EMPLOYEE'S REMEDIES

The application to the Tribunal

We have seen in the preceding chapters that employees (with a few exceptions) have a right not to be unfairly dismissed. If an employee is dismissed and he feels that such dismissal is unfair, he may try and negotiate with his employers and reach some form of settlement either to be reinstated in his job or to receive compensation. The significance of settlements without there being a formal Tribunal decision are considered in the next chapter (see page 333). If, of course, the employee is represented by a recognised Trade Union, then the Union will put forward representations on his behalf. If it is not possible to reach a settlement in this way, then the employee can apply to an Industrial Tribunal. The format and procedures of the Industrial Tribunals are dealt with in the next chapter. It is, however, important to note at this stage that any such application to a Tribunal has to be presented **within three months** from " the effective date of termination " (as previously defined —see page 213).

Paragraph 21(4) of Schedule 1 to the TUALRA provides that the Tribunal cannot consider a complaint of unfair dismissal " unless it is presented to the Tribunal before the end of the period of three months beginning with the effective date of termination or within such further period as the Tribunal considers reasonable in a case where it is satisfied that it was not reasonably practicable for the complaint to be presented within the period of three months ".

A considerable number of cases have reached the Courts and the Tribunals dealing with when it is **" not reasonably practicable "** for an employee to present his complaint. Many of

these cases arose out of the similar provisions in the Industrial
Relations Act 1971 where the time limit was in fact only four
weeks.

It has been held that the provisions of this paragraph go to
the jurisdiction of the Tribunal, *i.e.* this is not a matter which
the Tribunal or even the parties to the action if they both agree
can waive. If the application is not lodged in time, then the
Tribunal has no jurisdiction to deal with it. The only exception
to this is where the Tribunal is satisfied that it was not reasonably practicable for the complaint to be presented within the
period of three months.

At one stage doubts even arose as to the meaning of the
word " **presented** ". It was then held by the NIRC in the case
of *Hammond v. Haigh Castle & Co. Ltd.* [1973] ICR 148 that
a complaint is " presented " to an Industrial Tribunal when it
is received at the Central Office of the Industrial Tribunals.
Contrary to certain other general legal principles, the claim is
not presented simply by the act of posting it to the Tribunal.
This does, therefore, effectively reduce the time limit to a small
extent. Thus, an application arriving on the 28th day of the
28 day time limit (when this was in force) was held to be out
of time. If, however, the time limit expires on a Sunday or
Bank Holiday on which the Tribunal offices are closed, it will
be extended until the next day on which those offices are open.
In certain special circumstances, it has been held that abnormal
postal delays can extend the time limit in favour of the
employee.

As far as the words " **reasonably practicable** " are concerned many of the early decisions (when the time limit was
only 28 days) turned on whether the employee knew of his rights
regarding unfair dismissal and, at that time, it was held that if
an employee did not know of his rights then it would follow
that it was not " practicable " for him to apply in time. It is
felt, however, that it will now be very difficult indeed for an
employee to establish that he does not know of his rights.
During the last four years a considerable amount of publicity
has been given to the unfair dismissal rights and, in addition,
when a dismissed employee goes along to his local office of the

Department of the Employment to deal with such things as unemployment benefit, he will normally also be given a leaflet telling him about his rights with regard to dismissal.

An employee who is confined to bed due to illness or injury may be able to show that it was not practicable for him to apply in time, although, here again, his disability would have to apply for virtually the whole of the three month period.

The leading case in this part of the law is now *Dedman v. British Building & Engineering Appliances Ltd.* [1974] ICR 53. This was a decision of the Court of Appeal and related to the original four week limitation period.   The Court there reviewed the earlier decisions.   Lord Denman, M.R. indicated that the words " not practicable " should be given a liberal interpretation in favour of the employee; he felt that a strict construction would give rise to much injustice.   Despite this, the Court held that if an employee knew or was put on enquiry as to his rights then it was practicable for him to have presented his complaint within the time limit.   If, however, he did not know of his rights and there was nothing to put him on enquiry, then it was " not practicable ".   Lord Denning added that if the employee went to " skilled advisers " (*e.g.* a Solicitor or a Trade Union Official) and those advisers made a mistake, then it would be " practicable " for him to send off the application in time, and the Tribunal could not then entertain the application. " If a man engages skilled advisers to act for him—and they mistake the time limit and present it too late—he is out.   His remedy is against them ".   In this respect, however, clerks at the Employment Exchange are not treated as " skilled advisers "; if they make a mistake, the applicant may be allowed further time.

If, of course, the employee is misled by his employer about certain material facts which do affect the dismissal, then this could be a reason for extending the time limit.   Similarly, if the employer asks the employee not to take further action whilst the employer considers whether anything can be done, then it is unlikely that the employer will be able to rely on the application being out of time.

If an employee is for any reason doubtful about whether he should lodge his application, *e.g.* because negotiations are still taking place with his employers or he is exercising his rights under a domestic appeals procedure or because he is waiting trial on a criminal charge, then, rather than run the risk of being out of time with his Tribunal application, he should make the application and then apply for an adjournment. If he does not do this, he may be " out of time ". In those circumstances, there will normally be no problem at all about the granting of a reasonable adjournment.

Perhaps, the final word should be left to Sir John Donaldson in the case of *Hammond v. Haigh Castle & Co. Ltd.* (referred to above)—

" Practicability in this context falls to be considered in the light of the general standards of ordinary people working in industry. Accordingly the question which members of Tribunals have to ask themselves is ' would a jury composed of ordinary men and women employed in industry consider that in all the circumstances it was practicable for the complaint to have been presented within the time limit? ' ".

Subject to the above, employers who receive a copy of an application made to the Industrial Tribunal alleging unfair dismissal should at the outset watch out for the three month time limit; if the application is out of time, then this should be pleaded by the employer in the Notice of Appearance (see page 340).

It will have been noted that in other parts of employment legislation (including in particular the various new rights under the Employment Protection Act 1975) reference is also made to applications being made to a Tribunal within various set periods (very often three months) or " if that is not reasonably practicable within such further period as is reasonable ". It would seem that those provisions will be interpreted in a similar way to the provision referred to above and contained in Schedule 1 of the TUALRA.

Since 1st June 1976 it is also possible for an employee to lodge an application to a Tribunal alleging unfair dismissal even prior to the dismissal itself. By virtue of an amendment introduced by the EPA (Sched. 16, Part III, para. 21) the

Tribunal can consider a complaint where an employee has been dismissed with notice but where the notice period has not yet expired. Prior to this change in the law a premature application, *i.e.* one made before the effective date of termination of the employment could not be considered by the Tribunal.

THE REMEDIES

If the Industrial Tribunal finds that an employee has been unfairly dismissed then it will make an award in favour of the employee; that award can be one of the following three awards:

1. Reinstatement.
2. Re-engagement.
3. Compensation.

Considerable amendments have been made to this part of the law by the provisions of the Employment Protection Act 1975—in particular sections 71 to 76. This part of the EPA came into force on 1st June 1976. Under the EPA changes, there is much more emphasis placed on giving the employee an opportunity to get his job back than was previously the case. Prior to 1st June 1976, there were in practice very few cases in which reinstatement or re-engagement was recommended. The vast majority of cases were dealt with by way of an award of compensation.

We will now consider each of the remedies, dealing with reinstatment and re-engagement together.

1. REINSTATEMENT AND RE-ENGAGEMENT

Section 71 of the EPA deals with the making of an Order for reinstatement or re-engagement.

Before this can be done, the Tribunal must have made a finding of unfair dismissal; having done this, the Tribunal must explain to the employee that an Order for reinstatement or re-engagement can be made and it should also explain the circumstances in which such an order may be made. When this has been done, the Tribunal must ask the employer whether he wishes the Tribunal to make such an Order. (Under the law prior to 1st June 1976 this requirement was not obligatory and, in practice, it was exceptional for the Tribunal to ask an employee whether he wanted his job back). If the employee then expresses a wish that he would like his job back the Tribunal **may** make an Order. It is apparent that, at this stage, the Tribunal has a discretion.

(a) Reinstatement

In exercising its discretion with regard to making an Order for reinstatement the Tribunal has to take into account the following considerations—

(i) whether the **employee wishes** to be reinstated.

(ii) whether it is **practicable for the employer** to comply with an Order for reinstatement.

(iii) where the **employee caused or contributed** to some extent to the dismissal, whether it would be **just** to order his reinstatement.

The question of **practicability** was a factor in the previous legislation. It does not mean simply " possible ". The Tribunal will take into account such things as the interests of the business and they will also take into account the feeling of fellow employees, e.g. if the reinstatement of the employee will have the effect of the whole work force coming out on strike, it is unlikely that an Order for reinstatement will be made—see *Coleman v. Magnet Joinery Ltd.* [1974] ICR 25 where it was held that the Tribunal should consider the consequences of re-engagement in the industrial relations scene in which it would take place and that since, in that case, re-engagement would promote further strife it was not " practicable " in the circumstances to make such a recommendation.

Section 71(8) specifically provides that where the employer has engaged a permanent replacement for a dismissed employee the Tribunal shall not take that fact into account in determining whether it is practicable to comply with an Order for reinstatement—unless the employer can show that he could not arrange for the dismissed employee's work to be done without engaging a permanent replacement or that he did engage the replacement after the lapse of a reasonable period without having heard from the dismissed employee that he wished to be reinstated and that when the employer engaged the replacement it was no longer reasonable for him to arrange for his work to be done except by a permanent replacement.

The **reinstatement order** itself will be an order that the employer shall treat the employee in all respects as if he had not been dismissed and this will include giving the employee any improvements in wages, terms and other conditions that might have come into force since his actual dismissal. The Order will also specify—

(a) any monies due (including arrears of pay) for the period between the date of termination of employment and the date of reinstatement.

(b) any rights and privileges (including seniority and pension rights) which must be restored to the employee and

(c) the date by which the Order must be complied with.

As far as arrears of pay under (a) above are concerned, the Tribunal must take into account any sums received by the employee between the two dates by way of wages in lieu of notice; any ex-gratia payments made by the employer; any wages paid in respect of employment with another employer; and also " such other benefits as the Tribunal thinks appropriate in the circumstances ". It is felt that these latter words will also include any Social Security Benefits obtained by the employee.

(b) Re-engagement

Here again (as with reinstatement) the Tribunal in exercising its discretion has to take into account the three factors referred to above, although they are worded slightly differently. The Tribunal will in the first instance have had to consider whether to make a reinstatement order. It is only if the Tribunal decides not to do this that it will consider whether to make an Order for re-engagement. In reaching this decision, the following considerations have to be taken into account—

(i) any wish expressed by the employee as to the nature of the Order to be made.

(ii) whether it is **practicable for the employer** or a successor or associated employer to comply with an Order for re-engagement and

(iii) where the **employee caused or contributed** to some extent to the dismissal, whether it would be **just** to order his re-engagement and if so on what terms.

Except in the last mentioned case where the employee has been guilty of contributory fault, the order for re-engagement must be on terms which are, so far as is reasonably practicable, as favourable as an order for reinstatement.

As with the reinstatement order, the Tribunal cannot, except in the exceptional circumstances referred to on page 316, take into account the fact that a permanent replacement has been engaged since the dismissal.

The **re-engagement order** itself will order either the employer or a successor of the employer or an associated employer to engage the employee in " employment comparable to that from which he was dismissed or other suitable employment ".   No further guidance is given in the EPA with regard to these words and any further interpretation can only be left to Tribunal decisions.   The Order itself will specify the terms on which re-engagement is to take place and they will include—

(a) the identity of the employer.

(b) the nature of the employment.

(c) the remuneration for the employment.

(d) any amount payable by the employer in respect of monies (including arrears of pay) for the period between the dates of termination of employment and the date of re-engagement.   As with reinstatement, certain monies received by the employee must be taken into account by the Tribunal.

(e) any rights and privileges (including seniority and pension rights) which must be restored to the employee and

(f) the date by which the Order must be complied with.

Non-compliance with the Tribunal's Order

It will have been noted above that the EPA provisions refer throughout to an **order** for reinstatement or re-enagement. Under the previous TUALRA provisions the Tribunal could only **recommend** reinstatement or re-engagement. Even now, however, the Tribunal **cannot force** an employer to take back an employee. Nor, it seems, will refusal to obey an order be treated as contempt of court. There are, however, **severe financial sanctions** imposed on an employer who fails to comply with an order for either reinstatement or re-engagement. These sanctions are contained in section 72 of the EPA.

If the employer only complies **in part** with a reinstatement or re-engagement order but does not comply fully with that order then the Tribunal will make an award of **compensation** in favour of the employee of such amount as it thinks fit having regard to the loss sustained by the employee in consequence of the failure to comply fully with the terms of that Order. The compensation here cannot exceed the normal TUALRA limit of £5,200 (Sched. 1, para. 20(1)).

If, however, the employer **fails completely** to comply with an order for reinstatement or re-engagement, then the position becomes much more serious from the employer's point of view. In these circumstances, the award of compensation becomes in effect a **three tier award—**

(a) there will be the " basic award " of compensation (as to which see page 322) up to a maximum of £2,400.

(b) there may be a compensatory award (as to which see page 323) up to a maximum of £5,200 and

(c) there will be an additional award of compensation (see *below*) to be paid by the employer to the employee; this will vary according to the circumstances but could be as much as £4,160.

Many employers have still not appreciated that these figures are cumulative and that in certain circumstances (admittedly rather exceptional circumstances) the total compensation awarded against them could reach the sum of £11,760.

The basic award and compensatory award are dealt with on pages 321 to 327.

Further attention must now be paid to the **additional compensation** referred to in (c) above. This additional award will be made unless the employer satisfies the Tribunal that it was not practicable to comply with the order. The onus here will be on the employer. Presumably, the factors relating to practicability and referred to on page 316 above will be taken into account. If the employer cannot meet this burden of proof, then the Tribunal is bound by the EPA to make the additional award which will be either—

(i) where the dismissal was an unfair dismissal because of " inadmissible reasons " (*i.e.* dismissal for membership or non-membership of a Trade Union or for taking part in the activities of an independent Trade Union) or where the dismissal was an unlawful act of discrimination either under the Sex Discrimination Act 1975 or the Race Relations Act 1976 then the additional compensation will be not less than 26 or more then 52 weeks pay.

(ii) in any case other than those referred to above, the additional compensation will be not less than 13 or more than 26 weeks pay.

In either case there is a limit of £80 in respect of a week's pay (which again is as defined in Part II of Schedule 4 to the EPA— see Appendix III—page 360, *post*).

The Tribunal seems to be left with a discretion as to where it " pitches " the compensation award as between the number of weeks referred to in respect of any additional award of compensation, although the absolute minimum is 13 weeks. Decisions of the Tribunal will, therefore, be awaited with interest.

Here again, the fact that an employer has engaged a permanent replacement for a dismissed employee will not be taken into account in determining whether it was practicable for the employer to comply with a reinstatement or re-engagement order unless, of course, the employer can show that he could not carry on without engaging a replacement.

Section 73(6) provides that if the employee has " unreasonably prevented " an order for reinstatement or re-engagement from being complied with then the Tribunal shall take that conduct into account as a failure on the part of the employee to mitigate his loss. This provision applies not only in the case of a total failure to comply with an order but also in the case of a partial failure.

As indicated previously, although the employer can still refuse to reinstate or re-engage an employee, he obviously does so now at his peril. Employers should, before they actually appear before the Tribunal, consider the matter very carefully and be prepared to deal with questions put to them by the Tribunal relating to reinstatement or re-engagement.[1]

2. COMPENSATION

The Employment Protection Act has also made considerable changes to the law regarding compensation for unfair dismissal. Again, these changes came into force on 1st June 1976.

It is now made very clear by the legislation that once the Tribunal has found in favour of the employee it must first consider the question of reinstatement or re-engagement. The provisions regarding compensation only come into play as a secondary matter to the question of giving the employee his job back. It is felt that this is one of the most important amendments introduced by the Employment Protection Act. As indicated above, very few recommendations of reinstatement or re-engagement were made prior to 1st June 1976. It has been calculated that during the first three years after the introduction of the unfair dismissal rights Tribunals only made recommendations of reinstatement or re-engagement in about 2% of the cases that were heard. Under the EPA provisions, this percentage is bound to increase substantially.

Section 72(5) of the EPA provides that if the Tribunal finds in favour of the employee and makes no order with regard to reinstatement or re-engagement then the Tribunal will make an

---

[1] Tribunals now have specific power to award costs against an employer whose failure, without a special reason, to adduce reasonable evidence in a re-instatement or re-engagement case causes an adjournment (The Industrial Tribunals (Labour Relations) (Amendment) Regulations 1976).

award of compensation for unfair dismissal. The compensation is to be calculated in accordance with sections 73 to 76. Those sections then provide that the award shall be a two tier award—a basic award and a compensatory award.

Basic Award

The aim of the basic award is to try and ensure that all employees are treated at least as favourably as if they had been dismissed for redundancy purposes. Indeed, the award itself is very much based on the redundancy payment provisions. The award will normally be a minimum of two weeks pay and the maximum sum payable (as for redundancy purposes) will be £2,400, this sum being based on the fact that years of service over 20 years will not count for calculating the basic award nor is weekly pay taken into account in excess of the sum of £80 per week. In certain special redundancy cases, *i.e.* where an employee is dismissed for redundancy but does not receive a redundancy payment because of his unreasonable refusal of suitable alternative employment or because of his renewal or re-engagement under a new contract, the basic award will simply be two weeks' pay. Similarly, where the amount to be calculated in accordance with the following paragraphs is in fact less than two weeks' pay, then the Tribunal will in fact make an award equal to two weeks' pay.

Subject to the above provisions, the amount of the basic award is dealt with exactly as for a redundancy payment (see page 185). The Tribunal calculates the length of continuous employment of the employee as at the effective date of termination of the employment and will then make an award as follows:—

(a) 1½ weeks' pay for each year of employment in which the employee was aged 41 or over.

(b) 1 week's pay for each year of employment in which the employee was aged 22 or over but under the age of 41 and

(c) half a week's pay for each year of employment in which the employee was aged 18 or over but below the age of 22.

Provisions similar to the redundancy payment provisions regarding employees during their 64th (in the case of a man) and 59th (in the case of a woman) year are contained in section 74(7) (see page 185, *above*).

If the Tribunal finds that the dismissal was to any extent caused or contributed to by any action of the employee it will (except where the dismissal was because of redundancy) reduce the amount of the basic award by such proportion as it considers just and equitable. The award cannot, however, for this reason be reduced below the two weeks' pay referred to above.

The amount of the basic award must also be reduced by the amount of any redundancy payment actually awarded by a Tribunal or paid by the employer to the employee, whether this is pursuant to the Redundancy Payments Act 1965 or otherwise. Under this heading, therefore, the basic award could be reduced to a nil award.

By virtue of section 77(1) of the EPA account must also be taken of any award already made to the employee under the Sex Discrimination Act 1975.

One of the results of the new provisions relating to the basic award is that Tribunals will no longer have to take into account in assessing " general " compensation the employee's lost redundancy payment rights. These will already be covered by the basic award itself.

Compensatory Award

In addition to the basic award, the Tribunal will make a compensatory award. This is referred to in section 76 of the EPA. The amount of the award will be " such amount as the Tribunal considers **just and equitable** in all the circumstances having regard to the **loss** sustained by the complainant in consequence of the dismissal in so far as that loss is attributable to action taken by the employer ".

General principles are laid down which are, in the main, in line with those which have been in existence since 1972.

No compensation will be awarded for the manner of the dismissal unless there is cogent evidence that the manner of the dismissal caused the employee financial loss.

N2

The loss will include any expenses reasonably incurred by the employee in consequence of the dismissal and also the loss of any benefit which he might reasonably be expected to have had but for the dismissal.

The normal rule applies that the employee must **mitigate** his loss and failure to do so will be taken into account by the Tribunal. Similarly, if the Tribunal finds that the dismissal was to any extent **caused or contributed to** by any action of the employee it will reduce the amount of the compensatory award by such proportion as it considers just and equitable.

As far as compensation for loss of redundancy rights are concerned, if the employee has received—either by virtue of the Redundancy Payments Act or otherwise—a sum of money in excess of the amount that could be awarded under the basic award, then that excess will be deducted from the amount of any compensatory award.

There is the usual ceiling of £5,200 for compensation under this head and if there has also been an award under the Sex Discrimination Act 1975 the ceiling of £5,200 will apply to the aggregate of the compensatory award and the award under the Sex Discrimination Act.

Under section 76(5) no account can be taken of any pressure which was exercised on the employer to dismiss the employee by calling or organising in any way a strike or other industrial action or threatening to do so; the question of the loss sustained by the employee by virtue of the employer's action has to be determined as if no such pressure had been exercised.

In the main, the wording of section 76 of the EPA is on very similar lines to the previous provisions of the TUALRA (Sched. 1, para. 19). There are, therefore, various guide-lines already laid down by existing decided cases. One of the earliest—and still possibly the most important—compensation case was *Norton Tool Co. Ltd. v. Tewson* [1972] ICR 501. The " *Norton Tool Co. Ltd.*" case is still followed by Tribunals when they endeavour to quantify the **loss sustained** by the employee. The loss will, of course, be the net loss to the employee. As far as the loss itself is concerned the Tribunal will in the first instance look at the employee's immediate loss of earnings, *i.e.*

they will calculate what his normal average weekly earnings would be after deducting tax, National Insurance and other deductions or contributions and will then multiply this net figure by the number of weeks from the date of termination of his employment to the date of the hearing before the Tribunal or the date on which he obtained other employment, if this is prior to the Tribunal hearing. If at the date of hearing the employee has not obtained other employment, then the Tribunal will try and assess how long it will be before the person does get another job. They will take into account the age of the employee and his qualifications and experience and also the general economic situation both in the country, in the particular area where the man lives and works and in the particular industry concerned. When the Tribunal has assessed this, it will again multiply the number of weeks during which it estimates that the employee will remain unemployed by the amount of the employee's normal net earnings. This will then give a figure in respect of loss of earnings, both immediate and future.

The Employment Appeal Tribunal has now confirmed that in assessing compensation an Industrial Tribunal should take into account, as one of the circumstances, the personal characteristics of the person dismissed, provided they existed at the date of the dismissal. Thus the age and state of health of the employee will be very relevant (*Fougere v. Phoenix Motor Co. Ltd.* [1976] IRLR 259).

In calculating the **loss of earnings,** the Tribunals will take into account the loss of various benefits, *e.g.* all fringe benefits that go along with the actual job. These will include luncheon vouchers, provision of a company car (particularly where there is no restriction on the private use of such car), medical insurance, pension contributions, free accommodation, etc. In addition, such items as bonuses, tips and profit sharing schemes will also be taken into account. It will, of course, be for the employee to prove these matters. One of the more complicated items under this head relates to **pension rights.** Tribunals have used different methods of assessing the value of lost pension rights. One method has been simply to work out the contributions made both by employer and employee, adding to these some estimate of contributions for the future, and then awarding the sum as part of the compensation. The other method, which may involve evidence from an actuary, is to calculate the pension that will be received by the employee and then to calculate the pension that he would have received had he continued working until normal retirement age; having done this, the Tribunal then try and assess the sum of money that would be required in order to put the employee in as good a position with regard to his pension as he would have been in had he continued in employment until normal retirement age.

As noted previously, the Tribunal can also award any **expenses** reasonably incurred by the employee as a result of his dismissal. This will not include the legal costs of taking the matter to the Tribunal. Expenses can, however, include the cost of moving house necessitated by obtaining a new job and also the actual expenses incurred in looking for a new job, *e.g.* telephone calls, travelling, etc.

The question of lost redundancy rights will now be covered by the basic award and has already been referred to on page 322, *above*. In the *Norton Tool Co. Ltd.* case an award (equal to approximately one week's pay) was given to the employee in respect of his future loss of the right not to be unfairly dismissed. At that time, of course, the qualifying period was two years. It is now only 26 weeks and little or nothing is now being awarded by Tribunals under this head. Some Tribunals will also make an award to take into account the employee's rights to notice under the Contracts of Employment Act 1972, *e.g.* if a person has been employed for five years (thus being entitled to five weeks' notice to terminate his contract) and is then dismissed it will be another five years before he is back in that position. Here again, however, it is probable that only a nominal award will be made by a Tribunal.

The next stage in the Tribunal's deliberations in assessing compensation will be to make certain **deductions** from the employee's loss. The Tribunal will certainly deduct in full any **National Insurance** benefits that the employee either has received or could have received, had he applied.[1] Tax rebates will also be deducted, particularly if they have been received by the employee. If an employee has received money in lieu of notice, this will either be deducted or, more often, the Tribunal will only begin to calculate the loss as from when the period to which the pay relates has expired. In practice, if no proper notice (or less than the proper notice) has been given the Tribunals will take this into account in awarding compensation—although strictly this is not really within their jurisdiction (see page 238).

Having made the above deductions, there are then two final matters (which have already been touched on) which may be taken into account and which may reduce the award—one is **contributory fault** and the other is **mitigation.**

Contributory Fault

The general common law principle is confirmed in section 76(6) of the EPA whereby the Tribunal, if it finds that the dismissal was to any extent caused or contributed to by any action of the employee, must reduce the amount of the compensatory award. The reduction will be by such proportion as the Tribunal considers just and equitable. The basic award may be similarly reduced—except where the dismissal was by reason of redundancy.

Under this head it is for the employer to satisfy the Tribunal that the employee did in fact contribute to his own loss. This is a matter which normally the Tribunal will take into account themselves. The matter should, however, be specifically referred to by the employer in his appearance before the Tribunal; having submitted that the dismissal was in fact fair, he should go on to say (particularly in cases of misconduct) that the employee was himself to a large extent responsible for his own dismissal and that this should be taken into account by the Tribunal in reaching a decision. The Tribunals have given a very wide interpretation to the question of contributory fault. Conduct which has been taken into account includes taking part in industrial action, refusing to obey reasonable

---

1 Certainly, this was the case until 1st June 1976. Since that date the effect of the Social Security (Unemployment, Sickness and Invalidity Benefit) Amendment (No. 2) Regulations 1976 is that Tribunals will not deduct anything for unemployment benefit after the date of an unfair dismissal award.

and lawful orders, violence and dishonesty. The conduct
itself must be blameworthy in some way. There have even
been a few cases where the contribution by the employee has
been held to be 100% and he has, therefore, received no compensation at all, *e.g. Maris v. Rotherham County Borough
Council* [1974] IRLR 147 where the employee was convicted
of rendering fraudulent claims for expenses to his employers,
although he was ultimately dismissed on other grounds.

It does, however, seem that the *Maris* case was exceptional—
the unfair dismissal was of what might be called a " technical "
character. In *Cooper v. British Steel Corporation* [1975] ICR
454, Phillips, J. reduced a Tribunal's assessment of contributory
fault from 95% to 70% and indicated that only " in except-
tional cases where there are some special facts " should there
be a contribution anywhere near 100%. Tribunals must
always remember that if they are considering compensation at
all they will have already made a finding that the dismissal was
" unfair ". Again, it is impossible to generalise.

In reaching its decision under this head the Tribunal will
look at the realities of the situation to see to what extent, if
any, the employee has contributed to his own ultimate
dismissal.

It has already been noted (see page 272) that misconduct
discovered after the dismissal will not help the employer to
establish that the dismissal itself was fair. Discovery of such
misconduct can, however, affect compensation and will be
taken into account by the Tribunals. Strictly, this should not
be done under the heading of contributory fault but under the
general heading relating to the loss sustained. Having said
this, however, Tribunals do often tend to deal with the matter
under this particular head.

It has already been seen that, as far as the basic award is
concerned this cannot be reduced below two weeks' pay by
virtue of the fact that the employee contributed to his own
dismissal.

The maximum amount of compensation that can be awarded
in respect of the compensatory award is £5,200 and this figure
will only become relevant **after** any relevant reduction has been

made in respect of the contributory fault of the employee. The maximum limit only comes into operation after all other deductions and adjustments (as referred to above) have been taken into account. In theory, therefore, it is possible for the Tribunal to order a reduction due to the contributory fault of the employee and yet still make a maximum award.

Mitigation

The general rule applicable to all claims for damages is that it is the duty of a person who has been " wronged " to mitigate his loss. This rule is confirmed in relation to unfair dismissal by section 76(4) of the EPA. If the employee has failed to mitigate his loss, then the Tribunal may reduce the compensatory award that they would otherwise make in his favour.

Obviously, the best way to mitigate the loss is for the employee to find another job at the same level of remuneration. If by the time of the Tribunal hearing the employee has not found another job, he will have to give evidence to the Tribunal to show what efforts he has made to find other employment. The employer should be prepared at the Tribunal hearing to ask questions on this particular point and, if he can, to give evidence himself about job possibilities in the area or in the particular trade or industry concerned. In any event, the Tribunal is entitled to act on its own knowledge of local conditions and the local employment situation.

The obligation on the employee is that he should act reasonably in order to mitigate his loss. It may not be reasonable to take the very first job that comes along. On the other hand, it will probably be wrong for the employee to wait until he can find a job giving him the same level of pay. He may have to be prepared to accept a lower paid job. The difference will be taken into account by the Tribunal in assessing the compensation.

On occasions the employer himself offers some form of employment to the employee. If the employee refuses this offer, then the employer may put forward that the employee has refused to mitigate his loss. In this event, the Tribunal will look at all the circumstances. If the offer of the new job is at a much lower rate of pay or is a job with a much lower status, then they may hold that the employee did not act unreasonably in refusing the offer[1]; similarly this could be the case where the employee due to the dismissal has lost all faith and confidence in his employer.

If the Tribunal finds that the employee has not mitigated his loss, then it may make a percentage deduction from the compensatory award or it may calculate the earnings which they assess that the employee should have received had he secured another job within the time which the Tribunal feel is reasonable.

The employee must begin to try and find other employment even during the period of the notice he has received from the employer.   Having said this, if he does get another job within the notice period, this does not absolve the employer from giving to the employee the correct amount of notice or paying him money in lieu.

" The employee who is energetic enough—and lucky enough —to get a new job does not have to bring into account the wages that he was paid by his new employers during that period " (Phillips, J. in *Blackwell v. GEC Elliott Process Automation Ltd.* [1976] IRLR 144).

It will be noted that the principle is different from the **wrongful dismissal** position (see page 233) where credit must be given for anything earned during the notice period.

In **unfair dismissal** cases the point initially caused some difficulty, but it was ultimately clarified by Sir John Brightman in *Everwear Candlewick Ltd. v. Isaac* [1974] ICR 525 as follows:—

" If an employee is unfairly dismissed without due notice and without pay in lieu of notice, he is *prima facie* entitled to compensation equal to his net pay for the proper period of the notice. No deduction is to be made for anything which the employee may earn elsewhere, for example, from another employer, during the period for which he should have received notice.   If an employee is dismissed without due notice but receives a sum which is equal to his pay for a shorter period than the requisite notice, that sum is to be taken into account in the sense that the employee will not receive compensation for loss of wages during that (short period),

---

[1] See the case of *Basnett v. Jackson* referred to on p. 233.

but will receive compensation for loss of wages during the balance of the proper period of notice and no deduction is to be made for anything which the employee earns elsewhere during the requisite period of notice. If an employee is dismissed without due notice but is given by his employer a sum which actually exceeds his net pay for the due period of notice, he obviously receives no compensation for loss of wages during the period of notice because he has lost none, but he is bound to bring into account any additional sum which has been paid to him by his former employer. We underline the words ' by his former employer '. The position would be different if during the period of due notice he had received money from another employer ".

Difficulties can arise both in assessing compensation and in the question of mitigation where the employee decides that he will not seek other employment but will set up a business on his own account. It is impossible to generalise in this particular matter and each case will depend on its own particular facts and circumstances. The employee must, however, be able to give very clear evidence as to why he has decided not to seek further employment.

In practice, very few cases of importance have arisen with regard to mitigation of the employee's loss. Presumably, this is because the vast majority of employees who have lost their employment do immediately begin to seek other work; if they do not find another job quickly, it is more than likely that this is due to the current economic conditions at the time either generally throughout the country or in a particular area or industry.

Finally, it should be mentioned that the Tribunal itself has no power to enforce payment of any award of compensation (either basic award or compensatory award) that may be made. Enforcement proceedings have to be brought in the ordinary courts. As will be seen in the next chapter, either party has a right to appeal from the decision of an Industrial Tribunal and this right has to be exercised within 42 days from the date of the decision. It would seem, therefore, that an employee cannot really take formal action to recover any compensation until that period of time has elapsed. Once that time has elapsed and assuming no appeal has been lodged, then if the money still remains unpaid, then the employee can commence separate proceedings for recovery of the money in the County Court or, if the sum exceeds the present County Court limit of £1,000, in the High Court.

It has already been seen, however, that the EPA does contain provisions under which it may be possible to enforce an award through the Tribunal if and when the jurisdiction of the Tribunals is extended (see page 238).

PART VI

INDUSTRIAL TRIBUNALS

CHAPTER 24

THE INDUSTRIAL TRIBUNAL—
BEFORE, DURING AND AFTER

Before considering the procedures and powers of the Industrial Tribunals, it is perhaps appropriate to consider whether it is possible for an employer to prevent an employee taking a case to the Tribunal. Assuming that the employee has the necessary qualification rights in respect of his particular claim (whether it be for unfair dismissal, a redundancy payment or any other matter referred to in the previous chapters) then in general it is not possible for the employer to prevent the employee exercising his rights. As has been noted previously, it is not possible to contract out of the provisions of the legislation.

Settling " out of court "

Particularly in dismissal cases, however, an employer may wish, despite a proposed dismissal of an employee, to treat that employee fairly and reasonably. In particular, he may have in mind to pay to that employee a reasonable amount of compensation. Can the employer do this and make it a term that the employee will not then apply to a Tribunal? Basically, the answer is that this cannot be done—or at least, if the condition is imposed, the employee can subsequently ignore it. Even if the employee signs a receipt " in full and final settlement of all claims that I may have arising out of termination of my employment " this will **not** prevent him applying to an Industrial Tribunal and claiming unfair dismissal. This is

because such a receipt would in fact be an " agreement "
purporting to preclude a person from presenting a complaint
to a Tribunal (TUALRA, Sched. 1, para. 32(1)).[1] Employers
may, however, take some consolation from the fact that if the
above situation does arise and the employee still applies to the
Tribunal, then the Tribunal will normally take into account
when assessing compensation any monies that have already been
paid to the employee.

There is, however, one way round this problem—a way, it
might be added, which does not seem to be well known to
many employers. This is to use the services of a Conciliation
Officer. Paragraph 32(2)(d) excludes from the contracting out
restriction " any agreement to refrain from presenting a complaint . . . where in compliance with a request . . . a Conciliation Officer has taken action ".

Under paragraph 26(4) of Schedule 1 the Conciliation Officer
is under a duty to make his services available in an effort to
promote a settlement where an employee has ceased to be
employed in circumstances where he claims that he was unfairly
dismissed but before any complaint has been lodged with the
Industrial Tribunal and where he is requested (either by the
employer or the employee) to make such services available.

It is, of course, well known that the Conciliation Officer
will " come on the scene " once an application has been lodged
with the Tribunal. The above provisions, however, provide
that at any time after the dismissal the Conciliation Officer can
be approached (either by the employer or by the employee)
and can then assist in reaching a settlement. If such a settlement is reached with the consent and approval of the Conciliation Officer, this will be final and binding on both parties
and the employee will not subsequently be able to take the
matter to a Tribunal.

It is suggested that this possibility is worth exploring in
cases where an employer wishes to pay a reasonable sum of
money to an employee but, at the same time, only wishes to do
so if he can be sure that he will not subsequently be involved
before an Industrial Tribunal. In that situation, the employer

---

[1] See, for example, the EAT decision in *Council of Engineering Institutions v.
Maddison* [1976] IRLR 389.

can immediately after the dismissal contact the Conciliation Officer. In practice, this can even be done just prior to or at the same as the actual dismissal.

Section 118 of the **Employment Protection Act 1975** contains very similar provisions and in general prevents contracting out of the EPA. Again, however, an exception to this is any agreement to refrain from instituting or continuing any proceedings where the Conciliation Officer has been involved and a settlement is agreed with him. This is relevant in relation to the various employee rights introduced by the EPA.

It will be remembered (see page 234) that as far as a claim for **wrongful dismissal** is concerned it is still possible to pay a sum of money to an employee and to obtain from him a receipt in full and final settlement which, provided that the receipt was given without undue influence or pressure, will then prevent that employee from bringing Court proceedings.

The Conciliation Officer

The Conciliation Officer will mainly " come on the scene " when an employee makes an application to an Industrial Tribunal in respect of any situation where the employee has rights under any aspect of Employment Law legislation as referred to in the preceding chapters of this book.

The Conciliation Officer is in fact now a designated Officer of the Advisory Conciliation and Arbitration Service (referred to throughout the EPA as " the Service " but generally referred to as the ACAS). The ACAS became an independent body under the Employment Protection Act on 1st January 1976. Prior to that date, there had been since 2nd September 1974 a Conciliation and Advisory Service under the Department of Employment.

The main duties of the ACAS are referred to in sections 1 to 6 of the EPA and they cover Conciliation, Arbitration, Advice, Enquiries into questions relating to industrial relations generally and the drawing up of Codes of Practice.

In particular, section 2(4) of the EPA provides that the ACAS shall designate officers to perform the functions of Conciliation Officers in respect of matters which are or could be the subject of proceedings before an Industrial Tribunal. This sub-section is, therefore, the formal designation of the Conciliation Officer.

The general aim of the ACAS is to promote the improvement of industrial relations and in particular to encourage the extension of collective bargaining. Where a trade dispute exists the ACAS can offer its assistance to the parties to the dispute with a view to bringing about a settlement.

Apart from the situation referred to above where an employer or employee may specifically request help from a Conciliation Officer, the most normal method of involvement of such an officer will be after the employee has presented his complaint to an Industrial Tribunal. A copy of the complaint is sent to the ACAS and the Conciliation Officer will normally then get in touch with both parties. In some areas, the ACAS will send a printed form to the parties asking them to indicate whether it is a matter in which conciliation is felt to be useful.

Where a complaint has been presented to an Industrial Tribunal it is the duty of the Conciliation Officer to endeavour to promote a settlement of the complaint without it being determined by an Industrial Tribunal either if he is requested to do so by either party or if, in the absence of any such request, he considers that he could act with a reasonable prospect of success (see TUALRA, Sched. 1, para. 26(2) and EPA, s. 108(3)).

Neither of the parties is under any obligation to speak to or negotiate with the Conciliation Officer. A refusal to do this will not be known by or reported to any third party and, in particular, it will not come to the knowledge of the Industrial Tribunal. Similarly, anything communicated to a Conciliation Officer in connection with the performance of his functions is not admissible in evidence in any proceedings before an Industrial Tribunal, except with the consent of the person who communicated it to him. The parties can, therefore, remain " uninhibited " in their discussions with the Conciliation Officer.

There is really nothing to be lost by discussing the matter with the Conciliation Officer and, in many cases, a great deal can be gained. From the employer's point of view, the Conciliation Officer can be very useful in acting as an intermediary in helping to achieve a reasonable settlement. In many cases, the employer may well feel—particularly in the light of the more stringent provisions of the EPA relating to reinstatement and re-engagement—that serious consideration should be given to trying to agree a settlement via the Conciliation Officer, *e.g.* if the matter can be settled by payment of a reasonable compensation sum. Any such settlement will be noted in writing, signed by the parties and countersigned by the Conciliation Officer and that will then be an end of the matter; the employee will not then be able to re-open the matter by referring it to a Tribunal.

One other factor that should be mentioned in relation to discussions with a Conciliation Officer is that it is very often possible during those discussions to discover some more detailed information about the other side's case.

The Industrial Tribunal

In recent years Industrial Tribunals have become one of this country's largest " growth industries ". They were originally established under the provisions of section 12 of the Industrial Training Act 1964. They still have jurisdiction under that Act (although this is now very seldom used in practice), under the Redundancy Payments Act 1964, the Contracts of Employment Act 1972, the Trade Union and Labour Relations Act 1974, the Equal Pay Act 1970, the Sex Discrimination Act 1975, the Employment Protection Act 1975 and various other statutes. The most important part of the Tribunals' work is, of course, now the various aspects of employment law referred to in the preceding chapters of this book. To give an example of the growth and importance of the Tribunals applications in recent years have increased enormously—in England and Wales alone there were 14,890 applications in 1974, and 32,734 applications in 1975. Not all such applications reach a formal hearing—indeed, approximately two thirds of them are withdrawn or settled after conciliation.

During 1976 (taking into account the most recent legislation) it is anticipated that in the region of 55,000 applications will be made to Industrial Tribunals.

It will be remembered that Tribunals still do not have jurisdiction to deal with claims for damages for breach of contract
and for wrongful dismissal but that this is now provided for
by section 109 of the EPA. It is not at present known when the
Lord Chancellor will bring this section into force. Until this
is done we are left with the present unsatisfactory position
where, for example, a Tribunal can declare what notice an
employee was entitled to under his Contract of Employment
but cannot award the appropriate sum to the applicant, who
then has to commence separate proceedings in the County
Court.

Tribunals normally sit with three members, the Chairman
being legally qualified and having with him two lay members
appointed by the Employment Secretary from a Trade Union
panel and an Employers' panel. The Tribunals have regional
offices (where the cases are also heard) in most of the major
cities in the country.

The proceedings are informal and anyone can appear before
the Tribunal. An employee can either appear for himself or
he can be represented by a friend or by a Trade Union Official
or, of course, by a lawyer. Legal Aid is not at present available
for the actual hearing before the Tribunal, although it is
possible (subject to the normal Legal Aid financial limits) for
an employee to obtain Legal Aid for all advice prior to the
hearing, for preparation of the application to the Tribunal and
also for preparation of a form of written representation that
the employee can then lodge with or hand to the Tribunal.

The proceedings and the administration of the Tribunals are
mainly governed by the Industrial Tribunals (Labour Relations)
Regulations 1974.

An excellent summary of the functions of Industrial Tribunal
was given by Phillips, J. in a recent appeal case (*Watling v.
William Bird & Son Contractors Ltd.* [1976] ITR 70) when he
said—

    " . . . these matters have been entrusted for solution, not to
    the regular courts, but to industrial tribunals presided over by a
    lawyer but otherwise composed of representatives of employers
    and representatives of employees, the three together exercising

discretion and judgment which is suitable to them in their function as what the Court of Appeal has described as that of an ' industrial jury ', because they have the immense advantage of having experience in these questions, and they have the enormous advantage, which is difficult to exaggerate in this kind of case, of seeing the complaintant, of seeing the employers, of really being able to get the feel of the whole matter, sizing it up and coming to a judgment ".

The employee's application

Applications by an employee always have to be made within a certain period of time. This has been referred to under the various appropriate headings in preceding chapters, e.g. an application for unfair dismissal has normally to be lodged within three months of the date of termination of the employment (see page 311).

It will also be remembered that employees with 26 weeks service now also have a right to ask for a written statement of the reasons for their dismissal, provided they do this within 14 days of the date of the dismissal. If this is refused, the employee can apply to an Industrial Tribunal. In certain cases, it seems that this procedure may well be used by employees before they lodge their main application, e.g. alleging unfair dismissal.

There is a set application form to be used by an employee— Form IT1. This can be obtained from the Department of Employment offices, from any Employment Exchange or from the Central Office of the Industrial Tribunals. It is possible (although not really desirable from the employee's point of view) not to use the set form but to apply in writing to the Tribunal. This will be acceptable provided that the application in writing contains details of the name and address of the employee, the name and address of the employers, the grounds on which relief is sought and the question for determination by the Tribunal.

As indicated previously, the Tribunals aim to be informal. If, therefore, the employee makes a mistake in part of the application form, e.g. by naming the wrong employer, the Tribunals do have power to amend the application at the date of hearing. They will do this if they are satisfied that there was a genuine mistake and that the amendment will not cause injustice or hardship to the employer. If an application for such an amendment is made at the hearing itself and the employer feels that he is prejudiced by this, he can apply for an adjournment.

It is not now necessary on Form IT1 to specify exactly the Act of Parliament under which the employee claims relief, *e.g.* Redundancy Payments Act 1965, Sex Discrimination Act 1975, etc. The employee simply has to state in his own words the grounds on which relief is sought. The outcome of this is that an application alleging unfair dismissal may well ultimately be dealt with by the Tribunal as an application for a redundancy payment and/or unfair dismissal.

It has already been noted (see page 314) that since 1st June 1976 it is possible in the case of claim arising out of his dismissal for an employee to lodge his application before the period of notice has actually expired.

As soon as the IT1 is received by the Central Office of the Industrial Tribunals, a copy will be sent to the employer named in that form. The employee can withdraw his application at any time either of his own accord or after a settlement has been achieved. If a case is withdrawn, it will sometimes be recorded in the Tribunal records as having been " dismissed ". On other occasions, the terms of a settlement may be recorded as the decision itself.

The employer's reply

Once the employer receives a copy of Form IT1 he has only 14 days from the date of receipt to send in his Notice of Appearance (normally on Form IT3). This is most important from the point of view of the employer. If this is not done, the employer will not be entitled to be heard and the case will proceed without him even being informed of the date of hearing. In fact, the 14 day limit is not treated quite as strictly as the time limit in respect of applications by an employee. It does not go to the very root of the Tribunal's jurisdiction. The Tribunal has a wide discretion to extend the 14 day limit. Despite this, if employers are in difficulties in lodging a reply within the 14 days, then they should either lodge a very short and simple reply by way of a straight denial of the claim or they should write to the Tribunal within the 14 day period asking for further time to be allowed to them. Such an application will normally be granted.

Form IT3 requires the employer to give his reasons for refuting the claim of the employee. Here again, the official form does not **have** to be used, although it is better to do so. If, however, the form is not used, the reply must be in writing and it must set out the full name and address of the employer and must state whether or not he intends to resist the application and, if so, on what grounds.

Although the employer is under an obligation to state the grounds on which he resists the application of the employee, so that the employee is aware of the " general nature of the defence ", it may be policy in many cases for the employer to keep that information to the absolute minimum. If this is done, however, it should be borne in mind that the Tribunal does have power to order the employer to give further particulars of his case (see page 342).

Preliminary matters

Rule 4 of the 1974 Regulations deals with various matters that can arise prior to the actual hearing. As indicated previously, the aim is that proceedings should be informal. On the other hand either of the parties can seek further detailed information before the actual hearing. In particular, they can ask the Tribunal to make an order for **discovery of documents.** This order will call upon the other side to give a list of all relevant documents in their possession and to make them available for inspection or to supply copies. In most cases, however, this can be done on an amicable basis, *e.g.* the contract of employment relating to the employee or details of a pension scheme will normally be released by an employer on request from the employee or his advisers. Other important documents could include clock cards, medical notes, job and performance appraisals, etc. Production of documents will be ordered even if to do so will cause the employer considerable work and expense.

In addition, either side can ask for **further and better particulars** of the other's case. If, therefore, the employee has not made it clear exactly what he is alleging, the employer should ask the Tribunal to make an order calling upon the employee to give these further particulars. This procedure has not in the past been used very regularly and it seems that greater attention could be paid to the advantages of using this procedure.

In view of a recent ruling of the Employment Appeal Tribunal, it seems that Tribunals will now be more ready to order further and better particulars of an employer's case to enable the employee to know properly the details of the case he has to meet. Although " unnecessary legalism " should not be encouraged, it should not be avoided at the cost of failing to do justice (Phillips, J. in *White v. University of Manchester*—26th May 1976).

Finally, either party can apply either for a **witness order** or for an order for **production of documents.** These orders will normally be granted by the Tribunal without any difficulty whatsoever. If there is any problem about a particular witness order, the Tribunal can ask to be satisfied that the order is in fact necessary and that the evidence to be given by the witness will be relevant to the issues (*Dada v. Metal Box Co. Ltd.* [1974] ICR 559).

The hearing

The date, time and place of the hearing will be fixed by the Tribunal and the parties must be given at least 14 days' notice of the hearing. The practice of Tribunals with regard to adjournments seems to vary. In general, Tribunals seem to be rather more strict with regard to adjournments than is the High Court. The general experience seems to be that unless an application for an adjournment is made as soon as the date of hearing is received, it will be difficult to get an adjournment unless some very good reason indeed (*e.g.* time required for further conciliation) can be put forward.

The hearing itself will be in public unless it would be against the interests of national security to allow the evidence to be given in public or unless the hearing of evidence is likely to consist of information which the person could not disclose without contravening an Act of Parliament or is information which has been communicated to him in confidence or information the disclosure of which would be seriously prejudicial to the interests of any undertaking in which he works. In practice, it is very unusual indeed for proceedings to be in private.

Normally, of course, both sides will attend the hearing. As an alternative to this, however, a party can submit written representations to the Tribunal and then not appear himself. If he does this the written representations must be provided at least seven days before the hearing and a copy must be provided to the other party. It is obvious that written representations will carry less weight than evidence actually given by a party, in particular because in the case of written representations the party is not available for cross examination.

If a party does not attend at all, the regulations do not specifically provide that this fact will be held " against him ". The Tribunal do have power to dispose of the case in the absence of that party or they can adjourn the hearing to a later date. If the Tribunal does decide to deal with the case, then the actual form lodged by that party (IT1 or IT3) will be treated as " written representations " on his behalf as referred to above.

It has already been noted that parties can either appear themselves or they can be represented by a friend, an official from a Trade Union or Employers' Association or by a Solicitor or Barrister.

The **procedure** at the hearing is that each party will be allowed to make an opening statement, to give evidence, to call witnesses, to cross examine the other party's witnesses and to make a final address to the Tribunal. Evidence is normally given on oath, but witnesses can " affirm ". The strict rules of evidence do not apply and it is, therefore, possible to introduce " hearsay " evidence, although less weight will be attached to this by the Tribunal.

In most of the matters considered in the preceding chapters, it will be the employer who will have to present his case first. This will, however, depend on the particular issue and on the burden of proof. For example, in redundancy and unfair dismissal matters, if the dismissal itself is not in dispute, then the burden of proof is on the employer and he will have to present his case first. If, however, the dismissal is in dispute, the employee will have to prove the dismissal and he will present his case first; if the complaint in respect of any of the " employee rights " is outside the time limit, then again, the employee will have to prove that it was not reasonably practicable for him to present the application in time and, again, he will go first; finally, if the employee is, for example, alleging that he has been dismissed for an inadmissible reason, he will have to present his case first and prove the reason.

As far as the **decision** of the Tribunal is concerned, this will very often be given informally at the end of the hearing, unless the case has been very lengthy and/or complicated. The formal decision will, however, always be promulgated in writing and this is the official decision. This will normally be about two to three weeks from the actual date of hearing. A date will be stamped on the formal written decision and this will be the date when the written decision is issued. It is this date which is relevant for such things as an appeal or a review of the decision (see pages 348 and 345).

The decision of the Tribunal can be a majority decision; if there are only two members sitting, then the Chairman's view will prevail.

Costs

The regulations provide that a Tribunal shall not normally award costs but they may do so where in its opinion a party to any proceedings has acted **frivolously or vexatiously.** These words have been interpreted narrowly and it is very unusual indeed for an order for costs to be made. If an order is made, it will normally be in a specified sum (probably not more than £30) although the Tribunal does have power to award costs to be taxed.

Subject to the above provisions, the Tribunal does have a discretion as to the question of costs. In *E. T. Marler Ltd. v. Robertson* [1974] ICR 72 it was stated by Sir Hugh Griffiths as follows—

" if the employee knows that there is no substance in his claim and that it is bound to fail, or if the claim is on the face of it so manifestly misconceived that it can have no prospect of success, it may be deemed frivolous and an abuse of the procedure of the Tribunal to pursue it. If an employee brings a hopeless claim not with any expectation of recovering compensation but out of spite to harass his employers or for some other improper motive, he acts vexatiously, and likewise abuses the procedure. In such cases the Tribunal may and doubtless usually will award costs against the employee ".

Although the above is without doubt a correct statement of the law, it is apparent that this statement is very seldom applied in practice by the Tribunals. More recently, the Employment Appeals Tribunal has expressed the view that the rule as to costs may be a little too restrictive.

Separate Regulations have also now been introduced under which Tribunals can award costs against an employer whose failure, without reasonable excuse, to adduce reasonable evidence in reinstatement or re-engagement cases, causes an adjournment of the hearing.[1]

After the Decision

If the decision is in fact accepted by the parties then that is obviously an end of the matter. If the decision is not acceptable there are two alternatives—(a) to apply for a review or (b) to appeal.

Application for a review

The rights of a party to apply for a review of the decision of a Tribunal have been little used and it is felt that they are not widely known. The procedure can be very useful in that it is speedy and cheap, as compared with a full Appeal. Having said this, however, it is most unlikely that, on a review, the decision of the Tribunal will be completely reversed. It can, however, be extremely useful if it is felt that the Tribunal has erred in some part of its decision, *e.g.* as to the amount of compensation awarded.

---

[1] See footnote to p. 321.

The position is covered by Rule 9 of the 1974 Regulations. An application for a review can be made either at the hearing or within 14 days from the date of entry of the decision on the Register. There are only five possible grounds for a review and these are as follows:—

(a) where the decision was wrongly made as a result of error on the part of the Tribunal staff.

(b) where a party did not receive notice of the proceedings.

(c) where the decision was made in the absence of a party entitled to be heard.

(d) where new evidence has become available since the decision and its existence could not have been reasonably known or foreseen.

(e) where the interests of justice require a review.

There is only jurisdiction to entertain one application under any one of the above provisions.

As to **new evidence** the principles laid down in *Ladd v. Marshall* [1954] 3 All E.R. 745 apply and the evidence will only be admitted if three conditions are complied with—

(i) it was not previously available.

(ii) it has an important influence on the case.

(iii) it is credible.

All three of these conditions must be complied with.

Tribunals seem to be very strict in applying these provisions and there are very few cases where new evidence has been admitted after the original hearing.

In *Bateman v. British Leyland U.K. Ltd.* [1974] ICR 403 a review was in fact allowed in a case where the " new evidence " was that only two weeks after the original Tribunal decision the employee was made redundant in his new job; the Tribunal, on the review, increased the award of compensation and this was upheld by the Appeal Court (NIRC).

No review will, however, be allowed if the evidence was available at the original hearing. Thus, in a redundancy case (*Flint v. Eastern Electricity Board* [1975] ICR 395) the employee did not at the original hearing give evidence relating to his ill health (arthritis and bad leg) when the Tribunal were considering whether an offer of alternative employment, involving more walking, had been unreasonably refused. The application to review the decision was refused because the evidence had been available all along. The applicant also failed to get a review under ground (*e*) (" interests of justice "). Phillips, J., at the end of his decision, indicated that it was desirable that the rule as to reviews should be re-written, in the hope that it might be " made rather clearer in what circumstances a tribunal may, and in what circumstances it may not, order a review ".

In *McGregor v. Gibbings Amusements Ltd.* [1975] ITR 64 a Tribunal granted a review where subsequent to the original decision the employers obtained evidence that the employee had been defrauding them during the course of his employment. The compensation of £150 was reduced to a NIL award.

The " interests of justice " ground is intended to be a residual category designed to confer a wide discretion on Industrial Tribunals. Having said this, applications under this head are again granted very sparingly by Tribunals. It has, on several occasions, been stated that the Tribunal must also take into account " the interests of the general public that proceedings of this kind should be as final as possible ". It should, therefore, only be in unusual cases that the employee is allowed to have " a second bite of the cherry "—see Phillips, J. in the *Flint v. Eastern Electricity Board* case (*above*). If it is sought to review the compensation awarded, this will only be allowed if the basis of the decision has been falsified so as to invalidate the original decision.

One of the practical problems about applying for a review is that the matter will invariably be considered and heard by the same Tribunal which heard the original case itself. It is for this reason that it is most unlikely that a party will be able to persuade the Tribunal to change its mind completely on a particular decision.

Appeal

An appeal from an Industrial Tribunal will only lie on a question of law arising from a decision of the Tribunal. Since 31st March 1976 the appeal will lie to the Employment Appeal Tribunal (EAT). This has very similar composition, status and powers to the old National Industrial Relations Court (NIRC). Any appeal must be lodged within 42 days of the date of the decision of the Tribunal (as indicated above, this date being the date stamped on the written decision). Extensions of time will only be granted in rare and exceptional circumstances. The rules and procedures for the Employment Appeal Tribunal are governed by the Employment Appeal Tribunal Rules 1976. These stress the informality of the Tribunal and the desirability of conciliation at all stages of the proceedings. Again, costs will only be awarded where it appears that any proceedings were " unnecessary improper or vexatious or where there has been unreasonable delay or other unreasonable conduct in bringing or conducting the proceedings ". The late abandonment of a " hopeless " appeal was held by the NIRC to be " other unreasonable conduct " Legal Aid will be available for proceedings in the EAT in the same way as for proceedings in the normal Courts.

The EAT will normally sit in divisions of three with a lawyer Chairman, being a High Court Judge nominated by the Lord Chancellor. The lay members will be members who have special knowledge or experience of industrial relations either as representatives of employers or as representatives of workers and they will be drawn from panels of employers' representatives and Union representatives.

As indicated above, an appeal can only lie on a matter of law. There can be a very thin dividing line between what is a question of law and what is a question of fact. For example, a finding of fact can be an error in law if that finding is one which no Tribunal, properly directing itself, could reasonably have made. If, however, there was ample evidence to support the Tribunal's finding, there will be no error in law.

It is not enough on appeal to show that the Tribunal could have decided the point differently—or indeed that the appellate body may well themselves have decided it differently. The appellant must be able to show that only one conclusion was open to the Industrial Tribunal and that the Tribunal did not take it. If more than one conclusion was possible, it is a " grey area " and there will not normally be an error in law.

On an appeal fresh evidence cannot be introduced if it was already available at the original hearing.

Tribunals should give full reasons for each part of their decision so that the parties can know why the tribunal has decided as it has and also so that the appellate court will be able to determine precisely upon what grounds the decision has been reached. Similarly, if compensation is awarded, full details of how the figure has been assessed and calculated should be stated by the Tribunal. Failure to do this will be an error in law.

Thus, a person claiming that there is an error in law must establish one of three things:—

(1) that the Tribunal misdirected itself in law or misapplied the law or

(2) that the Tribunal misunderstood the facts or misapplied the facts or

(3) that, although the Tribunal apparently directed itself properly in law and did not mistate or misunderstand or misapply the facts, the decision was " perverse ", *i.e.* there was no evidence to justify the conclusion reached by the Tribunal.

The National Industrial Relations Court did issue a practice direction in July 1973 to the effect that if appeals were lodged which involved no question of law whatsoever, the Court might take the view that the appellant had been guilty of unreasonable conduct instituting the appeal and thus make an order for costs or expenses against him. That direction was upheld by the High Court (which dealt with appeals in the interim period between the abolition of the NIRC and the establishment of the EAT) in the case of *Dacres v. Walls Meat Co. Ltd.* [1976] ICR 44. It would seem, therefore, that this principle will probably also now be applied under the Employment Appeal Tribunal Rules 1976.

Appendix I

Extract from

THE SEX DISCRIMINATION (QUESTIONS AND REPLIES) ORDER 1975

SCHEDULE 1
THE SEX DISCRIMINATION ACT 1975 s. 74(1)(a)
QUESTIONNAIRE OF PERSON AGGRIEVED)

To..(*name of person to be questioned*)

of .... (*address*)

1.—(1) I........................(*name of questioner*) of..(*address*) consider that you may have discriminated against me contrary to the Sex Discrimination Act 1975.

(2) (*Give date, approximate time and a factual description of the treatment received and of the circumstances leading up to the treatment.*)

(3) I consider that this treatment may have been unlawful [because......................
....(*complete if you wish to give reasons, otherwise delete*)].

2. Do you agree that the statement in paragraph 1(2) above is an accurate description of what happened? If not, in what respect do you disagree or what is your version of what happened?

3. Do you accept that your treatment of me was unlawful discrimination by you against me?
If not—

    (a) why not,

    (b) for what reason did I receive the treatment accorded to me, and

    (c) how far did my sex or marital status affect your treatment of me?

4. (*Any other questions you wish to ask.*)

5. My address for any reply you may wish to give to the questions raised above is [that set out in paragraph 1(1) above] [the following address........................
....].

....(*signature of questioner*)

....(*date*)

N.B.—By virtue of section 74 of the Act this questionnaire and any reply are (subject to the provisions of the section) admissible in proceedings under the Act and a court or tribunal may draw any such inference as is just and equitable from a failure without reasonable excuse to reply within a reasonable period, or from an evasive or equivocal reply, including an inference that the person questioned has discriminated unlawfully.

SCHEDULE 2
THE SEX DISCRIMINATION ACT 1975 s. 74(1)(b)
REPLY BY RESPONDENT

To..(*name of questioner*)

of ....(*address*)

1. I.............................(*name of person questioned*) of.........................(*address*)
hereby acknowledge receipt of the questionnaire signed by you and dated
...............................which was served on me on...(*date*).

2. [I agree that the statement in paragraph 1(2) of the questionnaire is an accurate description of what happened.]

[I disagree with the statement in paragraph 1(2) of the questionnaire in that
....]

3. I accept/dispute that my treatment of you was unlawful discrimination by me against you.

[My reasons for so disputing are.. The reason why you received the treatment accorded to you and the answers to the other questions in paragraph 3 of the questionnaire are...]

4. (*Replies to questions in paragraph 4 of the questionnaire.*)

[5. I have deleted (in whole or in part) the paragraph(s) numbered.........................
above, since I am unable/unwilling to reply to the relevant questions in the correspondingly numbered paragraph(s) of the questionnaire for the following reasons...]

....(*signature of person questioned*)

....(*date*)

Appendix II

CALCULATION OF PERIOD OF EMPLOYMENT

The phrase " **continuous employment** " or reference to an employee being " **continuously employed** " arise in many aspects of employment law. In particular, most of the employee's rights do not arise at all until that employee has been " continuously employed " for a specified minimum period, *e.g.* 26 weeks in the case of unfair dismissal; two years in the case of redundancy; and so on.

An employee's entitlement to redundancy pay and to a specified minimum period of notice required to terminate his contract of employment is also based on the length of his " continuous employment ".

For all those purposes there is a special—and at times rather technical—definition of " continuous employment ". The definition is based on **Schedule 1 to the Contracts of Employment Act 1972**, which has, with effect from 1st June 1976, been amended by the Employment Protection Act 1975 (Sched. 16, Pt. II).

The definitions and provisions of Schedule 1 are incorporated by reference into the other relevant employment statutes, *e.g.* para. 30(1) of Schedule 1 to the Trade Union and Labour Relations Act 1974; para. 1(1) of Schedule 1 to the Redundancy Payments Act 1965; and section 126(5) of the Employment Protection Act 1975.

Thus, it is Schedule 1 to the 1972 Act which is vital and it is this Schedule (as amended and interpreted) that should be considered. Reference in this Appendix to numbered paragraphs are to those paragraphs in **Schedule 1 to the 1972 Act.**

Continuous Employment

In all the statutes referred to above, there is a presumption of continuity. For example, section 126(5) of the EPA provides that—

" for the purposes of any proceedings brought under or by virtue of this Act, a person's employment during any period shall, unless the contrary is shown, be presumed to have been continuous ".

Similar provisions are contained in para. 30(2) of the TUALRA and section 9(2)(*a*) of the RPA.

This presumption can be of great benefit to the employee. He will be assumed to have been continuously employed unless the employer can show that this is not the case. The burden of proof here is placed firmly on the employer. If he is unable to produce evidence to rebut the presumption and to show that the employment was " broken ", then the employment in question will be held to be continuous.

Normal working week

At the present time any week in which the employee is employed for 16 hours or more will count in computing a period of employment (para. 3). Similarly, any week during the whole or part of which the employee's relations with the employer are governed by a contract of employment which normally involves employment for 16 hours or more weekly shall count in computing a period of employment (para. 4).

Thus, " part-time " employees, i.e. those who are employed for less than 16 hours per week are excluded from most of the employee rights referred to in this book.

The EPA contains provisions (Sched. 16, Pt. II, paras. 13 and 14) whereby the original " definition " of " part-time " was reduced to 16 hours with effect from 1st February, 1977.

Under the EPA provisions the position is now as follows:—

(1) any week in which the employee is employed for 16 hours or more will count in computing a period of employment.

(2) if the contract of employment normally involves work for 16 hours or more weekly and this is reduced to 8 hours or more weekly then the later " 8 hour " weeks will still count in computing a period of employment and they will not break the continuity of the employment provided that not more than 26 such weeks shall count for this purpose.

(3) if an employee has been continuously employed for a period of 5 years or more, he shall be treated as a " full-time " employee (i.e. more than 16 hours weekly) if throughout that period he has worked for an employer under a contract of employment which normally involves employment for 8 hours or more, but less than 16 hours weekly.

(4) once an employee has been continuously employed for the relevant period qualifying him for a particular right under the legislation, he will be regarded as continuing to satisfy that requirement until in a week subsequent to that time his relations with his employer are governed by a contract normally involving employment for less than 8 hours weekly.

o

It will be seen from the above that the references in Schedule 1 are to a contract of employment " which normally involves employment " for more than the specified amount of time. In other words, it is what is **normal under the contract** of employment that is important—not the actual number of hours worked in a particular week. Thus, if an employee is put on short time during a slack period it will be the number of hours **normally** worked under his contract that will count for these purposes. Similarly, if an employee happens to arrive early or to work late, these additional hours will not be taken into account.

In calculating the number of hours of employment in a week, meal breaks do not count. A " week " for these purposes means a week ending with a Saturday. There is a special provision (para. 11(2)) dealing with employees who are required by virtue of their job to live on the premises where they work (*e.g.* the caretaker of a building); the hours of employment for such an employee are the hours during which he is on duty or during which his services may be required.

In certain circumstances, a temporary absence from work will not break the continuity. This is the effect of paragraph 4 referred to above. Again, the vital factor is whether during a particular week (or part of a week) the relationship of employee and employer was governed by a contract of employment which normally involved employment for more than the specified amount of time. Obviously, the absence of an employee on holiday will not break continuity. Similarly, absence due to sickness or due to a temporary lay-off will not break continuity, provided that the contract of employment is not terminated and provided that the employee in due course does return to his job. There are in fact also special provisions with regard to sickness or injury which will be considered under the next heading.

It should also be noted that paragraph 4 of Schedule 1 specifically refers to the whole **or part of** a week. This particular aspect of the paragraph has caused problems for Industrial Tribunals in assessing, for example, whether an employee has served for the necessary 26 week qualifying period for the purposes of unfair dismissal in a situation where he has been dismissed during the last week of the 26 week period. Conflicting Tribunal decisions have been resolved by the case of *Coulson v. City of London Polytechnic* [1976] ITR 121. In that particular case, the employee started work on 1st October 1974 (which was a Tuesday) and his contract terminated on 24th March 1975 (which was a Monday). The employee claimed that he had been unfairly dismissed and to establish such a claim he had to show in the first instance that he had been continuously employed for a period of not less than 26 weeks ending with the effective date of termination (*see* TUALRA, Sched. 1, para. 10(a)). 26 weeks from

1st October, calculated on a calendar basis, did not expire until 31st March. The employee's submissions were upheld by the Appeal Tribunal—the Tuesday, Wednesday, Thursday and Friday worked by the employee in his first week of employment counted as one week in accordance with paragraph 4 (that being " part of " a week); that first week gave him 25 weeks employment; since the employee also worked on the day of his dismissal (which was a Monday) that was also a week during part of which his relations with his employers were governed by a contract of employment within paragraph 4 and, therefore, that week also counted in computing the period of his employment and gave him the necessary 26 weeks. The decision of the Appeal Tribunal was, therefore, that in calculating the 26 week qualifying period of employment which entitles a dismissed employee to claim compensation for unfair dismissal, paragraph 4 applied so as to enable the employee to take into account the whole of the week in which his employment started and the whole of the week in which his employment was terminated. A similar method is also appropriate for calculating the qualifying period for a redundancy payment.

Breaks in employment

The basic principle is that a legal break in the employment will break continuity for the purposes of the schedule. If, therefore, there is such a break, the computation of the period of service of the employee will have to start all over again.

There are, however, certain circumstances dealt with in the schedule to the 1972 Act involving " temporary absences " of one sort or another and these absences will not constitute a break in the employment and, moreover, the period of the absence itself will normally count towards the period of continuous service. These circumstances are as follows:—

(1) **Sickness or injury**—paragraph 5(1) provides that if in any week the employee is, for the whole or the part of that week, incapable of work in consequence of sickness or injury that week shall . . . count as a period of employment. Paragraph 5(2) goes on to say that not more than 26 weeks shall count under this head. This provision applies when the contract of employment itself comes to an end, e.g. where the employee is dismissed during his absence due to ill health and he then subsequently goes back to the same employer within the 26 week period.

A legal decision prior to the Employment Protection Act 1975 held that absence from work due to pregnancy was not an absence due to " sickness ". It will be seen, however, that there is now a special provision introduced with regard to absence due to pregnancy.

(2) **Temporary cessation of work.**—If in any week the employee
is, for the whole or part of the week, absent from work on
account of a temporary cessation of work that week shall
. . . count as a period of employment. This will not, however, apply to a temporary cessation of work on account of a
strike in which the employee takes part.

Here again, this applies even if the employee's contract of
employment has been brought to an end during the temporary
cessation of work. It will be noted that there is no 26 week
limit as there is in respect of the absence due to sickness or
injury. Perhaps, one of the most interesting—and possibly
surprising—decisions under this head is the High Court case
of *The Bentley Engineering Co. Ltd. v. Crown and Miller*
[1976] ICR 225. In this case, after being made redundant
by their original employers, the two employees were out of
work for 21 months and 2 years respectively. During that
time, one of them took other employment. Subsequently,
they were re-engaged by The Bentley Engineering Co. Ltd.
(which was an associated company of their original employer).
At a later date, they were again made redundant. The High
Court (Mr. Justice Phillips) upheld the decision of the Industrial Tribunal and found that continuity of service had not
been broken and that the employees were entitled to have
their service with their original employer taken into account
in the calculation of their redundancy payment. The learned
judge in this case admitted that it might at first sight appear
that absences of such lengths and in such circumstances (particularly where one employee had taken up another job) could
almost be ruled out of account as possibly constituting
absences on account of a " temporary cessation of work ".
The law, however, is that the Tribunal must look at the
matter " as the historian of a completed chapter of events and
not as a journalist describing events as they occur from day
to day ". Things, as they unfold, seem quite different from
the way in which they are seen when one looks back and
considers the whole of the chapter in context. " What at
the time seems to be permanent may turn out to be temporary,
and what at the time seems to be temporary may turn out to
be permanent."

Three questions are posed by the provisions relating to a
temporary cessation of work—

(*a*) was there a cessation of the employee's work or job?

(*b*) was the employee absent on account of that cessation?
and

(*c*) was the cessation a temporary one?

The *Bentley Engineering Co. Ltd.* case confirmed that those are the correct questions to be asked. At the same time, however, the Court stressed that at the end of the day one must go back to the words of the statute itself.

There are several reported decisions on this aspect of the law, particularly for redundancy purposes. Each case must, however, turn on its own particular facts and circumstances.

(3) **Special arrangement or custom.**—Paragraph 5(1)(*c*) in effect provides that if in any week the employee is, for the whole or part of the week, absent from work in circumstances such that, by arrangement or custom, he is regarded as continuing in the employment of his employer for all or any purposes, then that week shall . . . count as a period of employment.

One example under this particular head is the case where an employer " lends " a workman to another employer for a short period with the intention or understanding that the workman will return to work with the original employer. Here again, no specific time limit is laid down as it is in the case of absence due to sickness or injury. The burden of proof here will lie on the employer to show that no arrangement or custom existed.

An example of such a custom or arrangement arose where an employee of the National Coal Board worked for a different employer for about 19 months but remained in the NCB pension scheme; he was held to have continuity of employment for the whole period (*Wishart v. National Coal Board* (1974) ICR 460).

(4) **Service with the Armed Forces.**—Paragraph 8 of the Schedule contains special provisions relating to employees who had to serve a period of National Service. National Service came to an end in 1962 and this provision will, therefore, only deal with breaks in employment prior to that date. Under the National Service Act 1948 certain employees were entitled to apply to their former employer for a job within a period of six months from the ending of their service. The effect of paragraph 8 is that the absence during National Service is not a break in employment; the periods of service with the employer prior to National Service are added to the period of re-employment after the employee returns to work. It will be noted that this is rather different from the provisions previously considered where the absence itself counts as continuous employment.

(5) **Pregnancy.**—By virtue of an amendment introduced by the Employment Protection Act 1975—with effect from 1st June 1976—the absence of an employee for the whole or part of any week when such absence is " wholly or partly because of

pregnancy or confinement " will nevertheless count as a period of employment.

(6) **Industrial Disputes.**—Absence from work due to a strike or lock-out may be dealt with as a possible temporary absence from work and thus may not break the continuous employment. Special provisions are in addition contained in paragraphs 6 and 7 with regard to strikes and lock-outs. The effect of these provisions is that if an employee is absent from work either because he took part in a strike or because of a lock-out by the employer then, although the period of absence will not itself be taken into account in calculating the length of the employment, such absence will not have the effect of breaking the continuity of the employment. As with the National Service provisions, the continuous employment before the strike or lock-out and the employment after the strike or lock-out will be added together. It should be noted that if the employee does not himself take part in the strike, but if he is laid off work because there is a strike and no work is available, then it is more than likely that his absence will be dealt with as a " temporary cessation of work " (see paragraph (2) above).

(7) **Change of employer.**—Paragraph 9 of the Schedule provides that the provisions of that Schedule relate only to employment by the one employer. Having said this, there are in effect the following exceptions:—

(a) if a trade or business is transferred from one person to another, the period of employment of an employee in that trade or business at the time of the transfer counts as a period of employment with the transferee of the business and the transfer will not break the continuity of the period of employment. The more important aspects of this provision are considered on page 179 with regard to redundancy.

(b) if under an Act of Parliament one body corporate is substituted for another as the employer, then the employee's period of employment is not broken.

(c) if on the death of an employer the employee is taken into the employment of the personal representatives or trustees of the deceased employer, then the death does not break the continuity of the period of employment and the employee's period of employment continues to run.

(d) if there is a change in the partners who employ any person, the employee's period of employment at the time of the change shall count as a period of employment with the partners after the change and that change

will not break the continuity of the period of employment. It has, however, been held that there is no
" change of partners " where one of two partners
leaves since, following the change, there is only a sole
proprietor left; thus, there will be no continuity (see
Harold Fielding Ltd. v. Mansi (1974) ICR 347).

(e) if an employee of one employer is taken into the
employment of another employer who, at that time, is
an **associated employer** of the first mentioned employer,
then the period of employment continues to run and
the change of employer will not break the continuity.
For these purposes, under an amendment introduced
by the EPA, any two employers are to be treated as
associated if one is a company of which the other
(directly or indirectly) has control or if both are companies of which a third person (directly or indirectly)
has control.

Appendix III

NORMAL WORKING HOURS AND CALCULATION OF A WEEK'S PAY

Many of the employee's rights ultimately involve a payment to him (either as an entitlement or by an order of an Industrial Tribunal), the payment being geared to " a week's pay ". This in itself is dependent on calculating what are the " normal working hours " of that employee.

For example, under the Employment Protection Act 1975 such matters as guarantee payments and maternity pay are linked to a calculation based on " a week's pay ". In addition, section 85 of the EPA (which section came into force on 1st June 1976) also provides that the methods of calculating " normal working hours " and " a week's pay " as set out in the EPA are now effective for the purposes of the Redundancy Payments Act 1965, the Contracts of Employment Act 1972 and the Trade Union and Labour Relations Act 1974.

The detailed regulations relating to these definitions are contained in Schedule 4 of the EPA.

Normal Working Hours

Part I of Schedule 4 to the EPA deals with " normal working hours ".

In many cases, the position is quite straightforward. The contract of an employee will provide for a fixed number of hours to be worked in a particular week, e.g. a 40 hour week; if this is the case, then these hours are treated as the employee's " normal working hours ". If there are in fact no normal working hours, then calculation of the " week's pay " is dealt with separately (see *below*).

With regard to overtime, the position is a little more complicated. Effectively, however, if, as is very often the case, the contract simply provides for a specified number of hours, but also states that if the employee works additional hours he will be paid at an overtime rate then, in that case, it is the specified number of hours which will be the " normal working hours "; in that case overtime hours are not included. In some contracts of employment, however,

[360]

the employee is bound under his contract to work for a certain number of overtime hours and, if this is the case, then it is the total number of hours specified in the contract (including the "compulsory" overtime hours) which will then constitute "normal working hours".

A Week's Pay

Detailed provisions regarding calculation of a "week's pay" are contained in Part II of Schedule 4 of the EPA.

The provisions of this part of the 4th Schedule appear to be a little complicated. The effect of the provisions is, however, as follows:—

(1) If there are normal working hours (as already defined) and if the remuneration of the employee does not vary with the amount of work done then the amount of a week's pay is the amount which is payable under the contract of employment. This is the straightforward case and there should be no problems. This will not, for example, cover an employee who is paid on a piece work basis.

(2) If there are normal working hours (as previously defined) for an employee and the amount of the week's pay does vary with the amount of work done in the week or other relevant period, the "week's pay" shall be the amount of remuneration for the number of normal working hours in a week calculated at the average hourly rate of remuneration payable by the employer to the employee in respect of the period of 12 weeks ending with the last complete week before the calculation date. The schedule specifically provides that references to remuneration varying with the amount of work done will include references to remuneration which may include any commission or similar payment which varies in amount. Thus, this particular example will cover the employee who is paid on a piece work basis or who is paid on commission. It will be seen that in practice what will happen here is that for the 12 week period the average hourly rate of remuneration will be worked out and then that figure will be multiplied by the number of "normal working hours".

(3) If there are "normal working hours" for an employee and he is required under his contract to work during those hours either on days of the week or at times of the day which differ from week to week or over a longer period so that the remuneration payable for any week varies according to the incidents of those days or times, then the amount of "a week's pay" will be the amount of remuneration for the average weekly number of normal working hours at the average hourly rate of remuneration. Here again, this is

calculated on the basis of a 12 week period immediately prior to the calculation date. The first calculation will be to work out the average number of hours worked each week over the 12 week period and then to assess the average hourly rate of pay assessed over that period; having done this the average hourly rate of remuneration will be multiplied by the average weekly number of " normal working hours ". Very often, of course, overtime will not be taken into account unless, of course, this falls within the strict definition of " normal working hours " (see *above*).

(4) In the calculations referred to under (2) and (3) above (relating to the 12 week average) only hours when the employee was actually working and only remuneration payable for such hours, is taken into account. Thus, if the employee is not paid for any part of the 12 week period, it may be necessary to take into account earlier weeks (para. 5(1)).

(5) If there are no normal working hours for an employee, the amount of " a week's pay " will be the amount of that employee's average weekly remuneration in the period of 12 weeks as referred to previously. Thus, in this particular situation, it is simply necessary to calculate the average of the employee's weekly remuneration for the period referred to.

(6) Paragraph 7 of Schedule 4 deals with the situation where an employee has not been employed for a sufficient period to enable a calculation to be made under any of the foregoing provisions. Paragraph 7 provides that " the amount of a week's pay shall be an amount which fairly represents a week's pay ". Further guidance is contained in the paragraph which states that the foregoing provisions of the schedule should be applied as far as this is possible and a Tribunal should have regard to various considerations, including any remuneration received by the employee in question, the amount offered to the employee as remuneration in respect of the particular job in question, the remuneration received by other persons engaged in " relevant comparable employment " either with the same employer or with other employers.

(7) In arriving at an average hourly rate or average weekly rate of remuneration under the schedule account must be taken of work done for a former employer within the 12 week period if the employment with that employer ranks as " continuous employment " (as to which see Appendix II, page 352, *ante*).

(8) For the purposes of Schedule 4 " week " means a week ending with Saturday, except in the case of an employee whose

remuneration is calculated weekly by a week ending with some other day, in which case the week will be taken as ending with that other day.

Appendix IV

DISCIPLINARY PRACTICE AND PROCEDURES

Draft Code of Practice issued under the Employment Protection Act 1975

Under section 6(1) of the Employment Protection Act 1975 the Advisory Conciliation and Arbitration Service (ACAS) may issue Codes of Practice containing practical guidance for the purpose of promoting the improvement of industrial relations.

A draft Code of Practice has been issued on Disciplinary Practice and Procedures. Under section 6(3) of the EPA the ACAS is bound to publsh a draft for consultation and to consider any representations made on it. The draft may then be modified before it is transmitted to the Secretary of State for Employment for approval and laid before Parliament. The draft (referred to in this Appendix) is intended to replace paragraphs 130 to 133 of the 1972 Code (see page 303, *above*). Comments on the draft Code had to be submitted to the ACAS by 3rd September 1976. It would seem, therefore, that the Code will not be in force until some time in 1977. Until Parliamentary approval is obtained to the new Code, the provisions of paragraphs 130 to 133 of the 1972 Code will still be applicable.

The draft Code seeks to give practical guidance on how to draw up disciplinary rules and procedures and how to operate them effectively. Its aim is to help employers and Trade Unions as well as individual employees and this is regardless of the size of the organisation in which they work.

It has already been noted (see page 39) that under the Contracts of Employment Act 1972 employers must now provide written information for their employees about certain aspects of their disciplinary rules and procedures. The aim is to help promote fairness and order in the treatment of individuals and in the conduct of industrial relations. The draft Code stresses that the primary responsibility lies with management. Having said this, the aim should be to secure the maximum involvement of employees and all levels of management in the formulation of disciplinary rules and procedures. In particular, Trade Union officials should participate in formulating and agreeing those procedural arrangements and disciplinary rules.

The basic rules should be those which are necessary for the efficient safe performance of work and for the maintenance of satisfactory relations within the work force and between employees and management. They will vary according to particular circumstances, e.g. the size of the establishment, the type of work, etc. Sometimes, particular jobs will require special rules. The draft Code states that unnecessary rules should be avoided and that in preparing rules a balance should be drawn between clarity (in order not to render the rules meaningless) and flexibility (in order to leave room for mitigating circumstances). Rules should be readily available, e.g. by posting them on notice boards or by including them in a handbook issued to employees. Employees should be left in no doubt as to the type of misconduct which is serious enough to warrant either suspension pending investigation or even instant dismissal. In practice, rules the breach of which is serious enough to warrant suspension or dismissal should be separated from those which are dealt with through a warnings procedure.

Essential features of disciplinary procedures

Paragraph 11 of the draft Code recommends that Disciplinary Procedures should:—

(a) provide for speedy operation.

(b) be in writing.

(c) specify to whom they apply.

(d) state the range of disciplinary actions which can be taken.

(e) specify who has the authority to take the various forms of disciplinary action, ensuring that immediate superiors do not normally have the power to dismiss without reference to more senior management.

(f) provide for the individual to be informed of the complaint against him and give him the opportunity to state his case before a decision is reached.

(g) give the individual the right to be accompanied by a representative of his choice at any stage.

(h) provide for a written warning or penalty to be acknowledged in writing by the individual or for the written communication to be handed to him in the presence of his representative.

(i) ensure that, except for serious misconduct, no employee is dismissed for a first breach of discipline.

(*j*) provide for suspension to ensure that, except in special circumstances, no dismissal takes effect until the case has been carefully investigated.

(*k*) provide a right of appeal to some level of management, joint committee or independent third party, not previously directly involved in the case.

(*l*) ensure that the individual is given the reason for any penalty imposed.

(*m*) ensure that the individual is informed of his right of appeal.

The procedure in operation

It will be noted from the above that much greater stress is placed on **suspension** than is the case under paragraphs 130 to 133 of the 1972 Code of Practice.

Indeed, the draft Code recommends that after the supervisor or manager has investigated a particular disciplinary matter and has interviewed the employee, giving him the opportunity to state his case and advising him of his rights under the procedure, then even in a case of serious misconduct for which the rules provide for summary dismissal, " the first step should normally be suspension whilst the case is investigated ". During this process, the employee should be entitled to all his rights under the procedure.

Assuming that this part of the draft Code is approved and brought into force, it will be interesting to see how Industrial Tribunals deal with cases that come before them where, in a case of serious misconduct, the employee is instantly dismissed without first being suspended. It does seem that under the draft Code instant dismissal will only be acceptable in cases of " serious misconduct " (the 1972 Code refers to " gross misconduct ") and in " special circumstances " (see paragraph 11(*j*) *above*).

The draft Code recommends that in cases other than those of alleged serious misconduct the normal procedure should be as follows:—

(*a*) in the case of minor offences the immediate supervisor should give an oral warning for the purpose of improving future performance.

(*b*) if further action proved necessary, or if the issue were more serious, there should be a written warning setting out the circumstances.

(*c*) further misconduct might warrant a final written warning which should contain a statement that any recurrence would lead to suspension or dismissal or some other penalty, as the case may be.

(*d*) the final step might be disciplinary transfer, or disciplinary suspension without pay (but only if these are allowed for by an express or implied condition of the contract of employment), or dismissal, according to the nature of the misconduct. Suspension without pay should not be used needlessly and should not normally be for a prolonged period.

Details of any disciplinary action should be given in writing to the employee and, if he so wishes, to his representative. At the same time, the employee should be told of his right of appeal, how to make it and to whom. When deciding what action to take, employers should bear in mind the need to satisfy the test of reasonableness in all the circumstances and should take into account any mitigating factors.

Provisions similar to part of paragraph 133 of the 1972 Code are included with regard to disciplinary action against a Trade Union official; it is recommended that no action (other than possibly an oral warning) should be taken until all the circumstances of the case have been discussed with a senior Trade Union representative or full-time official.

With regard to possible appeals, it is recommended that the appeals procedure should be kept separate from the normal grievance procedures. It is also noted that independent arbitration is sometimes an appropriate means of resolving disciplinary issues.

It is recommended that **records** should be kept, setting out the nature of any breach of disciplinary rules, the action taken and the reasons for it, whether an appeal was lodged, its outcome and any subsequent developments. These records should be carefully safeguarded and kept confidential. Except in special circumstances, breaches of discipline should be removed from an employee's record " after an appropriate period of satisfactory conduct ".

Finally, the draft Code states that rules and procedures should be reviewed periodically in the light of developments in employment law or industrial relations practice. Such amendments and any additional rules should only be introduced after full discussion with employees' representatives and after reasonable notice has been given and all employees have been informed.

It is felt that the draft Code does not envisage any major departure from the provisions of paragraphs 130 to 133 of the 1972 Code. The draft Code does, however, go into the matter in rather more detail and one major difference in emphasis seems to relate to the provision for suspension pending a full investigation.

TIME OFF FOR TRADE UNION DUTIES AND ACTIVITIES

DRAFT CODE OF PRACTICE

Under sections 57 and 58 of the EPA trade union members and trade union officials are allowed to have " reasonable " time off for the purpose of taking part in trade union activities and trade union duties respectively (see pages 99 to 103).

What is " reasonable " will depend mainly on the provisions of a Code of Practice issued by ACAS. The above sections will only come into force as and when the Code has been approved by the Secretary of State for Employment and laid before Parliament.

The Draft Code issued as a consultative document—although not legally binding until approved as above—does show what is likely to be considered to be " reasonable " time off. It is not intended that the provisions of the Code should disturb existing agreements or arrangements relating to time off.

The Draft Code deals with the following matters:—

1. **Duties of Trade Union Officials**

   An official's duties are those duties recognised by the union and related to the joint agreements or customary arrangements for consultation, collective bargaining, and grievance handling, where such matters concern the employer or an associated employer and his employees. To perform these duties properly an official should be permitted to take paid time off during working hours for such purposes as:

   (*a*) collective bargaining with any level of management;

   (*b*) meetings with members called to inform them of the outcome of negotiations or consultations with management;

   (*c*) meetings with other lay officials or full-time union officers to discuss business of an industrial relations nature;

   (*d*) interviews with and on behalf of union members on grievance and discipline matters;

(e) appearing on behalf of constituents before an outside body on industrial relations matters;

(f) explanations to new employees of the role of the union in the workplace industrial relations structure.

The amount of time officials will need to spend on duties will differ according to the size of the establishment, the number of officials, the number of members, the range of duties and the calls made upon officials. An official should be permitted to take paid time off during working hours for the amount of time necessary to complete his or her duties in an effective and responsible manner. Difficulties over the amount of time off officials should be able to have can be avoided by prior agreement between the union(s) and the employer concerned.

Special arrangements need to be made for officials who work unsocial hours either on a regular or rotating basis, so that their hours of work do not prevent them from carrying out their duties effectively.

2. Training of Officials

The Draft Code stresses that formal training, as well as practical experience, is necessary. The training must, however, be relevant and should also be approved by the TUC or the official's union. It is accepted that not every training course will be the same.

Every official who has duties concerned with industrial relations should be permitted to take paid time off from work for initial basic industrial relations training. Paid time off should also be permitted for further industrial relations training where an official has special responsibilities or where such training is necessary to meet circumstances such as changes in the structure or topics of negotiation at the place of employment or legislative changes affecting industrial relations.

Basic training should be arranged as soon as possible after the appointment of the official. Further training should be undertaken as and when the need arises.

Trade Unions are asked to give management " at least a few weeks' notice " of the course it has approved. In addition the number of officials attending training courses should be reasonable in the circumstances, taking into account the availability of relevant courses and the operational requirements of the employer.

3. Trade Union Activities

Trade Union activities are those activities relating to the running of and participation in the affairs of the union.

The Draft Code deals with the active participation of **union officials** in union activities and stresses that time off should be given for such things as executive committee meetings, the annual conference and certain external bodies, *e.g.* Industrial Training Boards.

Employees who are members of recognised unions also need the opportunity to participate in their unions' affairs. Such participation enables them to know and influence their union policy and to communicate with their representatives. It encourages a sound union structure at the workplace and effective communication and collective representation.

Members should be permitted to take time off during working hours for such purposes as voting in union elections. There may also be occasions when unions wish to hold meetings of members during working hours, for example to report back on negotiations with management. Where union activities would involve a large proportion of employees at the work place at any one time, management and unions should agree on a mutually convenient time which minimises the effects on production; for example, towards the end of the shift or the working week or just before or after a meal break. Every effort should be made to avoid the unnecessary prolongation of such activities.

4. Conditions relating to Time Off

The Draft Code recommends that management should make available facilities to enable union officials to perform their duties efficiently and to communicate effectively. Examples of recommended facilities include accommodation for meetings, access to a telephone, notice boards and, if appropriate, typing and duplicating facilities and storage for correspondence and files.

Paragraph 5.3 of the Draft Code states as follows:—

" It is management's responsibility to make the operational arrangements for time off. To minimise problems, management may wish to place certain officials on work from which their temporary absence will not cause serious delay to work-flows, output, or services. This should be done by joint agreement. Where appropriate, management should agree with the union on arrangements for other employees to cover the work of officials or members taking time off."

The union official and union member have a responsibility to use their time off from work conscientiously and efficiently. They should not unduly or unnecessarily prolong the time they are absent from work.

Where the union wishes to hold meetings of members during working hours it should seek to agree the arrangements with management as far in advance as practicable. When a number of members require time off at any one time the union should agree to leave at work such members as are essential for safety or operational reasons, for example to keep offices open to the public or to provide necessary manning in a continuous process firm.

Management may want time off work for union duties or activities to be deferred because, for example, safety or serious operational problems would ensue if time off were taken at a particular time. The reasons for postponement should be made clear and parties should endeavour to agree on an alternative time for the union duty or activity.

5. **Industrial Action**

The Draft Code states that both management and unions have a responsibility to use agreed procedures to avoid industrial action and the hope is expressed that the time off provisions will facilitate this—particularly where communication and co-operation between management and unions are in danger of breaking down.

6. **Agreements**

The Draft Code seems to recommend formal agreements relating to time off. Such agreements should include:—

(*a*) the arrangements for notifying management when time off is sought;

(*b*) the occasions for which time off is required by union officials on a regular basis and the amounts of time for such occasions where this is practicable;

(*c*) the arrangements for the release of officials for industrial relations training;

(*d*) the time off arrangements for officials working unsocial hours;

(*e*) the arrangements for time off for union activities;

(*f*) the arrangements for handling disputes on time off.

It must be stressed that this Appendix deals with extracts from the present Draft Code issued for consultation. It may be, therefore, that certain parts of the Code will be amended before it is finally approved by Parliament.

SUMMARY OF RIGH

NOTE: The following chart comprises only a brief summary of the vari
   point. The reader is, therefore, urged to use the chart only as a
   text.

Additional copies of this summary, printed on thin card may be obtained

THE RIGHTS OF THE EMPLOYEE and date of introduction	QUALIFYING PERIOD and CONDITIONS of Entitlement
1. Particulars of terms of employment —CEA, s. 4 (position since 1 June 76.)	13 weeks' continuous employment.
2. Equal pay—" the equality clause " —Equal Pay Act 1970, as set out in SDA, Schedule 1, Part II. (29 December 75.)	None, but there must be "like work " or " job rated as equivalent ".
3. No discrimination on grounds of sex or marital status—SDA. (29 December 75.)	None.
4. No discrimination on grounds of race, colour, etc.—RRA. ( )	None.

TS OF EMPLOYEES

ous rights of an employee. It is not intended to deal with every relevant guide and to check the detailed position with the relevant part of the

from the Publishers.

Excluded categories (see page 382 for details of numbered classes)	Entitlement and/or Remedies	Reference to Text
1, 2, 4, 6, 7 and 9.	Industrial Tribunal can declare what particulars should be delivered.	pp. 36-47
None.	Industrial Tribunal can— (a) declare employee's rights. (b) award arrears of remuneration up to a maximum of 2 years.	pp. 49-58
None, but see pp. 7 to 11 for certain specific exclusions.	Industrial Tribunal can— (a) declare employee's rights. (b) recommend that employer takes certain action. (c) award compensation up to £5,200.	pp. 3-11, 15-26, 59-64
None—but see pp. 13 to 15 for certain specific exclusions.	Industrial Tribunal can— (a) declare employee's rights. (b) recommend that employer takes certain action. (c) award compensation up to £5,200.	pp. 11-26, 64

[373]

THE RIGHTS OF THE EMPLOYEE and date of introduction	QUALIFYING PERIOD and CONDITIONS of Entitlement
5. Itemised pay statement—EPA, s. 81. (6 April 77.)	None.
6. Trade union membership and activities—EPA, s. 53. (1 June 76.)	None.
7. Time off for Trade Union officials —EPA, s. 57. (? 1977)	None, but official must be from a recognised independent trade union.
8. Time off for Trade Union members —EPA, s. 58. (? 1977)	None, but union must be a recognised independent trade union.
9. Time off for certain public duties— EPA, s. 59. (? 1977)	None, but duties limited to J.P., local councillor, Tribunal member, etc.
10. Time off to look for work or for training—EPA, s. 61. (1 June 76.)	(a) 2 years' continuous employment. (b) Given notice of dismissal due to redundancy.

Excluded categories (see page 382 for details of numbered classes)	Entitlement and/or Remedies	Reference to Text
1, 3, 4, 6 and 7.	Industrial Tribunal can— (a) declare rights of parties. (b) order employer to repay " unnotified deductions " up to 13 weeks.	pp. 125-128
1, 3 and 4.	Industrial Tribunal can— (a) declare rights of employee. (b) award compensation (no maximum limit).	pp. 96-99
1, 3, 4 and 6.	Right to reasonable time off with pay to carry out industrial relations duties or to undergo certain training. If refused, Industrial Tribunal can award compensation.	pp. 101-103
1, 3, 4 and 6.	Right to reasonable time off without pay to take part in trade union activities. If refused, Industrial Tribunal can award compensation.	pp. 99-101
1, 3, 4, 6 and 7.	Right to reasonable time off without pay. If refused, Industrial Tribunal can award compensation.	pp. 129-132
1, 2, 3, 4, 6 and 7.	Right to reasonable time off. If refused, Industrial Tribunal can award up to 2/5ths of a week's pay.	pp. 201-204

THE RIGHTS OF THE EMPLOYEE and date of introduction	QUALIFYING PERIOD and CONDITIONS of Entitlement
11. Medical suspension pay—EPA, s. 29. (1 June 76.)	(a) 4 weeks' continuous employment. (b) Suspended from work in consequence of certain specified medical requirements. (c) Still fit and available for work.
12. Guarantee payment—EPA, s. 22. (1 February 77.)	(a) 4 weeks' continuous employment. (b) Employee has one or more " workless days ".
13. Maternity Pay—EPA, s. 35. (6 April 77.)	(a) 2 years' continuous employment. (b) Employed until 11th week before expected confinement. (c) Informs employer 3 weeks before she leaves that she will be absent because of pregnancy.

Excluded categories (see page 382 for details of numbered classes)	Entitlement and/or Remedies	Reference to Text
1, 2, 3, 4, 5 and 6.	One week's pay for each week of suspension up to 26 weeks.	pp. 120-124
1, 2, 3, 4, 5 and 6. Also not applicable if:— (a) workless day caused by trade dispute or (b) employee unreasonably refuses offer of suitable alternative work or (c) employee does not comply with reasonable requirements ensuring availability of his services.	One day's pay (not exceeding £6) for each workless day— maximum of 5 days per quarter (February, May, August and November).	pp. 150-155
1, 3, 4 and 6.	Pay equal to 90% of a week's pay less National Insurance Maternity Allowance. Maximum—6 weeks. Maximum pay—£80 per week. (N.B.—100% rebate to employers.)	pp. 108-113

THE RIGHTS OF THE EMPLOYEE and date of introduction	QUALIFYING PERIOD and CONDITIONS of Entitlement
14. Reinstatement in job after maternity—EPA, s. 35. (1 June 76.)	(a) 2 years' continuous employment. (b) Employed until 11th week before expected confinement. (c) Informs employer 3 weeks before she leaves that she will be absent because of pregnancy. (d) Informs employer at same time as (c) that she intends to return to work. (e) Returns within 29 weeks from the confinement (possible 4 weeks' extension in case of ill-health).
15. Redundancy consultation and protective award—EPA, ss. 99 to 107. (8 March 76.)	None, but EPA consultation is only with a recognised independent trade union.
16. Redundancy pay—R.P.A. (5 August 65.)	(a) 2 years' continuous employment. (b) Dismissed for redundancy.

Excluded categories (see page 382 for details of numbered classes)	Entitlement and/or Remedies	Reference to Text
1, 3, 4 and 6.	If not allowed to return, rights as for unfair dismissal and/ or redundancy.	pp. 113-119
2, 3, 4, 5 and 7.	If employer in default— (*a*) Trade Union can apply to Industrial Tribunal which can make a " protective award " entitling employees to remuneration for 28, 60, or 90 days as appropriate. (*b*) If Secretary of State not consulted employer can be prosecuted or can lose part of his redundancy rebate (up to 10%).	pp. 191-201
1, 2, 3, 4, 6, 8, 9 and 10.	Statutory entitlement based on years of service (see p. 185). Maximum—£2,400.	pp. 145-148, 157-163

THE RIGHTS OF THE EMPLOYEE and date of introduction	QUALIFYING PERIOD and CONDITIONS of Entitlement
17. Unfair Dismissal — TUALRA, Schedule 1, para. 4. (28 February 72.)	26 weeks' continuous employment (unless dismissal for " inadmissible reason ", *e.g.* involvement in Trade Union activities).
18. Written statement of reasons for dismissal—EPA, s. 70. (1 June 76.)	26 weeks' continuous employment.
19. Notice to terminate contract of employment, CEA, s. 4. (position since 1 June 76.)	4 weeks' continuous employment.
20. Rights to payment on Insolvency of employer, EPA, s. 64. (20 April 76.)	None.

Excluded categories (see page 382 for details of numbered classes)	Entitlement and/or Remedies	Reference to Text
1, 2, 3, 4, 6 and 8.	Industrial Tribunal can order reinstatement or re-engagement or compensation. Maximum compensation— (a) £2,400 basic award. (b) £5,200 compensatory award. (c) £4,160 for failure to comply with reinstatement order.	pp. 246-332
1, 2, 3, 4 and 6.	If not supplied on request, Industrial Tribunal will award 2 weeks' pay.	pp. 241-243
2, 4, 5, 6, 7 and 9.	Employee entitled to 1 week's notice if employed under 2 years and thereafter 1 week for each year of service up to a maximum of 12. Industrial Tribunal can declare the rights of the parties.	pp. 228-229
1, 2, 3, 4 and 7.	Employee entitled to receive certain payments (e.g. 8 weeks' pay, 6 weeks' holiday pay, basic Unfair Dismissal award) direct from the Redundancy Fund.	pp. 207-211

POSSIBLE EXCLUDED CATEGORIES

(**N.B.**—This list is to be read only in conjunction with the Chart
set out above.)

1. Where the employer is the **husband or wife** of the employee.

2. **Registered dock workers** (not being work which is not dock work as
   defined by a scheme under the Dock Workers (Regulation of Employment) Act 1946).

3. Employment as master or as a member of the crew of a **fishing vessel**
   where the employee is not remunerated otherwise than by a share in
   the profits or gross earnings of the vessel.

4. Employment where under his contract of employment the employee
   ordinarily works outside Great Britain.

   (N.B.—(*a*) special provisions with regard to employment on
   board ship and on oil rigs, etc.—see p. 252.

   (*b*) slightly different definitions of " work outside Great
   Britain " are found in the different Acts—the detailed
   text of the book should, therefore, be checked in this
   respect.)

5. Employment under a contract for a **fixed term of 12 weeks** or less or
   employment under a contract in respect of a specific task which is
   not expected to last more than 12 weeks, unless in either case the
   employee has been continuously employed for more than 12 weeks

6. Employment under a contract which normally involves employment
   for **less than 16 hours weekly** (or 8 hours if continuously employed
   for 5 years).

   (N.B.—This " exclusion " will sometimes arise not as a specific
   exclusion but by virtue of the definition of " continuous
   employment "—see p. 353.)

7. **Merchant seamen.**

8. Where employee has **attained 65** (if male) or 60 (if female) or has
   attained **the normal retiring age** for an employee holding the position
   which he held.

9. **Crown servants.**

10. **Domestic servants** who are " **close relatives** " of the employer and
    who are employed in a private household (see p. 161).

INDEX

A

PAGE

Abroad, working—*see* " Overseas employment ".

Absence without leave... 285

ACAS—*see* " Advisory, Conciliation and Arbitration Service ".

Advertisements 6, 21

Advisory, Conciliation and Arbitration Service:
   Conciliation 335-337
   Discrimination 15
   Disclosure of information 76
   Terms and conditions of employment 86-90

Agreed procedure 292

Alternative employment, offers of ... 105-106, 121, 154, 162, 168, 172-173, 180, 281, 296

Appeals:
   disciplinary decisions, from 40
   Industrial Tribunal, from 331, 348-349

Appeals procedure 40, 309

Appeal Tribunal, Employment 348-349

Appearance, Notice of... 340-341

Applications to Industrial Tribunal 311-315, 339-340

Apprentices 208

" Appropriate time " 97, 262

Aptitude... 275-277

Arbitration 304, 367

Armed Forces, service with 357

Armed Services... 10

Arrears of pay 206, 208

Articled Clerks 208

Associated employers 38, 50, 105, 174, 179, 359

B

Ballot 72

Basic award 208, 322-323

Breach of Code of Practice 302, 306-308

Breach of contract:
   by employee—*see* " Conduct ".
   by employer 137, 216-219
   inducement of 90-94

PAGE

Breaks in employment... 355-359
Burden of proof:
    continuity of employment 353
    discrimination 16, 24
    equal pay 50-52
    inadmissible reasons 261
    Industrial Tribunal, before 344
    redundancy 163, 164, 241
    unfair dismissal... ... ... 241, 257, 271, 300
    unfair selection for redundancy 291-292, 294
Business:
    cessation of 164, 166
    moving the place of 167-169
    transfer of 166

C

CAC—*see* " Central Arbitration Committee ".
Capability 258, 274-281
Central Arbitration Committee:
    disclosure of information 80
    equal pay 54
    terms and conditions of employment 89-90
    union recognition 73-74
Cessation of business 164, 166
Charities... ... ... 10, 14
Clocking in 285
Close relatives 45, 161, 250
Closed shop 83-86, 268
Codes of Practice:
    Disciplinary practice and procedures 286, 364-367
    Disclosure of information 76-79
    Industrial Relations ... 31, 32, 39, 41, 69, 70, 71, 75, 99, 138, 192,
        201, 229, 241, 279, 295, 302-304, 306, 307, 309, 364
    Race Relations 13
    Time off... ... ... 100, 102, 130, 368-371
    Union recognition 69-70
Collective Agreements ... 33-34, 41, 94, 136, 150, 154, 160, 168, 190, 201, 292
Collective Bargaining 68, 71, 75, 77
Commission:
    Equal Opportunities 6, 17-21, 53
    Racial Equality... ... ... 13, 17, 18-21
Company directors 158
Compensation:
    basic award 208, 322-323
    compensatory award 323-327
    contributory fault 327-329
    deductions 326
    discrimination 16
    equal pay 53
    expenses 326
    fringe benefits 325

Compensation—*continued* PAGE
    injured feelings 17
    mitigation 324, 329-332
    unfair dismissal... 321-332
    wrongful dismissal 231-235
Compensatory award 323-327
Conciliation—*see* " Advisory, Conciliation and Arbitration Service ".
Conciliation Officers 15, 255, 334-337
Conduct... ... ... 171, 258, 282-290
" Conscientious objectors "—*see* " Religious belief ".
Consistency 309
Constructive dismissal... ... ... 137, 214, 216-219, 284, 301
Consultation, redundancy 191-201
Continuous employment 37, 38, 158, 179, 204, 352-359
Contract, inducement of breach of 90-94
Contracting out 97, 119, 160, 189, 201, 216, 253, 333
Contracts of employment:
    changes in terms 42-43, 283
    definition of 247
    disciplinary rules 39-40, 364-367
    express terms 31-32, 135
    fixed term 160, 163
    implied terms 32-33, 136, 283
    notice to terminate 39, 228, 237
    statutory particulars 36-41
        excluded categories 44-46
        sanctions 46-47
    suspension 135-140
Contributory fault 323, 324, 327-329
Convictions:
    dismissal, as reason for 286
    " spent " 26-28
Co-operation, lack of 284-285
Costs 344-345
Counter-inflation 48
Criminal liability of employers ... 7, 15, 17-18, 19, 28-29, 46, 82, 113
Criminal offences 230, 286
Crown servants... ... ... 46, 160, 382
Custom and practice 136
Customary arrangement 292

D

Damage to property 230
Damages—*see* " Compensation ".
Death 221
Debts, priority of 206
Decency or privacy 9

PAGE

Directors	158
Disabled persons, employment of	28-29
Disciplinary practice and procedures	303-305, 364-367
Disciplinary rules	31, 39-40, 364-367
Disclosure of information:	
Employment Protection Act 1975	75-80
Industry Act	80-82
Discovery of documents	341
Discrimination:	
Racial	11-15, 21, 64
advertisements	13, 21
Code of Practice	13
Commission for Racial Equality	13, 18-21
direct	12
exceptions	13-15
genuine occupational qualifications	13-14
indirect	12
injunctions	19-20
non-discrimination notices	19
questionnaires	24-25, 65
Sanctions:	
Commission	18-21
criminal liability	17
Industrial Tribunals	15, 63
Sex:	
advertisements	6, 21
benefits, facilities and services	62
detrimental treatment	62-63
direct	4
Equal Opportunities Commission	6, 17-21, 53
exceptions	7-11
genuine occupational qualifications	8-10
indirect	5
injunctions	19-20
non-discrimination notices	19
positive	11
promotion, transfer and training	60-62
questionnaires	24-25, 65, 350-351
Victimisation	63-64
Disharmony	298
Dishonesty	230, 285-288, 327
Disloyalty	285, 298
Dismissal:	
automatically fair	267-270
consent, by	220
constructive	137, 214, 216-219, 284, 301
definition	163, 212
lay-off	134
operation of law, by	220-225
pregnancy, due to	104-107
reasons for	165, 240-243
sex discrimination	60
short-time	134

Dismissal—*continued*   PAGE
  strike, when employee on 269
  summary 229-231
  unfair—*see* " Unfair dismissal ".
  wrongful—*see* " Wrongful dismissal ".
Disobedience 230, 282-284, 327
Dissolution of partnership 221
Dock workers 45, 122, 151, 161, 196, 204, 210, 243, 252, 382
Domestic servants 161
Driving disqualification 297
Drunkenness 289

E

Economic necessity of employer 299
Effective date of termination 213, 311
Employee:
  definition 157, 158, 247
  discrimination against 3-15, 59-65
  dismissal—*see* " Dismissal ".
  engagement of 3-29
  rights of 66-67, 372-382
Employer:
  " associated " 38, 50, 105, 174, 179, 359
  change of 358
  claims against employee 235-236
  obligations of 66-67, 372-382
  responsibility for employees 25-26
Employment:
  continuity of—*see* " continuous employment ".
  outside Great Britain 98, 101, 108, 122, 126, 382
  terms and conditions of 86-90
Employment Appeal Tribunal 348-349
Equal pay 48-58
  cases decided 54-58
  Central Arbitration Committee 54
  equality clause 49
  job evaluation 52
  " like work " 39, 51
  remedies of employees 53
  work rated as " equivalent " 52
Equal Opportunities Commission 6, 17-21, 53
Express terms 31-32, 135, 168

F

Fair dismissal 85, 267-270
Fishing vessels, employment on ... 98, 100, 108, 122, 126, 131, 151, 161,
  197, 204, 210, 243, 252, 282
Fixed term contracts 160, 163, 190, 213, 216, 226, 253-254
Frustration 221-225, 278
Further and better particulars 342

G

PAGE

Genuine occupational qualifications:
    racial discrimination 13-14
    sex discrimination 8-11
Goodwill 180
Great Britain, employment outside—see " Overseas employment ".
Grievance procedure 40-41
Gross misconduct 229, 285, 288, 289, 304, 366
Guarantee payments 137, 142, 150-155, 376-377
    amount 152-153
    defences to claim 153-154
    excluded categories 151
    insolvency, position on 206
    limitations 153
    sanctions 155
Guaranteed pay agreements 149-150, 154

H

Health of employee 175, 278-281
    See also " Sickness and injury ".
Holiday entitlement and pay 38, 206, 208
Hours of work 32, 38, 152, 171, 186
Husband or wife as employer... 45, 98, 100, 108, 122, 126, 131, 151, 161, 204,
                                    210, 243, 250, 382

I

Ill-health—see " Sickness and injury ".
Implied terms 32-33, 136, 283
Imprisonment 222, 289
Inadmissible reasons 103, 249, 250, 259-262, 320
Incompatability... ... ... 281, 289, 298
Inducement of breach of contract 90-94
Industrial disputes 358, 371
Industrial Tribunals—see " Tribunals ".
Information Agreements 77-78
Injunctions 19-20, 231
Insolvency:
    definition 207
    employee's rights on 207-209
    excluded categories 210-211
    priority of debts 206
    remedies of employee 209
Instant dismissal—see " Summary dismissal ".
Interests of justice 346-347
Interim relief 103, 262-267

PAGE

Interviews 22

Itemised pay statements:
    employee's rights 125-126
    excluded categories 126
    sanctions 127

J

Job appraisals 276
Job evaluation 52
Job specifications 276
Job title 39

L

Language 230, 288
" Last in, first out " 292-293
Lay-off 133-140, 143-148
Legal Aid 338, 348
Length of service 309
" Like work " 39, 51
Liquidation 221
    and see " Insolvency ".

Lock-outs 270, 358
Loss of earnings 325

M

Manner of dismissal 323

Maternity Pay:
    amount 110
    conditions of entitlement 108-109
    excluded categories 108
    Fund, rebate from 112
    sanctions 111

Maternity Pay Fund 112-113

Maternity rights 104-119
    contracting out 119
    dismissal due to pregnancy 104-107, 281
    maternity pay—see " Maternity Pay ".
    right to return to work after pregnancy 113-119
    suitable alternative employment, offers of 105-106
    temporary replacements 117

Medical evidence 280

Medical Suspension Pay:
    amount 123
    conditions of entitlement 120
    dismissals 123

Medical Suspension Pay—*continued* PAGE
    excluded categories 121-122
    insolvency, rights on 206
    sanctions 124
Membership of trade union 96-99
Merchant seamen—*see* " Seamen ".
Midwives 10
Ministers of religion 10
Misconduct—*see* " Conduct " and " Gross misconduct ".
Mitigation of loss 233, 324, 329-332
Money in lieu of notice 215

N

National Insurance benefits 326
National security 15, 98, 270
Negligence 230, 275
New evidence 346
Non-discrimination notices 19
Normal retiring age 250
Normal working hours 152, 186, 187, 360-361
Normal working week 353
Notice to terminate employment 39, 214, 227-229, 237
Notice of Appearance 340-341

O

" Off-duty " conduct 289
Offer of alternative employment ... 105-106, 121, 154, 162, 168, 172-173,
    180, 281, 296
Originating Application 339-340
Overseas employment ... 10, 14, 45-46, 98, 101, 108, 122, 126, 131, 151, 161,
    197, 204, 211, 243, 251, 382
Overtime 32, 38, 186, 282, 284

P

Particulars, further and better 342
Partnership 221
" Part-time " employees ... 44-45, 100, 108, 122, 126, 131, 151, 204, 243,
    249, 353, 382
Pay:
    contract of employment 38
    definition of a " week's pay "... ... ... 110, 144, 152, 186, 360-363
    disclosure of information 77
    equal pay—*see* " Equal pay ".
    guaranteed pay 149-155

PAGE

Pay—*continued*
    itemised pay statements 125-128
    maternity 108-113
    medical suspension pay 120-124
Pensions and pension schemes 38, 50, 206, 208
Pension rights 325
Physiology 8
Place of work 167, 168, 175
Police 10, 14, 247, 252
Practicable—*see* " Reasonably practicable ".

Pregnancy:
    continuity of employment 357
    discrimination due to 8
    dismissal due to 104-107, 281
    See also " Maternity Pay " and " Maternity Rights ".

Pressure on employer to dismiss 295
Previous employment 37, 182
Priority of debts 206
Prison—*see* " Imprisonment ".

Prison Service 10
Private households 7, 13
" Probation ", employee on 274, 277
Procedure agreements 254, 292, 305
Proceedings—*see* " Tribunals " and " Criminal liability of employers ".
Promotion 60-61, 277
Proof—*see* " Burden of proof ".
Protective award 103, 197-201, 206, 295
Public duties, time off for 129-132
Publishers of advertisements 7

Q

Qualifications:
    genuine occupational 8-11, 13-14
    lack of 258, 274, 277-278
Qualifying periods of employment 372-382
    Contracts of Employment Act statement 42
    Dismissal due to pregnancy 107
    Equal pay 50
    Guarantee payments 151
    Itemised pay statement 125
    Maternity pay 108
    Medical suspension pay 120
    Notice to terminate employment 228
    Reasons for dismissal 241
    Redundancy pay 158
    Re-instatement after pregnancy 114
    Time off to look for work 202
    Unfair dismissal 103, 248
Questionnaires 24-25, 65, 350-351

R

PAGE

Race Relations—*see* " Discrimination ".

Racial Discrimination—*see* " Discrimination ".

Reasonable notice 227, 237

" Reasonably practicable " 311-315

Reasons for dismissal 165, 240-243, 258-262, 271-299, 309

Rebates:
    Maternity Pay 112
    Redundancy Pay 187-190, 200

Receivership 221

Recognition of trade union 68-74

Recruitment 6, 21

Redundancy 156-190
    acceptance of offer of new employment 176
    amount of redundancy payment 185-187
    cessation of business 164, 166
    conditions of entitlement 162, 163
    consultation 191-201
    contracting out 160, 189-190
    definition 163-164
    dismissal by virtue of 290-296
    excluded categories 158-162
    lay-off 145-148
    moving the place of business 167-169
    non-redundancy dismissal reasons 170-172
    offer of alternative employment 172
    proof of 164-166
    protective award 197-201
    qualifying period 158
    rebate to employer 187-190, 200
    reduction in work 169-170
    refusal of offer of new employment 173-176
    short-time 145-148
    selection for 259, 291
    suitable employment 174
    time limits 183
    time off to look for work 201-204
    transfer of business 179-182
    trial period 177-179
    unfair dismissal 290-296

Redundancy Fund 187, 205, 207, 209, 210

Re-engagement 265, 317-321

References 244-245, 276, 310

Refusal of offer of new employment 173-176

Rehabilitation of offenders 26-28

Re-instatement:
    interim relief, by way of 262-267
    non-compliance with Tribunal order 319-321
    pregnancy, after 113-119
    unfair dismissal, after 315-317

Relatives—*see* " Close relatives " and " Husband or wife as employer ".

Religious belief, objection to joining trade union on grounds of ... 85, 97, 262, 268

PAGE

Remedies:
contract of employment particulars 46
disclosure of information 80-82
discrimination 15-17, 20-21, 63
equal pay 53
guarantee payment 155
insolvency, rights on 207
itemised pay statement 127-128
maternity pay 113
medical suspension pay 124
reasons for dismissal 242-243
redundancy consultation 197-199
redundancy pay 183-184
re-instatement after pregnancy 117-119
terms and conditions of employment 88-90
time off:
    public duties 132
    trade union members 101
    trade union officials 102-103
    work, to look for 203
trade union membership and activities 98-99
unfair dismissal... ... ... 107, 315-332
union recognition 71-74
wrongful dismissal 231-232

Remuneration—see " Pay ".

Replacements 117, 123, 316

Representations in writing 320, 343

Resignations 219-220

Retirement 8, 50, 159, 250

Retraining 202, 277

Review:
Tribunal decision, of 345-347
Wages, of 276

Right to work 138-140

S

Safety 283
Safety committees 95
Salary reviews 276, 310
Seamen 14, 45, 126, 196, 204, 211
Secretary of State 196, 200, 207, 209, 252
Security, national 15, 98, 270
Self-employed 158, 248
Serious misconduct—see " Gross misconduct ".
Service agreements 41
Settlement of employee's claim 234, 255, 333-337
Settling " out of court " 333-337
Sex Discrimination—see " Discrimination ".
Shop—see " Closed Shop ".

PAGE

Short term employees 46, 121, 151, 197, 382

Short-time 133, 140-148

Sickness and injury:
    break in employment 355
    dismissal by reason of 278-281
    frustration of contract 223-225, 278
    medical suspension pay 120-124
    pay 224, 279
    terms of employment 38

Single-sex establishments 9

Skill of employee 275-277

Small firms:
    disclosure of information 76
    racial discrimination 13
    sex discrimination 7
    unfair dismissal... ... ... 253, 309

Special circumstances 195, 197

Special reasons 293

Specific performance 231

Sports 10, 14

Status 175

Statute, breach of 258, 296-297

Stealing 285

Strikes 172, 236, 269, 358

Substantial reason, some other 297-299

Suitable alternative employment:
    dismissal due to pregnancy 105-106
    guarantee payment 154
    medical suspension pay 121
    redundancy 162, 168, 172

Summary dismissal 229-231

Suspension:
    full pay, on 137
    lay-off and short-time 135
    medical suspension 120-124
    pending investigations 288, 366
    terms of contract 135

Swearing 230, 288

T

Take-overs 276

Tax rebates 326

Temporary absence from work 354

Temporary cessation of work... 356

Temporary replacements 117, 123

Termination of employment—see " Dismissal ".

  PAGE

Terms and conditions of employment:
  Central Arbitration Committee 74, 80
  changes in   283
  general level of terms and conditions   87-88
  recognised terms and conditions   87
  see also " Contract of Employment ".

Time keeping   285

Time off:
  Code of Practice   368-371
  insolvency rights   206
  public duties   129-132
  trade union members   99-101
  trade union officials   101-103
  work, to look for   201-204

Title of job   39

Trade dispute 91, 154, 236

Trade Union:
  activities...   ...   . 97, 100, 103, 261, 369-370
  closed shop   83-86
  definition   68
  disclosure of information to   75-80
  interim relief   262-267
  membership   96-99
  recognition of   68-74
  religious beliefs...   ...   . 85, 97, 262, 268
  specified independent   268
  terms and conditions of employment   88
  time off for members 99, 369
  time off for officials 101, 368
  training 369
  union membership agreement...   83-86

Training...   ...   . 60-61, 310, 369

Transfer 60-61

Transfer of business   179-182

" Trial ", employee on...   274

Trial period 142, 173, 176, 177-179, 218

Tribunals:
  appeal from 331, 348-349
  application to 311-315, 339-340
  breach of contract cases   238
  Commission, application by   20-21
  constitution of 338
  costs   344-345
  decisions of   344
  discrimination 15-17
  equal pay   53
  establishment of   337
  guarantee payments   155
  hearings before 342-344
  insolvency rights   210
  interim relief   262-267
  itemised pay statements   127
  maternity pay   111
  medical suspension pay   124
  notice of appearance   340-341

Tribunals—*continued* PAGE

    originating application... 339-340
    preliminary matters 341-342
    protective award 197, 199
    " reasonably practicable " 311-315
    reasons for dismissal 240-243
    redundancy payments 183
    review of decision 345-347
    time off 101, 102, 132, 203
    trade union membership and activities 98-99
    unfair dismissal... 311-315

U

Unemployment benefit 326

Unfair dismissal:
    application to Industrial Tribunal 311-315
    basic award 322-323
    breach of statutory duty 296-297
    burden of proof 257, 271
    capability, lack of 274-281
    compensation 321-332
    compensatory award 323-327
    conduct 282-290
    contracting out 253-256
    excluded categories 247-252
    inadmissible reasons 259-262
    interim relief 262-267
    reasonableness 300-310
    reasons 258-262, 271-299
    redundancy 290-296
    re-engagement 317-318
    re-instatement 315-317
    religious belief 262, 268
    remedies... 311-332
    settling " out of court " 333-337
    some other substantial reason 297-299
    warnings... 304-306

Union—*see* " Trade Union ".

Union membership agreement 83-84, 255, 268

Unnotified deductions 127

V

Victimisation 63-64
Violence 230, 288, 327

W

Wages—*see* " Pay ".
Warnings 166, 192, 275, 280, 285, 295, 304-306, 366
Week's pay 110, 144, 152, 186, 198, 360-363
Welfare services 9, 14
Wife as employer—*see* " Husband or wife as employer ".

PAGE

Witness orders 342
Work:
    equivalent value, of 52
    like work 51
    right to 138-140
Working to rule 284
Workless day 151
Works rules 34-35, 41
Wrongful dismissal 226-239
    compensation for 232-235
    notice entitlement 227-229
    relationship with unfair dismissal 238-239
    remedies for 231-232